Inventing the Organizations of the 21st Century

Inventing the Organizations of the 21st Century

edited by Thomas W. Malone, Robert Laubacher and
Michael S. Scott Morton

The MIT Press
Cambridge, Massachusetts
London, England

This book was set in Times Roman by SNP Best-set Typesetter Ltd., Hong Kong and was printed and bound in the United States of America.

Library of Congress Cataloging-in-Publication Data

Inventing the organizations of the 21st century/Thomas W. Malone, Robert Laubacher, and Michael S. Scott Morton, editors.
   p. cm.
   An initiative of MIT's Sloan School of Management.
   Includes bibliographical references and index.
   ISBN 0-262-13431-4 (hc: alk. paper)—ISBN 0-262-63273-X (alk. paper)
   1. Industrial management. 2. Strategic planning. 3. Industrial organization. 4. Corporations.
I. Malone, Thomas W. II. Laubacher, Robert. III. Scott Morton, Michael S. IV. Sloan School of Management.

HD31 .I68 2003
658—dc21

2002023963

Contents

Acknowledgments

The following corporate sponsors of MIT's "Initiative on Inventing the Organizations of the 21st Century" provided financial and organizational support for the research on which this book was based:

Founding sponsors

- British Telecommunications (U.K.)
- EDS/A. T. Kearney (U.S.)
- National Westminster Bank (U.K.)

Major sponsors

- Norwegian Business Consortium (a collaboration involving Norsk Hydro, Norwegian Confederation of Business and Industry, Norwegian School of Management and Telenor)
- Union Bank of Switzerland

Regular sponsors

- AMP (U.S.)
- Eli Lilly (U.S.)
- Ericsson (Sweden)
- LG Electronics (South Korea)
- McKinsey & Company (U.S.)
- Siemens-Nixdorf (Germany)
- Siemens Private Communication Systems (Germany)

We would like to give special thanks to the following individuals from sponsor companies for their help and support: Dan Moorhead, Elisa O'Donnell, Kerry Scott, Bruce Bond, Tim Jones, Gerhard Schulmeyer, Ragnhild Sohlberg, Nathaniel Foote, and Brook Manville.

Many of the people who made significant contributions to the 21st Century Initiative are authors of the chapters in this volume or are listed in the acknowledgments sections of those chapters. It is worth mentioning separately, however, the following people who played continuing roles in the Initiative:

Co-directors Thomas W. Malone, Michael S. Scott Morton

Executive directors Robert Russman Halperin, Ed Heresniak, Roanne Neuwirth

We would like to give special thanks to Robert Halperin, the 21st Century Initiative's first executive director. Without him, it is likely that this Initiative would never have happened.

Full-time project research staff   Robert Laubacher

MIT faculty steering committee   Thomas Malone, Michael Scott Morton, Jack Rockart, Peter Senge, Bengt Holmström, Wanda Orlikowski, John Carroll.

MIT core faculty group (includes members of faculty steering committee plus the following)   Deborah Ancona, Lotte Bailyn, Erik Brynjolfsson, Charlie Fine, Tom Kochan, Don Lessard, John Sterman, JoAnne Yates.

Other MIT faculty members and researchers who undertook research in the Initiative or participated in working groups and sponsor meetings   Harold Abelson, Thomas Allen, Michael Cusumano, Randall Davis, John de Figuereido, Chrysanthos Dellarocas, William Hanson, David Hardt, Paul Healey, Rebecca Henderson, William Isaacs, Richard Lester, John Little, Stuart Madnick, Robert McKersie, Thomas Magnanti, Jeffrey Meldman, Daniel Nyhart, Nelson Repenning, Daniel Roos, Julio Rotemberg, George Roth, Ed Schein, Maureen Scully, Warren Seering, John Sterman, David Tennenhouse, Sherry Turkle, John van Maanen, Stephen Ward.

MIT research scientists and doctoral students who participated in 21st Century Initiative events   Joseph Bailey, Martha Broad, Guk-Hun Cho, Paul Gallagher, Andreas Gast, William Lehr, Sharon Eisner Gillett, Scott Rockart.

We would like to thank Lester Thurow and Glen Urban, who provided important encouragement and support as Deans of the MIT Sloan School of Management during the time of the Initiative. We also thank Robert McKersie and Tom Allen, the Deputy Deans for research during the Initiative. We are grateful to Meg Christian, Chris Foglia, Maria Byerly, and Pat White, for providing administrative support during the Initiative and to Peggy Nagel and Heather Snow for providing editorial assistance during the preparation of the manuscript.

I INTRODUCTION

1 Inventing the Organizations of the 21st Century

Now and then in human history, there come periods of dramatic change. After an era of relative stability, many things are suddenly transformed, seemingly all at once, in profound ways. Looking back on such times, we realize that the choices made during the transition laid the foundations for a new era—for better or for worse. The Industrial Revolution was one such period, and to a lesser degree, so were the years just after World War II and after the fall of communism in the Soviet Union.

We believe we have now entered such a period of momentous change in the ways businesses are organized. Buzzwords from the 1980s and 1990s like "downsizing" and "reengineering" gave us a hint of what was to come, and the dot-com bubble of the late 1990s gave us a premature—but partly correct—sense of the scope of the changes still in store for us.

Buffeted today by powerful forces like deregulation and globalization, rapid advances in computer and communications technologies, and the increasing education and affluence of people around the world, we now face profound choices about how we organize work. These choices are not a simple matter of selecting from a few well-understood alternatives. Instead, some of the most important choices involve possibilities we haven't even imagined yet. In fact, the factors transforming the business world today are making it possible to organize work in ways that have never before been possible in history.

To take full advantage of these new ways of organizing, we first have to invent them. Successful invention requires more than just knowledge and creativity. It also requires a sense of values. If you are only trying to *predict* what is going to happen, what you want doesn't matter very much. But if you are trying to *invent* new things, your own values and desires are very important indeed.

To achieve the full potential of the opportunities that face us, therefore, we need to think deeply about what we really want—as individuals, as organizations, and as societies—and to imagine creatively how new technologies and new ways of organizing work can help us achieve those things. In other words, we need to invent the organizations that we, and our children, will inhabit for the rest of the twenty-first century.

It was in this spirit that we undertook a five-year research initiative at the MIT Sloan School of Management called "Inventing the Organizations of the 21st Century." It is in the same spirit that we offer in this book some of the major results of that initiative's work. The Initiative included more than 20 MIT faculty members and researchers from many different academic disciplines. It was sponsored by a dozen leading international corporations from many different industries and countries. Together, our mission was "not only to understand emerging ways of working, but also to invent entirely new and more effective approaches and put them into practice."

Before proceeding to the Initiative's results, it is useful to reflect on how we got to where we are today. To do that, we need to look at the hierarchical corporations that dominated the global economy throughout most of the twentieth century and at the forces that are now leading them to change.

The 20th-Century Organization

The corporation is an institution so familiar that we take its existence for granted. Yet large firms of the sort we have today simply did not exist as recently as the first half of the nineteenth century. Even in the industrializing nations of Europe and North American, localized agriculture and craft production remained the core of the economy. The most advanced enterprises of the age—textile factories operating water- or steam-powered looms, New England shipping firms plying the East Asian trade routes—were organized as small partnerships, whose legal structure and financial practices would have been familiar to the Italian merchants of the Renaissance. Commerce proceeded across well-established networks; manufactured goods and imports from overseas moved from cities into the hinterland via complex webs of wholesalers and local merchants (Chandler 1977).

In the second half of the nineteenth century, the building of railroad and telegraph systems in the United States led to the creation of organizations with unprecedented financial and administrative scale. These were the first modern corporations. After the Civil War, the United States rail and telegraph network was completed, providing for the first time ready access to a market that was national in scope, plus a mode of communication to manage far-flung operations. This enabled, by the end of the nineteenth century, the development of large-scale mass production in the U.S. and the rise of the first giant, vertically integrated industrial enterprises (Chandler 1977). The completion of rail and telegraph networks in Europe and Japan led to the rise of national markets and large mass-production firms in those regions as well (Chandler 1990).

These early corporations began as single-product firms. Over the last quarter of the nineteenth century, through a combination of economic adaptation and emulation of leading firms, a rough consensus emerged about how the large corporation should be organized. They typically featured a handful of major departments with specific functional expertise—purchasing, engineering, manufacturing, logistics, finance—with the employees inside each unit organized in hierarchical bureaucracies. The whole was overseen by a small senior management group, which set overall direction and coordinated interactions between the functional units. This structure came to be known by later students of organization as the unitary form, or sometimes, more simply, as a functional hierarchy (Williamson 1975, chapter 8).

Over the first decades of the twentieth century, many such single-business firms began to migrate into new product areas. This greater level of complexity required new organizational principles. Fitfully, over the first quarter of the new century, another structure emerged—the multidivisional form. The multidivisional corporation featured a series of separate business units, each producing a portfolio of related products and having the requisite set of functional hierarchies. A headquarters group oversaw the lines of businesses and assumed responsibility for a series of central corporate activities, the most important being allocation of capital among the divisions (Chandler 1962).

A key feature of the modern corporation was the separation of the firm's owners—the shareholders—from its managers—the cadre of experts responsible for overseeing day-to-day operations. Over the course of the late nineteenth and early twentieth centuries, management gradually established itself as a profession, with the rise of separate schools, specialized publications, and recognized sub-fields with their own distinct career paths.

The rise of the corporation triggered a period of wrenching social change as the railroad timetable and demands of the assembly line supplanted the rhythms of field and workshop. Millions streamed from the countryside to take jobs in city factories (Handlin 1951), which were the site of bitter, often violent, labor strife. The violence ranged from local clashes between workers and police to revolutionary upheaval that toppled national governments in Europe on several occasions, most notably with the Russian Revolution in 1917. While not the proximate cause, the social and economic upheaval spurred by the rise of mass production greatly contributed to the tensions that ignited war in 1914. The direst crisis of the modern corporate system, the Great Depression of the 1930s, led directly to the outbreak of the Second World War.

Over the first half of the twentieth century, as this upheaval was churning, groups of social reformers, labor activists, personnel managers inside firms, academics, and government officials across the industrial world worked out a series of arrangements to reconcile the existence of the large mass-production firm with the needs of workers and society. The details differed from nation to nation, but the common elements of this accommodation included union recognition, the national government assuming a referee role in labor-management relations, and forms of social insurances to mitigate the risks faced by individual workers (Jacoby 1985, Brody 1993,

Jacoby 1993). After World War II, these reforms brought an end to virulent labor unrest and solidified the place of the large corporation in modern industrial society. A relatively stable corporate system held sway in North America, Western Europe, and Japan for the next quarter-century.

This system featured several key characteristics. In major industries, there was oligopolistic competition among a handful of large firms operating primarily in national markets, many of which were heavily regulated. Shareholders were for the most part wealthy individuals or large financial institutions, content to leave management alone as long as they delivered stability and modest returns. At most large firms, an implicit contract existed between workers and their employers; employees offered loyal service in return for job security and opportunities for advancement. Collective bargaining agreements were either in place or were emulated across broad sectors of the economy, and ensured that workers shared in the broad productivity gains enjoyed by the industrial economies during this period (Cappelli 1999, chapter 2; Osterman 1999, pp. 21–32). Senior management's energies were devoted to positioning their business units in their respective product markets, deciding which were "cash cows" to be milked, "stars" to be fed, or "dogs" to be sold off (Ghemawat 2002).

This consensus left some out, most notably women and minorities. But for a good part of the population in the industrial world, it worked well, leading to a widespread diffusion of prosperity throughout the 1950s and 1960s and into the 1970s. A version of this corporate form also spread to the newly industrializing countries of the Far East—Korea, Taiwan, Singapore and its cousins in Southeast Asia—bringing a promise of broad-based prosperity there.

Perhaps the high-water mark of this arrangement came in 1976. In December of that year, a *New York Magazine* article speculated that by century's end, the editors of *Fortune* would be unable to compile their annual list of the 500 largest American firms, because with the anticipated progress of mergers and conglomeration, there would be only 479 independent companies left (Tobias 1976, Useem 1996a).

The Old Order Upended

Even as some voiced concern about the future plight of *Fortune*'s editors, a series of developments had begun to undo the post-war corporate order. The twin oil shocks of the 1970s ushered in an era of sluggish economic growth and high inflation throughout the industrial world. As national economies limped along, many observers came to question the fundamental underpinnings of the post-war order.

One influential critique claimed that the combination of regulation in product markets and institutionalized collective bargaining created systemic rigidities that stifled growth and innovation (Yergin and Stanislaw 1998, chapters 4–5). Another contended that corporate management teams were insufficiently attentive to shareholders' interests. The adherents of this position argued that managers needed a greater financial stake in the firms they ran to align incentives properly (Jensen and Meckling 1976).

With the election of Margaret Thatcher as British prime minister in 1979 and Ronald Reagan as U.S. president in 1980, the first of these critiques became a guiding force behind public policy. Deregulation swept through a series of British and American industries—oil and gas, trucking, aviation, telecommunications, banking—spurring unfettered competition in some of these sectors for the first time ever. With the subsequent evolution of the common European market into a more tightly federated European Union, deregulation eventually spread across the continent (Yergin and Stanislaw, chapters 4, 11–12).

The European and Japanese economies had been fully reconstructed by this time as well and were aggressively exporting to the United States in key sectors, most notably autos and consumer electronics. U.S. firms responded in kind, which served to trigger an ever-widening spiral of global competition.

Spurred by deregulation, a series of financial and management innovations emerged, most notably leveraged buyouts and incentive compensation for managers, that more closely aligned the interests of shareholders and management. At the same time, shares increasingly came to be concentrated in the hands of a group of institutional investors—primarily pension fund and mutual fund managers—who competed fiercely to deliver the highest returns. This new class of investors was far more demanding than the shareholders of the post-war era and exerted pressure on managers to deliver financial results on a quarterly basis (Useem 1996b).

While these developments were shifting the framework within which business was run, a series of new technologies—low-cost jet travel and air transport, packetized freight shipping, cheap long-distance phone service, overnight package delivery, the fax machine and, most importantly, the PC and computer network—made it vastly easier and cheaper to move people, goods and information (Butler *et al.* 1997).

The combined result of these changes was twofold. The business world became far more competitive, and tools were available that allowed firms to compete in new ways. The locus of senior management attention moved away from thinking about the product divisions' positions vis-à-vis the external environment. The action instead began to center inside the functional units, as managers asked questions about the arrangement of the shop floor, the R&D lab, the sales force, and about the interactions between these groups. Out of this new emphasis came a series of novel management concepts—total quality, lean manufacturing, re-engineering—that gained great currency and challenged central aspects of the traditional corporate model.

By the early 1990s, some of the leading names in the old corporate firmament had stumbled in the new, more demanding business environment. The editors of *Fortune*, far from struggling to find 500 candidates to fill out the their annual roster of leading firms, were documenting the travails of major U.S. companies that formerly seemed impregnable. Their May 1993 issue featured a cover story on the troubles then afflicting IBM, General Motors and Sears—among the most prominent American corporations of the twentieth century. To dramatize the plight of these companies, and the larger forces that seemed to be undermining the traditional corporation as an institution, the cover of this issue of *Fortune* depicted IBM, GM, and Sears as three tottering dinosaurs (Loomis 1993).

What's Happening Now?

Today, the changes that began in the 1980s and 1990s are in full swing, working their way through business after business and industry after industry. New IT tools are constantly enabling new ways for firms to compete, and the notched up-competitive environment creates the pressure that pushes companies to adopt new practices.

Start-up firms and the new venture sector, for example, are vastly more important than in the past. This phenomenon emerged first in Silicon Valley and along Boston's Route 128, and subsequently took root in high-tech districts in other parts of the United States and the world. The new venture sector represents a novel way of doing business that in its leanness and agility departs in significant ways from the traditional hierarchical approaches (Saxenian 1994). The spectacular success of firms like Apple and Microsoft in the 1980s and early 1990s only made the organizational model embodied by the new venture sector more prominent and influential. Not all startups survive. Many of the new firms launched during the dot-com craze, for instance, did not have the attributes needed to compete over the long term. But others were successful and carried on the legacy of the PC-era startups—eBay is one of the most prominent examples.

An even more extreme development than the rising profile of startups has been e-lancing—electronically connected freelancing—in which individuals or small teams link up over the Internet to collaborate on a project basis (Malone and Laubacher 1998). The techniques of e-lancing were used by the programmers who created Linux and other open-source software applications. And a group of recent startups—guru.com, elance.com and freeagent.com—have created global Internet marketplaces where talent is bought and sold on a project basis.

At the same time, large organizations, in many cases responding to the setbacks they faced in the 1980s and 1990s, have been decentralizing and doing less internally. Inspired by the example of ABB and GE (Taylor 1991, Bartlett and Ghoshal 1993), many global companies underwent major restructurings in the 1990s, breaking up unwieldy product divisions into a series of small, relatively autonomous units, each with responsibility for its own profit-and-loss statement. Inside business units, there has been a move to team-based work, with many of the teams operating across, and in the process undermining, the old functional hierarchies. In addition, there has been growing reliance on temporary project teams inside large firms. The overall result has been to push decision-making and accountability to lower levels in the organizations. At the same time, large firms have focused on what they do exceptionally well and have shed activities they cannot perform better than their competitors (Prahalad and Hamel 1990). As a result, big companies are relying on contractors and outsourcing relationships to do much work that was formerly undertaken inside the firm.

Given the growing prominence of small startups and large companies' increasing reliance on contracting and outsourcing, inter-firm relationships have become much more important than in the past. The most prominent such relationships are not the short-term, opportunistic buyer-seller ties that tended to characterize component markets in the industrial era, but rather, longer-standing links driven by a desire to pursue mutual interests over years or even decades. This has led to a move away from oligopolistic competition among stand-alone firms selling individual products and toward new kinds of networked industry structures (Powell 1990). These structures are called "supply chains" in established sectors like autos. To Silicon Valley insiders they're known as industry "ecosystems." Such webs often develop around a lead firm, a company with a strong position or one that has established an industry-wide technical standard. Around these lead firms are clustered groups of suppliers and "complementors," companies that buy or sell complementary products and services (Brandenburger and Nalebuff 1996). Similar clusters can develop when a group of firms collaborate to provide customers with tailored solutions comprised of bundles of related products and services (Foote *et al.* 2001).

In all, the late twentieth century has seen a trend toward the externalization of functions by large firms and decentralization of activities still undertaken internally. Functions formerly administered bureaucratically inside the walls of the firm are now contracted out or handled through long-term partnership arrangements. Matters decided in the past by the senior leadership of large business units are now the province of managers inside smaller, autonomous units; formerly monolithic factory floors are now run by independent work teams.

This movement toward externalization and decentralization has been pronounced; but the same factors that have driven that trend—advances in technology, more stringent competition—also drive the business systems of today to operate at previously unimaginable scale. Global mergers are creating huge firms selling into global product markets. Yet even these massive firms are subject to the organizational innovations of the time: internal disaggregation, partnerships with members of industry ecosystems or supply chains, reliance on the new venture sector to develop new products or technologies. In sectors like technology and pharmaceuticals, feverish merger activity has been accompanied by continued close ties with partners and innovative startups. The extreme embodiment of these new organizational principles is the so-called "virtual company," where a small core is linked by technology to a web of partners. The much-examined tech firms Dell and Cisco embody this concept in scaled-up form. New startups and e-lancing represent the most granular versions.

So as the twenty-first century begins, business organizations, paradoxically, appear simultaneously large and small, global in overall reach, but with that reach often achieved through a stitching together of small pieces—either business units under a corporate umbrella or a group of value chain partners—working together in a patchwork, linked manner.

History of the Initiative

What is really happening with all these changes? Where are they taking us? And what choices do we have for the future? To help answer these questions, we began the MIT Initiative on "Inventing the Organizations of the 21st Century" in 1994. Three existing Sloan School research centers—the Center for Coordination Science (CCS), the Center for Information Systems Research (CISR) and Organizational Learning Center (OLC)[1]—jointly launched the Initiative.

The Initiative had two major constituencies: MIT researchers who were interested in the changes going on and where they might lead, and executives from sponsor firms with a parallel interest from the practitioner's perspective. The three founding sponsors were British Telecommunications, EDS/A. T. Kearney and National Westminster Bank. They were joined by a larger group of global firms active in a broad range of industries—AMP, Eli Lilly, Ericsson, LG Electronics, McKinsey &

Company, Siemens Private Communication Systems, Siemens-Nixdorf, Union Bank of Switzerland—and the Norwegian Business Consortium (a collaboration involving Norsk Hydro, the Norwegian Confederation of Business and Industry, the Norwegian School of Management, and Telenor). The researchers provided frameworks for thinking about the issues and a set of specific projects in which to anchor the larger themes of the Initiative. The executives from sponsor firms provided funding and ongoing input about the direction of the overall Initiative and of specific projects.

The Initiative itself worked as loose confederation of research projects. More than 20 MIT faculty members and researchers carried out individual projects under the Initiative's umbrella. In addition, MIT researchers and sponsors collaborated on several special projects in areas of mutual interest. In one special project, for instance, consultants from A. T. Kearney, along with an internal task force from an A. T. Kearney client, worked closely with an MIT research team to develop novel approaches to redesigning the client's hiring process.

Three faculty working groups also met to discuss specific issues. One addressed firm boundaries and transfer pricing; another met over the course of an academic year to think about the possible evolution of research universities in the twenty-first century. A third group met to reflect upon the social and value implications of new organizational practices, and produced a "Manifesto for the Organizations of the 21st Century," which is included in this volume.

Three integrating projects—the Process Handbook, the Interesting Organizations Database, and Scenarios of 21st Century Organizations—worked to pull together cross-Initiative themes. The Process Handbook project developed a systematically structured database of knowledge about business activities using insights from coordination science. Applications include process invention and knowledge management. The Interesting Organizations Database project gathered information on organizations with characteristics that were "unusual today, but likely to become more common in the future." Brief descriptions of more than 250 organizations were collected in a Web-based repository, and more detailed information was gathered on a subset of those organizations. The Scenarios project asked the question, "What might the dominant forms of business organization look like in the year 2015?" The project began in 1994 with a series of sessions involving a core team of MIT researchers, facilitated by experienced scenario planners. The initial scenarios that grew out of that effort were then discussed and refined over the next two years in more than a dozen meetings with MIT researchers, Sloan students and executives from sponsor firms and other large companies. Results from each of these integrating projects are included in this volume as well.

The Initiative held regular meetings of researchers and sponsors. Executive Meetings, where a particular issue was discussed in depth, included topics like "Decentralization and the Role of Technology" and "Values: What Do We Really Want?" Broad research reviews were also held periodically, where the MIT researchers presented reports on the range of work being undertaken in connection with the Initiative.

After five years of activity, the Initiative on "Inventing the Organizations of the 21st Century" formally ended with a summary meeting in November 1999, just before the dawn of the new millennium (Andrews 1999). Many of the projects begun as part of the Initiative, however, have continued in other forms, and the research themes that characterized the Initiative continue to be central to much of our ongoing work at MIT.

Outline of the Book

In the remainder of this book, the results of the Initiative's work are organized into three main sections:

- What is changing?
- What can you do about it?
- What do you want in the first place?

The first of these sections, "What Is Changing?," has two parts. One, "Why Are Things Changing?," involves the broad environmental forces that have been driving transformation of the business world in recent years and theoretical frameworks for understanding them. The other, "How Are Things Changing?," involves specific examples of the new organizational practices that are emerging.

The second section, "What Can You Do About It?," also has two primary parts. The first, "Inventing New Strategies," focuses on how the business landscape that has emerged in recent years has created novel ways of gaining competitive advantage. The latter, "Inventing New Organizations," focuses on how firms can create and manage the fluid structures that information technologies enable and competitive realities demand.

The final section, "What Do You Want in the First Place?," is closely tied to the spirit of invention that animated our Initiative in the first place. If we are truly going to invent the future, and not just predict it, we need to know what goals we are trying to achieve. In the case of business, we believe there is a profound opportunity to invent organizations that help achieve a broader range of human goals than just the purely economic ones many firms have emphasized in our recent past. The last section of the book reflects on what human values we want our businesses to serve, and gives examples of how new kinds of organizations can help achieve those values.

The articles included in this volume are by researchers from a variety of disciplines—business history, economics, industrial relations, information systems, operations research, organization studies, strategy. In selecting the articles, however, we have sought works that, while strongly grounded in their respective disciplines, are still understandable by those with backgrounds in other fields. Our goal was a book that is broadly accessible across academic disciplines, and of interest to practicing managers as well. We hope that we can help stimulate broad discussion about these issues, not only among researchers from many different fields, but also among managers, consultants, and others in business today. Most of all, we hope that this volume can help all of us invent organizations for the twenty-first century that will not only be more economically productive but also more humanly desirable.

Note

1. The Organizational Learning Center was later spun out from MIT as the Society for Organizational Learning (SOL).

References

Andrews, Fred, 1999. Merger Mania Got You Down? So, Start Thinking Small. *New York Times*, December 1, C1.

Bartlett, Christopher, and Sumantra Ghoshal. 1993. Beyond the M-Form: Toward a Managerial Theory of the Firm. *Journal of Strategic Management* 14 (Winter Special Issue): 23–46.

Brandenburger, Adam, and Barry J. Nalebuff. 1996. *Co-opetition*. New York: Doubleday.

Brody, David. 1993. Workplace contractualism in comparative perspective. In *Industrial Democracy in America: The Ambiguous Promise*, edited by Nelson Lichtenstein and Howell John Harris. Cambridge: Woodrow Wilson Center Press and Cambridge University Press, 176–205.

Butler, Patrick, Ted W. Hall, Alistair M. Hanna, Lenny Mendonca, Byron Auguste, James Manyika, and Anumpam Sahay. 1997. A revolution in interaction. *McKinsey Quarterly* (1): 4–23.

Cappelli, Peter. 1999. *The New Deal at Work: Managing the Market-Driven Workforce*. Boston: Harvard Business School Press.

Chandler, Alfred D., Jr. 1962. *Strategy and Structure: Chapters in the History of the Industrial Enterprise*. Cambridge, Mass.: MIT Press.

Chandler, Alfred D., Jr. 1977. *The Visible Hand: The Managerial Revolution in American Business*. Cambridge, Mass.: Belknap Press of the Harvard University Press.

Chandler, Alfred D., Jr. with the assistance of Takashi Hikino. 1990. *Scale and Scope: The Dynamics of Industrial Capitalism*. Cambridge, Mass.: Belknap Press of the Harvard University Press.

Foote, Nathaniel W., Jay Galbraith, Quentin Hope, and Danny Miller. 2001. Making solutions the answer. *McKinsey Quarterly* (3): 84–93.

Ghemawat, Pankaj. 2002. Competition and Business Strategy in Historical Perspective. *Business History Review* 76 (Spring): 37–74.

Handlin, Oscar. 1951. *The Uprooted: The Epic Story of the Great Migrations that made the American People*. Boston: Little, Brown.

Jacoby, Sanford M. 1985. *Employing Bureaucracy: Managers, Unions, and the Transformation of Work in American Industry, 1900–1945*. New York: Columbia University Press.

Jacoby, Sanford M. 1993. Pacific ties: industrial relations and employment systems in Japan and the United States since 1900. In *Industrial Democracy in America: The Ambiguous Promise*, edited by Nelson Lichtenstein and Howell John Harris. Cambridge: Woodrow Wilson Center Press and Cambridge University Press, 206–248.

Jensen, Michael C., and William H. Meckling. 1976. Theory of the Firm: Managerial Behavior, Agency Costs and Ownership Structure. *Journal of Financial Economics* 3 (October): 305–360.

Loomis, Carol J. 1993. Dinosaurs? *Fortune*, May 3, 36–42.

Malone, Thomas W., and Robert J. Laubacher. 1998. The Dawn of the E-lance Economy. *Harvard Business Review* 76 (September–October): 145–152.

Osterman, Paul. 1999. *Securing Prosperity—The American Labor Market: How it Has Changed and What to Do about It*. Princeton, N.J.: Princeton University Press.

Powell, Walter W. 1990. Neither Market Nor Hierarchy: Network Forms of Organization. *Research in Organizational Behavior* 12: 295–336.

Prahalad, C. K., and Gary Hamel. 1990. The Core Competence of the Corporation. *Harvard Business Review* 68 (May–June): 79–91.

Saxenian, AnnaLee. 1994. *Regional Advantage: Culture and Competition in Silicon Valley and Route 128*. Cambridge, Mass.: Harvard University Press.

Taylor, William. 1991. The Logic of Global Business: An Interview with ABB's Percy Barnevik. *Harvard Business Review* 69 (March–April): 91–105.

Tobias, Andrew. 1976. The Merging of the "Fortune 500." *New York Magazine*, December 20, 23–25 ff.

Useem, Michael. 1996a. Corporate Education and Training. In *The American Corporation Today*, edited by Carl Kaysen. New York and Oxford: Oxford University Press, 292–326.

Useem, Michael. 1996. *Investor Capitalism: How Money Managers are Changing the Face of Corporate America*. New York: Basic Books.

Williamson, Oliver E. 1975. *Markets and Hierarchies; Analysis and Antitrust Implications: A Study in the Economics of Internal Organization*. New York: Free Press.

Yergin, Daniel, and Joseph Stansislaw. 1998. *The Commanding Heights: The Battle between Government and the Marketplace that is Remaking the Modern World*. New York: Simon & Schuster.

II WHAT IS CHANGING?

Many factors have been changing business organizations in recent years: globalization, deregulation, the growing pace of innovation, the increasing education and affluence of people, and new technologies. This section focuses on how these factors are affecting and will affect organizations and how they will shape the choices we have in creating the organizations of the future.

Of all these factors, one stands out as especially important: new technologies, especially new information technologies. These new technologies have been advancing at a remarkable rate over the past few decades. Moore's Law, which predicts that the power of microchips will double every 18 months, has held true since the mid-1960s and appears likely to continue for the foreseeable future. Bandwidth, the capacity to move data over communications networks, has doubled every two years since the late 1970s.

Technological advances alone don't directly change business, but these technological developments have also been key enablers for many other factors that are spurring business change (like globalization, faster innovation, and increasing education). Thus these new technologies have been—directly and indirectly—both enablers and drivers for many of the organizational changes that are sweeping through the business world today.

Why Are Things Changing?

The relationship between organizations and the forces that are reshaping them—especially information technology—is by no means simple. We begin with a subsection—Why Are Things Changing?—that includes three perspectives on this relationship.

The first chapter in this subsection is a theoretical essay by Bengt Holmström and John Roberts on what determines the boundaries of a firm. This article reviews some of the classic works on the economics of organization, a field that examines why economic activity is sometimes managed inside large firms and sometimes through external market-based transactions. Holmström and Roberts note that the most influential past work on this question has focused primarily on what economists call the "hold-up problem"—a situation where one party makes an investment and the other party can then "hold them up" when bargaining about how to share the returns from that investment. Holmström and Roberts go on to show that many recent organizational developments—supply chain links within Japanese *keiretsu*, long-term exclusive contracting relationships, the alliances and interconnections that prevail in networked industries, certain kinds of sales force and franchising arrangements, the use of spin-offs, knowledge transfer, and the leveraging of brands inside large firms—cannot be understood by consideration of the hold-up problem alone. Past work on the economics of organization was oriented toward issues that arose in traditional multidivisional corporations. Such an approach is no longer adequate to address the range of emerging organizational forms, many of which involve activities formerly undertaken inside the firm now being governed by interactions between firms. Holmström and Roberts point out that the longstanding approach of organizational economists, which was to consider the implications of a one-time transaction between two players, needs to be augmented by new thinking, which takes into account a long-term series of interactions among many players.

Next is an article by Thomas Malone on how information technology affects decision-making in organizations. The key message is that information technology, by dramatically decreasing the costs of communication, is enabling much more decentralized ways of organizing work. This means smaller, more decentralized firms and "empowerment" and delegation of decisions within hierarchical organizations. But as Malone notes, this relationship is not always straightforward. History has shown that advances in information technology have sometimes led to more centralization, sometimes to more decentralization. Malone resolves this seeming paradox though a simple model that plots the costs of transmitting information—communication costs—against the value of remote information. The model reveals that if other factors are equal, organizations will tend to move through a three-stage process as communications costs go down. At the first stage, when communications costs are high, independent, decentralized decision-making is favored. As costs drop, there comes a point where centralized decision-making works better. And as costs drop still more, decentralized, connected structures prevail. This progression has parallels in the historical development of business organizations over the past two centuries—from the small, disconnected partnerships of the early nineteenth century; to the large corporations that arose in the mid-nineteenth century and dominated through most of the twentieth; to the decentralized organizations that began to emerge at the end of the twentieth century.

Malone shows that the connected, decentralized organizations enabled by today's new technologies have many advantages. When given more freedom and, at the same time, provided with the right communications tools, front-line workers can be empowered to make decisions based on local information to which only they have access; at the same time, the autonomy they've been granted tends to make them more enthusiastic, committed, and creative. In a growing number of situations in our knowledge-based economy, these factors are likely to be critical to success.

The first section ends with an article by Erik Brynjolfsson and Lorin Hitt that shows IT associated with a wide range of complementary organizational changes, in particular decentralization inside firms and greater reliance on external relationships. The authors go on to show that these changes have been associated with significant gains in efficiency.

Brynjolfsson and Hitt cite empirical studies that link high levels of IT investment with a range of innovative organizational practices inside companies—granting greater autonomy to more highly skilled workers, smaller firm size and less vertical integration. These attributes tend to occur together as "clusters" of reinforcing organizational characteristics. Lay parlance instinctively recognized this phenomenon in the late 1990s when it termed firms that operated in this way as part of the "new economy," as contrasted with the "old economy" approach reliant on practices of the mass production era—lots of physical capital and hierarchical command-and-control structures. The article also shows how IT has enabled greater reliance on relations between firms, for example, in tighter supply chain linkages or the more intimate ties with customers associated with mass-customization, build-to-order business models.

Brynjolfsson and Hitt then marshal evidence that these IT-enabled approaches are more productive than the mass-production-era practices they supplanted. They cite a number of firm- and industry-level studies, including their own, that demonstrate a correlation between IT investment and increases in productivity, especially when the IT investment is combined with the kinds of organizational changes recounted above.

Finding evidence that IT has contributed to productivity increases in the economy as a whole has proven more difficult, leading economists to speak of a so-called "productivity paradox." Brynjolfsson and and Hitt argue that two unique characteristics of IT create problems for productivity accounting. First, purchases of IT equipment are associated with a need to build complex organizational capabilities to use that equipment properly. The costs of building these organizational skills can exceed the initial costs of IT hardware and software by a ratio of ten to one or more. Second, the benefits associated with IT are frequently intangible—things like higher quality, greater variety or convenience, and higher levels of customer service. Today's productivity accounting does not handle either of these factors well, leading to a significant understatement of the productivity benefits of IT, which Brynjolfsson and Hitt estimate may be on the order of 1 percent per annum or more. Even with these accounting problems, official measurements of labor productivity in the U.S. economy still moved strongly upward in the late 1990s, to levels unseen since the 1960s.

These three articles don't constitute the final word on why organizations are changing, but they suggest the range of issues that need to be considered and the complexity of the relationships involved. They also provide some tantalizing glimpses of where we are headed.

How Are Things Changing?

The next subsection—How Are Things Changing?—looks in more detail at where we are headed. An important goal of this subsection is to stretch your thinking about what is possible.

The subsection opens with an article by Thomas Malone and Robert Laubacher that explores in detail a provocative scenario of radical decentralization. They call this scenario the "e-lance economy" where "e-lance" is a term they coined to mean "electronically connected freelancers." The basic idea explored in this chapter is that much of the work done in the past inside large, hierarchical corporations may in the future be done by temporary combinations of very small companies or independent contractors. An important implication of such a development could be radical changes in management practices. The example of the Internet—a vast, global system with no central leadership that is enabled by a handful of simple technical standards—is illustrative. There will still be a need for managers, but the role will differ considerably from that which existed inside the traditional hierarchical firm. Managing in an e-lance world will involve influencing and coordinating networks that no one can really control. Also, a likely prerequisite of a radically decentralized e-lance economy is broad acceptance of standards of various kinds—ranging from technical specifications such as those that allow communication between computers on the World Wide Web to sets of widely agreed-upon cultural assumptions—the "rules of the games"—to allow effective interaction among people.

The next chapter, also by Malone and Laubacher, broadens our view of what is possible by exploring two possible extreme scenarios on the dimension of firm size. It grew out of the 21st Century Initiative's scenarios project, which attempted to envision what the dominant form of business organization would be in the year 2015. The first of the scenarios ("Small companies, large networks") is described only briefly in this excerpt because we have already seen it described in detail as the "e-lance economy." The other scenario is the opposite extreme: companies so large that they assume the character of "virtual countries." This scenario explores what the world might look like if companies became far larger and more pervasive in their employees' lives but at the same time grew more decentralized in their internal decision-making—so decentralized that employees were able to elect their own managers at every level of the hierarchy, much as voters elect the leaders of their governments today.

The real world of the future will likely include elements of both scenarios. In fact, the distinctions between large and small firms may even blur and become less important. The point of scenarios such as these is to help expand our thinking about the range of possibilities.

Another way of expanding our thinking about what is possible is to look at intriguing examples of things that are already happening today. That is the focus of the last chapter in this section, in which Michael S. Scott Morton describes the "Interesting Organizations Database." This project compiled a collection of examples of organizations that are "unusual today, but likely to become more common in the future." This approach, which involved looking at novel practices, then thinking about whether they could become more widespread in the future, became a way of seeing and thinking that had influence in other 21st Century Initiative projects as well. After initially gathering data on more than 250 companies, Scott Morton focused his efforts on a group of eight large firms that had been radically transformed through innovative use of information technologies. These examples show both the possible pitfalls and the potential breakthrough benefits of IT-enabled transformation—what Scott Morton calls "digitalization."

Taken together, these articles offer a snapshot view of the twenty-first century organization. Inside the firm, increasingly skilled workers will operate more and more autonomously, relying on extensive links with colleagues inside the organization and close ties with suppliers, partners, and customers. In some cases, the key unit will be a decentralized, global corporation; in others, a network of suppliers and partners will comprise a virtual "extended enterprise." In still other instances, small teams and independent e-lancers, collaborating on a project basis, will actually constitute a temporary "firm" that will dissolve when the work is complete. High-speed networks will stitch together the whole, providing rich, real-time communication between computers and people and enabling a system that's both flexible and efficient.

Why Are Things Changing?

2 The Boundaries of the Firm Revisited

Bengt Holmström and John Roberts

Why do firms exist? What is their function, and what determines their scope? These remain the central questions in the economics of organization. They are also central questions for business executives and corporate strategists. The worldwide volume of corporate mergers and acquisitions exceeded $1.6 trillion in 1997. It is hard to imagine that so much time, effort, and investment bankers' fees would be spent on adjusting firm boundaries unless there was some underlying economic gain. Indeed, the exceptional levels of merger and acquisition activity over the past two decades are a strong indication that economically significant forces do determine organizational boundaries.

The study of firm boundaries originated with the famous essay by Coase (1937), who raised the question of why we observe so much economic activity inside formal organizations if, as economists commonly argue, markets are such powerful and effective mechanisms for allocating scarce resources. Coase's answer was in terms of the costs of transacting in a world of imperfect information. When the transaction costs of market exchange are high, it may be less costly to coordinate production through a formal organization than through a market.

In large part thanks to the work of Williamson (1975, 1985), recent decades have seen a resurgence of interest in Coase's fundamental insight that firm boundaries can be explained by efficiency considerations. Our understanding of firm boundaries has been sharpened by identifying more precisely the nature and sources of transaction costs in different circumstances. In the process, the focus of attention has shifted away from the coordination problems originally emphasized by Coase and toward the role of firm boundaries in providing incentives. In particular, the most influential work during the last two decades on why firms exist, and what determines their boundaries, has been centered on what has come to be known as the "hold-up problem."

The classic version of the hold-up story is told by Klein, Crawford, and Alchian (1978); its essence is modeled in Grout (1984). One party must make an investment to transact with another. This investment is relation-specific; that is, its value is appreciably lower (perhaps zero) in any use other than supporting the transaction between the two parties.[1] Moreover, it is impossible to draw up a complete contract that covers all the possible issues that might arise in carrying out the transaction and could affect the sharing of the returns from the investment. The classic example, cited by Klein, Crawford, and Alchian (1978), involves the dies used to shape steel into the specific forms needed for sections of the body of a particular car model (say, the hood or a quarter panel). These dies are expensive—they can cost tens of millions of dollars. Further, they are next-to-worthless if not used to make the part in question. Suppose the dies are paid for and owned by an outside part supplier. Then the supplier will be vulnerable to hold-up. Because any original contract is incomplete, situations are very likely to arise after the investment has been made that require the two parties to negotiate over the nature and terms of their future interactions. Such *ex post* bargaining[2] may allow the automobile man-ufacturer to take advantage of the fact that the dies cannot be used elsewhere to force a price reduction that grabs some of the returns to the investment that the supplier had hoped to enjoy. The supplier may then be unwilling to invest in the specific assets, or it may expend resources to protect itself against the threat of hold-up. In either case, inefficiency results: Either the market does not bring about opti-mal investment, or resources are expended on socially wasteful defensive measures. Having the auto company own the dies solves the problem.

If the supply relationship faces more extensive hold-up problems, the best solu-tion may be vertical integration, with all the parts of the body being procured inter-nally rather than outside. The organization and governance structure of a firm are thus viewed as a mechanism for dealing with hold-up problems.

The next section of the paper will review the two strains of work that have dom-inated the research on the boundaries of the firm: transaction cost economics and property rights theory. Both theories, while quite different in their empirical impli-cations, focus on the role of ownership in supporting relationship-specific invest-ments in a world of incomplete contracting and potential hold-ups. There is much to be learned from this work.

In this essay, however, we argue for taking a much broader view of the firm and the determination of its boundaries. Firms are complex mechanisms for coordi-nating and motivating individuals' activities. They have to deal with a much richer variety of problems than simply the provision of investment incentives and the reso-lution of hold-ups. Ownership patterns are not determined solely by the need to provide investment incentives, and incentives for investment are provided by a variety of means, of which ownership is but one. Thus, approaches that focus on one incentive problem that is solved by the use of a single instrument give much too limited a view of the nature of the firm, and one that is potentially misleading.

We support our position first by pointing to situations where relationship-specific investments appear quite high and contracting is incomplete, yet the patterns of ownership are hard to explain either with transaction cost theory or property rights models. The comparison of traditional procurement and subcontracting practices across the U.S. and Japanese automobile industries is the best and most detailed these costs quite clearly relate not to one single transaction, but to the whole collection of transactions that the hierarchy covers (Milgrom and Roberts 1992, pp. 32–33).

Finally, Williamson treats market trade as a default that is assumed superior to within-organization trade unless levels of uncertainty, frequency, and asset specificity are high enough to pull the transaction out of the market. Because the market is the default, its benefits are not spelled out as clearly as its costs. In transactions cost economics, the functioning market is as much a black box as is the firm in neoclassical microeconomic theory. An assortment of conditions has been adduced by Williamson and others to limit firm size—costs of bureaucracy, the weakening of individual incentives, the hazards of internal politicking, and so on—but none of these costs is easy to measure, and (perhaps for this reason) they have not played much of an empirical role.[4]

A major strength of the modern property rights approach, pioneered by Grossman and Hart (1986),[5] is that it spells out the costs and benefits of integration in a manner that does not rely on the presence of an impersonal market. The theory takes ownership of non-human assets as the defining characteristic of firms. A firm is exactly a set of assets under common ownership. If two different assets have the same owner, then we have a single, integrated firm; if they have different owners, then there are two firms and dealings between them are market transactions. Decisions about asset ownership—and hence firm boundaries—are important because control over assets gives the owner bargaining power when unforeseen or uncovered contingencies force parties to negotiate how their relationship should be continued. The owner of an asset can decide how it should be used and by whom, subject only to the constraints of the law and the obligations implied by specific contracts. Assets become bargaining levers that influence the terms of new agreements and hence the future payoffs from investing in the relationship. In contrast to transactions cost economics, the standard property rights models assume that *all* bargaining, including any that occurs after investments are made, is efficient. Thus, everything turns on how ownership affects initial investments, but unlike Klein *et al.* (1978), it is essential that these investments are non-contractible.[6]

To illustrate, in Hart and Moore (1990) each agent makes (non-contractible) investments in human capital that are complementary with a set of non-human assets. Each agent necessarily owns his or her own human capital. The ownership of the non-human assets, however, affects the incentives to invest in human capital. Once the investment is made, *ex post* bargaining determines the allocation of the returns from the investments. This bargaining is assumed to give each party—that is, the buyer B or the seller S—what it could have obtained on its own, V_B or V_S, plus a share of the surplus created by cooperation.

Specifically, payoffs take the form $P_i = V_i + \frac{1}{2}(V - V_i - V_j)$, i, j = B, S, where as before V is the capitalized value of cooperation. Ownership influences the separation payoffs V_B and V_S, since the owner of a particular asset gets to deny the other party the use of it if cooperation is not achieved. Ownership does not influence V, since all assets are in use when the parties cooperate. Neither party's investment affects the other's separation payoff, because if they do not cooperate then neither has access to the other's human capital and the investment in it.

Individual incentives to invest are driven by the derivatives of the payoff functions P_B and P_S. If $V \equiv V_B + V_S$ for all levels of investment, then individual returns to investments coincide exactly with the social returns, as measured by the derivatives of V. This case corresponds to a competitive market, because no extra value is created by the particular relationship between B and S; both parties would be equally well off if they traded with outsiders. In general, however, the social returns and the individual returns differ, resulting in inefficient investments. In particular, if the payoff functions are supermodular,[7] so that the payoff to incremental investment by one party is increasing in both the volume of non-human assets available to that party and the amount of the other party's investment, then there is underinvestment. One can strengthen the incentives of one party by giving that party control over more assets, but only at the expense of weakening the incentives of the other party. There is a trade-off, because ownership shares cannot add up to more than 100 percent. This trade-off determines the efficient allocation of ownership.

Several conclusions follow from this model. For instance, as investment by the buyer B becomes more important (for generating surplus V) relative to investments by the seller S, B should be given more assets. B should be given those assets that make V_B most sensitive to B's investment. If an asset has no influence on B's investment it should be owned by S. For this reason, no outsider should ever own an asset—that would waste bargaining chips that are precious for incentive provision. For the same reason, joint ownership—meaning that both parties have the right to veto the use of the asset—is never optimal. As a consequence, assets that are worthless unless used together should never be separately owned.

While these implications regarding joint ownership, outside ownership, and co-ownership of perfectly complementary assets are often stressed, it is important to keep in mind that they are easy to overturn by slight changes in assumptions. For instance, joint ownership may be desirable when investments improve non-human assets. Third-party control can be desirable if, otherwise, parties would invest too much in improving their outside opportunities to strengthen their bargaining positions (Holmström and Tirole 1991, Holmström 1996, Rajan and Zingales 1998). And most conclusions are sensitive to the particular bargaining solution being used (de Meza and Lockwood 1998). What does survive all variations of the model is the central idea that asset ownership provides levers that influence bargaining outcomes and hence incentives.

In contrast to Williamson's three-factor framework, there is no uncertainty in this model. Frequency plays no role either (although it can be introduced with interesting results, as in Baker, Gibbons, and Murphy 1997, or Halonen 1994). Most strikingly, the *level* of asset specificity has no influence on the allocation of ownership. The predictions of the model remain unchanged if one increases the total surplus V by adding an arbitrarily large constant to it, because investments are driven by marginal, not total, returns. This is problematic for empirical work, partly because margins are hard to observe when there are no prices and partly because some of the key margins relate to returns from hypothetical investments that in equilibrium are never made. Indeed, as Whinston (1997) has noted, the extensive empirical research geared to testing Williamson's three-factor framework casts no light on the modern property rights models.

As noted earlier, a virtue of the property rights approach is that it simultaneously addresses the benefits *and* the costs of ownership. Markets are identified with the right to bargain and, when necessary, to exit with the assets owned. This greatly clarifies the market's institutional role as well as its value in providing entrepreneurial incentives. On the other hand, firms are poorly defined in property rights models and it is not clear how one actually should interpret the identities of B and S. In an entrepreneurial interpretation, B and S are just single individuals, but this seems of little empirical relevance. If, on the other hand, firms consist of more than one individual, then one has to ask how one should interpret the unobserved investments (in human capital) that cannot be transferred. An even more fundamental question is why firms, as opposed to individuals, should own any assets. At present, the property rights models are so stylized that they cannot answer these questions.[8]

Investment Incentives are Not Provided by Ownership Alone

There is no doubt that hold-up problems are of central concern to business people. In negotiating joint venture agreements, venture capital contracts or any of a number of other business deals, much time is spent on building in protections against hold-ups. At the same time, such contracts are *prima facie* evidence that hold-up problems do not get resolved solely by integration of buyer and seller into a single party—the firm. Indeed, there seems to be something of a trend today toward disintegration, outsourcing, contracting out, and dealing through the market rather than bringing everything under the umbrella of the organization. This trend has seen the emergence of alternative, often ingenious solutions to hold-up problems.

Japanese Subcontracting

The pattern of relations between Japanese manufacturing firms and their suppliers offers a prominent instance where the make-buy dichotomy and related theorizing have been less than satisfactory. Although the basic patterns apply in a number of industries (including, for example, electronics), the practices in the automobile industry are best documented (Asanuma 1989, 1992). These patterns have spread from Japan to the auto industry in the United States and elsewhere, and from autos to many other areas of manufacturing. These practices feature long-term, close relations with a limited number of independent suppliers that seem to mix elements of market and hierarchy. Apparently, these long-term relations substitute for ownership in protecting specific assets.

Two points of contrast in the treatment of specific investments between traditional U.S. practice and the Japanese model present particular problems for the received theory. The first concerns investments in designing specialized parts and components. Traditional U.S. practice featured either internal procurement or arm's-length, short-term contracting. Design-intensive products were very often procured internally (Monteverde and Teece 1982).[9] When products were outsourced, the design was typically done by the auto-maker, with the drawings being provided to the suppliers. This pattern is what hold-up stories would predict, for the investment in design is highly specific and probably cannot be protected fully by contracts; thus, external suppliers will not make such relationship-specific investments, for fear that they will be held up by buyers after their investments are in place. In stark contrast, it is normal practice for Japanese auto firms to rely on their suppliers to do the actual design of the products supplied. The design costs are then to be recovered through the sale price of the part, with the understanding that this price will be adjusted in light of realized volumes.

A second contrast: Traditional U.S. practice has been that physical assets specific to an auto-maker's needs are owned by the auto-maker. This clearly applies in the case of internally procured items, but it also holds in cases where the assets are used by the external supplier in its own factory. For example, the dies used in making a particular car part will belong to the auto-maker, even though they are used in the supplier's plant on the supplier's presses. Again, this accords well with the transaction cost story of potential hold-up by the auto-maker.[10] In Japan, in contrast, these specific investments are made by the supplier, who retains ownership of the dies. This would seem to present the auto-maker with temptations to appropriate the returns on these assets, once the supplier has made the relationship-specific investment. Moreover, because the Japanese auto manufacturers typically have a very small number of suppliers of any part, component or system, the supplier would also seem to be in a position to attempt opportunistic renegotiation by threatening to withhold supply for which there are few good, timely substitutes.

The Japanese pattern is directly at odds with transaction cost theory. Meanwhile, the divergence in ownership of the dies between the two countries presents problems for attempts to explain ownership allocation solely in terms of providing incentives for investment.[11]

In Japanese practice, explicit contracting is not used to overcome the incentive problems involved in outsourced design and ownership of specific assets. In fact, the contracts between the Japanese auto-makers and their suppliers are short and remarkably imprecise, essentially committing the parties only to work together to resolve difficulties as they emerge. Indeed, they do not even specify prices, which instead are renegotiated on a regular basis. From the hold-up perspective, the prospect of frequent renegotiations over the prices of parts that are not yet even designed would certainly seem problematic.

The key to making this system work is obviously the long-term, repeated nature of the interaction.[12] Although supply contracts are nominally year-by-year, the shared understanding is that the chosen supplier will have the business until the model is redesigned, which lasts typically four or five years. Moreover, the expectation is that the firms will continue to do business together indefinitely. There has been very little turnover of Japanese auto parts suppliers: over a recent eleven-year period, only three firms out of roughly 150 ceased to be members of *kyohokai*, the association of first-level Toyota suppliers (Asanuma 1989).

The familiar logic of repeated games, that future rewards and punishments motivate current behavior, supports the on-going dealings.[13] An attempted hold-up would presumably bring severe future penalties. As importantly, the amount of future business awarded to a supplier is linked to ratings of supplier performance. The auto companies carefully monitor supplier behavior—including cost reductions, quality levels and improvements, general cooperativeness, and so on—and frequent redesigns allow them to punish and reward performance on an on-going basis. In this sense, supplier relationships in Japan are potentially *less*, not more, locked in than in the traditional U.S. model, where at the corresponding point in the value chain, the supplier is typically an in-house division or department.

Having a small number of suppliers is crucial to the Japanese system. It reduces the costs of monitoring and increases the frequency of transacting, both of which strengthen the force of reputation. Also, the rents that are generated in the production process do not have to be shared too widely, providing the source for significant future rewards. This logic underlies the normal "two-supplier system" used at Toyota. There is more than one supplier to permit comparative performance evaluation, to allow shifting of business as a reward or punishment, to provide insurance against mishaps, and perhaps to limit the hold-up power of each supplier, but the number is not chosen to minimize hold-ups.

The relationship is marked by rich information sharing, including both schedules of production plans necessary for just-in-time inventory management and also details of technology, operations, and costs. The auto-makers also assist the suppliers in improving productivity and lowering costs: Technical support engineers are a major part of the auto-makers' purchasing staff, and they spend significant amounts of time at the suppliers' facilities. All this in turn means that potential information asymmetries are reduced, which presumably facilitates both performance evaluation and the pricing negotiations.[14]

Perhaps the major problem in the system may be that the auto-makers are inherently too powerful and thus face too great a temptation to misbehave opportunistically. Indeed, many Japanese observers of the system have interpreted it in terms of the auto-makers' exploitation of their power. One counterbalance to this power asymmetry is the supplier association, which facilitates communication among the suppliers and ensures that if the auto company exploits its power over one, all will know and its reputation will be damaged generally. This raises the cost of misbehavior. In this regard, the fact that Toyota itself organized an association of the leading suppliers for its Kentucky assembly plant is noteworthy (Milgrom and Roberts 1993).

An alternative solution to this imbalance would be for the auto-maker to own the dies, as in the United States. Here a property rights explanation may be useful: Under this arrangement, the supplier would not have the same incentives to maintain the dies, since it must be very hard to contract over the amount of wear and tear and its prevention.[15]

Mini-mills, Exclusive Sourcing, and Inside Contracting

Another significant shift in the organization of production is illustrated by Nucor, the most successful steel maker in the United States over the past 20 years. Nucor operates mini-mills, which use scrap (mainly car bodies) as raw material for steel production. After an initial technological breakthrough, Nucor started to expand aggressively (Ghemawat 1995). The strategy required much capital, and to save on capital outlays, Nucor decided to outsource its entire procurement of steel scrap. Traditionally, mini-mills had integrated backwards, partly to secure an adequate supply of raw material and partly because sourcing entails substantial know-how and so was considered "strategically critical." Chaparral Steel, another big mini-mill operator, continues to be integrated backwards, for instance.

In a break with the tradition, Nucor decided to make a single firm, the David J. Joseph Company (DJJ), its sole supplier of scrap. Total dependence on a single supplier would seem to carry significant hold-up risks, but for more than a decade, this relationship has been working, smoothly and successfully. Unlike in the Japanese subcontracting system, there are certain contractual supports. Prices are determined by a cost-plus formula to reflect market conditions, and an "evergreen" contract specifies that the parties have to give warning (about half a year in advance) if they intend to terminate the relationship. Even so, there is plenty of room for opportunism. Despite transparent cost accounting (essentially, open books), DJJ can misbehave, since realized costs need not be the same as potential costs. Asset specificity remains significant even with the six-month warning period, since a return to traditional sourcing and selling methods would be quite disruptive and expensive for both sides. Indeed, one reason why the partnership has been working so well may be the high degree of mutual dependence: Nucor's share of DJJ's scrap business is estimated to be over 50 percent.

The success of Nucor's organizational model has led other mini-mills to emulate and refine it. In England, Co Steel has gone as far as relying on its sole supplier to make ready-to-use "charges," the final assemblage of materials to go into the steel-making ovens. The production technology for charges is quite complicated: About twenty or thirty potential ingredients go into each mixture, with the mix depending on the desired properties of the final product, and big cost savings can be had by optimizing the use of the different inputs. This activity entails much know-how and requires extensive information exchange with the steel plant to match inputs with final product demand. The charges must be prepared by the supplier on Co Steel's premises, both for logistical reasons and to facilitate information sharing. In transaction cost economics, such a cheek-by-jowl situation would be an obvious candidate for integration. Yet, the industry is moving in the direction of disintegration in the belief that specialization will save on costs by eliminating duplicate assets, streamlining the supply chain, and providing better incentives for the supplier through improved accountability.

Related experiments of "inside contracting" include Volkswagen's new car manufacturing plant in Brazil, where the majority of the production workers in the factory are employees, not of Volkswagen, but of subcontractors that provide and install components and systems on the cars as they move along the line. It is too early to tell whether other firms will return to inside contracting, which used to be quite common in the United States up to World War I (Buttrick 1952), and whether such a move will be successful. But evidently, even potentially large hold-up problems have not deterred recent experimentation.

Airline Alliances

Another illustration of close coordination without ownership is provided by airline alliances, which have proliferated in recent years. Coordinating flight schedules to take advantage of economies of scope requires the parties to resolve an intricate set of issues, particularly ones related to complex "yield management" decisions on how to allocate seats across different price categories and how to shift prices as the flight date approaches. Information and contracting problems abound, and it is hardly surprising that tensions occasionally surface. For instance, KLM and Northwest Airlines recently ran into a dispute that had to be resolved by dismantling their cross-ownership structure. But interestingly, this did not prevent KLM and Northwest from deepening their commitment to their North Atlantic alliance by agreeing to eliminate, over a period of years, all duplicate support operations in the United States and Europe. With the completion of this deal, KLM and Northwest have made themselves extraordinarily interdependent in one of the most profitable segments of their business. A 13-year exclusive contract, with an "evergreen" provision requiring a three-year warning before pull-out, is the main formal protection against various forms of opportunism, but undoubtedly the real safeguard comes from the sizable future rents that can be reaped by continued good behavior.

Why don't the two airlines instead integrate? Regulations limiting foreign ownership and potential government antitrust objections are a factor, as may be tax considerations. However, an explanation we have been given is that airline cultures (and labor unions) are very strong and merging them is extremely difficult. Pilot seniority is a particularly touchy issue.

Contractual Assets and Network Influence

In property rights theory, the boundaries of the firm are identified with the ownership of assets, but in the real world, control over assets is a more subtle matter. "Contractual assets" can often be created rather inexpensively to serve some of the same purposes that the theory normally assigns to ownership: to provide levers that give bargaining power and thereby enhance investment incentives. What we have in mind here are contracts that allocate decision rights much like ownership; for instance, exclusive dealing contracts such as Nucor's, or licensing agreements of various kinds. Such "governance contracts" are powerful vehicles for regulating market relationships. With increased disintegration, governance contracts seem to have become more nuanced and sophisticated. They place firms at the center of a network of relationships, rather than as owners of a clearly defined set of capital assets.

BSkyB, a satellite broadcasting system in Rupert Murdoch's media empire, is an example of a highly successful organization that has created its wealth, not by owning physical assets, but by crafting ingenious contracts that have given it influence over an effective network of media players. Satellite broadcasting requires a variety of highly complementary activities, including acquisition and development of programming, provision of the distribution system (satellites, transmitters, and home receivers) and development of encryption devices (to limit reception to those who pay), all of which must be carried out before the service can be offered. Other similarly complex and innovative systems of complements, like electric lighting systems or early computer systems, were largely developed within a single firm. BSkyB instead relies on alliances with other firms. Topsy Tail is even more of a "virtual company." It employs three people, but has sales of personal appearance accessories (combs, hair clips and such) approaching $100 million. Topsy Tail conceives of new products, but essentially everything involved in developing, manufacturing, and distributing them is handled through an extensive contractual network. Benetton and Nike, to take some bigger and more conventional firms, also extensively rely on outsourcing and a small asset base. The critical asset in these cases is of course control of the brand name, which gives enormous power to dictate how relationships among the various players are to be organized.

Microsoft and the web of inter-firm relations centered around it provide another illustration. The stock market values Microsoft at around $250 billion, which is more than $10 million per employee. Surely very little of this is attributable to its ownership of physical assets. Instead, by leveraging its control over software standards, using an extensive network of contracts and agreements that are informal as well as formal and that include firms from small start-ups to Intel, Sony, and General Electric, Microsoft has gained enormous influence in the computer industry and beyond. We are not experts on Microsoft's huge network of relationships, but it seems clear that the traditional hold-up logic does poorly in explaining how the network has developed and what role it serves. If one were to measure asset specificity simply in terms of separation costs, the estimates for breaking up some of the relationships—say, separating Intel from Microsoft—would likely be large. Yet these potential losses do not seem to cause any moves in the direction of ownership integration.

A similar pattern can be observed in the biotechnology industry (Powell 1996). As in the computer industry, the activities of the different parties are highly inter-related, with different firms playing specialized roles in the development and marketing of different products. Most firms are engaged in a large number of partnerships; for instance, in 1996 Genentech was reported to have 10 marketing partnerships, 20 licensing arrangements, and more than 15 formal research collaborations (Powell 1996, p. 205). Significant relationship-specific investments are made by many parties, and potential conflicts must surely arise after these investments are in place. Yet the system works, thanks to creative contractual assets—patents and licensing arrangements being the oldest and most ingenious—but also to the force of reputation in a market that is rather transparent, because of the close professional relationships among the researchers.

Firm Boundaries are Responsive to More than Investment Incentives

The examples above make clear that there are many alternatives to integration when one tries to solve hold-up problems. The examples also suggest that owner-ship may be responsive to problems other than underinvestment in specific assets. Speaking broadly, the problems relate to contractual externalities of various kinds, of which hold-ups are just one.

Resolving Agency Problems

An example of how agency issues can affect the boundaries of an organization is whether a firm employs its sales force directly, or whether it uses outside sales agents. The best-known example here involves electronic parts companies, some of which hire their own sales agents while others sell through separate supply companies (Andersen 1985, Andersen and Schmittlein 1984). Originally, Andersen (1985) appears to have expected that the observed variation in this choice would relate to the degree of asset specificity—for example, the extent to which invest-ment by sales people with knowledge about products was specific to a particular company. Instead, measurement costs and agency concerns turned out to be central. An employee sales force is used when individual performance is difficult to measure and when non-selling activities (like giving customer support or gathering infor-mation about customers' needs) are important to the firm; otherwise, outside com-panies are used.

Holmström and Milgrom (1991, 1994) rationalize this pattern with a model of multi-task agency, in which sales people carry out three tasks: making current sales, cultivating long-term customer satisfaction, and gathering and relaying information on customer needs. If the latter two activities are important and if the three activities compete for the agent's time, then the marginal rewards to improved performance on each must be comparable in strength; otherwise, the ill-paid activities will be slighted. Because performance in non-selling activities is arguably hard to measure, it may be best to provide balanced, necessarily lower-powered incentives for all three activities.

Offering weak incentives to an outside sales agent can be problematic, however, because the agent may then divert all effort to selling other firms' products that come with stronger rewards for sales. With an employee, this problem can be handled with a salary and a low commission rate, because the employee's outside activities are more easily constrained and promotion and other broader incentives can be used within the firm to influence the agent's behavior.[16] This logic also explains why outside agents commonly receive higher commission rates than does an inside sales force.

A less familiar illustration of how ownership responds to agency concerns comes from multi-unit retail businesses. Some of these businesses are predominantly organized through traditional franchise arrangements, in which a manufacturer contracts with another party to sell its products in a dedicated facility, as in gasoline retailing. Others, including fast-food restaurants, hotels, and pest-control services, are organized in what is called "business concept" franchising. The franchiser provides a brand name and usually other services like advertising, formulae and recipes, managerial training, and quality control inspections, collecting a fee from the franchisee in return, but the physical assets and production are owned and managed by the franchisee. Sometimes franchisers (like McDonald's) own and operate a number of outlets themselves. Finally, other businesses are commonly organized with a single company owning all the multiple outlets and hiring the outlet managers as employees. Examples are grocery supermarkets and department stores. What accounts for such differences?

It is hard to see how the specificity of the assets—real estate, cash registers, kitchens, and inventories—differs between supermarkets and restaurants in such a way that transactions cost arguments would lead to the observed pattern. Indeed, the assets involved are often not very specific at all. Alternatively, applying the Hart-Moore property rights model here would involve identifying non-contractible investments that are unavailable to the other party if the franchise agreement is terminated or the store manager's employment should end. Noncontractible investments by the center in building the brand might qualify on the one hand, but in many cases it is hard to see what the investments of the operator might be. For example, a fast-food restaurant manager might invest in training the workers and building a clientele, but these investments would presumably still be effective even if the manager were replaced by another. Further, these should also be investments that vary across cases in such a way that it is more important to provide the strong incentives of ownership to the manager of the outlet in one case and to the central party in the other.[17]

An alternative approach based on the need to offer incentives for effort has been proposed by Maness (1996). This approach begins by noting that any elements of the retail outlet's financial costs that are sufficiently difficult to measure must accrue to the owner of the outlet as residual claimant, because they cannot be passed by contract to another party. Suppose then that all costs are non-contractible in this sense; that is, since the level or appropriateness of various costs cannot be well monitored from outside, such costs cannot be part of an agreed-upon contract. Then, the only possibility for payments from the owner to the other party is on the basis of revenues. Indeed, actual franchise fees are almost always based on revenues and not on costs (Maness, p. 102) and incentive pay for employee managers is also often based on sales. In such a structure, the employee-manager has no direct incentive to control costs under central ownership, while the franchiser has no incentives for cost reduction under local ownership. Because the efforts of either party might affect costs, this creates a potential inefficiency. The solution is to lodge ownership with the party to whom it is most important to give incentives for cost control. Maness then argues that cost control in a fast-food operation is more influenced by the local manager's efforts at staffing, training, controlling waste, and the like, while costs in supermarkets are most influenced by the inventory and warehousing system, which can be centrally managed. Thus, an explanation emerges for the observed patterns: Ownership is assigned to give appropriate incentives for cost control.

A more complex example involves gasoline retailing in the United States and Canada, which has been studied by Shepard (1993) and Slade (1996), respectively. They document a variety of contractual arrangements that are used in each country between the gasoline refining company and the station operator and, in the United States, significant variation in ownership of the station. While the physical assets used in gasoline retailing are quite specific to that use, a station can be switched from one brand to another with a little paint and new signs. Consequently, neither study attempted to explain the variation in contractual and ownership arrangements in terms of specific assets and hold-up.

Both studies find that the observed patterns are consistent with the arrangements being chosen to deal with problems of inducing effort and its allocation among tasks. These arrangements differ over the strengths of the incentives given to sell gasoline and other, ancillary services like repairs, car washes, and convenience store items. In turn, these ancillary services differ in the ease and accuracy of performance measurement. The observed patterns were generally consistent with their being selected to provide appropriately balanced incentives. For example, Shepard's (1993) work notes that in repair services, effort is hard to measure and, more importantly, monitoring the realized costs and revenues by the refiner may be tricky. This should make it less likely that the refinery will own the station and employ the operator, and more likely that an arrangement will be adopted where the operator is residual claimant on sales of all sorts, either owning the station outright or leasing it from the refiner on a long-term basis. This is what the data show. In Slade's (1996) data, the presence of repair did not affect the ownership of the station (essentially all the stations were refiner-owned). It did, however, favor leasing arrangements, where the operator is residual claimant on all sales, and diminished the likelihood of commission arrangements, which would offer unbalanced incentives because the operator is residual claimant on non-gasoline business but is paid only a small commission on gasoline sales. The presence of full service rather than just self-serve gasoline sales also favors moving away from the company-owned model, since it matches the returns to relationship-building with the costs, which are borne by the local operator.[18] However, adding a convenience store actually increases the likelihood of using company-owned and -operated stations in the U.S. data, which goes against this logic unless one assumes that monitoring of such sales is relatively easy.

Considering a broad variety of retailing businesses more generally, LaFontaine and Slade (1997) document that the contractual and ownership arrangements that are used are responsive to agency considerations.

Market Monitoring

Ownership also influences agency costs through changes in the incentives for monitoring and the possibilities for performance contracting. A firm that is publicly traded can take advantage of the information contained in the continuous bidding for firm shares. Stock prices may be noisy, but they have a great deal more integrity than accounting-based measures of long-term value. For this reason, stock-related payment schemes tend to be superior incentive instruments. This factor can come to play a decisive role in organizational design as local information becomes more important and firms are forced to delegate more decision authority to sub-units and lower-level employees. Such moves require stronger performance incentives and in many cases the incentives can be offered most effectively by spinning off units and exposing them to market evaluation.

This, at least, is the underlying philosophy of Thermo Electron Corporation and its related companies. Thermo is an "incubator." It finances and supports start-up companies and entrepreneurs within a modern-day variant of the conglomerate. As soon as a unit is thought to be able to stand on its own feet, it is spun off. A minority stake is offered to outside investors, with Thermo and its family of entrepreneurs (particularly the head of the new operation) retaining a substantial fraction. The principal owners of Thermo, the Hatsopolous brothers, make it very clear that getting to the spin-off stage is the final objective and a key element in their strategy to foster a true entrepreneurial spirit within the company. Besides making managerial incentives dependent on market information, spin-offs limit the amount of intervention that Thermo can undertake in the independent units. This, too, will enhance entrepreneurial incentives.[19]

While Thermo has been remarkably successful (at least until recently), few companies have emulated its strategy. One likely reason is that Thermo's approach requires real commitment not to interfere inappropriately in the management of the spun-off units, as this would undercut entrepreneurial incentives and would also destroy the integrity of the independent businesses in the eyes of outside investors. While laws protecting minority shareholders help to achieve this commitment to some extent, Thermo's founders have worked for more than a decade to establish a reputation for neither intervening excessively nor cross-subsidizing their units. Another reason may be that Thermo has enjoyed all the benefits of a booming stock market since the early 1980s; it is not clear how well Thermo's strategy would work in a flat stock market like the 1970s.

Knowledge Transfers and Common Assets

Information and knowledge are at the heart of organizational design, because they result in contractual and incentive problems that challenge both markets and firms. Indeed, information and knowledge have long been understood to be different from goods and assets commonly traded in markets. In light of this, it is surprising that the leading economic theories of firm boundaries have paid almost no attention to the role of organizational knowledge.[20] The subject certainly deserves more scrutiny.

One of the few economic theory papers to discuss knowledge and firm boundaries is Arrow (1975), who argued that information transmission between upstream and downstream firms may be facilitated by vertical integration. As we saw in the examples of Nucor and the case of Japanese subcontracting, however, this type of information transfer may actually work fairly well even without vertical integration. More significant problems are likely to emerge when a firm comes up with a better product or production technology. Sharing this knowledge with actual or potential competitors would be socially efficient and could in principle enrich both parties, but the dilemma is how to pay for the trade. Until the new ideas have been shown to work, the potential buyer is unlikely to want to pay a lot. Establishing the ideas' value, however, may require giving away most of the relevant information for free. Again, repeated interactions can help here; in fact, even competing firms engage in continuous information exchange on a much larger scale than commonly realized. An example is the extensive use of benchmarking, in which the costs of particular processes and operations are compared between firms. But when big leaps in knowledge occur, or when the nature of the knowledge transfer will involve ongoing investments or engagements, the issues become more complex. A natural option in that case is to integrate. Any claims about the value of knowledge are then backed up by the financial responsibility that comes with pairing cash flow and control rights.[21]

We think that knowledge transfers are a very common driver of mergers and acquisitions and of horizontal expansion of firms generally, particularly at times when new technologies are developing or when learning about new markets, technologies, or management systems is taking place. Given the current level of merger and acquisition activity, and the amount of horizontal rather than vertical integration, it seems likely that many industries are experiencing such a period of change. The trend toward globalization of businesses has put a special premium on the acquisition and sharing of knowledge in geographically dispersed firms.

Two organizations that we have studied in which the development and transfer of knowledge are particularly central are ABB Asea Brown Boveri, the largest electrical equipment manufacturer, and British Petroleum, the fourth-largest integrated oil company. Both firms see the opportunity to learn and to share information effectively as key to their competitive advantage, and both operate with extremely lean headquarters that are too small to play a central, direct role in transferring knowledge across units. ABB spends a huge amount of time and effort sharing technical and business information across its more than 1,300 business units around the world through a variety of mechanisms. This would hardly be possible if these businesses were not under the single ABB umbrella. Similarly, BP's 100 business units have been encouraged to share information extensively through "peer assists," which involve business units calling on people from other units to help solve operating problems. BP also has a network of different "federal groups," each of which encourages technologists and managers from units around the world to share knowledge about similar challenges that they face.

The problem with knowledge transfers can be viewed as part of the more general problem of free-riding when independent parties share a common asset. If bargaining is costly, the situation is most easily solved by making a single party responsible for the benefits as well as the costs of using the asset. Brand names are another example of common assets that typically need to be controlled by a single entity.

Concluding Remarks

It seems to us that the theory of the firm, and especially work on what determines the boundaries of the firm, has become too narrowly focused on the hold-up problem and the role of asset specificity. Think of arraying the set of coordination and motivation problems that the firm solves along one dimension of a matrix, and the set of instruments it has available along the other. Put the provision of investment incentives in Column 1 and ownership-defined boundaries in Row 1. Let an element of the matrix be positive if the corresponding instrument is used to solve the corresponding problem, and zero otherwise. So there is certainly a positive entry in Row 1, Column 1: ownership does affect incentives for investment. We have argued, however, that both the first column and the first row have many other positive elements; ownership boundaries serve many purposes and investment incentives are provided in many ways.

Admittedly, most of the evidence we have offered in support of this claim is anecdotal and impressionistic. Our stories are largely based on newspaper reports, case studies, and our own consulting work, and they are not the sort of systematic evidence one would ideally want. Nevertheless, we think that of the significant organizational change that seems to be taking place, only a small part can be easily understood in terms of traditional transactions cost theory in which hold-up problems are resolved by integration. Many of the hybrid organizations that are emerging are characterized by high degrees of uncertainty, frequency, and asset specificity, yet they do not lead to integration. In fact, high degrees of frequency and mutual dependency seem to support, rather than hinder, ongoing cooperation across firm boundaries. This issue deserves to be explored in future work.[22]

It is also questionable whether it makes sense to consider one transaction at a time when one tries to understand how the new boundaries are drawn. In market networks, interdependencies are more than bilateral, and how one organizes one set of transactions depends on how the other transactions are set up. The game of influence is a complicated one and leads to strategic considerations that transcend simple two-party relationships.

The property rights approach, with its emphasis on incentives driven by ownership, may be a good starting point for investigating these new hybrid structures.

These appear to be emerging in response to, among other things, an increase in the value of entrepreneurship and the value of human capital, both of which are features that the property rights approach can in principle model. But this approach also needs to expand its horizon and recognize that power derives from other sources than asset ownership, and that other incentive instruments than ownership are available to deal with the joint problems of motivation and coordination. We do not believe that a theory of the firm that ignores contracts and other substitutes for ownership will prove useful for empirical studies. The world is replete with alternative instruments and, as always, the economically interesting action is at the margin of these substitutions.

Acknowledgments

This chapter is reprinted with permission from *Journal of Economic Perspectives* 12, no. 4 (Fall 1998): 73–94. We thank Bradford De Long, Robert Gibbons, Oliver Hart, David Kreps, Timothy Taylor, and Michael Whinston for their helpful comments. We are also indebted to the members of the Corporation of the Future initiative at McKinsey & Company, especially Jonathan Day, with whom we have collaborated on the issues discussed here.

Notes

1. Thus, once the investment has been sunk, it generates quasi-rents—amounts in excess of the return necessary to keep the invested assets in their current use. There could, but need not be pure rents—returns in excess of those needed to cause the investment to be made in the first place.

2. The terms *ex ante* and *ex post*—"before the fact" and "after the fact"—are widely used in this literature. In the hold-up story, the investment must be made *ex ante*, before a binding agreement is reached, while the renegotiation is *ex post*, after the investment. More generally, the literature refers to negotiations that occur after some irreversible act, including the establishing of the relationship, as *ex post* bargaining.

3. Whinston (1997) takes a close look at the empirical distinctions of transactions cost theory and property rights theory.

4. This is changing. Recently, for example, influence cost ideas (Milgrom and Roberts 1988, 1990, Meyer, Milgrom, and Roberts 1992) have been used to explain observed inefficiencies in internal capital markets (Scharfstein 1998, Shin and Stulz 1998).

5. Hart and Moore (1990) and many others have developed the property rights approach further. See Hart (1995). Recent additions include DeMeza and Lockwood (1998) and Rajan and Zingales (1998). Holmström (1996) offers a critical commentary.

6. If the parties can contract on the investments, the assumption of efficient bargaining means that they will be made at the efficient levels, irrespective of ownership patterns.

7. Supermodularity of a function means that an increase in one argument increases the incremental return from all the other arguments. With differentiable functions, the cross-partials are all non-negative.

In the Hart-Moore model, supermodularity refers both to human capital and to assets, so that having more assets implies a higher marginal return to all investments. See Milgrom and Roberts (1994).

8. Holmström and Milgrom (1994) and Holmström (1996) argue that the function of firms cannot be properly understood without considering additional incentive instruments that can serve as substitutes for outright ownership. Employees, for instance, typically own no assets, yet they often do work quite effectively. In these theories asset ownership gives access to many incentive instruments and the role of the firm is to coordinate the use of all of them. That may also explain why non-investing parties, including the firm itself, own assets.

9. This pattern, however, did not become standard until decades after the founding of the industry. Earlier, something akin to the practices associated now with the Japanese was the norm. See Helper (1991).

10. An alternative story is more in the line of Williamson's earlier discussions emphasizing inefficiencies in *ex post* bargaining. The useful life of a die far exceeds the one-year contracting period. If the supplier owned the die, changing suppliers would require negotiating the sale of the die to the new supplier, and this could be costly and inefficient.

11. Interestingly, Toyota followed U.S. practice in supplying the dies used by at least some of the suppliers to its Kentucky assembly plant (Milgrom and Roberts 1993).

12. Taylor and Wiggins (1997) argue that these long-term relations are also the means used in the Japanese system to solve moral hazard problems with respect to quality.

13. Baker *et al.* (1997) present a formal analysis of the choice between external and internal procurement, taking into account the important fact that long-term relational contracts can be maintained both within a firm as well as across firms.

14. Strikingly, as automobile electronics have become more sophisticated and a greater part of the cost of a car, Toyota has ceased to rely exclusively on its former sole supplier, Denso, and has developed its own in-house capabilities in this area. Arguably, this was to overcome information asymmetries and their associated costs (Ahmadjian and Lincoln 1997). In contrast, see the discussion of the effects of Ford's complete reliance on Lear for developing seats for the redesigned 1997 Taurus (Walton 1997).

15. See Segal and Whinston, 1997, for a model in the property rights spirit that is relevant to these issues.

16. For a further discussion of the idea that low-powered incentives are a major virtue of firm organization and can help explain firm boundaries, see Holmström (1996).

17. See Lutz (1995) for a formal model of franchising along these lines.

18. A hold-up story is consistent with the fact that the presence of repair services favors dealer ownership over leasing arrangements in the U.S. data: A lessee who invests in building a clientele for repair work might worry that the refining company will raise the lease payments to appropriate the returns from this investment. This argument, however, does not do much to explain the pattern in the Canadian data, where the refiners own all the stations. One might also attempt to apply this logic to the choice between company-owned and leased stations by arguing that if the company owns the station it cannot motivate the employee-manager to invest in building a clientele because it will appropriate all the returns. However, this argument is not compelling without explaining how firms in other industries succeed in motivating their employees to undertake similar investments.

19. See Aghion and Tirole (1997) for a model along these lines. In general, the role of firm boundaries in limiting interventions by more senior managers, thereby improving subordinates' incentives in various ways, has been a basic theme in the influence cost literature (Milgrom and Roberts 1990, Meyer *et al.* 1992).

20. In contrast, researchers outside economic theory have made much of the role of knowledge. See, for instance, Teece *et al.* (1994).

21. Stuckey (1983), in his extraordinary study of the aluminum industry, reports that knowledge transfer was an important driver of joint ventures.

22. See Halonen (1994) for a first modeling effort along these lines.

References

Aghion, Philippe, and Jean Tirole. 1997. Formal and Real Authority in Organizations. *Journal of Political Economy* 105: 1–27.

Ahmadjian, Christina, and James Lincoln. 1997. Changing Firm Boundaries in Japanese Auto Parts Supply Networks. Draft, Columbia Business School.

Andersen, Erin. 1985. The Salesperson as Outside Agent or Employee: A Transaction Cost Analysis. *Marketing Science* 4: 234–254.

Andersen, Erin, and David Schmittlein. 1984. Integration of the Sales Force: An Empirical Examination. *Rand Journal of Economics* 15: 385–395.

Arrow, Kenneth. 1975. Vertical Integration and Communication. *Bell Journal of Economics* 6: 173–182.

Asanuma, Banri. 1989. Manufacturer-Supplier Relationships in Japan and the Concept of Relation-Specific Skill. *The Journal of the Japanese and International Economies* 3: 1–30.

Asanuma, Banri. 1992. Japanese Manufacturer-Supplier Relationships in International Perspective. In Paul Sheard, ed., *International Adjustment and the Japanese Economy*. St. Leonards, Australia: Allen & Unwin.

Baker, George, Robert Gibbons, and Kevin J. Murphy. 1997. Relational Contracts and the Theory of the Firm. Draft, Massachusetts Institute of Technology.

Buttrick, John. 1952. The Inside Contracting System. *Journal of Economic History* 12: 205–221.

De Meza, David, and Ben Lockwood. 1998. Does Asset Ownership Always Motivate Managers? Outside Options and the Property Rights Theory of the Firm. *Quarterly Journal of Economics* 113 (2): 361–386.

Ghemawat, Pankaj. 1995. Competitive Advantage and Internal Organization: Nucor Revisited. *Journal of Economics and Management Strategy* 3: 685–717.

Grossman, Sanford, and Oliver Hart. 1986. The Costs and Benefits of Ownership: A Theory of Lateral and Vertical Integration. *Journal of Political Economy* 94: 691–719.

Grout, Paul. 1984. Investment and Wages in the Absence of Binding Contracts: A Nash Bargaining Approach. *Econometrica* 51: 449–460.

Halonen, Maija. 1994. Reputation and Allocation of Ownership. STICERD Theoretical Economics Discussion Paper, London School of Economics.

Hart, Oliver. 1995. *Firms, Contracts, and Financial Structure*. Oxford: Clarendon Press.

Hart, Oliver, and John Moore. 1990. Property Rights and the Nature of the Firm. *Journal of Political Economy* 98: 1119–1158.

Helper, Susan. 1991. Strategy and Irreversibility in Supplier Relations: The Case of the U.S. Automobile Industry. *Business History Review* 65: 781–824.

Holmström, Bengt. 1996. The Firm as a Subeconomy. Draft, Department of Economics, Massachusetts Institute of Technology.

Holmström, Bengt, and Paul Milgrom. 1991. Multitask Principal-Agent Analyses: Incentive Contracts, Asset Ownership, and Job Design. *Journal of Law, Economics, and Organization* 7: 24–51.

Holmström, Bengt, and Paul Milgrom. 1994. The Firm as an Incentive System. *American Economic Review* 84: 972–991.

Holmström, Bengt, and Jean Tirole. 1991. Transfer Pricing and Organizational Form. *Journal of Law, Economics, and Organization* 7 (2): 201–228.

Klein, Benjamin, Robert Crawford, and Armen Alchian. 1978. Vertical Integration, Appropriable Rents, and the Competitive Contracting Process. *Journal of Law and Economics* 21: 297–326.

LaFontaine, Francine, and Margaret Slade. 1997. Retail Contracting: Theory and Practice. *Journal of Industrial Economics* 45: 1–25.

Lutz, Nancy. 1995. Ownership Rights and Incentives in Franchising. *Journal of Corporate Finance* 2: 103–131.

Maness, Robert. 1996. Incomplete Contracts and the Choice between Vertical Integration and Franchising. *Journal of Economic Behavior and Organization* 32: 101–115.

Meyer, Margaret, Paul Milgrom, and John Roberts. 1992. Organizational Prospects, Influence Costs and Ownership Changes. *Journal of Economics and Management Strategy* 1 (1): 9–35.

Milgrom, Paul, and John Roberts. 1988. An Economic Approach to Influence Activities and Organizational Responses. *American Journal of Sociology* 94 (supplement): S154–S179.

Milgrom, Paul, and John Roberts. 1990. Bargaining Costs, Influence Costs and the Organization of Economic Activity. In J. Alt and K. Shepsle, eds., *Perspectives on Positive Political Economy*. Cambridge: Cambridge University Press, 57–89.

Milgrom, Paul, and John Roberts. 1992. *Economics, Organization and Management*. Englewood Cliffs, N.J.: Prentice-Hall.

Milgrom, Paul, and John Roberts. 1993. Johnson Controls, Inc. Automotive Systems Group: The Georgetown Kentucky Plant. Stanford Graduate School of Business, Case S-BE-9.

Milgrom, Paul, and John Roberts. 1994. Comparing Equilibria. *American Economic Review* 84: 441–459.

Monteverde, Kirk, and David Teece. 1982. Supplier Switching Costs and Vertical Integration in the Automobile Industry. *Bell Journal of Economics* 13: 206–213.

Powell, Walter. 1996. Inter-Organizational Collaboration in the Biotechnology Industry. *Journal of Institutional and Theoretical Economics* 152 (1): 197–215.

Rajan, Raghuram, and Luigi Zingales. 1998. Power in a Theory of the Firm. *Quarterly Journal of Economics* 113 (2): 387–432.

Scharfstein, David. 1998. The Dark Side of Internal Capital Markets II: Evidence from Diversified Conglomerates. NBER Working Paper No. 6352.

Segal, Ilya, and Michael Whinston. 1993. Exclusive Dealing and Protection of Investments. Draft, Department of Economics, University of California, Berkeley.

Shepard, Andrea. 1993. Contractual Form, Retail Price, and Asset Characteristics. *Rand Journal of Economics* 24: 58–77.

Shin, Hyun-Han, and Rene M. Stulz. 1998. Are Internal Capital Markets Efficient? *Quarterly Journal of Economics* 113 (2): 531–552.

Slade, Margaret. 1996. Multitask Agency and Contract Choice: An Empirical Assessment. *International Economic Review* 37: 465–486.

Stuckey, John. 1983. *Vertical Integration and Joint Ventures in the Aluminum Industry*. Cambridge, Mass.: Harvard University Press.

Taylor, Curtis, and Steven Wiggins. 1997. Competition or Compensation: Supplier Incentives Under the American and Japanese Subcontracting Systems. *American Economic Review* 87: 4, 598–618.

Teece, David, Richard Rumelt, Giovanni Dosi, and Sidney Winter. 1994. Understanding Corporate Coherence, Theory and Evidence. *Journal of Economic Behavior and Organization* 23: 1–30.

Walton, Mary. 1997. *Car: A Drama of the American Workplace*. New York: W.W. Norton.

Whinston, Michael. 1997. On the Transaction Cost Determinants of Vertical Integration. Draft, Department of Economics, Northwestern University.

Williamson, Oliver. 1975. *Markets and Hierarchies: Analysis and Antitrust Implications*. New York: Free Press.

Williamson, Oliver. 1979. Transaction-Cost Economics: The Governance of Contractual Relations. *Journal of Law and Economics* 22: 233–271.

Williamson, Oliver. 1985. *The Economic Institutions of Capitalism*. New York: Free Press.

3 Is Empowerment Just a Fad? Control, Decision Making, and IT

Thomas W. Malone

Are you stifling innovation and creativity by trying to micromanage? Or are you operating your organization as many autonomous fiefdoms and missing the benefits of being one company? Should you give more autonomy to the people who work for you? Or perhaps you feel you should take more control and show "real" leadership?

Nagging questions like these indicate that some of the most difficult problems for managers are those of exercising control. A central issue for organizations in the twenty-first century will be how to balance top-down control with bottom-up empowerment.[1] For example, recent business rhetoric has focused so much on the importance of "empowering" workers that the term has become an almost meaningless cliché. Is the talk of empowerment just a fad? Or are fundamental changes making decentralized control increasingly desirable?

Our research suggests that the dramatically decreasing costs of information technology (IT) are changing the economics of organizational decision making, with the result that decentralized control is becoming more desirable in many situations. Moreover, our very notions of centralization and decentralization may be incomplete. When most people talk about decentralized organizations and empowerment, they mean relatively timid shifts of power within a fairly conventional, hierarchical structure. But these forms of empowerment go only halfway toward what is possible. To fully exploit the possibilities of new information technologies, we need to expand our thinking and see radically decentralized organizations—the Internet, all kinds of markets, and scientific communities, for example—as new models for organizing work in the twenty-first century.

Our research also suggests that a simple pattern underlies many future changes. As improvements in technology reduce communication and coordination costs, the most desirable way to make decisions moves through three stages. In the first stage, when communication costs are high, the best way to make decisions is via *independent, decentralized* decision makers. In the course of history, most economic decisions have been made this way—by people in largely independent tribes, villages, and towns.

As communication costs fall, however, it becomes desirable in many situations to bring remote information together, where *centralized* decision makers can have a broad perspective and therefore make better decisions than isolated, local decision makers can. The economic history of the twentieth century has been largely the story of this centralizing of decision making in large, global corporations. And, for many kinds of decisions, companies can still derive substantial benefits from centralization.

As communication costs continue to fall, however, there comes a point in many decision-making situations at which *connected, decentralized* decision makers are more effective. These decision makers can combine the best information from anywhere in the world with their own local knowledge, energy, and creativity. As the economy becomes increasingly based on knowledge work and creative innovation, and as new technologies make it possible to connect decentralized decision makers on a bigger scale than ever before, exploiting such opportunities for empowerment will surely be an important theme in the economic history of the next century.

Of course, many factors other than communication costs affect centralization and decentralization in organizations. Patterns of interpersonal trust, locations of decision-relevant information, personal motivations, prior distributions of power within the organization, government regulations, national cultures, organizational traditions, and individual personalities are all important.[2] In fact, in any given situation at any given point in time, combinations of these other factors can be much more important than communication costs in determining where decisions are made. My goal in this article is not to analyze the complex question of how all these factors interact in particular situations. Instead I will focus on a simpler question: What is the relationship between reducing communication costs over time and the economics of different decision-making structures?

Understanding this relationship is important for three reasons. First, it helps us understand conceptually the economic effects of reduced communication costs if all other factors remain constant. Second, it provides a possible explanation for a variety of well-known facts, such as broad historical trends in organizational structures during the past century. Finally, to the degree you believe that reduced communication costs enabled by IT are likely to be important in the future, this work suggests an effect those changes are likely to have.[3] Whether this factor actually turns out to be important is uncertain, of course. But if relentless improvements in IT continue to reduce communication costs by a factor of ten every few years—as they have been doing—shifts toward more decentralized empowerment are likely to continue.

How Will IT Affect Centralization and Decentralization?

In 1958, Leavitt and Whisler predicted that IT would lead to the elimination of middle managers and to greater centralization of decision making.[4] Since then, many others have speculated about how IT will affect centralization and decentralization in organizations; over the years, numerous changes have occurred in both directions. In some cases, IT appears to have led to more centralization; in other cases, to more decentralization; in still others, it appears to have had no effect at all on centralization.[5] Previous research, therefore, gives no clear indication of IT's effect on centralization and decentralization.

Much of this confusion results from lumping together two kinds of decentralization. When we distinguish between decentralized control by unconnected (that is, independent) decision makers and decentralized control by connected decision makers, a clearer pattern emerges.[6] Our research suggests that unconnected, decentralized decision makers should be common when communication costs are high. When communication costs fall, centralized decision making becomes more desirable. When they fall still further, connected, decentralized decision making becomes desirable in many situations.

The logic of this progression is derived from two simple assumptions:

1. New information technologies will significantly reduce communication costs.

2. Each stage in this progression requires more communication than the previous one, and in many situations, each stage has some other advantages over the previous stage.

In an era of decreasing communication costs, therefore, eventually each stage will reach a point at which its other advantages will be more important than its (diminishing) communication cost disadvantage.

Explaining History

This simple logic explains some of the most salient aspects of this century's economic history. According to this interpretation, the dramatic rise of large organizations in the past 100 years was motivated partly by the economic benefits of centralized decision making. In many instances, centralized decision makers could integrate diverse kinds of remote information efficiently and thus make better decisions than the unconnected, local decision makers they superseded.[7] Centralized decision making itself was made economically feasible by advances in information technologies (not just computers and telephones but also television, radio, and other innovations). For much of this century, in fact, centralization was the only game in town. And many managers believe it still has significant benefits—witness the recent megamergers of Disney with ABC and Chemical Bank with Chase Manhattan.

In the latter part of the century, however, another kind of change is beginning to occur. Many companies are flattening their organizations by removing layers of middle managers. The remaining managers, who are often supervising significantly more people now than their predecessors did, are delegating more decisions to subordinates—the "empowerment" of the 1990s. More employees find themselves with increased responsibilities, and more managers act like coaches who help employees solve problems, rather than decision makers who issue commands and monitor compliance.

In another transformation, more work is coordinated outside the boundaries of traditional, hierarchical organizations. With large companies outsourcing noncore activities, in many industries, small companies have more important roles. Virtual corporations, networked organizations, and other shifting alliances of people and organizations are performing work that single, large organizations once handled.

Why are these changes happening? Making decisions closer to the point at which they are actually carried out ("closer to the customer," for example) has advantages and provides economic motivations for decentralizing decision making. In many kinds of work, people are more energetic and creative if they have autonomy in both how they work and what they do. Moreover, local decision makers frequently have access to information that helps them make good decisions (customers' unstated preferences, for example) but is difficult to communicate to central decision makers. Yet decentralized decision makers also need the kind of information that helps centralized decision makers make better decisions in the first place. It is precisely the communication of this large amount of information to much bigger groups of decision makers that IT now makes possible at a cost and on a scale never seen before.

Before examining this logic in detail, let's look at one example: the evolution of retailing, especially in small towns in the United States.

Revolution in Retailing

For most of this century, the majority of retail stores in small towns were owned and operated at local (or regional) levels. "Mom and pop" operations were common, not only as grocery stores and restaurants, but also as clothing, hardware, toy, and many other types of stores. Decision making in such enterprises was necessarily decentralized to the local level. Because there was no higher-level management, each local store owner made key decisions on pricing, promotions, and product selection. And, for the most part, store owners made these decisions without knowing what was happening in other stores outside their area. It was an era of largely unconnected, decentralized decision making.

Into this seemingly placid scene came Sam Walton and Wal-Mart. By centralizing pricing, buying, and promotional decisions on a national level, Wal-Mart was able to deliver better-quality products for lower prices than most of its competitors—with the result that small towns across the United States are now filled with the empty hulls of local retail stores, driven out of business by a Wal-Mart down the street. Other factors played a role, too, but a key factor that enabled Wal-Mart to centralize its decision making was IT. With its famous state-of-the-art electronic ordering and inventory control systems, for instance, Wal-Mart introduced a new level of connected, centralized decision making into small-town retailing.

Following the three-stage pattern I introduced earlier, we might expect that some decisions would return eventually to local store managers. This has occurred, but with a big difference: Local managers now have access to national sales data and other information to help them make decisions. For example, Wal-Mart store managers have considerable autonomy in allocating space and ordering stock. Also, even though most pricing is done centrally, Wal-Mart identifies about 500 to 600 price-sensitive items for which local store managers can set their own prices, depending on what local competitors are doing.[8] Thus it appears that the next wave in retailing may already be happening at Wal-Mart: local managers using global information to make more decentralized decisions. As Wal-Mart's CIO put it: "I think the challenge . . . is to enable a chain as big as Wal-Mart to act like a hometown store, even while it maintains its economies of scale."[9]

An even more decentralized form of retailing is emerging on the Internet. Almost anyone can now set up a retail sales operation on the Internet and immediately have access to customers worldwide. Picture-Phone Direct, a mail-order reseller of desktop video-conferencing equipment, is one example. "When we started our business," reported founder Jeremy Goldstein, "we thought we would concentrate on the northeastern United States. But when we put our catalog on the Internet, we got orders from Israel, Portugal, and Germany. All of a sudden, we were a global company." Another example is the Internet Underground Music Archive; its Internet site provides music samples and information about hundreds of bands and soon expects to sell compact discs on-line for home delivery. The company's rationale, in part, is to provide a distribution channel for musicians whose work is not sold in mainstream music stores such as Tower Records.

In these examples, "local" retailers make their own decisions, without supervision from any national chain or any need to appeal to a mass market. Moreover, initially small retailers have access to global markets and thus the potential to expand rapidly and dramatically.

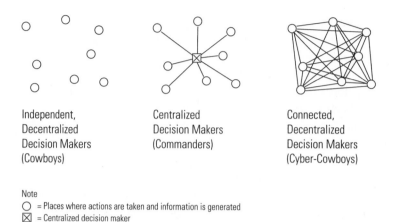

Independent,   Centralized   Connected,
Decentralized   Decision Makers   Decentralized
Decision Makers   (Commanders)   Decision Makers
(Cowboys)   (Cyber-Cowboys)

Note
○ = Places where actions are taken and information is generated
⊠ = Centralized decision maker

Figure 3.1
Three Decision-Making Structures

Factors Leading to Centralization and Decentralization

Why should the pattern I have suggested occur? To better understand my reasoning, it helps to look at the basic information flows for making decisions in different kinds of organizations.

Types of Decision-Making Structures

There are three basic types of decision-making structures: *independent, decentralized decision makers*; *centralized decision makers*; and *connected, decentralized decision makers* (see figure 3.1). For simplicity, I call them "cowboys," "commanders," and "cyber-cowboys."

Cowboys   By definition, independent, decentralized decision makers have relatively low needs for communication. Alone on a horse, a cowboy must make independent decisions based only on what he can see and hear in his immediate environment. Similarly, when local store managers set prices by using only the information available to them locally, they don't need nationwide information systems or long-distance telephone conversations. Independent, local banks make their own loan decisions; they don't need to confer with a national headquarters before approving a loan. Individual farmers who make their own decisions about planting and harvesting don't need to communicate with anyone else either.

The price these independent decision makers pay for simplicity of decision making, however, is that their decisions are relatively uninformed. They don't know what is happening elsewhere; they aren't learning from the experiences of people in other places; and they can't easily pool resources or take advantage of economies of scale.

Commanders   Centralized decision makers, on the other hand, have significantly higher communication needs. A military commander who wants to intelligently control troops from a distance needs information from scouts, the battlefield, and other sources. Likewise, "commanders" in companies need information from diverse sources to make informed decisions. For instance, the people who make decisions on national Wal-Mart prices need sales histories for the products they are pricing and detailed information about consumer tastes. Similarly, if a national bank sets its loan policies or advertising strategies at headquarters, it should communicate with local branches in order to do it well.

An obvious advantage of centralized decision making is that, with more information, people can often make better decisions. Managers can test pricing or promotion experiments in a few stores and use the results in others. They can share best practices among stores, identify the best suppliers, and capture economies of scale. Regional managers at Wal-Mart, for instance, share stories every week. As Sam Walton commented, "If they've been to that Panama City Beach store and seen a suntan cream display that's blowing the stuff out the door, they can share that with the other regionals for their beach stores."[10]

In some cases, new technologies make it possible for individualized, local decisions to be made at a national level. For example, until a few years ago, Mervyn's grouped its local stores into a dozen categories based on sales volume, then distributed inventory based on averages for the categories.[11] The problem with this approach was that individual stores varied greatly in the sizes and colors they sold. Some stores sold a lot of black jeans, while others needed traditional blue. To cope with these dilemmas, Mervyn's implemented a highly successful, centralized system that distributes to each store a mix of products, sizes, and colors matched precisely to local sales.

Cyber-Cowboys   Connected, decentralized decision makers generally require even more communication than centralized ones. I call them cyber-cowboys because they make autonomous decisions, but based on potentially vast amounts of remote information available through electronic or other networks. These decentralized decision makers sometimes cooperate with each other; other times they compete. In any case, relevant information needs to be brought not just to one central point but to all the decentralized decision makers.

Edward D. Jones & Co., a retail brokerage firm based in St. Louis, has 3,100 sales representatives nationwide reporting directly to the national head of sales. This very flat organization makes heavy use of IT. For instance, sales reps update files and download new product information from computers in St. Louis and call head-quarters frequently with client problems and questions. They are also in almost daily contact with headquarters via the company's television network, a direct link for new product information, training, motivation, and corporate culture.[12]

One aspect of this sales force structure is its highly motivated people. "The kind of people we attract are self-starters, entrepreneurial, type A personalities, the type who might otherwise be running their own businesses," says Doug Hill, head of sales and marketing, who provides product training and support to the sales force.[13] And what about quotas? "I don't have any quotas," says one sales rep. "I have a prof-itability responsibility for this territory." At Edward D. Jones, IT has enabled sig-nificant decentralization of decision-making authority while retaining the benefits of global information sharing.

More extreme examples of connected, decentralized decision making occur all the time in the interactions among buyers and sellers in a market. Whenever a company chooses to buy a product or a service from an outside supplier, rather than manufacture it internally, for example, it is using the decentralized structure of the marketplace, rather than its own hierarchical structure to coordinate production. In many cases, such market-based structures are cheaper, faster, or more flexible than internal production. For instance, two entrepreneurs compared the advantages of the vendor network in Silicon Valley with those of the larger, more vertically inte-grated firms on Massachusetts's Route 128:

"One of the things that Silicon Valley lets you do is minimize the costs associated with getting from idea to product. Vendors here can handle everything. If you specify something—or, as is often the case, if the vendor helps you specify it—you can get hardware back so fast that your time-to-market is incredibly short."[14] "There is a huge supply of contract labor—far more than on Route 128. If you want to design your own chips, there are a whole lot of people around who just do contract chip layout and design. You want mechanical design? It's here. There's just about any-thing you want in this infrastructure."[15]

By making potential markets larger and more efficient, IT can greatly increase the desirability of buying—rather than making—more and more things.[16] In the 1980s, for instance, computerized airline reservation systems allowed airline companies to outsource much of their sales function to independent travel agents. Today, there are on-line markets for all kinds of products—from electronic parts to insurance to consumer appliances. These markets are allowing decentralized decision makers in many autonomous companies to participate in global markets, with access to knowledge and customers from all over the world.

Factors Affecting Where Decisions Are Made

Many factors affect how decision-making power is distributed in organizations: government regulations, national cultures, organizational traditions, and individual personalities, to name a few. Three factors, however—*decision information*, *trust*, and *motivation*—are especially important in determining the economic desirability of making decisions in different places. Let's look at how IT relates to these three factors.

Decision Information   Making good decisions requires information. I have discussed how different decision-making situations have different needs for information. By reducing communication costs, IT makes structures that require more communication feasible where they would be impossible otherwise.

IT also makes distance less important in determining where decisions should be made by bringing information to decision makers wherever they are. But this does not mean that all decisions can be made anywhere with equal effectiveness. Some people are better at making certain decisions than others, and some kinds of information are inherently easier to communicate than others. A field salesperson can easily communicate the dollar volume of her sales last month, for example; she finds it much harder to communicate her sense—based on years of experience—of what kinds of new products customers want. It is easy to communicate the temperature of a container in a chemical refinery; it is hard to communicate the chemical reasoning for why a certain temperature is necessary. In general, information is easier to communicate if it is already explicit in some way—already written down, for example, or expressed in quantitative form. Information is more difficult to communicate—or "sticky"—if it is based on someone's experience or on implicit, qualitative impressions.[17]

One implication is that companies should use IT to bring decisions to where the most important sticky information is located. Or, to put it another way, companies should use IT to bring easily communicable information (financial data, news reports, and so forth) to people who have knowledge, experience, or capabilities that are hard to communicate (customer understanding, technical competence, or interpersonal skills).

Trust If I don't trust you, I don't want you to make decisions on my behalf. That very human attitude means that centralized decision makers will avoid delegating important decisions to local decision makers, and if they have to, they will try to control or monitor the local decision makers as much as possible.[18]

IT can increase trust (or deal with the lack of it) in several ways:

1. IT can make remote decision makers more effective. For example, Mrs. Fields Cookies can hire very young, inexperienced employees in its stores partly because it has centrally developed software that helps manage store operations at a very detailed level. The software helps determine quantities of ingredients and baking schedules based on seasonally and locally adjusted sales projections. It even suggests when store managers should go outside with free samples to entice customers.[19]

2. IT can help control and monitor remote decision makers more effectively. Several years ago, Otis Elevator Company replaced its decentralized service system with a centralized one, so trouble calls bypassed the field service offices. This allowed executives to spot a number of chronically malfunctioning elevators whose poor records had been buried for years in field-office files.[20]

3. IT can help socialize remote decision makers and engender loyalty. Edward D. Jones managers use the company's business television network to inculcate feelings of corporate identity and team spirit. By enabling personal contacts over long distances, electronic communication technologies (from telephones to e-mail to video-conferencing) can also inspire a spirit of community and a sense of loyalty in geographically dispersed organizations.[21]

Of course, not all such uses of IT are desirable in all situations, but they illustrate how IT can help increase trust or deal with the lack of it.[22] For example, IT can help central decision makers trust the local decision makers to implement their decisions more faithfully, or to make more decisions themselves. In that way, IT helps centralized systems become more decentralized. On the other hand, if a system is so decentralized that local decision makers make the major decisions, then IT can help local decision makers trust central decision makers (such as their centralized suppliers) more. In cases like that, IT enables more centralized systems, with some important decisions "delegated" to central decision makers.

Overall, therefore, the factor of trust leads to ambiguous predictions about the effects of IT on centralization. With regard to trust, IT can either increase or decrease centralization. In general, IT should lead to more mixed systems, with some important decisions made by central decision makers and others by local decision makers.

Motivation   The kind of energy and creativity that people bring to their work often depends on who makes the decisions about what they will do. For certain kinds of work (highly routine or purely physical work, for example), people may work harder when others tell them what to do. But, in general, a big factor that makes jobs more enjoyable is some degree of autonomy.[23] When people make their own decisions about how to do their work and how to allocate their time, they usually enjoy their jobs more and put more energy and creativity into their work. An important part of entrepreneurial motivation, for instance, is not just that you get to keep the rewards of your work but also that you make your own decisions.

Increased motivation, then, is one advantage of decentralizing decisions (and rewards) to local decision makers. Increased motivation, in turn, often leads to higher quality and more creativity in what people do. As more work becomes knowledge work and as innovation becomes increasingly critical to business success, this factor probably will become more important. Because IT can enable either more centralized or more decentralized systems, its effect on motivation is ambiguous.

How the Factors Work Together

The characteristics of different situations that are likely to make centralization or decentralization desirable can be used as a kind of checklist to decide which kind of decision making is desirable in a given situation (see table 3.1). Of all three factors, decision information has the clearest implications for costs and benefits. (table 3.2 summarizes the relative costs and benefits of the three different decision-making structures.) In general, cowboys should incur the lowest communication costs because they do the least communicating, followed by commanders, then cyber-cowboys. In addition, both commanders and cyber-cowboys enjoy the benefits of remote information, whereas cowboys do not.

The costs of the other two factors, trust and motivation, are more situation-dependent. The costs of lack of trust do not depend primarily on the type of decision-making structure but on how extensively important decisions are delegated. Similarly, the costs resulting from lack of motivation, initiative, and creativity depend on the kind of work being done. Because they are somewhat ambiguous, I have included these other two factors as part of the uncertainty concerning "all other costs." That category might also include the costs of actually making decisions (for example, the cost of salaries for decision makers) and the costs of economies of scale (or the lack thereof) that are realized by a particular decision-making structure.

How do these different kinds of costs trade off against each other for different decisions? Let's look first at the two dimensions about which we have the least ambiguity: (1) the value of the remote decision information used (that is, the cost of

Table 3.1
Choosing Centralization or Decentralization

Factor	Centralization is desirable when . . .	Decentralization is desirable when . . .
Decision information	Using remote information is valuable in decision making, and the information can be communicated to central decision makers at moderate cost	Local decision makers have access to important information that cannot be easily communicated to central decision makers *or* Remote information is not valuable in local decisions making *or* Remote information is valuable in decision making and is very inexpensive to communicate
Trust	Central decision makers don't want to (or cannot) trust local decision makers for important decisions	Local decision makers don't want to (or cannot) trust central decision makers for important decisions
Motivation	Local decision makers work harder or better when told what to do by someone else (likely to be less common in the future)	Local decision makers work harder or better when they make decisions for themselves (likely to be more common in the future)

Table 3.2
Costs of Various Decision-Making Structures

Decision-Making Structure	Costs of Communicating Remote Decision Information	Benefits of Considering Remote Decision Information	All Other Costs (Trust, Motivation, etc.)
Independent, Decentralized (Cowboys)	Low	Low	?
Centralized (Commanders)	Medium	High	?
Connected, Decentralized (Cyber-Cowboys)	High	High	?

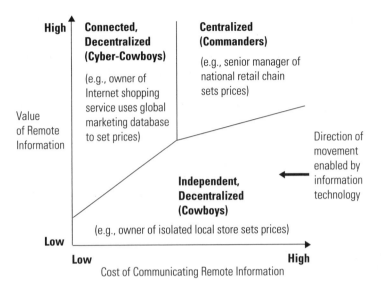

Figure 3.2
Desirable Decision-Making Structures for Different Kinds of Decisions

not considering it) and (2) the costs of communicating the remote decision information. Any decision can be plotted on a graph, depending on the average value of the remote information available and the average costs of communicating that information (see figure 3.2). For different regions of the graph, different decision-making structures are desirable. Of course, the exact shapes and locations of the regions depend on the nature of the various costs in the different decision-making structures. But the shapes and relative positions of the regions, shown in figure 3.2, follow mathematically from the assumptions in table 3.2, with one additional assumption: that the other costs of the cyber-cowboys are less than those of the commanders.[24]

That additional assumption would be true, for instance, in any situation in which the motivational advantages of having entrepreneurial, local decision makers make autonomous decisions are important. These motivational factors are usually important in all kinds of management situations and in most knowledge work (sales, marketing, finance, product development, and consulting). They are even important in many physical jobs, such as assembly line work, when creativity and innovation are valuable. This additional assumption would also be true whenever local decision makers have important information that is sticky (hard to communicate), such as knowing what customers really want or understanding subtle but critical aspects of new technologies.

If the "other costs" of cyber-cowboys are higher than the costs of commanders, however, then cyber-cowboys are never desirable, and the commanders' region extends all the way to the vertical axis. For instance, if the local decision makers are very unskilled, such as the young workers in Mrs. Fields stores, then it may never be desirable to decentralize some decisions.

In using figure 3.2, we see that decisions in which remote information is too expensive to communicate relative to its value for decision making should generally be left to local cowboys who already have the information. Even in centralized, national retail chains, for instance, local store managers usually decide whom to hire as clerks. But if the remote information is valuable enough, it may be worth paying significant communication costs to transmit it somewhere else for decision making. Accounting information about the amount of money received and spent in each store, for example, is of significant value in many kinds of business decisions and is almost always communicated elsewhere, whether for centralized decision making in a single place or decentralized decision making in multiple places.

IT and the Evolution of Centralization

The recognition that an important effect of IT is to reduce the costs of communicating many kinds of information produces a key insight (see figure 3.2). In general, we can expect decisions to move gradually leftward in the figure as the unit costs decline for communicating the information that people use. Thus the graph suggests that many decisions will pass through a stage of being centralized before eventually moving to a structure with decentralized, connected decision makers.

This progression will not always occur. For instance, in situations in which the remote information is of only moderate value (and the other costs of centralized control are high), we might see a transition from the cowboy structure directly to cyber-cowboy. Instead of creating a chain of their own local truck-repair shops, for example, Caterpillar developed a PC-based service that lets independent truck-repair shops use a national database of repair histories for individual truck engines.[25] Similarly, in situations where the remote information is even less valuable (and the costs of connected, decentralized decision making are also relatively high), the cowboy structure may be the most desirable, even when communication costs become zero. In the same way, if the other costs of cyber-cowboys are higher than those of commanders, then the cyber-cowboys would never be desirable and would not even appear on the graph.

In general, however, decreasing communication costs leads to movement along the path described when local decisions can be significantly improved with remote information and when either or both of the following are true:

1. Local decisions can be significantly improved by considering local information that is sticky or hard to communicate.

2. Local decision makers are significantly more enthusiastic, committed, and creative when they have more autonomy in their work.

While not true for all important decisions, these conditions appear to be true for many. Therefore, we can expect a significant long-term migration along the path described.

Radically Decentralized Organizations

When people talk about decentralization and empowerment, they usually mean delegating decisions to a lower level in a hierarchy. But what if power isn't delegated to lower levels but instead originates there? How much energy and creativity might be unlocked if all people in an organization feel in control? This more radical kind of decentralization may become more important in the future.

In a free market, for instance, no one at the top delegates decisions about what to buy or sell to the different players. Instead, a buyer and a seller can exchange almost anything on which they mutually agree (subject to their financial constraints and their abilities). The marvel of how overall coherence emerges from these countless decisions between two parties is what Adam Smith called the "invisible hand" of the market.

A similar kind of radical decentralization comes from the notion of *subsidiarity*. This principle of social philosophy, derived from Roman Catholic teaching, holds that any task should be performed in the smallest possible unit: for example, at the local level before the regional level, and at the regional level before the national level. The principle of subsidiarity is increasingly viewed as desirable for political organizations (for example, in the European Community) and in business organizations.[26]

In essence, this principle turns the whole notion of delegation upside down. Instead of all legitimate power being derived from the top of an organization and delegated down, all legitimate power originates at the bottom and is delegated up only when there are benefits in doing so.

The Decentralization Continuum

To understand these ideas more precisely, consider the following two dimensions of centralization: (1) Who makes the most important decisions?, and (2) Who can overrule the decisions made by others? We can use these two dimensions to develop a

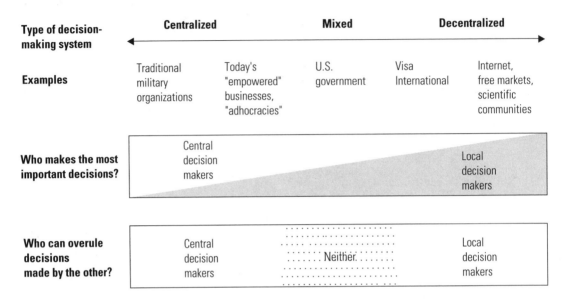

Type of decision-making system	Centralized		Mixed		Decentralized
Examples	Traditional military organizations	Today's "empowered" businesses, "adhocracies"	U.S. government	Visa International	Internet, free markets, scientific communities
Who makes the most important decisions?	Central decision makers				Local decision makers
Who can overrule decisions made by the other?	Central decision makers		Neither		Local decision makers

Figure 3.3
The Decentralization Continuum

decentralization continuum ranging from highly centralized systems at one end to highly decentralized systems at the other (see figure 3.3). (Of course, it is possible to have other combinations of these two factors, but most real-world examples fall somewhere along this continuum.)

In highly centralized systems, for example, central decision makers make most of the important decisions and can overrule most other decisions that they delegate to local decision makers. Traditional military organizations, for example, embody an extreme form of centralized control; high-ranking officers make all important decisions for their troops and can overrule their subordinates' most trivial decisions.[27] On the other hand, in highly decentralized systems, local decision makers make most of the important decisions and can overrule most decisions that they delegate to the central decision makers. For instance, Internet users can communicate however they want with other users, as long as their computers follow the standard protocols (or interconnection procedures) that the Internet governing boards have approved. A subgroup of users can even create a new protocol.

In between these two extremes are mixed systems, in which both central and local decision makers make some important decisions, and in which each makes certain decisions that cannot be overruled by the other. The U.S. Constitution, for instance, spells out a mixed system of relationships between the federal government and the state governments in which each has certain important powers that the other cannot overrule.

Most discussions about empowerment stop halfway, at the middle of the decentralization continuum. By definition, you cannot empower someone unless you have the right to make or overrule the decisions you are delegating. But radical decentralization is not something that people at the top do for people at the bottom; it is something that starts at the bottom.

Visa International An example of a radically decentralized organization in which the ultimate power rises from the bottom is Visa, whose users are its owners. Dee Hock, Visa founder, calls this company an "inverted holding company." Rather than one company that owns numerous others, Visa is a company owned by the banks and other institutions that issue Visa cards. They are simultaneously its owners and its customers. In many cases, they are also its suppliers.

The Visa organization was consciously designed as a "federal" system and includes a series of regional, national, and international organizations, each with its own members and board of directors.[28] Each organizational level receives its power from the levels below rather than from above. Decisions are made by votes at the various board levels, typically with a sixty- to ninety-day cycle for an issue to pass through all levels. For instance, Visa members have voted on a service charge to themselves for all Visa transactions and certain other transaction fees for processing services, if they choose to use them. However, the member organizations are free to use any Visa product, to leave the whole Visa organization if they so choose, and to offer competing products. (In fact, most banks offer the primary competing product, Mastercard.)

While such a highly decentralized structure would be inefficient for some purposes, it has been extremely successful for Visa. In the approximately twenty years since its founding, Visa has become a global organization with more than 23,000 member institutions, 300 million customers, and a $650 billion annual sales volume. More important, this decentralized structure has been able to provide essential centralized services (such as a global transaction clearinghouse and global brand management) for members that are, in many cases, direct competitors. From this fundamentally decentralized structure, therefore, a very successful global organization has emerged.

The Internet An even more extreme example of a decentralized structure is the Internet, which has no ownership relationships at all. The Internet has been doubling in size every year since 1988 and now has more than 30 million users. Clearly the Internet (or communication networks like it) will have a profound effect on how electronic commerce—and business, in general—is conducted in the next century. But in addition to being a technological enabler of other organizations, the Internet's technical architecture and governance structure themselves provide models for structuring highly decentralized organizations.

For example, no one is in charge of the Internet, and everyone is. No one, for instance, can unilaterally decide to shut the Internet down or deny access to any particular person or organization. Instead, anyone who follows the agreed-on rules for communicating on the Internet can connect to any other node and thus be connected to the entire worldwide network. And anyone who is connected to the network can be a service provider or a service user connected to anyone else. In the rare cases when Internet protocols need to be changed, a combination of elected and volunteer boards approves them. In addition, any group of users that wants to experiment with new protocols is free to do so. In fact, new protocols that the Internet boards adopt are generally accepted only after they have been widely— and successfully—used in experiments. The role of the "center" (that is, the standards boards) is simply to establish the framework through which its "members" interact—not to tell them what to do.

It is easy to imagine Internet-like principles being used in other kinds of organizations. For instance, even though global consulting firms such as McKinsey & Company are mixed organizations overall, they have structures that use some Internet-like principles. McKinsey has established a strong organizational culture that includes norms about selecting and promoting people and expectations for working with others. But its management does not tell individual partners what kind of work to do, which clients to work for, or which people to select for their teams. Instead, the partners make largely autonomous decisions about what they will do and how they will do it. When it works well, this highly decentralized effort—within the overall interaction framework that the firm provides—results in an extremely flexible, global organization.

Conclusion

Empowerment is currently one of the most popular business buzzwords. But is it just a fad? Will it soon pass the way of countless other business trends? The logic in this article shows why greater decentralization in business is not just a fad but a response to fundamental changes in the economics of decision making enabled by new information technologies. Of course, decentralization may never occur in some cases, and greater centralization may occur before increased decentralization in others. But in the knowledge-based economy that is emerging, globally connected, decentralized decision makers will play increasingly important roles. Figuring out how to design effective decentralized systems and how to manage the continually shifting balance between empowerment and control will not be easy. But I believe that mastering this challenge will be one of the most important differences between organizations that succeed in the next century and those that fail.

Acknowledgements

This chapter is reprinted with permission from *Sloan Management Review* 38, no. 2 (Winter 1997), 23–36. An earlier version was presented at the Harvard Business School Colloquium on "Multimedia and the Boundaryless World" to be published in S. P. Bradley and R. L. Nolan, eds., *Multimedia and the Boundaryless World*, Boston: Harvard Business School Press, 1997. Portions were also included in a presentation at the International Conference on Information Systems, G. M. Wyner and T. W. Malone, "Cowboys or Commanders: Does Information Technology Lead to Decentralization?," in Cleveland, Ohio, December 15–18, 1996. The author acknowledges the support of the MIT Center for Coordination Science and the MIT Initiative on Inventing the Organizations of the 21st Century, the excellent research assistance of Andrea Meyer, and helpful conversations with George Wyner, Erik Brynjolfsson, Art Kleiner, and Albert Wenger.

Notes

1. See, for example, Johansen, Saveri, and Schmid 1995.

2. See, for example, DiMaggio and Powell 1983; Galbraith 1991; Huber and McDaniel 1986; Markus 1983; Schein 1985; Scott 1992; Thompson 1967.

3. Our model is particularly intriguing in this regard because, unlike previous models (for example, Gurbaxani and Whang 1991), ours shows how a simple model can explain changes in both directions while nevertheless predicting a broad change in one direction in the long run.

4. Leavitt and Whisler 1958.

5. For summaries of previous research, see, for example, Attewell and Rule 1984; George and King 1991.

6. For a previous paper that makes this distinction, see Anand and Mendelson 1995.

7. See, for example, Chandler 1977.

8. Stevenson 1994; see also Anand and Mendelson 1995.

9. Fox 1994.

10. Walton and Huey 1993.

11. Dvorak, Dean, and Singer 1994.

12. Keenan 1994.

13. Ibid.

14. Denend 1994.

15. J. Kalb, quoted in Saxenian 1994, x.

16. See, for example, Malone, Yates, and Benjamin 1987.

17. von Hippel 1994.

18. For useful discussions of these issues, see, for example, Jensen and Meckling 1973; Gurbaxani and Whang 1991.

19. Richman 1987.

20. Stoddard 1986; see also Bruns and McFarlan 1987.

21. Keenan 1994.

22. For a description of how electronic and other communications media are used in different ways, see Daft and Lengel 1986.

23. See, for example, Hackman and Oldham 1980.

24. The mathematical proof of this result is given in Wyner and Malone 1996.

25. Sullivan 1995.

26. See, for example, Handy 1992.

27. Interestingly, even military organizations are now moving away from this extreme form of centralization. See, for example, Smith 1994.

28. See, for example, Breuner 1995; Nocera 1994.

References

Anand, K. S., and H. Mendelson. 1995. *Information and Organization for Horizontal Multimarket Coordination*. Stanford University, Graduate School of Business, Research Paper 1359.

Attewell, P., and J. Rule. 1984. Computing and Organizations: What We Know and What We Don't Know. *Communications of the ACM* 17: 1184–1192.

Breuner, E. F. 1995. Complexity and Organizational Structure: Internet and Visa International as Prototypes for the Corporation of the Future. MIT Sloan School of Management, unpublished master's thesis.

Bruns, W. J., and F. W. McFarlan. 1987. Information Technology Puts Power in Control Systems. *Harvard Business Review* 65 (September–October): 89–94.

Chandler, A. D., Jr. 1977. *The Visible Hand*. Cambridge, Mass.: Belknap Press.

Daft, R. L., and R. H. Lengel. 1986. Organizational Information Requirements, Media Richness and Structural Design. *Management Science* 32: 554–571.

Denend, L. 1994. 3Com Corp. In *Regional Advantage: Culture and Competition in Silicon Valley and Route 128*, by A Saxenian. Cambridge, Mass.: Harvard University Press.

DiMaggio, P. J., and W. W. Powell. 1983. The Iron Cage Revisited: Institutional Isomorphism and Collective Rationality in Organizational Field. *American Sociological Review* 48 (April): 147–160.

Dvorak, R., D. Dean, and M. Singer. 1994. Accelerating IT Innovation. *McKinsey Quarterly* 4: 123–135.

Fox, B. 1994. Staying on Top at Wal-Mart. *Chain Store Age Executive* 70 (April): 47.

Galbraith, J. R. 1977. *Organization Design*. Reading, Mass.: Addison-Wesley.

George, J. F., and J. L. King. 1991. Examining the Computing and Centralization Debate. *Communications of the ACM* 34 (July): 63–72.

Gurbaxani, V., and S. Whang. 1991. The Impact of Information Systems on Organizations and Markets. *Communications of the ACM* 34 (January): 59–73.

Hackman, J. R., and G. Oldham. 1980. *Work Redesign*. Reading, Mass.: Addison-Wesley.

Handy, C. 1992. Balancing Corporate Power: A New Federalist Paper. *Harvard Business Review* 70 (November–December): 59–73.

Huber, G. P., and R. R. McDaniel. 1986. The Decision-Making Paradigm of Organizational Design. *Management Science* 32: 572–589.

Johansen, B., A. Saveri, and G. Schmid. 1995. *21st Century Organizations: Reconciling Control and Empowerment*. Menlo Park, Calif.: Institute for the Future.

Jensen, M. C., and W. H. Meckling. 1973. Theory of the Firm: Managerial Behavior, Agency Costs, and Ownership Structure. *Journal of Financial Economics* 3: 305–360.

Keenan, Jr., W. 1994. Death of the Sales Manager. *Sales and Marketing Management* 146 (October): 66.

Leavitt, H. J., and T. L. Whisler. 1958. Management in the 1980s. *Harvard Business Review* 36 (November–December): 41–48.

Malone, T. W., J. Yates, and R. I. Benjamin. 1987. Electronic Markets and Electronic Hierarchies. *Communications of the ACM* 30 (June): 484–497.

Markus, M. L. 1983. Power, Politics, and MIS Implementation. *Communications of the ACM* 26 (June): 430–444.

Nocera, J. 1994. *A Piece of the Action*. New York: Simon & Schuster.

Richman, T. 1987. Mrs. Fields' Secret Ingredient. *Inc.* 9 (October): 65–72.

Saxenian, A. 1994. *Regional Advantage: Culture and Competition in Silicon Valley and Route 128*. Cambridge, Mass.: Harvard University Press.

Schein, E. H. 1985. *Organizational Culture and Leadership*. San Francisco: Jossey-Bass.

Scott, W. R. 1992. *Organizations: Rational, Natural, and Open Systems*. 3d ed. Englewood Cliffs, N.J.: Prentice-Hall.

Smith, L. 1994. New Ideas from the Army (Really). *Fortune*, September 19, 203–212.

Stevenson, M. 1994. The Store to End All Stores. *Canadian Business Review* 67 (May): 20–29.

Stoddard, D. 1986. Otisline. Harvard Business School, Case 9–186–304.

Sullivan, D. 1995. On the Road Again. *CIO Magazine*, January, 50–52.

Thompson, J. D. 1967. *Organizations in Action*. New York: McGraw-Hill.

von Hippel, E. 1994. Sticky Information and the Locus of Problem Solving: Implications for Innovation. *Management Science* 40: 429–439.

Walton, S., and J. Huey. 1993. *Sam Walton: Made in America*. New York: Bantam Books.

Wyner, G. M., and T. W. Malone. 1996. Cowboys or Commanders: Does Information Technology Lead to Decentralization? Cleveland, Ohio: Proceedings of the International Conference on Information Systems.

4 Beyond Computation: Information Technology, Organizational Transformation, and Business Performance

Erik Brynjolfsson and Lorin M. Hitt

How do computers contribute to business performance and economic growth?

Even today, most people who are asked to identify the strengths of computers tend to think of computational tasks like rapidly multiplying large numbers. Computers have excelled at computation since the Mark I (1939), the first modern computer, and the ENIAC (1943), the first electronic computer without moving parts. During World War II, the U.S. government generously funded research into tools for calculating the trajectories of artillery shells. The result was the development of some of the first digital computers with remarkable capabilities for calculation—the dawn of the computer age.

However, computers are not fundamentally number crunchers. They are symbol processors. The same basic technologies can be used to store, retrieve, organize, transmit, and algorithmically transform any type of information that can be digitized—numbers, text, video, music, speech, programs, and engineering drawings, to name a few. This is fortunate because most problems are not numerical problems. Ballistics, code breaking, parts of accounting, and bits and pieces of other tasks involve lots of calculation. But the everyday activities of most managers, professionals, and information workers involve other types of thinking. As computers become cheaper and more powerful, the business value of computers is limited less by computational capability, and more by the ability of managers to invent new processes, procedures, and organizational structures that leverage this capability. As this form of innovation continues to develop, the applications of computers are expected to expand well beyond computation for the foreseeable future.

The fundamental economic role of computers becomes clearer if one thinks about organizations and markets as information processors (Galbraith 1977, Simon 1976, Hayek 1945). Most of our economic institutions and intuitions emerged in an era of relatively high communications costs, limited computational capability, and related constraints. Information technology (IT), defined as computers as well as related digital communication technology, has the broad power to reduce the costs of coordination, communications, and information processing. Thus, it is not surprising that the massive reduction in computing and communications costs has engendered a substantial restructuring of the economy. Most modern industries are being significantly affected by computerization.

Information technology is best described not as a traditional capital investment, but as a "general purpose technology" (Bresnahan and Trajtenberg 1995). In most cases, the economic contributions of general purpose technologies are substantially

larger than would be predicted by simply multiplying the quantity of capital investment devoted to them by a normal rate of return. Instead, such technologies are
economically beneficial mostly because they facilitate complementary innovations.

Earlier general purpose technologies, such as the telegraph, the steam engine, and
the electric motor, illustrate a pattern of complementary innovations that eventually leads to dramatic productivity improvements. Some of the complementary
innovations were purely technological, such as Marconi's "wireless" version of
telegraphy. However, some of the most interesting and productive developments
were organizational innovations. For example, the telegraph facilitated the formation of geographically dispersed enterprises (Milgrom and Roberts 1990); while the
electric motor provided industrial engineers more flexibility in the placement
of machinery in factories, dramatically improving manufacturing productivity by
enabling workflow redesign (David 1990). The steam engine was at the root of a
broad cluster of technological and organizational changes that helped ignite the first
industrial revolution.

In this paper, we review the evidence on how investments in IT are linked to
higher productivity and organizational transformation, with emphasis on studies
conducted at the firm level. Our central argument is twofold: first, that a significant
component of the value of IT is its ability to enable complementary organizational
investments such as business processes and work practices; second, that these investments, in turn, lead to productivity increases by reducing costs and, more importantly, by enabling firms to increase output quality in the form of new products
or in improvements in intangible aspects of existing products like convenience,
timeliness, quality, and variety.[1]

There is substantial evidence from both the case literature on individual firms and
multi-firm econometric analyses supporting both these points, which we review and
discuss in the first half of this paper. This emphasis on firm-level evidence stems in
part from our own research focus but also because firm-level analysis has significant measurement advantages for examining intangible organizational investments
and product and service innovation associated with computers.

Moreover, as we argue in the latter half of the paper, these factors are not well
captured by traditional macroeconomic measurement approaches. As a result,
the economic contributions of computers are likely to be understated in aggregate-
level analyses. Placing a precise number on this bias is difficult, primarily because
of issues about how private, firm-level returns aggregate to the social, economy-wide
benefits and assumptions required to incorporate complementary organizational
factors into a growth accounting framework. However, our analysis suggests that
the returns to computer investment may be substantially higher than what is

assumed in traditional growth accounting exercises, and the total capital stock (including intangible assets) associated with the computerization of the economy may be understated by a factor of ten. Taken together, these considerations suggest the bias is on the same order of magnitude as the currently measured benefits of computers.

Thus, while the recent macroeconomic evidence about computers contributions is encouraging, our views are more strongly influenced by the microeconomic data. The micro data suggest that the surge in productivity that we now see in the macro statistics has its roots in over a decade of computer-enabled organizational invest-ments. The recent productivity boom can in part be explained as a return on this large, intangible, and largely ignored form of capital.

Case Examples

Companies using IT to change the way they conduct business often say that their investment in IT complements changes in other aspects of the organization. These complementarities have a number of implications for understanding the value of computer investment. To be successful, firms typically need to adopt computers as part of a "system" or "cluster" of mutually reinforcing organizational changes (Milgrom and Roberts 1990). Changing incrementally, either by making computer investments without organizational change, or only partially implementing some organizational changes, can create significant productivity losses as any benefits of computerization are more than outweighed by negative interactions with existing organizational practices (Brynjolfsson, Renshaw, and Van Alstyne 1997). The need for "all or nothing" changes between complementary systems was part of the logic behind the organizational re-engineering wave of the 1990s and the slogan "Don't Automate, Obliterate" (Hammer 1990). It may also explain why many large-scale IT projects fail (Kemerer and Sosa 1991), while successful firms earn significant rents.

Many of the past century's most successful and popular organizational practices reflect the historically high cost of information processing. For example, hierarchi-cal organizational structures can reduce communications costs because they mini-mize the number of communications links required to connect multiple economic actors, as compared with more decentralized structures (Malone 1987, Radner 1993). Similarly, producing simple, standardized products is an efficient way to utilize inflexible, scale-intensive manufacturing technology. However, as the cost of auto-mated information processing has fallen by more than 99.9 percent since the 1960s, it is unlikely that the work practices of the previous era will also be the same ones that best leverage the value of cheap information and flexible production. In this spirit, Milgrom and Roberts (1990) construct a model in which firms' transition from "mass production" to flexible, computer-enabled, "modern manufacturing" is driven by exogenous changes in the price of IT. Similarly, Bresnahan (1999) and Bresnahan, Brynjolfsson, and Hitt (2000) show how changes in IT costs and capabilities lead to a cluster of changes in work organization and firm strategy that increases the demand for skilled labor.

In this section we will discuss case evidence on three aspects of how firms have transformed themselves by combining IT with changes in work practices, strategy, and products and services; they have transformed the firm, supplier relations, and the customer relationship. These examples provide qualitative insights into the nature of the changes, making it easier to interpret the more quantitative econometric evidence that follows.

Transforming the Firm

The need to match organizational structure to technology capabilities and the challenges of making the transition to an IT-intensive production process is concisely illustrated by a case study of "MacroMed" (a pseudonym), a large medical products manufacturer (Brynjolfsson, Renshaw, and Van Alstyne 1997). In a desire to provide greater product customization and variety, MacroMed made a large investment in computer integrated manufacturing. These investments also coincided with an enumerated list of other major changes including: the elimination of piece rates, giving workers authority for scheduling machines, decision rights, process and workflow innovation, more frequent and richer interactions with customers and suppliers, increased lateral communication and teamwork, and other changes in skills, processes, culture, and structure (see table 4.1).

However, the new system initially fell well short of management expectations for greater flexibility and responsiveness. Investigation revealed that line workers still retained many elements of the now-obsolete old work practices, not from any conscious effort to undermine the change effort, but simply as an inherited pattern. For example, one earnest and well-intentioned worker explained that "the key to productivity is to avoid stopping the machine for product changeovers." While this heuristic was valuable with the old equipment, it negated the flexibility of the new machines and created large work-in-process inventories. Ironically, the new equipment was sufficiently flexible that the workers were able to get it to work much like the old machines! The strong complementarities within the old cluster of work

Table 4.1
Work Practices at MacroMed as Described in the Corporate Vision Statement
Introduction of computer-based equipment was accompanied by an even larger set of complementary changes

Principles of "old" factory	Principles of the "new" factory
• Designated equipment	• Flexible computer-based equipment
• Large WIP and FG inventories	• Low inventories
• Pay tied to amount produced	• All operators paid same flat rate
• Keep line running no matter what	• Stop line if not running at speed
• Thorough final inspection by QA	• Operators responsible for quality
• Raw materials made in-house	• All materials outsourced
• Narrow job functions	• Flexible job responsibilities
• Areas separated by machine type	• Areas organized in work cells
• Salaried employees make decisions	• All employees contribute ideas
• Hourly workers carry them out	• Supervisors can fill in on line
• Functional groups work independently	• Concurrent engineering
• Vertical communication flow	• Line rationalization
• Several management layers (6)	• Few management layers (3–4)

practices and within the new cluster greatly hindered the transition from one to the other.

Eventually, management concluded that the best approach was to introduce the new equipment in a "greenfield" site with a handpicked set of young employees who were relatively unencumbered by knowledge of the old practices. The resulting productivity improvements were significant enough that management ordered all the factory windows painted black to prevent potential competitors from seeing the new system in action. While other firms could readily buy similar computer-controlled equipment, they would still have to make the much larger investments in organizational learning before fully benefiting from them and the exact recipe for achieving these benefits was not trivial to invent (see Brynjolfsson, Renshaw, and Van Alstyne 1997 for details). Similarly, large changes in work practices have been documented in case studies of IT adoption in a variety of settings (e.g., Hunter, Bernhardt, Hughes, and Skuratowitz 2000; Levy, Beamish, Murnane, and Autor 2000; Malone and Rockart 1992; Murnane, Levy, and Autor 1999; Orlikowski 1992).

Changing Interactions with Suppliers

Due to problems coordinating with external suppliers, large firms often produce many of their required inputs in-house. General Motors is the classic example of a company whose success was facilitated by high levels of vertical integration.

However, technologies such as electronic data interchange (EDI), Internet-based procurement systems, and other interorganizational information systems have significantly reduced the cost, time, and other difficulties of interacting with suppliers. For example, firms can place orders with suppliers and receive confirmations electronically, eliminating paperwork and the delays and errors associated with manual processing of purchase orders (Johnston and Vitale 1988). However, even greater benefits can be realized when interorganizational systems are combined with new methods of working with suppliers.

An early successful interorganizational system is the Baxter ASAP system, which lets hospitals electronically order supplies directly from wholesalers (Vitale and Konsynski 1988, Short and Venkatraman 1992). The system was originally designed to reduce the costs of data entry—a large hospital could generate 50,000 purchase orders annually which had to be written out by hand by Baxter's field sales representatives at an estimated cost of $25–35 each. However, once Baxter computerized its ordering and had data available on levels of hospital stock, it took increasing responsibility for the entire supply operation: designing stock room space, setting up computer-based inventory systems, and providing automated inventory replenishment. The combination of the technology and the new supply chain organization substantially improved efficiency for both Baxter (no paper invoices, predictable order flow) and the hospitals (elimination of stockroom management tasks, lower inventories, and less chance of running out of items). Later versions of the ASAP system let users order from other suppliers, creating an electronic marketplace in hospital supplies.

ASAP was directly associated with cost savings on the order of $10 million to $15 million per year, which allowed them to rapidly recover the $30 million up-front investment and ~$3 million annual operating costs. However, management at Baxter believed that even greater benefits were being realized through incremental product sales at the 5,500 hospitals that had installed the ASAP system, not to mention the possibility of a reduction of logistics costs borne by the hospitals themselves, an expense which consumes as much as 30 percent of a hospital's budget.

Computer-based supply chain integration has been especially sophisticated in consumer packaged goods. Traditionally, manufacturers promoted products such as soap and laundry detergent by offering discounts, rebates, or even cash payments to retailers to stock and sell their products. Because many consumer products have long shelf lives, retailers tended to buy massive amounts during promotional periods, which increased volatility in manufacturing schedules and distorted manufacturers' view of their market. In response, manufacturers sped up their packaging changes to discourage stockpiling of products and developed internal audit departments to monitor retailers' purchasing behavior for contractual violations (Clemons 1993).

To eliminate these inefficiencies, Procter and Gamble (P&G) pioneered a program called "efficient consumer response" (McKenney and Clark 1995). In this approach, each retailer's checkout scanner data goes directly to the manufacturer; ordering, payments, and invoicing are fully automated through electronic data interchange; products are continuously replenished on a daily basis; and promotional efforts are replaced by an emphasis on "everyday low pricing." Manufacturers also involved themselves more in inventory decisions and moved toward "category management," where a lead manufacturer would take responsibility for an entire retail category (say, laundry products), determining stocking levels for its own and other manufacturers' products, as well as complementary items.

These changes, in combination, greatly improved efficiency. Consumers benefited from lower prices, and increased product variety, convenience, and innovation. Without the direct computer-computer links to scanner data and the electronic transfer of payments and invoices, they could not have attained the levels of speed and accuracy needed to implement such a system.

Technological innovations related to the commercialization of the Internet have dramatically decreased the cost of building electronic supply chain links. Computer-enabled procurement and on-line markets make possible a reduction in input costs through a combination of reduced procurement time and more predictable deliveries, which reduce the need for buffer inventories and reduce spoilage for perishable products; reduced price due to increasing price transparency and the ease of price shopping; and reduced direct costs of purchase order and invoice processing. These innovations are estimated to lower the costs of purchased inputs by 10 percent to 40 percent depending on the industry (Goldman Sachs 1999).

Some of these savings clearly represent a redistribution of rents from suppliers to buyers, with little effect on overall economic output. However, many of the other changes represent direct improvements in productivity through greater production efficiency and indirectly by enabling an increase in output quality or variety without excessive cost. To respond to these opportunities, firms are restructuring their supply arrangements and placing greater reliance on outside contractors. Even General Motors, once the exemplar of vertical integration, has reversed course and divested its large internal suppliers. As one industry analyst recently stated, "What was once the greatest source of strength at General Motors—its strategy of making parts in-house—has become its greatest weakness" (Schnapp 1998). To get some sense of the magnitude of this change, the spinoff in 1999 of Delphi Automotive Systems, only one of GM's many internal supply divisions, created a separate company that by itself has $28 billion in sales.

Changing Customer Relationships

The Internet has opened up a new range of possibilities for enriching interactions with customers. Dell Computer has succeeded in attracting customer orders and improving service by placing configuration, ordering, and technical support capabilities on the Web (Rangan and Bell 1998). It coupled this change with systems and work practice changes that emphasize just-in-time inventory management, build-to-order production systems, and tight integration between sales and production planning. Dell has implemented a consumer-driven build-to-order business model, rather than using the traditional build-to-stock model of selling computers through retail stores, which gives Dell as much as a 10 percent advantage over its rivals in production cost. Some of these savings represent the elimination of wholesale distribution and retailing costs. Others reflect substantially lower levels of inventory throughout the distribution channel. However, a subtle but important by-product of these changes in production and distribution is that Dell can be more responsive to customers. When Intel releases a new microprocessor, as it does several times each year, Dell can sell it to customers within seven days compared to eight weeks or more for some less Internet-enabled competitors. This is a non-trivial difference in an industry where adoption of new technology and obsolescence of old technology is rapid, margins are thin, and many component prices drop by 3–4 percent each month.

Other firms have also built closer relations with their customer via the Web and related technologies. For instance, Web retailers like Amazon.com provide personalized recommendations to visitors and allow them to customize numerous aspects of their shopping experience. As described by Denise Caruso, "Amazon's on-line account maintenance system provides its customers with secure access to everything about their account at any time. [S]uch information flow to and from customers would paralyze most old-line companies." Merely providing Internet access to a traditional bookstore would have had a relatively minimal impact without the cluster of other changes implemented by firms like Amazon.

An increasingly ubiquitous example is using the Web for handling basic customer inquiries. For instance, UPS now handles a total of 700,000 package tracking requests via the Internet every day. It costs UPS 10¢ per piece to serve that information via the Web vs. $2 to provide it over the phone (Seybold and Marshak 1998). Consumers benefit too. Because customers find it easier to track packages over the Web than via a phone call, UPS estimates that two-thirds of the Web users would not have bothered to check on their packages if they did not have Web access.

Large-Sample Empirical Evidence on IT, Organization, and Productivity

The case study literature offers many examples of strong links between IT and investments in complementary organizational practices. However, to reveal general trends and to quantify the overall impact, we must examine these effects across a wide range of firms and industries. In this section we explore the results from large-sample statistical analyses. First, we examine studies on the direct relationship between IT investment and business value. We then consider studies that measured organizational factors and their correlation with IT use, as well as the few initial studies that have linked this relationship to productivity increases.

IT and Productivity

Much of the early research on the relationship between technology and productivity used economy-level or sector-level data and found little evidence of a relationship. For example, Roach (1987) found that while computer investment per white-collar worker in the service sector rose several hundred percent from 1977 to 1989, output per worker, as conventionally measured, did not increase discernibly. In several papers, Morrison and Berndt examined Bureau of Economic Analysis data for manufacturing industries at the two-digit SIC level and found that the gross marginal product of "high tech capital" (including computers) was less than its cost and that in many industries these supposedly labor-saving investments were associated with an increase in labor demand (Berndt and Morrison 1995, Morrison 1996). Robert Solow (1987) summarized this kind of pattern in his well-known remark: "[Y]ou can see the computer age everywhere except in the productivity statistics."

However, by the early 1990s, analyses at the firm level were beginning to find evidence that computers had a substantial effect on firms' productivity levels. Using data from more than 300 large firms over the period 1988–1992, Brynjolfsson and Hitt (1995, 1996) and Lichtenberg (1995) estimated production functions that use the firm's output (or value-added) as the dependent variable and use ordinary capital, IT capital, ordinary labor, IT labor, and a variety of dummy variables for time, industry, and firm.[2] The pattern of these relationships is summarized in figure 4.1, which compares firm-level IT investment with multifactor productivity (excluding computers) for the firms in the Brynjolfsson and Hitt (1995) dataset. There is a

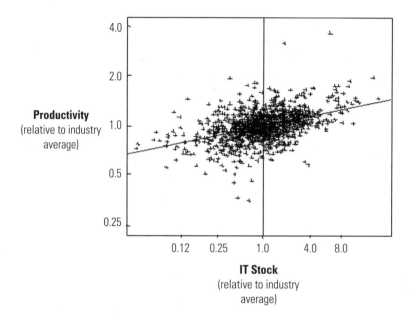

Figure 4.1
Productivity versus IT Stock (capital plus capitalized labor) for Large Firms (1988–1992) adjusted for industry

clear positive relationship, but also a great deal of individual variation in firms' success with IT.

Estimates of the average annual contribution of computer capital to total output generally exceed $0.60 per dollar of capital stock, depending on the analysis and specification (Brynjolfsson and Hitt 1995, 1996; Lichtenberg 1995; Dewan and Min 1997). These estimates are statistically different from zero, and in most cases significantly exceed the expected rate of return of about $0.42 (the Jorgensonian rental price of computers—see Brynjolfsson and Hitt 2000). This suggests either abnormally high returns to investors or the existence of unmeasured costs or barriers to investment. Similarly, most estimates of the contribution of information systems labor to output exceed $1 (and are as high as $6) for every $1 of labor costs.

Several researchers have also examined the returns to IT using data on the use of various technologies rather than the size of the investment. Greenan and Mairesse (1996) matched data on French firms and workers to measure the relationship between a firm's productivity and the fraction of its employees who report using a personal computer at work. Their estimates of computers' contribution to output are consistent with earlier estimates of the computer's output elasticity.

Other micro-level studies have focused on the use of computerized manufacturing technologies. Kelley (1994) found that the most productive metal-working plants use computer-controlled machinery. Black and Lynch (1996) found that plants where a larger percentage of employees use computers are more productive in a sample containing multiple industries. Computerization has also been found to increase productivity in government activities both at the process level, such as package sorting at the post office or toll collection (Muhkopadhyay, Surendra, and Srinivasan 1997) and at higher levels of aggregation (Lehr and Lichtenberg 1998).

Taken collectively, these studies suggest that IT is associated with substantial increases in output. Questions remain about the mechanisms and direction of causality in these studies. Perhaps instead of IT causing greater output, "good firms" or average firms with unexpectedly high sales disproportionately spend their windfall on computers. For example, while Doms, Dunne, and Troske (1997) found that plants using more advanced manufacturing technologies had higher productivity and wages, they also found that this was commonly the case even before the technologies were introduced.

Efforts to disentangle causality have been limited by the lack of good instrumental variables for factor investment at the firm level. However, attempts to correct for this bias using available instrumental variables typically increase the estimated coefficients on IT even further (for example, Brynjolfsson and Hitt 1996, 2000). Thus, it appears that reverse causality is not driving the results: Firms with an unexpected increase in free cash flow invest in other factors, such as labor, before they change their spending on IT. Nonetheless, there appears to be a fair amount of causality in both directions—certain organizational characteristics make IT adoption more likely and vice versa.

The firm-level productivity studies can shed some light on the relationship between IT and organizational restructuring. For example, productivity studies consistently find that the output elasticities of computers exceed their (measured) input shares. One explanation for this finding is that the output elasticities for IT are about right, but the productivity studies are underestimating the input quantities because they neglect the role of unmeasured complementary investments. Dividing the output of the whole set of complements by only the factor share of IT will imply disproportionately high rates of return for IT.[3]

A variety of other evidence suggests that hidden assets play an important role in the relationship between IT and productivity. Brynjolfsson and Hitt (1995) estimated a firm fixed effects productivity model. This method can be interpreted as dividing firm-level IT benefits into two parts: One part is due to variation in firms' IT investments over time, the other to firm characteristics. Brynjolfsson and Hitt found that in the firm fixed effects model, the coefficient on IT was about 50 percent lower, compared to the results of an ordinary least squares regression, while the coefficients on the other factors, capital and labor, changed only slightly. This change suggests that unmeasured and slowly changing organizational practices (the "fixed effect") significantly affect the returns to IT investment.

Another indirect implication from the productivity studies comes from evidence that effects of IT are substantially larger when measured over longer time periods. Brynjolfsson and Hitt (2000) examined the effects of IT on productivity *growth* rather than productivity *levels*, which had been the emphasis in most previous work, using data that included more than 600 firms over the period 1987 to 1994. When one-year differences in IT are compared to one-year differences in firm productivity, the measured benefits of computers are approximately equal to their measured costs. However, the measured benefits rise by a factor of two to eight as longer time periods are considered, depending on the econometric specification used. One interpretation of these results is that short-term returns represent the direct effects of IT investment, while the longer-term returns represent the effects of IT when combined with related investments in organizational change. Further analysis, based on earlier results by Schankermann (1981) in the R&D context, suggested that these omitted factors were not simply IT investments that were erroneously misclassified as capital or labor. Instead, to be consistent with the econometric results, the omitted factors had to have been accumulated in ways that would not appear on the current balance sheet. Firm-specific human capital and "organizational capital" are two examples of omitted inputs that would fit this description.[4]

A final perspective on the value of these organizational complements to IT can be found using financial market data, drawing on the literature on Tobin's q. This approach measures the rate of return of an asset indirectly, based on comparing the stock market value of the firm to the replacement value of the various capital assets it owns. Typically, Tobin's q has been employed to measure the relative value of observable assets such as R&D or physical plant. However, as suggested by Hall (1999, 1999b), Tobin's q can also be viewed as providing a measure of the total quantity of capital, including the value of "technology, organization, business practices, and other produced elements of successful modern corporation." Using an approach along these lines, Brynjolfsson and Yang (1997) found that while $1 of ordinary capital is valued at approximately $1 by the financial markets, $1 of IT capital appears to be correlated with between $5 and $20 of additional stock market value for Fortune 1000 firms using data spanning 1987 to 1994. Since these results largely apply to large, established firms rather than new high-tech startups, and since they predate most of the massive increase in market valuations for technology stocks in the late 1990s, these results are not likely to be sensitive to the possibility of a recent "high-tech stock bubble."

A more likely explanation for these results is that IT capital is disproportionately associated with other intangible assets like the costs of developing new software, populating a database, implementing a new business process, acquiring a more highly skilled staff, or undergoing a major organizational transformation, all of which go uncounted on a firm's balance sheet. In this interpretation, for every dollar of IT capital, the typical firm has also accumulated between $4 and $19 in additional intangible assets. A related explanation is that firms must occur substantial "adjustment costs" before IT is effective. These adjustment costs drive a wedge between the value of a computer resting on the loading dock and one that is fully integrated into the organization.

The evidence from the productivity and the Tobin's q analyses provides some insights into the properties of IT-related intangible assets, even if we cannot measure these assets directly. Such assets are large, potentially several multiples of the measured IT investment. They are unmeasured in the sense that they do not appear as a capital asset or as other components of firm input, although they do appear to be unique characteristics of particular firms as opposed to industry effects. Finally, they have more effect in the long term than the short term, suggesting that multiple years of adaptation and investment are required before their influence is maximized.

Direct Measurement of the Interrelationship between IT and Organization

Some studies have attempted to measure organizational complements directly, and to show either that they are correlated with IT investment, or that firms that combine complementary factors have better economic performance. Finding correlations between IT and organizational change, or between these factors and measures of economic performance, is not sufficient to prove that these practices are complements, unless a full structural model specifies the production relationships and demand drivers for each factor. Athey and Stern (1997) discuss issues in the empirical assessment of complementarity relationships. However, after empirically evaluating possible alternative explanations and combining correlations with performance analyses, complementarities are often the most plausible explanation for observed relationships between IT, organizational factors, and economic performance.

The first set of studies in this area focuses on correlations between use of IT and extent of organizational change. An important finding is that IT investment is greater in organizations that are decentralized and have a greater level of demand for human capital. For example, Bresnahan, Brynjolfsson, and Hitt (2000) surveyed approximately 400 large firms to obtain information on aspects of organizational structure like allocation of decision rights, workforce composition, and investments in human capital. They found that greater levels of IT are associated with increased delegation of authority to individuals and teams, greater levels of skill and education in the workforce, and greater emphasis on pre-employment screening for education and training. In addition, they find that these work practices are correlated with each other, suggesting that they are part of a complementary work system.[5]

Research on jobs within specific industries has begun to explore the mechanisms within organizations that create these complementarities. Drawing on a case study on the automobile repair industry, Levy, Beamish, Murnane, and Autor (2000) argue that computers are most likely to substitute for jobs that rely on rule-based decision making while complementing non-procedural cognitive tasks. In banking, researchers have found that many of the skill, wage, and other organizational effects of computers depend on the extent to which firms couple computer investment with organizational redesign and other managerial decisions (Hunter, Bernhardt, Hughes, and Skuratowitz 2000; Murnane, Levy, and Autor 1999). Researchers focusing at the establishment level have also found complementarities between existing technology infrastructure and firm work practices to be a key determinant of the firm's ability to incorporate new technologies (Bresnahan and Greenstein 1997); this also suggests a pattern of mutual causation between computer investment and organization.

A variety of industry-level studies also shows a strong connection between investment in high technology equipment and the demand for skilled, educated workers (Berndt, Morrison, and Rosenblum 1992; Berman, Bound, and Griliches 1994; Autor, Katz, and Krueger 1998). Again, these findings are consistent with the idea that increasing use of computers is associated with a greater demand for human capital.

Several researchers have also considered the effect of IT on macro-organizational structures. They have typically found that greater levels of investment in IT are associated with smaller firms and less vertical integration. Brynjolfsson, Malone, Gurbaxani, and Kambil (1994) found that increases in the level of IT capital in an economic sector were associated with a decline in average firm size in that sector, consistent with IT leading to a reduction in vertical integration. Hitt (1999), examining the relationship between a firm's IT capital stock and direct measures of its vertical integration, arrived at similar conclusions. These results corroborate earlier case analyses and theoretical arguments that suggested that IT would be associated with a decrease in vertical integration because it lowers the costs of coordinating externally with suppliers (Malone, Yates, and Benjamin 1987; Gurbaxani and Whang 1991; Clemons and Row 1992).

One difficulty in interpreting the literature on correlations between IT and organizational change is that some managers may be predisposed to try every new idea and some managers may be averse to trying anything new at all. In such a world, IT and a "modern" work organization might be correlated in firms because of the temperament of management, not because they are economic complements. To rule out this sort of spurious correlation, it is useful to bring measures of productivity and economic performance into the analysis. If combining IT and organizational restructuring is economically justified, then firms that adopt these practices as a system should outperform those that fail to combine IT investment with appropriate organizational structures.

In fact, firms that adopt decentralized organizational structures and work structures do appear to have a higher contribution of IT to productivity (Bresnahan, Brynjolfsson, and Hitt 2000). For example, for firms that are more decentralized than the median firm (as measured by individual organizational practices and by an index of such practices), have, on average, a 13 percent greater IT elasticity and a 10 percent greater investment in IT than the median firm. Firms that are in the top half of *both* IT investment and decentralization are on average 5 percent more productive than firms that are above average only in IT investment or only in decentralization.

Similar results also appear when economic performance is measured as stock market valuation. Firms in the top third of decentralization have a 6 percent higher market value after controlling for all other measured assets; this is consistent with the theory that organizational decentralization behaves like an intangible asset. Moreover, the stock market value of a dollar of IT capital is between $2 and $5 greater in decentralized firms than in centralized firms (per standard deviation of the decentralization measure), and this relationship is particularly striking for firms that are simultaneously extensive users of IT and highly decentralized as shown in figure 4.2 (Brynjolfsson, Hitt, and Yang 2000).

The weight of the firm-level evidence shows that a combination of investment in technology and changes in organizations and work practices facilitated by these technologies contributes to firms' productivity growth and market value. However, much work remains to be done in categorizing and measuring the relevant changes in organizations and work practices, and relating them to IT and productivity.

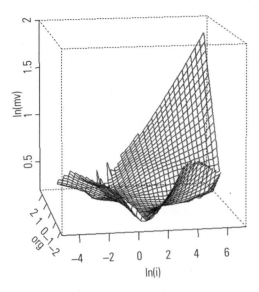

Figure 4.2
Market Value as a function of IT and Work Organization
This graph was produced by non-parametric local regression models using data from Brynjolfsson, Hitt, and Yang (2000). Note: *I* represents computer capital, *org* represents a measure of decentralization and *mv* is market value.

The Divergence of Firm-Level and Aggregate Studies on IT and Productivity

While the evidence indicates that IT has created substantial value for firms that have invested in it, it has been a challenge to link these benefits to macroeconomic performance. A major reason for the gap in interpretation is that traditional growth accounting techniques focus on the (relatively) observable aspects of output, like price and quantity, while neglecting the intangible benefits of improved quality, new products, customer service, and speed. Similarly, traditional techniques focus on the relatively observable aspects of investment, such as the price and quantity of computer hardware in the economy, and neglect the much larger intangible investments in developing complementary new products, services, markets, business processes, and worker skills. Paradoxically, while computers have vastly improved the ability to collect and analyze data on almost any aspect of the economy, the current computer-enabled economy has become increasingly difficult to measure using conventional methods. Nonetheless, standard growth accounting techniques provide a useful benchmark for the contribution of IT to economic growth.

Studies of the contribution of IT concluded that technical progress in computers contributed roughly 0.3 percentage points per year to real output growth when data from the 1970s and 1980s were used (Jorgenson and Stiroh 1995, Oliner and Sichel 1994, Brynjolfsson 1996).

Much of the estimated growth contribution comes directly from the large quality-adjusted price declines in the computer-producing industries. The nominal value of purchases of IT hardware in the United States in 1997 was about 1.4 percent of GDP. Since the quality-adjusted prices of computers decline by about 25 percent per year, simply spending the same nominal share of GDP as in previous years represents an annual productivity increase for the real GDP of 0.3 percentage points (that is, $1.4 \times .25 = .35$). A related approach is to look at the effect of IT on the GDP deflator. Reductions in inflation, for a given amount of growth in output, imply proportionately higher real growth and, when divided by a measure of inputs, for higher productivity growth as well. Gordon (1998, p.4) calculates that "computer hardware is currently contributing to a reduction of U.S. inflation at an annual rate of almost 0.5 percent per year, and this number would climb toward one percent per year if a broader definition of IT, including telecommunications equipment, were used."

More recent growth-accounting analyses by the same authors have linked the recent surge in measured productivity in the U.S. to increased investments in IT. Using similar methods as in their earlier studies, Oliner and Sichel (2000) and Jorgenson and Stiroh (1999) find that the annual contribution of computers to output growth in the second half of the 1990s is closer to 1.0 or 1.1 percentage points per year. Gordon (2000) makes a similar estimate. This is a large contribution for any single technology, although researchers have raised concerns that computers are primarily an intermediate input and that the productivity gains are disproportionately visible in computer-producing industries as opposed to computer-using industries. For instance, Gordon notes that after he makes adjustments for the business cycle, capital deepening and other effects, there has been virtually no change in the rate of productivity growth outside of the durable goods sector. Jorgenson and Stiroh ascribe a larger contribution to computer-using industries, but still not as great as in the computer-producing industries.

Should we be disappointed by the productivity performance of the downstream firms?

Not necessarily. Two points are worth bearing in mind when comparing upstream and downstream sectors. First, the allocation of productivity depends on the quality-adjusted transfer prices used. If a high deflator is applied, the upstream sectors get credited with more output and productivity in the national accounts, but the downstream firms get charged with using more inputs and thus have less productivity. Conversely, a low deflator allocates more of the gains to the downstream sector. In both cases, the increases in the total productivity of the economy are, by definition, identical. Since it is difficult to compute accurate deflators for complex, rapidly changing intermediate goods like computers, one must be careful in interpreting the allocation of productivity across producers and users.[6]

The second point is more semantic. Arguably, downstream sectors are delivering on the IT revolution by simply maintaining levels of measured total factor productivity growth in the presence of dramatic changes in the costs, nature, and mix of intermediate computer goods. This reflects a success in costlessly converting technological innovations into real output that benefits end consumers. If "mutual insurance" maintains a constant nominal IT budget in the face of 50 percent IT price declines over two years, it is treated in the national accounts as using 100 percent more real IT input for production. A commensurate increase in real output is required merely to maintain the same measured productivity level as before. This is not necessarily automatic since it requires a significant change in the input mix and organization of production. In the presence of adjustment costs and imperfect output measures, one might reasonably have expected measured productivity to initially *decline* in downstream sectors as they absorb a rapidly changing set of inputs and introduce new products and services.

Regardless of how the productivity benefits are allocated, these studies show that a substantial part of the upturn in measured productivity of the economy as a whole can be linked to increased real investments in computer hardware and declines in their quality-adjusted prices. However, there are several key assumptions implicit in economy- or industry-wide growth accounting approaches which can have a substantial influence on their results, especially if one seeks to know whether investment in computers is increasing productivity as much as alternate possible investments. The standard growth accounting approach begins by assuming that all inputs earn "normal" rates of return. Unexpected windfalls, whether the discovery of a single new oil field, or the invention of a new process which makes oil fields obsolete, show up not in the growth contribution of inputs but as changes in the multifactor productivity residual. By construction, an input can contribute more to output in these analyses only by growing rapidly, not by having an unusually high net rate of return.

Changes in multifactor productivity growth, in turn, depend on accurate measures of final output. However, nominal output is affected by whether firm expenditures are expensed, and therefore deducted from value-added, or capitalized and treated as investment. As emphasized throughout this paper, IT is only a small fraction of a much larger complementary system of tangible and intangible assets. However, current statistics typically treat the accumulation of intangible capital assets, such as new business processes, new production systems, and new skills, as expenses rather than as investments. This leads to a lower level of measured output in periods of net capital accumulation. Second, current output statistics disproportionately miss many of the gains that IT has brought to consumers such as variety, speed, and convenience. We will consider these issues in turn.

The magnitude of investment in intangible assets associated with computerization may be large. Analyses of 800 large firms by Brynjolfsson and Yang (1997) suggest that the ratio of intangible assets to IT assets may be ten to one. Thus, the $167 billion in computer capital recorded in the U.S. national accounts in 1996 may have actually been only the tip of an iceberg of $1.67 trillion of IT-related complementary assets in the United States.

Examination of individual IT projects indicates that the 10:1 ratio may even be an underestimate in many cases. For example, a survey of enterprise resource planning projects found that the average spending on computer hardware accounted for less than 4 percent of the typical start-up cost of $20.5 million, while software licenses and development were another 16 percent of total costs (Gormley et al. 1998). The remaining costs included hiring outside and internal consultants to help design new business processes and to train workers in the use of the system. The time of existing employees, including top managers, that went into the overall implementation was not included, although it too is typically quite substantial.

The up-front costs were almost all expensed by the companies undertaking the implementation projects. However, insofar as the managers who made these expenditures expected them to pay for themselves only over several years, the non-recurring costs are properly thought of as investments, not expenses, when considering the impact on economic growth. In essence, the managers were adding to the nation's capital stock not only of easily visible computers, but also of less visible business processes and worker skills.

How might these measurement problems affect economic growth and productivity calculations? In a steady state, it makes little difference, because the amount of new organizational investment in any given year is offset by the "depreciation" of organizational investments in previous years. The net change in capital stock is zero. Thus, in a steady state, classifying organizational investments as expenses does not bias overall output growth as long as it is done consistently from year to year. However, the economy has hardly been in a steady state with respect to computers and their complements. Instead, the U.S. economy has been rapidly adding to its stock of both types of capital. To the extent that this net capital accumulation has not been counted as part of output, output and output growth have been underestimated.

The software industry offers a useful example of the impact of classifying a category of spending as expense or investment. Historically, efforts on software development have been treated as expenses, but recently the government has begun recognizing that software is an intangible capital asset. Software investment by U.S. businesses and governments grew from $10 billion in 1979 to $159 billion in 1998 (Parket and Grimm 2000). Properly accounting for this investment has added 0.15 to 0.20 percentage points to the average annual growth rate of real GDP in the 1990s. While capitalizing software is an important improvement in our national accounts, software is far from the only, or even most important, complement to computers.

If the wide array of intangible capital costs associated with computers were treated as investments rather than expenses, the results would be striking. According to some preliminary estimates from Yang (2000), building on estimates of the intangible asset stock derived from stock market valuations of computers, the true growth rate of U.S. GDP, after accounting for the intangible complements to IT hardware, has been increasingly underestimated by an average of over 1 percent per year since the early 1980s, with the underestimate getting worse over time as net IT investment has grown. Productivity growth has been underestimated by a similar amount. This reflects the large net increase in intangible assets of the U.S. economy associated with the computerization that was discussed earlier. Over time, the economy earns returns on past investment, converting it back into consumption. This has the effect of raising GDP growth as conventionally measured by a commensurate amount even if the "true" GDP growth remains unchanged.

While the quantity of intangible assets associated with IT is difficult to estimate precisely, the central lesson is that these complementary changes are significant and cannot be ignored in any realistic attempt to estimate the overall economic contributions of IT.

The productivity gains from investments in new IT are underestimated in a second major way: failure to account fully for quality change in consumable outputs. It is typically much easier to count the number of units produced than to assess intrinsic quality—especially if the desired quality may vary across customers. A significant fraction of value of quality improvements due to investments in IT—like greater timeliness, customization, and customer service—is not directly reflected as increased industry sales, and thus is implicitly treated as nonexistent in official economic statistics.

These issues have always been a concern in the estimation of the true rate of inflation and the real output of the U.S. economy (Boskin *et al.* 1997). If output mismeasurement for computers were similar to output mismeasurement for previous technologies, estimates of long-term productivity trends would be unaffected (Baily and Gordon 1988). However, there is evidence that in several specific ways, computers are associated with an increasing degree of mismeasurement that is likely to lead to increasing underestimates of productivity and economic growth.

The production of intangible outputs is an important consideration for IT investments whether in the form of new products or improvements in existing products. Based on a series of surveys of information services managers conducted in 1993, 1995, and 1996, Brynjolfsson and Hitt (1997) found that customer service and sometimes other aspects of intangible output (specifically quality, convenience, and timeliness) ranked higher than cost savings as the motivation for investments in information services. Brooke (1992) found that IT was also associated with increases in product variety.

Indeed, government data show many inexplicable changes in productivity, especially in the sectors where output is poorly measured and where changes in quality may be especially important (Griliches 1994). Moreover, simply removing anomalous industries from the aggregate productivity growth calculation can change the estimate of U.S. productivity growth by 0.5 percent or more (Corrado and Slifman 1999). The problems with measuring quality change and true output growth are illustrated by selected industry-level productivity growth data over different time periods, shown in table 4.2. According to official government statistics, a bank today is only about 80 percent as productive as a bank in 1977; a health care facility is only 70 percent as productive and a lawyer only 65 percent as productive as they were 1977.

Table 4.2
Annual (measured) Productivity Growth for Selected Industries
Calculation by Gordon (1998) based on dividing BEA gross output by industry figures by BLS hours worked by industry for comparable sectors

Industry	1948–1967	1967–1977	1977–1996
Depository Institutions	.03%	.21%	−1.19%
Health Services	.99%	.04%	−1.81%
Legal Services	.23%	−2.01%	−2.13%

Source: Partial reproduction from Gordon (1998, Table 3).

These statistics seem out of touch with reality. In 1977, all banking was conducted at the teller windows; today, customers can access a network of 139,000 ATMs 24 hours a day, 7 days a week (Osterberg and Sterk 1997), as well as a vastly expanded array of banking services via the Internet. The more than tripling of cash availability via ATMs required an incremental investment on the order of $10 billion compared with over $70 billion invested in physical bank branches. Computer-controlled medical equipment has facilitated more successful and less invasive medical treatment. Many procedures that previously required extensive hospital stays can now be performed on an outpatient basis; instead of surgical procedures, many medical tests now use non-invasive imaging devices such as x-rays, MRI, or CT scanners. Information technology has supported the research and analysis that has led to these advances plus a wide array of improvements in medication and outpatient therapies. A lawyer today can access much wider range of information through on-line databases and manage many more legal documents. In addition, some basic legal services, such as drafting a simple will, can now be performed without a lawyer using inexpensive software packages such as Willmaker.

One of the most important types of unmeasured benefits arises from new goods. Sales of new goods are measured in the GDP statistics as part of nominal output, although this does not capture the new consumer surplus generated by such goods, which causes them to be preferred over old goods. Moreover, the Bureau of Labor Statistics has often failed to incorporate new goods into price indices until many years after their introduction; for example, it did not incorporate the VCR into the consumer price index until 1987, about a decade after they began selling in volume. This leads the price index to miss the rapid decline in price that many new goods experience early in their product cycle. As a result, the inflation statistics overstate the true rise in the cost of living, and when the nominal GDP figures are adjusted using that price index, the real rate of output growth is understated (Boskin *et al.* 1997). The problem extends beyond new high tech products, like personal digital assistants and handheld Web browsers. Computers enable more new goods to be developed, produced, and managed in all industries. For instance, the number of new products introduced in supermarkets has grown from 1,281 in 1964, to 1,831 in 1975, and then to 16,790 in 1992 (Nakamura 1997); the data management requirements to handle so many products would have overwhelmed the computerless supermarket of earlier decades. Consumers have voted with their pocketbooks for the stores with greater product variety.

This collection of results suggests that IT may be associated with increases in the intangible component of output, including variety, customer convenience, and service. Because it appears that the amount of unmeasured output value is increasing with computerization, this measurement problem not only creates an underestimate of output level, but also errors in measurement of output and productivity growth when compared with earlier time periods which had a smaller bias due to intangible outputs.

Just as the Bureau of Economic Analysis successfully reclassified many software expenses as investments and is making quality adjustments, perhaps we will also find ways to measure the investment component of spending on intangible organizational capital and to make appropriate adjustments for the value of all gains attributable to improved quality, variety, convenience, and service. Unfortunately, addressing these problems can be difficult even for single firms and products, and the complexity and number of judgments required to address them at the macroeconomic level is extremely high. Moreover, because of the increasing service component of all industries (even basic manufacturing), which entails product and service innovation and intangible investments, these problems cannot be easily solved by focusing on a limited number of "hard to measure" industries—they are pervasive throughout the economy.

Meanwhile, however, firm-level studies can overcome some of the difficulties in assessing the productivity gains from IT. For example, it is considerably easier at the firm level to make reasonable estimates of the investments in intangible organizational capital and to observe changes in organizations, while it is harder to formulate useful rules for measuring such investment at the macroeconomic level.

Firm-level studies may be less subject to aggregation error when firms make different levels of investments in computers and thus could have different capabilities for producing higher value products (Brynjolfsson and Hitt 1996, 2000). Suppose a firm invests in IT to improve product quality and consumers recognize and value these benefits. If other firms do not make similar investments, any difference in quality will lead to differences in the equilibrium product prices that each firm can charge. When an analysis is conducted across firms, variation in quality will contribute to differences in output and productivity, and thus will be measured as increases in the output elasticity of computers. However, when firms with high quality products and firms with low quality products are combined together in industry data (and subjected to the same quality-adjusted deflator for the industry), both the IT investment and the difference in revenue will average out, and a lower correlation between IT and (measured) output will be detected. Interestingly, Siegel (1997) found that the measured effect of computers on productivity was substantially increased when he used a structural equation framework to directly model the errors in production input measurement in industry-level data.

However, firm-level data can be an insecure way to capture the social gains from improved product quality. For example, not all price differences reflect differences in product or service quality. When price differences are due to differences in market power that are not related to consumer preferences, then firm-level data will lead to inaccurate estimates of the productivity effects of IT. Similarly, increases in quality or variety (e.g., new product introductions in supermarkets) can be a by-product of anti-competitive product differentiation strategies, which may or may not increase total welfare. Moreover, firm-level data will not fully capture the value of quality improvements or other intangible benefits if these benefits are ubiquitous across an industry, because then there will not be any inter-firm variation in quality and prices. Instead, competition will pass the gains on to consumers. In this case, firm-level data will also understate the contribution of IT investment to social welfare.

Conclusion

Concerns about an IT "productivity paradox" were raised in the late 1980s. Over a decade of research since then has substantially improved our understanding of the relationship between IT and economic performance. The firm-level studies in particular suggest that, rather than being paradoxically unproductive, computers have had an impact on economic growth that is disproportionately large compared to their share of capital stock or investment, and that this impact is likely to grow further in coming years.

In particular, both case studies and econometric work point to organizational complements such as new business processes, new skills, and new organizational and industry structures as a major driver of the contribution of IT. These complementary investments, and the resulting assets, may be as much as an order of magnitude larger than the investments in the computer technology itself. However, they go largely uncounted in our national accounts, suggesting that computers have made a much larger real contribution to the economy than previously believed.

The use of firm-level data has cast a brighter light on the black box of production in the increasingly IT-based economy. The outcome has been a better understanding of the key inputs, including complementary organizational assets, as well as the key outputs including the growing roles of new products, new services, quality, variety, timeliness, and convenience. Measuring the intangible components of complementary systems will never be easy. But if researchers and business managers recognize the importance of the intangible costs and benefits of computers and undertake to evaluate them, a more precise assessment of these assets needn't be beyond computation.

Acknowledgments

This chapter is reprinted with permission from *Journal of Economic Perspectives* 14, no. 4 (Fall 2000): 23–48. Portions also appear in *MIS Review* and in an edited volume, *The Puzzling Relations Between Computer and the Economy*, Nathalie Greenan, Yannick Lhorty, and Jacques Mairesse, eds., MIT Press, 2001.

The authors thank David Autor, Brad DeLong, Robert Gordon, Shane Greenstein, Dale Jorgenson, Alan Krueger, Dan Sichel, Robert Solow, Kevin Stiroh, and Timothy Taylor for valuable comments on (portions of) earlier drafts. This work was funded in part by NSF Grant IIS-9733877.

Notes

1. For a more general treatment of the literature on IT value see reviews by Attewell and Rule (1984), Brynjolfsson (1993), Wilson (1995), and Brynjolfsson and Yang (1996). For a discussion of the problems in economic measurement of computers contributions at the macroeconomic level see Baily and Gordon (1988), Siegel (1997), and Gullickson and Harper (1999).

2. These studies assumed a standard form (Cobb-Douglas) for the production function, and measured the variables in logarithms. In general, using different functional forms, such as the transcendental logarithmic (translog) production function, has little effect on the measurement of output elasticities.

3. Hitt (1996) and Brynjolfsson and Hitt (2000) present a formal analysis of this issue.

4. Part of the difference in coefficients between short and long difference specifications could also be explained by measurement error (which tends to average out somewhat over longer time periods). Such errors-in-variables can bias down coefficients based on short differences, but the size of the change is too large to be attributed solely to this effect (Brynjolfsson and Hitt 2000).

5. Kelley (1994) found that the use of programmable manufacturing equipment is correlated with several aspects of human resource practices.

6. It is worth noting that if the exact quality change of an intermediate good is mismeasured, then the total productivity of the economy is not affected, only the allocation between sectors. However, if computer-using industries take advantage of the radical change in input costs and quality to introduce new quality levels (or entirely new goods) and these changes are not fully reflected in final output deflators, then total productivity will be affected. In periods of rapid technological change, both phenomena are common.

References

Athey, S., and S. Stern. 1997. An Empirical Framework for Testing Theories about Complementarities in Organizational Design. Mimeo, MIT.

Attewell, P., and J. Rule. 1984. Computing and Organizations: What We Know and What We Don't Know. *Communications of the ACM* 27 (12): 1184–1192.

Autor, D., L. F. Katz, and A. B. Krueger. 1998. Computing Inequality: Have Computers Changed the Labor Market? *Quarterly Journal of Economics* 113 (4): 1169–1213.

Baily, M. N., and R. J. Gordon. 1988. The Productivity Slowdown, Measurement Issues, and the Explosion of Computer Power. In *Brookings Papers on Economic Activity*, W. C. Brainard and G. L. Perry, eds. Washington, D.C.: Brookings Institution, 347–431.

Berman, E., J. Bound, and Z. Griliches. 1994. Changes in the Demand for Skilled Labor within U.S. Manufacturing Industries. *Quarterly Journal of Economics* 109 (May): 367–398.

Berndt, E. R., and C. J. Morrison. 1995. High-tech Capital Formation and Economic Performance in U.S. Manufacturing Industries: An Exploratory Analysis. *Journal of Econometrics* 65: 9–43.

Berndt, E. R., C. J. Morrison, and L. S. Rosenblum. 1992. High-Tech Capital, Economic Performance and Labor Composition in U.S. Manufacturing Industries: An Exploratory Analysis. MIT Working Paper 3414EFA.

Black, S. E., and L. M. Lynch. 1996. How to Compete: The Impact of Workplace Practices and IT on Productivity. Harvard University and U.S. Department of Labor, Washington, D.C., September.

Boskin, Michael J., Ellen R. Dulberger, Robert J. Gordon, Zvi Griliches, and Dale Jorgenson. 1997. The CPI Commission: Findings and Recommendations. *American Economic Review* 87 (2): 78–83.

Bresnahan, T., E. Brynjolfsson, and L. Hitt. 2000. IT, Workplace Organization and the Demand for Skilled Labor: A Firm-level Analysis. Mimeo, MIT, Stanford, and Wharton.

Bresnahan, T. F., and M. Trajtenberg. 1995. General Purpose Technologies: "Engines of Growth?" *Journal of Econometrics* 65: 83–108.

Bresnahan, T. F., and S. Greenstein. 1997. Technical Progress and Co-Invention in Computing and in the Use of Computers. *Brookings Papers on Economic Activity: Microeconomics* (January): 1–78.

Bresnahan, T. F. 1999. Computerization and Wage Dispersion: An Analytic Reinterpretation. *Economic Journal* 109 (456): 381–389.

Brooke, G. M. 1992. The Economics of Information Technology: Explaining the Productivity Paradox. MIT Sloan School of Management Center for Information Systems Research Working Paper No. 238.

Brynjolfsson, E. 1993. The Productivity Paradox of Information Technology. *Communications of the ACM* 35 (12): 66–77.

Brynjolfsson, E. 1996. The Contribution of Information Technology to Consumer Welfare. *Information Systems Research* 7 (3): 281–300.

Brynjolfsson, E., T. Malone, V. Gurbaxani, and A. Kambil. 1994. Does Information Technology Lead to Smaller Firms? *Management Science* 40 (12): 1628–1644.

Brynjolfsson, E., and L. Hitt. 1995. Information Technology as a Factor of Production: The Role of Differences Among Firms. *Economics of Innovation and New Technology* 3 (4): 183–200.

Brynjolfsson, E., and L. Hitt. 1996. Paradox Lost? Firm-level Evidence on the Returns to Information Systems Spending. *Management Science* 42 (4): 541–558.

Brynjolfsson, E., and L. Hitt. 1997. Breaking Boundaries. *Informationweek*, September 22: 54–61.

Brynjolfsson, E., and L. Hitt. 2000. Computing Productivity: Are Computers Pulling Their Weight? Mimeo, MIT and Wharton.

Brynjolfsson, E., and S. Yang. 1996. Information Technology and Productivity: A Review of the Literature. *Advances in Computers* 43: 179–214.

Brynjolfsson, E., and S. Yang. 1997. The Intangible Benefits and Costs of Computer Investments: Evidence from Financial Markets. *Proceedings of the International Conference on Information Systems*, Atlanta.

Brynjolfsson, E., A. Renshaw, and M. V. Alstyne. 1997. The Matrix of Change. *Sloan Management Review*, 38 (Winter): 37–54.

Brynjolfsson, E., L. Hitt, and S. K. Yang. 2000. Intangible Assets: How the Interaction of Information Systems and Organizational Structure Affects Stock Market Valuations. Mimeo, MIT and Wharton. A previous version appeared in the *Proceedings of the International Conference on Information Systems*, Helsinki, Finland, 1998.

Clemons, Eric K., Matt E. Thatcher, and Michael C. Row. 1995. Identifying sources of re-engineering failures: A study of the behavioral factors contributing to reengineering risks. *Journal of Management Information Systems* 12 (2): 9–36.

Clemons, Eric K. 1993. Re-engineering the Sales Function: Re-engineering Internal Operations, Teaching Case, Wharton School.

Corrado, C., and L. Slifman. 1999. Decomposition of Productivity and Unit Costs. *American Economic Review* 89 (2): 328–332.

David, P. A. 1990. The Dynamo and the Computer: A Historical Perspective on the Modern Productivity Paradox. *American Economic Review Papers and Proceedings* 1 (2): 355–361.

Dewan, S., and C. K. Min. 1997. Substitution of Information Technology for Other Factors of Production: A Firm-level Analysis. *Management Science* 43 (12): 1660–1675.

Doms, Mark, Timothy Dunne, and Kenneth R. Troske. 1997. Workers, Wages, and Technology. *Quarterly Journal of Economics* 112 (1): 253–290.

Galbraith, J. 1977. Organizational Design. Reading, Mass.: Addison-Wesley.

Gordon, Robert J. 1998. Monetary Policy in the Age of Information Technology: Computers and the Solow Paradox. Working Paper, Northwestern University.

Goldman Sachs. 1999. B2B: To Be or Not 2B? High Technology Group Whitepaper, November.

Gormley, J., W. Bluestein, J. Gatoff, and H. Chun. 1998. The Runaway Costs of Packaged Applications. *Forrester Report* 3 (5).

Greenan, N., and J. Mairesse. 1996. Computers and Productivity in France: Some Evidence. National Bureau of Economic Research Working Paper 5836, November.

Griliches, Z. 1994. Productivity, R&D and the Data Constraint. *American Economic Review* 84 (2): 1–23.

Gullickson, W., and M. J. Harper. 1999. Possible Measurement Bias in Aggregate Productivity Growth. *Monthly Labor Review* 122 (February): 47–67.

Gurbaxani, V., and S. Whang. 1991. The Impact of Information Systems on Organizations and Markets. *Communications of the ACM* 34 (1): 59–73.

Hall, R. E. 1999. The Stock Market and Capital Accumulation. NBER Working Paper No. 7180.

Hall, R. E. 1999b. Reorganization. NBER Working Paper No. 7181.

Hammer, M. 1990. Re-engineering Work: Don't Automate, Obliterate. *Harvard Business Review* 68 (July–August): 104–112.

Hitt, L. 1996. *Economic Analysis of Information Technology and Organization*. Unpublished doctoral dissertation, MIT Sloan School of Management.

Hitt, Lorin M. 1999. Information Technology and Firm Boundaries: Evidence from Panel Data. *Information Systems Research* 10 (9): 134–149.

Hunter, Larry W., Annette Bernhardt, Katherine L. Hughes, and Eva Skuratowicz. 2000. It's Not Just the ATMs: Firm Strategies, Work Restructuring, and Workers' Earnings in Retail Banking. Mimeo, Wharton School.

Johnston, H. Russell, and Michael R. Vitale. 1988. Creating Competitive Advantage with Interorganizational Information Systems. *MIS Quarterly* 12 (2): 153–165.

Jorgenson, Dale W., and Kevin Stiroh. 1995. Computers and Growth. *Journal of Economics of Innovation and New Technology* 3: 295–316.

Jorgenson, Dale W., and Kevin Stiroh. 1999. Information Technology and Growth. *American Economic Review, Papers and Proceedings* 89 (2): 109–115.

Kelley, Maryellen R. 1994. Productivity and Information Technology: The Elusive Connection. *Management Science* 40 (11): 1406–1425.

Kemerer, C. F., and G. L. Sosa. 1991. Systems Development Risks in Strategic Information Systems. *Information and Software Technology* 33 (3): 212–223.

Lehr, W., and F. R. Lichtenberg. 1998. Computer Use and Productivity Growth in Federal Government Agencies 1987–92. *Journal of Industrial Economics* 46 (2): 257–279.

Levy, Frank, Anne Beamish, Richard J. Murnane, and David Autor. 2000. Computerization and Skills: Examples from a Car Dealership. Mimeo, MIT and Harvard.

Lichtenberg, F. R. 1995. The Output Contributions of Computer Equipment and Personnel: A Firm-Level Analysis. *Economics of Innovation and New Technology* 3: 201–217.

Malone, T. W., J. Yates, and R. I. Benjamin. 1987. Electronic Markets and Electronic Hierarchies. *Communications of the ACM* 30 (6): 484–497.

Malone, Thomas W. 1987. Modeling Coordination in Organizations and Markets. *Management Science* 33 (10): 1317–1332.

McKenney, J. L., and T. H. Clark. 1995. Procter and Gamble: Improving Consumer Value through Process Redesign. Harvard Business School Case Study 9-195-126.

Milgrom, P., and J. Roberts. 1990. The Economics of Modern Manufacturing: Technology, Strategy, and Organization. *American Economic Review* 80 (3): 511–528.

Morrison, Catherine J. 1996. Assessing the Productivity of Information Technology Equipment in U.S. Manufacturing Industries. *Review of Economics & Statistics* 79 (3): 471–481.

Mukhopadhyay, Tridas, Rajiv Surendra, and Kannan Srinivasan. 1997. Information Technology Impact on Process Output and Quality. *Management Science* 43 (12): 1645–1659.

Murnane, Richard J., Frank Levy, and David Autor. 1999. Technological Change, Computers, and Skill Demands: Evidence from the Back Office Operations of a Large Bank. Mimeo, NBER Economic Research Labor Workshop, June.

Nakamura, L. I. 1997. The Measurement of Retail Output and the Retail Revolution. Paper presented at the CSLS Workshop on Service Sector Productivity and the Productivity Paradox, Ottawa, Canada, April.

Oliner, S. D., and Sichel, D. E. 1994. Computers and Output Growth Revisited: How Big is the Puzzle? *Brookings Papers on Economic Activity: Microeconomics* (2): 273–334.

Orlikowski, W. J. 1992. Learning from Notes: Organizational Issues in Groupware Implementation. In *Conference on Computer Supported Cooperative Work*, J. Turner and R. Kraut, eds. Toronto: Association for Computing Machinery, 362–369.

Osterberg, William P., and Sandy A. Sterk 1997. Do more banking offices mean more banking services? *Economic Commentary (Federal Reserve Bank of Cleveland)*, 1–5.

Radner, R. 1993. The Organization of Decentralized Information Processing. *Econometrica* 62: 1109–1146.

Rangan, V., and M. Bell. 1998. *Dell Online*. Harvard Business School Case Study 9-598-116.

Roach, Stephen S. 1987. America's Technology Dilemma: A Profile of the Information Economy. *Morgan Stanley Special Economic Study*, April.

Schankerman, M. 1981. The Effects of Double-Counting and Expensing on the Measured Returns to R&D. *Review of Economics and Statistics* 63: 454–458.

Schnapp, John. 1998. An Old Strategy is Backfiring at G.M. *New York Times*, July 12, section 3, 12.

Seybold, Patricia, and Ronni Marshak. 1998. *Customers.com: How to Create A Profitable Business Strategy for the Internet & Beyond*. New York: Times Books.

Siegel, Donald. 1997. The Impact of Computers on Manufacturing Productivity Growth: A Multiple-Indicators Multiple-Causes Approach. *Review of Economics & Statistics* 79 (1): 68–78.

Short, James E., and N. Venkatraman. 1992. Beyond Business Process Redesign: Redefining Baxter's Business Network. *Sloan Management Review* 34 (1): 7–20.

Simon, Herbert A. 1976. *Administrative Behavior*. New York: Free Press, 3rd edition.

Solow, R. M. 1987. We'd Better Watch Out. *New York Times Book Review*, July 12, 36.

Vitale, M., and B. Konsynski. 1988. Baxter Healthcare Corp.: ASAP Express. Harvard Business School Case 9-188-080.

Wilson, Diane D. 1995. IT Investment and Its Productivity Effects: An Organizational Sociologist's Perspective on Directions for Future Research. *Economics of Innovation and New Technology* (3): 235–251.

How Are Things Changing?

5 The Dawn of the E-Lance Economy

Thomas W. Malone and Robert Laubacher

In October of 1991, Linus Torvalds, a 21-year-old computer-science student at the University of Helsinki, made available on the Internet a kernel of a computer operating system he had written. Called Linux, it was a rudimentary version of the ubiquitous UNIX operating system, which for more than a decade had been a mainstay of corporate and academic computing. Torvalds encouraged other programmers to download his software—for free—and use it, test it, and modify it as they saw fit. A few took him up on the offer. They fixed bugs, tinkered with the original code, and added new features, and they too posted their work on the Internet.

As the Linux kernel grew, it attracted the attention of more and more programmers, who contributed their own ideas and improvements. The Linux community grew steadily, soon coming to encompass thousands of people around the world, all sharing their work freely with one another. Within three years, this loose, informal group, working without managers and connected mainly through the Internet, had turned Linux into one of the best versions of UNIX ever created.

Imagine, now, how such a software development project would have been organized at a company like IBM or Microsoft. Decisions and funds would have been filtered through layers of managers. Formal teams of programmers, quality assurance testers, and technical writers would have been established and assigned tasks. Customer surveys and focus groups would have been conducted, their findings documented in thick reports. There would have been budgets, milestones, deadlines, status meetings, performance reviews, approvals. There would have been turf wars, burnouts, overruns, delays. The project would have cost an enormous amount of money, taken longer to complete, and quite possibly produced a system less valuable to users than Linux.

For many executives, the development of Linux is most easily understood (and most easily dismissed) as an arcane story of hackers and cyberspace—a neat *Wired* magazine kind of story, but one that bears little relevance to the serious world of big business. This interpretation, while understandable, is shortsighted. What the Linux story really shows us is the power of a new technology—in this case, electronic networks—to fundamentally change the way work is done. The Linux community, a temporary, self-managed gathering of diverse individuals engaged in a common task, is a model for a new kind of business organization that could form the basis for a new kind of economy.

The fundamental unit of such an economy is not the corporation but the individual. Tasks aren't assigned and controlled through a stable chain of management, but rather are carried out autonomously by independent contractors. These electronically connected freelancers—e-lancers—join together into fluid and temporary networks to produce and sell goods and services. When the job is done—after a day, a month, a year—the network dissolves, and its members become independent agents again, circulating through the economy, seeking the next assignment.

Far from being a wild hypothesis, the e-lance economy is, in many ways, already upon us. We see it not only in the development of Linux but also in the evolution of the Internet itself. We see it in the emergence of virtual companies, in the rise of outsourcing and telecommuting, and in the proliferation of freelance and temporary workers. Even within large organizations, we see it in the increasing importance of ad-hoc project teams, in the rise of "intrapreneurs," and in the formation of independent business units.[1]

All these trends point to the devolution of large, permanent corporations into flexible, temporary networks of individuals. No one can yet say exactly how important or widespread this new form of business organization will become, but judging from current signs, it is not inconceivable that it could define work in the twenty-first century as the industrial organization defined it in the twentieth. If it does, business and society will be changed forever.

Businesses of One

Business organizations are, in essence, mechanisms for coordination. They exist to guide the flow of work, materials, ideas, and money, and the form they take is strongly affected by the coordination technologies available. Until a hundred or so years ago, coordination technologies were primitive. Goods and messages were transported primarily by foot, horse, or boat, and the process was slow, unreliable, and often dangerous. Because there was no efficient way to coordinate disparate activities, most people worked near their homes, often by themselves, producing products or services for their neighbors. The business organizations that did exist—farms, shops, foundries—were usually small, comprising a few owners and employees. When their products had to reach distant consumers, they did so through a long series of transactions with various independent wholesalers, jobbers, shippers, storekeepers, and itinerant peddlers.

It was not until the second half of the nineteenth century, after railroad tracks had been laid and telegraph lines strung, that large, complex organizations became possible. With faster, more dependable communication and transportation, businesses could reach national and even international markets, and their owners had the means to coordinate the activities of large and dispersed groups of people. The hierarchical, industrial corporation was born, subsuming a broad array of functions and, often, a broad array of businesses, and it quickly matured to become the dominant organizational model of the twentieth century.

Despite all the recent talk of decentralized management, empowered employees, and horizontal processes, the large, industrial organization continues to dominate the economy today. We remain in the age of multinational megacompanies, and those companies appear to be rushing to meld into ever larger forms. The headlines of the business press tell the story: Compaq buys Digital. WorldCom buys MCI. Citibank merges with Travelers. Daimler-Benz acquires Chrysler. British Airways allies with American Airlines (which in turn allies with US Airways). Some observers, projecting this wave of consolidation into the future, foresee a world in which giant global corporations replace nations as the organizing units of humanity. We will be citizens of Sony or Shell or Wal-Mart, marching out every day to do battle with the citizens of Philips or Exxon or Sears.

Such a scenario certainly seems plausible. Yet when we look beneath the surface of all the M&A activity, we see signs of a counterphenomenon: the disintegration of the large corporation. People are leaving big companies and either joining much smaller companies or going into business for themselves as contract workers, freelancers, or temps. Twenty-five years ago, one in five U.S. workers was employed by a *Fortune* 500 company. Today the ratio has dropped to less than one in ten. The largest private employer in the United States is not General Motors or IBM or UPS. It's the temporary-employment agency Manpower Incorporated, which in 1997 employed 2 million people. While big companies control ever larger flows of cash, they are exerting less and less direct control over actual business activity. They are, you might say, growing hollow.

Even within large corporations, traditional command-and-control management is becoming less common. Decisions are increasingly being pushed lower down in organizations. Workers are being rewarded not for efficiently carrying out orders, but for figuring out what needs to be done and then doing it. Some large industrial companies like Asea Brown Boveri and British Petroleum have broken themselves up into scores of independent units that transact business with one another almost as if they were separate companies. And in some industries, like investment banking and consulting, it is often easier to understand the existing organizations not as traditional hierarchies but as confederations of entrepreneurs, united only by a common brand name.

What underlies this trend? Why is the traditional industrial organization showing evidence of disintegration? Why are e-lancers proliferating? The answers lie in the basic economics of organizations. Economists, organizational theorists, and business historians have long wrestled with the question of why businesses grow large or stay small. Their research suggests that when it is cheaper to conduct transactions internally, within the bounds of a corporation, organizations grow larger, but when it is cheaper to conduct them externally, with independent entities in the open market, organizations stay small or shrink. If, for example, the owners of an iron smelter find it less expensive to establish a sales force than to contract with outside agencies to sell their products, they will hire salespeople, and their organization will grow. If they find that outside agencies cost less, they will not hire the salespeople, and their organization will not grow.

The coordination technologies of the industrial era—the train and the telegraph, the automobile and the telephone, the mainframe computer—made internal transactions not only possible but also advantageous. Companies were able to manage large organizations centrally, which provided them with economies of scale in manufacturing, marketing, distribution, and other activities. It made economic sense to directly control many different functions and businesses and to hire the legions of administrators and supervisors needed to manage them. Big was good.

But with the introduction of powerful personal computers and broad electronic networks—the coordination technologies of the twenty-first century—the economic equation changes. Because information can be shared instantly and inexpensively among many people in many locations, the value of centralized decision making and expensive bureaucracies decreases. Individuals can manage themselves, coordinating their efforts through electronic links with other independent parties. Small becomes good.

In one sense, the new coordination technologies enable us to return to the preindustrial organizational model of tiny, autonomous businesses—businesses of one or of a few—conducting transactions with one another in a market. But there's one crucial difference: electronic networks enable these microbusinesses to tap into the global reservoirs of information, expertise, and financing that used to be available only to large companies. The small companies enjoy many of the benefits of the big without sacrificing the leanness, flexibility, and creativity of the small.

In the future, as communications technologies advance and networks become more efficient, the shift to e-lancers promises to accelerate. Should that indeed take place, the dominant business organization of the future may not be a stable, permanent corporation but rather an elastic network that may sometimes exist for no more than a day or two. When a project needs to be undertaken, requests for proposals will be transmitted or electronic want ads posted, individuals or small teams will respond, a network will be formed, and new workers will be brought on as their particular skills are needed. Once the project is done, the network will disband. Following in the footsteps of young Linus Torvalds, we will enter the age of the temporary company.

The Temporary Company

From the 1920s through the 1940s, the movie business was controlled by big studios like MGM and Columbia. The studios employed actors, directors, screenwriters, photographers, publicists, even projectionists—all the people needed to produce a movie, get it into theaters, and fill the seats. Central managers determined which films to make and who would work on them. The film industry was a model of big-company, industrial organization.

By the 1950s, however, the studio system had disintegrated. The power had shifted from the studio to the individual. Actors, directors, and screenwriters became free-lancers, and they made their own choices about what projects to work on. For a movie to be made, these freelancers would join together into a temporary company, which would employ different specialists as needed from day to day. As soon as the film was completed, the temporary company would go out of existence, but the various players would, in time, join together in new combinations to work on new projects.

The shift in the film business from permanent companies to temporary companies shows how entire industries can evolve, quite rapidly, from centralized structures to network structures. And such transformations are by no means limited to the idiosyncratic world of Hollywood. Consider the way many manufacturers are today pursuing radical outsourcing strategies, letting external agents perform more of their traditional activities. The computer-display division of the Finnish company Nokia, for example, chose to enter the U.S. display market with only five employees. Technical support, logistics, sales, and marketing were all subcontracted to specialists around the country. The fashion accessories company Topsy Tail, which has revenues of $80 million but only three employees, never even touches its products through the entire supply chain. It contracts with various injection-molding companies to manufacture its goods; uses design agencies to create its packaging; and distributes and sells its products through a network of independent fulfillment houses, distributors, and sales reps. Nokia's and Topsy Tail's highly decentralized operations bear more resemblance to the network model of organization than to the traditional industrial model.

For another, broader example, look at what's happened to the textile industry in the Prato region of Italy. In the early 1970s, Massimo Menichetti inherited his family's business, a failing textile mill. Menichetti quickly broke up the firm into eight separate companies. He sold a major portion of equity—between one-third and one-half—to key employees, and he required that at least 50 percent of the new companies' sales come from customers that had not been served by the old company. Within three years, the eight new businesses had achieved a complete turn-around, attaining significant increases in machine utilization and productivity.

Following the Menichetti model, many other big mills in Prato broke themselves up into much smaller pieces. By 1990, more than 15,000 small textile firms, averaging fewer than five employees, were active in the region. The tiny firms built state-of-the-art factories and warehouses, and they developed cooperative ventures in such areas as purchasing, logistics, and R&D, where scale economies could be exploited. Textile production in the area tripled during this time, despite the fact that the textile industry was in decline throughout the rest of Europe. And the quality of the products produced in the Prato region rose as innovation flourished. Textiles from Prato have now become the preferred material for fashion designers around the world.

Playing a key role in the Prato textile industry are brokers, known as *impannatori,* who act as conduits between the small manufacturing concerns and the textile buyers. The impannatori help coordinate the design and manufacturing process by bringing together appropriate groups of businesses to meet the particular needs of a customer. They have even created an electronic market, which serves as a clearinghouse for information about projected factory utilization and up-coming requirements, allowing textile production capacity to be traded like a commodity.

The Prato experience shows that an economy can be built on the network model, but Prato, it could be argued, is a small and homogenous region. How would a complex, diverse industry operate under the network model? The answer is: far more easily than one might expect. As a thought experiment, let's take a journey forward in time, into the midst of the twenty-first century, and see how automobiles, the archetypal industrial product, are being designed.

General Motors, we find, has split apart into several dozen separate divisions, and these divisions have outsourced most of their traditional activities. They are now small companies concerned mainly with managing their brands and funding the development of new types and models of cars. A number of independent manufac-turers perform fabrication and assembly on a contract basis for anyone who wants to pay for it. Vehicles are devised by freelance engineers and designers, who join together into small, ever-shifting coalitions to work on particular projects. A coali-tion may, for example, focus on engineering an electrical system or on designing a chassis, or it may concentrate on managing the integration of all of the subsystems into complete automobiles.

These design coalitions take many forms. Some are organized as joint ventures; some share equity among their members; some are built around electronic markets that set prices and wages. All are autonomous and self-organizing, and all depend on a universal, high-speed computer network—the descendant of the Internet—to connect them to one another and exchange electronic cash. A highly developed venture-capital infrastructure monitors and assesses the various teams and provides financing to the most promising ones.

In addition to being highly efficient, with little managerial or administrative overhead, this market-based structure has spurred innovation throughout the automotive industry. While much of the venture capital goes to support traditional design concepts, some is allocated to more speculative, even wild-eyed, ideas, which if successful could create enormous financial rewards. A small coalition of engineers may, for example, receive funds to design a factory for making individualized lighting systems for car grilles. If their idea pans out, they could all become multimillionaires overnight. And the next day, they might dissolve their coalition and head off to seek new colleagues and new challenges.

Over the past few years, under the auspices of the Massachusetts Institute of Technology's initiative on Inventing the Organizations of the 21st Century, we have worked with a group of business professors and executives to consider the different ways business might be organized in the next century.[2] The automotive design scenario we've just laid out was discussed and refined by this group, and we subsequently shared it with managers and engineers from big car companies. They not only agreed that it was a plausible model for car design but also pointed out that the auto industry was in some ways already moving toward such a model. Many automakers have been outsourcing more and more of their basic design work, granting ever greater autonomy to external design agencies.

A shift to an e-lance economy would bring about fundamental changes in virtually every business function, not just in product design. Supply chains would become *ad hoc* structures, assembled to fit the needs of a particular project and disassembled when the project ended. Manufacturing capacity would be bought and sold in an open market, and independent, specialized manufacturing concerns would undertake small batch orders for a variety of brokers, design shops, and even consumers. Marketing would be performed in some cases by brokers, in other cases by small companies that would own brands and certify the quality of the merchandise sold under them. In still other cases, the ability of consumers to share product information on the Internet would render marketing obsolete; consumers would simply "swarm" around the best offerings. Financing would come less from retained earnings and big equity markets and more from venture capitalists and interested individuals. Small investors might trade shares in *ad hoc*, project-based enterprises over the Internet. Business would be transformed fundamentally. But nowhere would the changes be as great as in the function of management itself.

The Transformation of Management

In the mid-1990s, when the Internet was just entering the consciousness of most business executives, the press was filled with disaster stories. The Internet, the pundits proclaimed, was about to fall into disarray. Traffic on the World Wide Web was growing too fast. There were too many Web sites, too many people on-line. Demand was outstripping capacity, and it was only a matter of months before the entire network crashed or froze. It never happened. The Internet has continued to expand at an astonishing rate. Its capacity has doubled every year since 1988, and today more than 90 million people are connected to it. They use it to order books and flowers, to check on weather conditions in distant cities, to trade stocks and commodities, to send messages and spread propaganda, and to join discussion groups on everything from soap operas to particle physics.

So who's responsible for this great and unprecedented achievement? Who oversaw what is arguably the most important business development of the last 50 years? No one. No one controls the Internet. No one's in charge. No one's the leader. The Internet grew out of the combined efforts of all its users, with no central management. In fact, when we ask people whether they think the Internet could have grown this fast for this long if it had been managed by a single company—AT&T, for example—most say no. Managing such a massive and unpredictable explosion of capacity and creativity would have been beyond the skills of even the most astute and capable executives. The Internet *had* to be self-managed.

The Internet is the greatest model of a network organization that has yet emerged, and it reveals a startling truth: In an e-lance economy, the role of the traditional business manager changes dramatically and sometimes disappears completely. The work of the temporary company is coordinated by the individuals who compose it, with little or no centralized direction or control. Brokers, venture capitalists, and general contractors all play key roles—initiating projects, allocating resources, and coordinating work—but there need not be any single point of oversight. Instead, the overall results *emerge* from the individual actions and interactions of all the different players in the system.

Of course, this kind of coordination occurs all the time in a free market, where products ranging from cars to copying machines to soft drinks all get produced and consumed without any centralized authority deciding how many or what kinds of these products to make. More than two hundred years ago, Adam Smith called this kind of decentralized coordination the invisible hand of the market, and we usually take for granted that it is the most effective way for companies to interact with one another.

But what if this kind of decentralized coordination were used to organize all the different kinds of activities that today go on *inside* companies? One of the things that allows a free market to work is the establishment and acceptance of a set of standards—the "rules of the game"—that govern all the transactions. The rules of the game can take many forms, including contracts, systems of ownership, and procedures for dispute resolution. Similarly, for an e-lance economy to work, whole new classes of agreements, specifications, and common architectures will need to evolve.

We see this already in the Internet, which works because everyone involved with it conforms to certain technical specifications. You don't have to ask anyone for permission to become a network provider or a service provider or a user; you just have to obey the communication protocols that govern the Internet. Standards are the glue that holds the Internet together, and they will be the glue that binds temporary companies together and helps them operate efficiently.

To return to our auto industry scenario, car designers would be able to work independently because they would have on-line access to highly detailed engineering protocols. These standards would ensure that individual component designs are compatible with the overall design of the vehicle. Headlight designers, for example, would know the exact space allocated for the light assembly as well as the nature of any connections that need to be made with the electrical and control systems.

Standards don't have to take the form of technical specifications. They may take the form of routinized processes, such as we see today in the medical community. When doctors, nurses, and technicians gather to perform emergency surgery, they usually all know what process to follow, what role each will play, and how they'll interact with one another. Even if they've never worked together before, they can collaborate effectively without delay. In other cases, the standards may simply be patterns of behavior that come to be accepted as norms—what might today be referred to as the culture of a company or "the way things are done" in an industry.

One of the primary roles for the large organizations that remain in the future may be to establish rules, standards, and cultures for network operating partly within and partly outside their own boundaries. Some global consulting firms already operate in more or less this way. For example, McKinsey & Company has well-established norms about how people are selected and promoted and how they are expected to work together. Linked by the firm's culture, McKinsey partners operate quite autonomously, making independent decisions about what they will do and how they will do it. In this example, the value the firm provides comes mainly from the standards—the rules of the game—it has established, not from the strategic or operational skills of its top managers.

As more large companies establish decentralized, market-based organizational structures, the boundaries between companies will become much less important. Transactions within organizations will become indistinguishable from transactions between organizations, and business processes, once proprietary, will freely cross organizational boundaries. The key role for individuals—whether they call themselves managers or not—will be to play their parts in shaping a network that neither they nor anyone else controls.

Thinking About the Future

Most of what you've just read is, of course, speculative. Some of it may happen; some of it may not. Big companies may split apart, or they may stay together but adopt much more decentralized structures. The future of business may turn out to be far less revolutionary than we've sketched out, or it may turn out to be far more revolutionary. We're convinced, though, of one thing—an e-lance economy, though a radical concept, is by no means an impossible or even an implausible concept. Most of the necessary building blocks—high-bandwidth networks, data interchange standards, groupware, electronic currency, venture capital micromarkets—either are in place or are under development.

What is lagging behind technology is our imagination. Most people are not able to conceive of a completely new economy where much of what they know about doing business no longer applies. Mitch Resnick, a colleague of ours at MIT, says that most people are locked into a "centralized mind set." When we look up into the sky and see a flock of birds flying in formation, we tend to assume that the bird in front is the leader and that the leader is somehow determining the organization of all the other birds. In fact, biologists tell us, each bird is simply following a simple set of rules—behavioral standards—that result in the emergence of the organization. The bird in the front is no more important than the bird in the back or the bird in the middle. They're all equally essential to the pattern that they're forming.

The reason it's so important for us to recognize and to challenge the biases of our existing mind set is that the rise of an e-lance economy would have profound implications for business and society, and we should begin considering those implications sooner rather than later. An e-lance economy might well lead to a flowering of individual wealth, freedom, and creativity. Business might become much more flexible and efficient, and people might find themselves with much more time for leisure, for education, and for other pursuits. A Golden Age might dawn.

On the other hand, an e-lance economy might lead to disruption and dislocation. Loosed from its traditional moorings, the business world might become chaotic and cutthroat. The gap between society's haves and have-nots might widen, as those lacking special talents or access to electronic networks fall by the wayside. The safety net currently formed by corporate benefit programs, such as health and disability insurance, might unravel.[3] E-lance workers, separated from the communities that companies create today, may find themselves lonely and alienated. All of these potential problems could likely be avoided, but we won't be able to avoid them if we remain blind to them.

Twenty-four years from now, in the year 2022, the *Harvard Business Review* will be celebrating its one hundredth year of publication. As part of its centennial celebration, it may well publish a series of articles that look back on recent business history and contemplate the massive changes that have taken place. The authors may write about the industrial organization of the twentieth century as merely a transitional structure that flourished for a relatively brief time. They may comment on the speed with which giant companies fragmented into the myriad microbusinesses that now dominate the economy. And they may wonder why, at the turn of the century, so few saw it coming.

Acknowledgements

This chapter is reprinted with permission from *Harvard Business Review* 76, no. 5 (September–October 1998), 145–152.

Notes

1. For more about the influence of information technology on business organizations, see Malone, chapter 3 of this volume; Malone (1987); Malone and Rockart (1991).

2. See Laubacher and Malone (1997a).

3. Workers' guilds, common in the Middle Ages, may again rise to prominence, taking over many of the welfare functions currently provided by big companies; see Laubacher and Malone (1997b); Laubacher and Malone, chapter 17 of this volume.

References

Laubacher, Robert J., Thomas W. Malone, and the MIT Scenario Working Group. 1997a. Two Scenarios for 21st Century Organizations: Shifting Networks of Small Firms or All-Encompassing "Virtual Countries"? MIT Initiative on Inventing the Organizations of the 21st Century Working Paper No. 001, January, http://ccs.mit.edu/21c/21CWP001.html.

Laubacher, Robert J., and Thomas W. Malone. 1997b. Flexible Work Arrangements and 21st Century Worker's Guilds. MIT Initiative on Inventing the Organizations of the 21st Century Working Paper No. 004, October, http://ccs.mit.edu/21c/21CWP004.html.

Malone, Thomas W., JoAnne Yates, and Robert I. Benjamin. 1987. Electronic Markets and Electronic Hierarchies. *Communications of the ACM*, 30 (June): 484–497.

Malone, Thomas W., and John F. Rockart. 1991. Computers, Networks, and the Corporation. *Scientific American* 265 (September) 128–136.

6 Two Scenarios for 21st Century Organizations: Shifting Networks of Small Firms or All-Encompassing "Virtual Countries"?

Robert Laubacher, Thomas W. Malone, and the MIT Scenarios Working Group[1]

One of the key activities of MIT's Initiative on Inventing the Organizations of the 21st Century was developing a series of coherent scenarios of possible future organizations. The scenarios were not intended as predictions, but rather as visions of potential alternative ways of organizing work and structuring business enterprises in the next century. This chapter describes the results of the Initiative's scenario development activity.

Background and Approach

Scenario planning begins with the assumption that the future ultimately cannot be knowable with any certainty. Starting from this point, scenario planners set out to think deeply about the various potential futures that might emerge. The scenario process employs a range of techniques—research, brainstorming, story telling—and attempts to sketch a series of narrative accounts which delineate the boundaries of what could conceivably occur going forward.[2] Scenario planning was chosen as an approach for the 21st Century Initiative, since it provided a structured methodology for thinking about the environment in which future organizations will operate and the likely form those organizations might take.

Scenario Creation Group

The Scenario Creation Group was comprised of thirteen members of the MIT faculty and research staff (see list of members and their affiliations in the acknowledgments at the end of this chapter). Peter Schwartz of Global Business Network, a consulting firm that specializes in scenario planning, served as discussion facilitator. The Group held a series of during the spring of 1994 and framed an initial set of scenarios. The focus was:

- the world 20 years hence (approximately 2015),
- future ways of organizing work,
- issues likely to fall under the control of business enterprises, with government policy considered primarily insofar as it might affect business,
- business around the world, not just in the U.S.,
- effects of future organizational forms on both economic and non-economic aspects of life, and on both individuals and society.

Review by Faculty, Corporate Sponsors, and Others

In late spring 1994, these initial scenarios were the subject of a half-day meeting held by a Scenario Review Group comprised of ten additional Sloan faculty. Over the next two years, the scenarios were discussed by researchers, executives, and students at a series of events held by the 21st Century Initiative and meeting sponsored by other groups, both at MIT and elsewhere. In all, more than 500 people heard about and commented on the scenarios at more than 10 events.

Scenario Contents

In its scenario development activities, the MIT Working Group considered a variety of possible driving forces that might shape twenty-first century organizations, all of which could have served as the basis for intriguing scenarios. The Working Group chose to focus on one major uncertainty which emerged repeatedly in the discussions: the *size* of individual companies. This led to a set of scenarios that posed the question: Will organizations in the future be much larger, much smaller, or not very different in size from the organizations we know today? In order to stimulate creative thinking, the group imagined two extremes on this dimension: very small companies and very large companies.

Thus, the first scenario focuses on how work might be organized in ever-shifting networks of small firms and individual contractors; the second focuses on how work might be organized in huge, long-lasting, and all-encompassing holding companies. These two scenarios are called "Small Companies, Large Networks" and "Virtual Countries."

Even though these two scenarios were originally conceived of as extremes on the dimension of company size, it is also possible to think of them as extremes on the dimension of organizational *longevity*. The small companies in the first scenario can participate in very large, temporary networks of thousands of people. But these temporary organizations (or "virtual companies") may only exist for a few weeks, days, or hours until the project that brings the network together is completed. The large "virtual countries," on the other hand, expect to last for decades or even centuries while projects, people, and whole industries come and go within their boundaries.

Scenario One: Small Companies, Large Networks

Imagine that it is now the year 2015. . . .

The corporation of the late twentieth century was just a transitional form.[4] It lasted more than one hundred years, but few corporations of that kind remain today. Now, looking back at the "dinosaur" era in which General Motors, Microsoft, and Sony stalked the earth, we are most aware of the tiny "mammals"—entertainment production companies, construction project teams, and consultant workgroups—which operated without much public notice back in the 1990s, only to become the prototypes of today's modern organization.

Today, nearly every task is performed by autonomous teams of one to ten people, set up as independent contractors or small firms, linked by networks, coming together in temporary combinations for various projects, and dissolving once the work is done. When a project needs to be undertaken, requests for proposals are issued or jobs to be done are advertised, candidate firms respond, sub-contractors are selected, and workers are hired largely on an *ad hoc* basis.

Consider the design of automobiles.[5] In a typical project, a variety of independent firms form competing coalitions, to explore alternative designs for the electric system, the chassis, or the task of putting the car's subsystems together. Some of these firms are joint ventures; some share equity; some are built around electronic markets that set prices and wages. All are autonomous and self-organizing. All depend on the ubiquitous, high-bandwidth, transaction-heavy electronic network that connects them to each other. A highly-developed venture capital infrastructure identifies promising teams and provides financing.

Authority is still evident, but not through commands. A small "Chevrolet/Saturn" central company still has senior people who exercise their judgment by choosing where to invest their R&D, marketing, and production capital. But groups also try wild-eyed ideas that turn out to be very successful—and financially rewarding for their participants. For instance, one team of four people created a factory for nano-engineering individualized lighting systems for each car's grille. They bucked conventional wisdom when they built it, and all became millionaires in the process.

Even though this way of organizing work is extremely well-suited to rapid innovation and dynamically changing markets, the world would be a lonely and unsatisfying place if all our interactions were contractual. Therefore, we are all fortunate to have independent organizations for social networking, learning, reputation-building, and income smoothing. These communities evolved from professional societies, college alumni associations, unions, fraternities, clubs, neighborhoods, families, and churches. Many are similar to the writers' and actors' guilds of Hollywood. They help us save for retirement, and most of us pay a percentage of our income to our "guilds" as a voluntary form of unemployment insurance. It is here that we learn and update the skills of our professions, and share war stories and reputations. Perhaps most importantly, we derive much of our sense of identity and belonging from these stable communities that we call "home" as temporary projects come and go.

Shifting Task Networks with Stable Homes

There are two key elements of the "small firms" scenario: fluid networks for organizing tasks and the stable communities to which people belong as they move from project to project.

Examples of shifting task networks already exist. Film production and construction are organized in this way in the U.S., and the texile industry in the Prato region of Italy has thousands of small firms, most with five or fewer employees. Radical outsourcing, in which a firm keeps product development and high-level marketing functions in-house, then contracts out the rest of the value chain, is prevalent in the apparel industry and the computer sector in Silicon Valley and other high technology regions.[6] The preceding chapter of this volume, on the "e-lance economy," describes several examples of this kind in greater detail.

The second element of the Small Companies/Large Networks scenario is that existing or new organizations will step in to meet the "life maintenance" requirements—the need for health insurance, protection against unemployment and income fluctuation, professional development, and a sense of belonging and community—of those who work in networked organizations. In the developed world, these needs are now largely met by some combination of corporations and the state, with more of the burden carried by employers in the United States and Japan, more by governments in Western Europe.

The Small Companies/Large Networks scenario posits that these life maintenance needs will be met by a variety of other organizations, some of which are currently playing a part in one or another of these areas. The leading candidates for assuming these roles include: professional societies, unions, universities, alumni associations, churches, political parties, service clubs, fraternal orders, neighborhoods, and families/clans. There may also be opportunities for entrepreneurs to create new kinds of organizations to fill some or all of these life maintenance needs. Another possibility envisioned by the Scenario Working Group was that collections of families and individuals might pool their resources and form semi-communal living arrangements to fulfill non-economic needs and mitigate the potential harshness of a solely market-driven work environment.[7]

The "life maintenance" organizations of this scenario might look very much like the guilds of pre-industrial times or labor unions of the early years of the industrial revolution.[8] The potential for organizations of this sort is addressed in more detail in chapter 17 in this volume, on "the retreat of the firm and the rise of guilds."

Scenario Two: Virtual Countries[9]

Imagine that it is now the year 2015. . . .

The huge global conglomerate has emerged as the dominant way of organizing work. These *keiretsu*-style alliances, each with operating companies in almost every industry, have minimal national allegiance. Members of the same family work for Sony/Microsoft or General Electric/Toyota, and feel little loyalty to the United States or Japan. It would be considered disloyal and unusual for members of the same family to work at competing *keiretsu*. The alliances meet all our needs on a cradle-to-grave basis by providing income and job security, health care, education, social networking, and a sense of self-identity. Our organizations are as powerful and influential as nations, and we owe allegiance to them. They have no dominion over our land, but they control our much more significant assets—access to knowledge, the networks, and our livelihood. They even wage war on each other—using lawyers instead of armies, valiantly protecting the trademarks of our company.

These days, if you want to define me, you can ignore my geographic location; I can be stereotyped according to the company I work for, in whose service I expect to retire. My friends and family members from around the world all work for the same organization. Occasionally, although I work for Shell/Daewoo, I must ride a nonaligned airline, and I run across someone from Exxushita. We always converse, full of curiosity, but guarded—taking advantage of a rare opportunity to see ourselves as others see us.

Employees own the firms in which they work, through pension plans, stock options, employee participation contracts, and other vehicles. And just as the modern nation states ultimately turned to democracy, many of the corporations of the twenty-first century have moved to representative governance. Our firm is one—employee-shareholders have the right to elect the management of the company, not just the board of directors, but managers at almost every level throughout the organization. Decisions are made hierarchically, but every year, on election day, we choose from slates of managers who vow to do the best job for the company as a whole. Since our livelihoods depend on the choice, nearly all of us take advantage of the *keiretsu's* "open-book" financial reports, which provide a constantly-updated overview of the business's priorities and assets.

Some people think of this system as paternalistic and bureaucratic. But actually, there is very little "fat" in the system. Nepotism, ossified command structures, and sinecures don't last long, since everyone benefits from improved performance. Specialist "organization designers" travel through the massive alliances, brokering partnerships and helping make sure that people communicate effectively across boundaries. All of us tend to get along, because our companies attract people who agree with the prevailing attitudes. We all know the "Shell/Daewoo way," and we live and die according to it.

The Virtual Countries scenario has four major elements:

- large vertically- and horizontally-integrated firms;
- pervasive role of firms in employees' lives;
- employee ownership of firms;
- employee selection of firm management.

Large Vertically- and Horizontally-Integrated Firms

The second MIT scenario posits a world economy dominated by large conglomerates which operate globally across a number of industries. As with the present-day

Asian *keiretsu* arrangement, there will be a small number of core firms—large holding companies which sell products with widely recognized brand names—occupying a position at the center of the economy. These companies in turn will have a series of permanent or semi-permanent relationships with various smaller supplier firms, which will stand at the periphery of the system. The industry structure in most sectors will be oligopolistic, with a small number of major competitors holding dominant positions, and high entry barriers preventing upstarts from challenging the hegemony of market leaders.

The huge conglomerates envisioned in the Virtual Countries scenario could grow out of a continuation of the merger wave that has swept through the global business environment since the mid-1990s. The value of announced mergers involving U.S. firms totaled $519 billion in 1995 and $659 billion in 1996, by far surpassing the $353 billion registered in 1988, the previous peak year.[10] Recent mergers have been concentrated in industries affected by government deregulation—telecommunications, broadcasting, financial services, aviation, natural gas and electric utilities—or where public policy has directly or indirectly encouraged consolidation, as in the case of the aerospace and health care sectors. But the globalization of markets has also driven some mergers and led to the creation of numerous international joint ventures, such those which are in place in the airline industry.

Management theory of the last decade has emphasized the importance of firms staying tightly focused and relying on their "core competencies." This trend was largely a response to the conglomerate craze of the 1960s and 1970s, when many large firms diversified into areas entirely unrelated to their original businesses. In the sectors with the greatest volume of recent mergers, the activity has primarily involved the buying of competitors or diversification into closely related areas. The result has been rapid consolidation in a number of industries, often on a global scale. When a firm sells off a business unit unconnected to its central activities and buys an entity with a position in its core industry, the company is effectively substituting scope for scale.

One interpretation of the widespread substitution of scope for scale is that firms are responding to the increased competitive pressures created by the arrival of truly global markets. By this argument, companies are refocusing because their competitors will hurt them if they don't. Some observers believe that once the consolidation of major industries on a world-wide basis has run its course, and oligopolistic industry structures return, unrelated diversification may once again appear attractive, and a series of mergers could ensue to create a second generation of conglomerates, this time on a global scale. Such a sequence of events could serve as the means of forming the world-spanning conglomerates of the Virtual Countries scenario.

Another force that could drive the world toward a Virtual Countries future would be the legal system's inability or unwillingness to protect intellectual property. Should intellectual property laws be weak or confusing, or enforcement of them lax or ineffective, a greater degree of vertical integration may become a strategic imperative for firms whose products have significant knowledge content. Such an approach could become necessary because, in the absence of legal safeguards, capturing the value inherent in a piece of knowledge would require producing and selling a tangible product which physically embodied that knowledge. Under such circumstances, larger companies would be at an advantage, and there would be strong incentives to prevent important knowledge from passing outside the boundaries of the firm.

The management structure employed at the large conglomerates in the Virtual Countries scenario could vary. In some cases, a traditional hierarchy might be maintained, with tight top-to-bottom controls in place to ensure that consistent performance was achieved at operations located around the globe. Alternatively, the conglomerates might be structured in a more decentralized manner, with arm's-length agreements and transfer pricing arrangements characterizing transactions between operating divisions, and employees heavily incentivized by performance-based compensation and promotion schemes. In this scheme, the corporate headquarters would still play an important role in establishing the organization's overall mission and shaping its culture, and in facilitating collaboration between business units where appropriate.

An example of such an approach is the decentralized organizational structure adopted in the last decade by such firms as Asea Brown Boveri, General Electric, and Johnson and Johnson. In all three instances, the traditional multidivisional structure was set aside, and "focal units," consisting of between 200 and 500 employees, were created to operate more or less as autonomous businesses. A thin layer of corporate staff was retained, and the traditional ownership structure, with a single publicly traded corporation serving as a sort of vast holding company for the entire agglomeration, remained unchanged.[11]

Pervasive Role of Firm in Employees' Lives

In the Virtual Countries scenario, the conglomerates will assume full responsibility for meeting the "life maintenance" requirements of their employees. This will include first providing for tangible economic needs, through such means as a guarantee of lifetime employment, generous benefits packages, and retraining in the event that economic or technological changes make employees' skills obsolete. Affiliation with a large, respected company will also help employees meet more intangible needs: It will confer status and a sense of identity, and associating with colleagues at company-sponsored activities and events will become the primary social and recreational outlet of workers.

Employees will be expected to purchase goods and services only from company-affiliated firms. They will fly the company airline, purchase cars and appliances from company subsidiaries, subscribe only to the company-affiliated Internet-telecommunications-entertainment service. The *keiretsu* of Asia already exhibit some of the these characteristics. One member of a 21st Century Initiative sponsor discussion group told of an evening spent in Tokyo, where a Japanese salaryman entertaining foreign business associates showed them the list of company-approved products issued to all employees—and then ordered the brand of beer produced by his firm's subsidiary.

In the Virtual Countries scenario, ties to the company will extend far into employees' personal lives. Family members will tend to work for the same company, and attempts by young couples to marry across company lines will meet with disapproval from parents and co-workers, in the same way that marriages across racial, ethnic, or religious lines are now discouraged in many parts of the world.[12]

By providing completely for employees' life maintenance needs, the large firms will be assuming responsibility for many of the "safety net" functions performed by government in the Western European social democracies during the second half of the 20th century. With private firms taking on this larger role and also operating freely on a transnational basis, it is anticipated that the authority of government and the scope of its activities could be significantly reduced. In parts of world where one or a handful of industries are dominant, private firms may literally take on many of the former roles of the state, including the provision of defense and police protection. Such circumstances would entail the creation of a vastly expanded version of the company town, with the emergence of the "company region" or even "company country" as distinct possibilities.

Nationalism could well decline, as the allegiance citizens formerly felt for their countries gets translated into employees' expanded sense of loyalty to their companies. The notion of citizenship itself would likely become substantially less important—companies might begin issuing the equivalent of passports, allowing only their employees, or approved guests, to travel to regions where their facilities were located, much as firms now issue badges to staff and visitors to grant access to offices and factories.

Employee Ownership/Employee Selection of Firm Management

The Virtual Countries scenario assumes that employees would hold a controlling interest in the shares of most firms, either directly, through straightforward equity holdings, or indirectly, through employee pension funds. Another possibility envisioned in this scenario is that employees would select their firm's management themselves—either indirectly, through appointment of top management by the pension fund's managers, or directly, through employee elections of managers at all levels of the firm.[13]

The concept of employees holding significant stakes in their companies and exerting control over selection of management is an extrapolation from two recent mainstream trends. The first is the rising power of institutional investors and their increasing willingness to assert their will in matters of corporate governance.[14] The second is the somewhat less prominent movement toward employee ownership of companies. By year-end 1995, nearly 10,000 ESOPs were in existence in the U.S., involving more than 10 million employees. In most employee-owned firms, however, management operates relatively autonomously, with employees exerting limited control. The aggressive role taken in 1996 by United Airlines employees in pushing for a new CEO and blocking a proposed merger with USAir stands as a counterexample in which employees were quite engaged and exerted significant authority.[15]

A striking instance of employee ownership and selection of management is found in the group of worker cooperatives operating in and around the city of Mondragón in the Basque region of Spain. The first cooperative in Mondragón was started in 1956 by a group of five foundry workers inspired by the ideas of José María Arizmendiarrieta, a Basque priest. By the late 1980s there were nearly 100 worker cooperatives in and around Mondragón, employing over 20,000. The cooperatives jointly support a bank and technical institute. Employees elect members of a governing council, which in turn selects the management of each enterprise. A large percentage of profits from operations are split among workers in proportion to their salaries, with employees able to take the full amount from their profit-sharing accounts when they leave their firms.[16]

Another model that combines employee ownership and election of management is the partnership structure, common in professional service firms. Many large law, consulting, investment banking, and accounting practices are organized in this way, with the partners jointly owning the firm and also selecting the management team which runs it. While employees below the partner level are excluded from full participation, most are on a career track in which they are eligible to be considered for partnership. Though it does not involve all members of a company, the partnership nonetheless stands as a successful model of broad ownership and self-management within a firm. Selected features of the partnership approach could be incorporated in the more inclusive, firm-wide employee ownership and governance structures envisioned in the Virtual Countries scenario.

Some members of the Working Group expressed skepticism about the workability of employee election of management, voicing concerns that electioneering and cronyism would flourish. Those who saw such a practice being viable envisioned it as the extension of recent efforts at some large firms to distribute responsibility and accountability more widely throughout the organization. This line of thinking was based on the assumption that greater involvement by employees in decisions affecting their own work would grow into an interest in selecting first the managers responsible for overseeing their part of the organization, and eventually, top management of the firm as a whole.

Feasibility

To assess the robustness of the scenarios, the Working Group posed several questions. The first was: Are they feasible? A primary determinant of feasibility is the likely economic viability of the organizational forms the scenarios describe.

Questions about the underlying economics of business enterprises touch on a series of profound and complex issues: Why do certain firms grow large or stay small? What are the critical advantages of size? Are these advantages inherent, or are they tied to conditions unique to certain industries or certain stages of economic development? Economists and business historians have long wrestled with these questions. The fundamental insight behind much of their work has been that while the same transaction can either be internalized within a firm or take place through separate entities exchanging in the marketplace, the arrangement which typically emerges under a given set of circumstances is the one which results in the lowest overall costs.[17]

The Small Companies/Large Networks scenario envisions a world in which external transactions will be much cheaper and more efficient than they are today. The result is expected to be an organizational environment rich in external transactions, where the advantages of speed and flexibility so overshadow those of scale that almost no large, permanent organizations exist. The Virtual Countries world, by contrast, is one in which the advantages of scale which have driven the growth of large organizations in the past are assumed to continue, and indeed, to be amplified significantly—so much so that the number of external transactions will be quite limited, with most of the value chain for the production of goods and services retained inside the core firm and the family of suppliers which will together make up the "extended enterprise" of the large conglomerates.

Desirability

The second major question posed by the Working Group about its scenarios was: Are they desirable? Perspectives on the desirability of one scenario over another are likely to vary significantly by region and culture, and from individual to individual.

Autonomy vs. Community

The Small Companies/Large Networks scenario portrays a world with a myriad of choice. Work for many will be project-based, with free lance independent contractors able to bid for new assignments based on their circumstances and preferences, and flexible schedules and telecommuting the rule.

In the social realm, there would exist a wide range of organizations providing for a variety of needs—casual interaction, education, recreation, professional development, and health care and insurance protection. People would be free to become members of those organizations that best fit their personal requirements, and as a result, many might voluntarily join a variety of groups, none of which would be exclusively tied to their work. In the best case, these organizations might assume some of the characteristics of the voluntary associations described by Alexis de Tocqueville in his description of nineteenth-century American society. Social organizations of this sort have long formed the backbone of what political scientists term "civil society," an entity whose decline has recently been much lamented by students of American politics.[18]

Despite these positive aspects, the Small Companies/Large Networks world would also have its costs. Life spent as independent contractor could be perilous. There would be a continual need to find work, as well as the likelihood of significant down time between assignments. Some members of the MIT Scenario Working Group expressed concern that employees at networked firms and free lancing individuals might be required to invest so much of their effort searching for assignments that they would be able to devote only a fraction of the time a designer or engineer currently employed by a large firm spends working on creating actual products.

The Working Group also expressed concerns about social isolation and the potential lack of a sense of belonging to a larger community. Some members of the group feared that in the absence of mediating social institutions, a networked economy could lead to a Hobbesian future, where life could be solitary, nasty, brutish—and in the U.S., if there were no workable provisions for free lance workers to obtain health coverage—short.

In the end, the desirability of the Small Companies/Large Networks scenario will likely depend on whether existing or new organizations can take on the "life maintenance" role currently played by corporations and governments in providing economic security and fulfilling the function the large firm serves as a nexus for social interaction and professional development.

The future set out in the Virtual Countries scenario, where people's fate is so closely tied to large organizations, is likely to be viewed with dismay by those who place a high value on autonomy and choice. But individual freedom is prized most in the U.S.; in many parts of the world, security and community are valued more. In Asia, for example, where Confucian ethics still have a strong hold and the extended family retains significant influence, many might view the virtual country scenario as an attractive prospect. And one could envision a Virtual Countries future gaining approval from some in Europe as well, if, through a process of privatization, the conglomerates took over many of the major functions of the current welfare state.

If the Tocquevillian description of voluntary associations stands as a historical analogy to the Small Companies/Large Networks scenario, post-independence Singapore may stand as a cognate for the Virtual Countries world. Whether one prefers the rough and tumble of the nineteenth-century American frontier or the tightly planned and controlled prosperity of Singapore stands largely as a matter of cultural and personal preference. And the preference could well change over time— a renewal of the turmoil brought about by massive layoffs and downsizing of the early 1990s could make a more paternalistic scenario appear attractive to Americans.

Haves vs. Have-Nots

Another major concern expressed by members of the Scenario Working Group was the prospect of a sharp division of society into haves and have-nots. In the Small Companies scenario, the have-nots would consist of members of society who lacked the skills to plug into the electronic network or those who preferred secure employment and the prospect of not having to bid continually for work. As part of the scenario, it was posited that jobs might be created, either by government or private firms, in fields like elder care, which would attract people with these preferences. But there remains the strong prospect that many workers with these inclinations would remain well outside the networked mainstream. The Small Companies/Large Networks scenario might also work to exaggerate already existing tendencies toward polarization of income and wealth in society as a whole and winner-take-all outcomes in particular industries and professions.

The Virtual Countries scenario will have its own set of have-nots, but the excluded groups may have a different composition than those which will appear in the Small Companies world. In a Virtual Countries future, those unable to secure employment at one of the core global conglomerates would likely face significant difficulties. The government safety net would in all probability be smaller, or even non-existent, and employees of the big conglomerates would tend to work and socialize almost exclusively together. Life could be harsh and isolating for the unemployed.

And even those working at firms that are part of the conglomerates' extended supply chain may not receive the generous benefits or employment security enjoyed by members of the core firms, because companies on the periphery of the system will be unlikely to have the means to provide such amenities. This distinction between the status of employees at the core firms and those at the peripheral suppliers is already a feature of the Asian *keiretsu* arrangement.

Finally, another possibility raised by members of the Scenario Working Group was that the global conglomerates would keep a small core staff on a permanent basis and fill any other positions with temporary employees from a large pool of contingent workers. Many large U.S. firms in the 1990s already showed signs of moving toward this sort of hiring strategy.

Concluding Remarks

The scenarios project represented a forum within the 21st Century Initiative for MIT faculty and researchers to reflect upon how the organizations of the future might work. The scenarios project's intention was to provide a setting in which structured, informed speculation about possibilities for the future could occur. The hope was that this work would allow the choices which shape the future to be made in a more thoughtful and considered manner.

Acknowledgments

This chapter is an abridged version of MIT 21st Century Initiative Working Paper #001, January 1997. The full text of the working paper is available at http://ccs.mit.edu/21c/21CWP001.html.

The lead authors are grateful to members of the Scenarios Working Group for their contributions to the project. The members, and their MIT affiliations, were:

Scenario Creation Group

- Erik Brynjolfsson (Information Technology)
- John Carroll (Organizational Studies)
- Donald Lessard (Strategy)
- Stuart Madnick (Information Technology)
- Thomas Malone (Information Technology)
- Wanda Orlikowski (Information Technology)
- Sandy Pentland (Media Laboratory)
- Paul Resnick (Information Technology)
- Jack Rockart (Information Technology)
- Michael Scott Morton (Strategy)
- Maureen Scully (Industrial Relations)
- David Tennenhouse (Laboratory for Computer Science)

Scenario Review Group

- Deborah Ancona (Organizational Studies)
- Lotte Bailyn (Organizational Studies)
- Charles Fine (Operations Management)
- Mauro Guillén (Organizational Studies)
- Rebecca Henderson (Strategy)
- Richard Locke (Industrial Relations)
- Thomas Magnanti (Operations Research)
- Daniel Nyhart (Law)
- William Ocasio (Organizational Studies)
- JoAnne Yates (Communications)

We also thank Peter Schwartz, CEO of Global Business Network, for his contributions as facilitator of the Working Group.

Special thanks go to Robert Russman Halperin, who as Executive Director of the 21st Century Initiative, helped launch the scenario project and see it through its first two years.

The scenarios project was made possible by the financial support of the following 21st Century Initiative's sponsors:

Founding Sponsors
- British Telecom
- EDS/A.T. Kearney
- National Westminster Bank

Major Sponsor
- Union Bank of Switzerland

Regular Sponsors
- AMP
- Eli Lilly
- LG Electronics
- McKinsey & Company
- Siemens Nixdorf
- Siemens PCN

We also express gratitude to the many executives from sponsor firms and other companies, as well as scholars and experts from a variety of institutions, who commented on earlier versions of the MIT scenarios. In particular, we thank those who attended the MIT Industrial Liaison scenarios program in May 1994, the Sloan-Price Waterhouse Thought Summit in October 1994 and the MIT-Global Business Network WorldView meeting in November 1995.

We are also grateful to Charlie Fine, Bill Hanson, Bengt Holmström, Thomas Kochan, Wanda Orlikowski, and Jack Rockart of the Sloan faculty, David Tennenhouse of the MIT Laboratory for Computer Science, and Sloan doctoral students Andreas Gast and Albert Wenger, who generously commented on early drafts of this paper. The work was also informed by discussions in the 21st Century Initiative faculty seminar on Inter-organizational Relationships held during the Spring of 1996.

Notes

1. The MIT Scenario Working Group was comprised of a Scenario Creation and Scenario Review Group. Members of the two groups are listed in the acknowledgements.

2. On the history and methods of scenario planning, see Wack (1985a, 1985b); de Gues (1988); and Schwartz (1991). Kleiner (1996a) gives a brief history of the rise of scenario planning at Shell and its continuation by many of the Shell practitioners through their work at Global Business Network.

3. Several of the events where the 21st Century Initiative scenarios were discussed are described in Halperin (1994); CEO Thought Summit (1995); and Kleiner (1996b).

4. The narrative descriptions of both scenarios included in this chapter are excerpted and adapted from a report on a meeting jointly sponsored by the 21st Century Initiative and Global Business Network in November 1995; see Kleiner (1996b, 5–7).

5. An early version of the automobile industry scenario set out here appears in Malone (1993).

6. On the film industry in the vertically-integrated studio era, see Schatz (1988) and Bordwell *et al.* (1985); on the post-studio era, see Lewis (1985) and Pierson (1996). The Prato region's textile industry is described in Enright (1995); Jaikumar (1986); and Voss (1994). The apparel industry's structure is recounted in Voss (1994), and Silicon Valley practices are discussed in Saxenian (1994) and Jackson (1996).

7. Sloan faculty member Maureen Scully created a series of vignettes dramatizing the possible fate of several character types—authoritarian CEO, "enlightened" senior manager, engineer, vocational trainer, unemployed inner city resident—under the two MIT scenarios, and these were presented, with the parts played by professional actors, at the MIT Industrial Liaison Program Symposium in May 1994; see Scully (1994).

8. The literature on unions and other organizations created by the industrial working class is vast. Two classic works addressing the early years of the industrial era are Thompson (1964) and Foner (1970).

9. The term "virtual countries" was brought to the attention of the MIT Scenario Working Group by executives at National Westminster Bank, one of the 21st Century Initiative's founding sponsors. The term was then used inside NatWest to refer to an organization that now possesses or might in the future attain some of the important characteristics of a nation-state. The European Union, for example, was referred to as a "virtual country" within NatWest. The NatWest usage was thus somewhat broader and more general than the quite specific meaning applied to the term in the MIT scenarios.

10. See Kramer (1997); cited figures were based on global data collected by Securities Data Company on merger and acquisition activity, joint ventures and partnerships and venture funding.

11. Taylor (1991) discusses ABB's practices. The 21st Century Initiative's Interesting Organizations project examined GE and Johnson & Johnson; on the database, see chapter 7 of this volume. Bartlett and Ghoshal (1993) suggest that the innovative organizational forms put in place in recent years at ABB and a handful of other firms—GE, 3M, Toyota, Canon—represent a new model likely to replace the multidivisional structure that has been dominant for the last half-century.

12. The notion of a taboo against marriage between employees of different firms was explored by the science fiction writer William Gibson in his futuristic novel *Neuromancer*; see Gibson (1984).

13. The idea of employee election of managers was developed in detail by Bruce Sterling in his science fiction novel, *Islands in the Net*; see Sterling (1989).

14. On the growing influence of institutional investors, see Useem (1996). Another testament to the increasing assertiveness of employee pension fund managers is a piece by the general counsel of CALPERS, the California Public Employees Retirement System, contending that the pension funds' longer investment horizons will eventually prevail over the short-termism that resulted in the "hollowing out" of many U.S. companies in the 1990s. See Koppes (1996).

15. ESOP figures from National Center for Employee Ownership; see http://www.nceo.org.

16. Whyte and Whyte (1991) give an account of the rise and development of the Mondragón cooperatives. Thomas and Logan (1982) examine the economic performance of the cooperatives.

17. The seminal work on this subject in economics is Coase (1937). Williamson (1975) revisited the questions originally posed by Coase and triggered a wave of work on this set of issues. A good review of economists' work in this area is Holmström and Tirole (1989). Though he approaches the question from

a different perspective, the business historian Alfred Chandler attributes the rise of the modern corporation largely to the "internalization"—for the purpose of achieving economies of various sorts—within large firms of functions formerly performed by small firms transacting in arm's-length fashion in the marketplace; see Chandler (1977).

18. The work that initiated recent discussion about the decline of civil society was Putnam (1995). For a broad-ranging analysis of the possible causes for the decline, see Putnam (1996). Lemann (1996) presents an opposing point of view.

References

Bartlett, Christopher, and Sumantra Ghoshal. 1993. Beyond the M-Form: Toward a Managerial Theory of the Firm. *Journal of Strategic Management* 14 (Special Issue Winter): 23–46.

Bordwell, David, Janet Staiger, and Kristen Thompson. 1985. *The Classical Hollywood Cinema: Film Style and Mode of Production to 1960*. New York: Columbia University Press.

CEO Thought Summit. 1995. *Sloan Management Review* 36, (Spring): 13–21.

Chandler, Alfred D., Jr. 1977. *The Visible Hand: The Managerial Revolution in American Business.* Cambridge, Mass.: Belknap/Harvard University Press.

Coase, Ronald. 1937. The Nature of the Firm. *Econometrica* 4: 386–405.

de Gues, Arie P. 1988. Planning as Learning. *Harvard Business Review* 66 (March–April): 70–74.

Enright, Michael J. 1995. Organization and Coordination in Geographically Concentrated Industries. In *Coordination and Information: Historical Perspectives on the Organization of Enterprise*, National Bureau of Economic Research Conference Report, Naomi R. Lamoreaux and Daniel M. G. Raff, eds. Chicago: University of Chicago Press, 120–127.

Foner, Eric. 1970. *Free Soil, Free Labor, Free Men: The Ideology of the Republican Party before the Civil War.* New York: Oxford University Press.

Gibson, William. 1984. *Neuromancer.* New York: Ace.

Halperin, Robert Russman. 1994. Scenarios for 21st Century Organizations. MIT 21st Century Initiative Discussion Paper, October.

Holmström, Bengt R., and Jean Tirole. 1989. Theory of the Firm. In *Handbook of Industrial Organization*, vol. 1, Richard Schmalensee and Robert D. Willig, eds. Amsterdam: Elsevier, 61–133.

Jackson, Tim. 1996. Virtual Corporation with a Twist. *Financial Times*, February 5, 9.

Jaikumar, R. 1986. Massimo Menichetti. Harvard Business School Case Study 686–135.

Kleiner, Art. 1996a. Consequential Heresies: How "Thinking the Unthinkable" Changed Royal Dutch Shell. In *Scenario Thinking: Concepts and Approaches*, Emeryville, Calif.: Global Business Network.

Kleiner, Art. 1996b. *Twenty-First Century Organizations: Four Plausible Prospects.* Emeryville, Calif.: Global Business Network, 1996.

Koppes, Richard H. 1996. And in the Long Run We Should Win. *New York Times*, May 19, F13.

Kramer, Farrell. 1997. Mergers Roared Ahead in 1996, Set Records. *Boston Globe*, January 2, E1–E2.

Lemann, Nicholas. 1996. Kicking in Groups. *Atlantic Monthly*, April, 22–26.

Lewis, Jon. 1985. *"Whom God Wishes to Destroy—": Francis Coppola and the New Hollywood.* Durham, N.C.: Duke University Press.

Malone, Thomas W. 1993. Scenario: Information Technology and the Workplace. Aspen Institute Roundtable on Information Technology, August 4–8.

Pierson, John. 1996. *Spike, Mike, Slackers and Dykes: A Guided Tour Across a Decade of American Independent Cinema.* New York: Miramax/Hyperion.

Putnam, Robert D. 1995. Bowling Alone: America's Declining Social Capital. *Journal of Democracy* 6 (January): 65–78.

Putnam, Robert D. 1996. The Strange Disappearance of Civil Society. *The American Prospect*, no. 24 (Winter): 34–48.

Saxenian, AnnaLee. 1994. *Regional Advantage: Culture and Competition in Silicon Valley and Route 128.* Cambridge, Mass.: Harvard University Press.

Scully, Maureen. 1994. Scenario Scripts, or 10 Characters in Search of a Future. MIT 21st Century Initiative Discussion Paper, May.

Schatz, Thomas. 1988. *The Genius of the System: Hollywood Filmmaking in the Studio Era.* New York: Pantheon.

Schwartz, Peter. 1991. *The Art of the Long View: Planning for the Future in an Uncertain World.* New York: Doubleday Currency.

Sterling, Bruce. 1989. *Islands in the Net.* New York: Ace.

Taylor, William. 1991. The Logic of Global Business: An Interview with ABB's Percy Bavenick. *Harvard Business Review*, 69 (March–April): 91–105.

Thomas, Henk, and Chris Logan. 1982. *Mondragón: An Economic Analysis.* London: George Allen & Unwin.

Thompson, E. P. 1964. *Making of the English Working Class.* New York: Pantheon, 1964.

Useem, Michael. 1996. *Investor Capitalism: How Money Managers are Changing the Face of Corporate America.* New York: Basic Books.

Voss, Hanswerner. 1994. Virtual Organizations: The Future is Now. *Strategy and Leadership* 24 (July–August), 12–14.

Wack, Pierre. 1985a. Scenarios: Uncharted Waters Ahead. *Harvard Business Review* 63 (September–October): 72–79.

Wack, Pierre. 1985b. Scenarios: Shooting the Rapids. *Harvard Business Review* 63 (November–December): 139–150.

Whyte, William Foote, and Kathleen King Whyte. 1991. *Making Mondragón: The Growth and Dynamics of the Worker Cooperative Complex.* Cornell International Industrial and Labor Relations Report Number 14, 2nd edition. Ithaca, N.Y.: ILR Press.

Williamson, Oliver. 1975. *Markets and Hierarchies: Analysis and Antitrust Implications.* New York: Free Press.

7 The Interesting Organizations Project: Digitalization of the 21st Century Firm

Michael S. Scott Morton

Overview of the Interesting Organizations Project

Over the last decade, a series of rapid advances in information technology coincided with greatly increased turbulence in the business environment. This combination of technological and environmental change means that businesses face increasing complexity and novel problems. One natural result is that firms have a chance to rethink how they organize.

Scholars of organizations (Galbraith 1973; Chandler 1962) have written persuasively about the forces that determine a firm's structure. From this work it is clear that as the economics and nature of both information flows and production functions change, historical organizational structures and processes are no longer likely to remain optimal. This fact, however, also implies that changes in the business environment and technology give us new degrees of freedom in how we might organize the firm.

With this context in mind, the Interesting Organizations project was launched in 1994 as part of MIT's Initiative on Inventing the Organizations of the 21st Century. The project's objective was to look for evidence of interesting organizational change in the world of business practice. The underlying idea was that by looking broadly and openly, we could find new organizational forms that might look unusual today, but would be likely to become more common in the future.

A group of researchers affiliated with the 21st Century Initiative identified, and briefly documented, 261 organizations that formed the nucleus of the Interesting Organizations Data Base (IODB). These ranged across a wide spectrum of industries. Manufacturing (93 organizations) and services (73 organizations) together accounted for nearly two-thirds of the entries in the database. The remaining entries were spread broadly among retail/wholesale trade (36 organizations); financial services (30 organizations); telecommunications, transportation and utilities (21 organizations); other private firms (5 organizations); and government (3 organizations). More than 80 percent were U.S. firms; and less than one-third were large, widely recognized corporations. As might be expected in a database tracking novel business practices, most of the organizations included were young (established within 5 years) and small (fewer than 100 employees).

Through a series of discussions, the researchers involved with the project identified a group of themes to categorize the various dimensions of "interestingness" that the organizations in the database embodied. In some cases, the organizations exhibited novel structures, business models, patterns of control, or processes. In other instances, the attributes of the organization's product/service offerings were highly unusual. In still other cases, working conditions for employees of the organizations were the reason for inclusion.

A number of organizations that were entered into the database in the mid-1990s, when they were not widely known, went on to become widely celebrated in the business press in subsequent years. Among these was a group of organizations with highly decentralized structures and governance. Examples of such organizations include Visa International, whose story was widely disseminated in speeches and a book by its founder, Dee Hock (Hock 1999); Semco, a Brazilian manufacturing firm that helps its employees to form satellite enterprises in which both the parent firm and workers hold ownership stakes (Semler 1989, 1994, 1995); and the global network of software engineers that developed Linux, the personal computer operating system that has become the leading rival to Microsoft's Windows.

Another organization, Verifone, a maker of electronic equipment for verifying credit card transactions, was included because of its practice of handing off product development work from team to team across continents. At the end of its workday, a Verifone team in Europe would send its work electronically to a team in North America, who would pick up where the Europeans had left off. At the end of its day, the North American team, in turn, would hand off to an Asian team, who would continue the work and then hand off the to Europeans, starting the cycle again. Verifone came to be frequently cited as an example of 24-hour-a-day global product development (e.g. Galbraith 2000, chapter 10) and practices of this sort were broadly adopted in the late 1990s.

Other organizations in the database exhibited practices of great interest and with significant potential for the future, but have not yet become so widely known. A few examples from among these organizations give a sense of the database's breadth.

Perkin-Elmer is U.S.-based firm that has more than $1 billion in revenues from systems and analytic instruments used in such markets as biotechnology. The company uses a technique it terms "flocking" to decide which new product ideas to develop. Researchers who have an idea are free to seek out other researchers and try to persuade them to join the new project. If an idea can attract a critical mass of participants from the research staff, it's deemed worth pursuing. In this way, Perkin-Elmer taps into the knowledge and judgment of its own researchers to assess which projects are likely to be successful (Lissack 1996).

Ross/Flex is a U.S.-based manufacturer of air valves used to control industrial machinery. The company has pioneered an approach that allows customers to co-design the valves they want. Working with Ross's engineers and machinists, and using computer-aided design (CAD) software, customers can design a valve that exactly meets their specifications, in production runs as low as one (Alter 1994, Sheridan 1996).

Agile Web is a virtual enterprise comprised of 19 small manufacturing companies. The members agree to work together, with each firm contributing its particular expertise, on an as-needed basis, to respond to customer needs. When a customer need is identified, the group forms "resource teams" comprised of appropriate people from each member firm to address the opportunity. The system relies on members' willingness to exchange sensitive data and trust in each other (Mahajan 1995).

The initial IODB sample of firms was purely exploratory, a way to identify what our range of informants thought were "interesting" new organizational forms. But the firms were for the most part so small and so heterogeneous that although provocative, we could not use the database to find a broadly applicable theory that accounted for the organizational innovation that was occurring. We did, however, decide that these initial findings were intriguing enough that we should look for patterns in larger firms. Again, we first undertook an exploratory phase and looked at large firms in both manufacturing and services. The seven that were chosen had surfaced more than once in the business press as firms that had some interesting and novel dimensions. These seven large firms, and the reason for their inclusion, were:

• Boeing. Their 777 airplane took some novel approaches to development and manufacturing.

• Citibank Japan. Citibank's Japanese subsidiary made innovative use of technology to break into a lucrative segment of the retail banking market.

• GE. The story of GE's Web-based procurement system shows the potential power of exploiting a core back-office function.

• Lithonia. A producer of light fixtures, Lithonia was one of the earliest "networked" organizations

• 7-Eleven Japan. 7-Eleven has achieved remarkable success with a convenience store concept that was scaleable and very responsive to the consumer.

• Thermo Electron. Thermo Electron made use of a spin-out model to exploit intellectual capital.

• USAA Insurance. USAA used technology in innovative ways to get economies of scope.

These seven organizations were examined in more depth, through a review of academic sources and the business press and, in some cases, interviews.

Boeing

The story of why and how Boeing moved to a radically new design, development, and manufacturing process for its then next-generation wide-bodied commercial aircraft, the 777, has been documented extensively (Sabbagh 1998). There were several key factors that pushed Boeing to this step. One was the cost pressures Boeing's customers, the airlines, were facing. Extrapolating the traditional cost structure to this next-generation model resulted in a plane that was simply too expensive for airlines. In addition, Boeing now had another serious competitor, in the form of Airbus, for the first time since the 1960s. The environment thus placed severe constraints on Boeing. Business as usual was not going to be good enough.

At the core of Boeing's re-thinking was the concept of "design and build teams." This meant that Boeing would meld together the design and manufacturing engineers "into one tightly coupled team." With this approach came new processes that put all the relevant skills, regardless of organizational unit or position in the formal hierarchy, into one room to arrive at joint decisions.

All of this new structure and process was based on an enabling platform—a single, working database of the digitized aircraft. This not only ensured there was one continuously updated version of the plane as the design proceeded, it also allowed access from any physical location in the world and provided a host of related software tools that permitted dynamic three-dimensional views and other functionality to enhance the design and build process.

The investment in the infrastructure was massive. But ultimately the plane moved from concept to flight in record time and was a major success.

While the 777 was a great success, as was the process by which it was designed and built, Boeing had difficulty implementing practices pioneered on the 777 on its established aircraft programs. It appears that established mindsets and work practices coupled with the cost and effort of making the change to the existing programs has essentially blocked progress. A lesson from the Boeing case is that despite the undoubted power of technology, company-wide systemic change remains extremely hard to achieve.

Citibank Japan

Citibank has been an aggressive, yet focused, investor in IT ever since John Reed became influential in the firm, and eventually assumed the CEO position. In the U.S., Citibank's overall performance has generally been strong, but it is impossible

to break out the relative impact of IT, since country effects, the mix of loan portfo-
lios, and other factors make comparisons between banks, their use of IT, and its relative impact very problematic. If one takes a particular country segment, however,
impacts can be seen more clearly. Citibank in Japan in the retail market is one such
example.[1] Citibank Japan's breakthrough came about as a result of a seeming
barrier—the impossibly high cost of establishing physical branches to reach retail
customers.

Citibank crafted an innovative deal with the Japanese post office to allow their
ATM machines on their premises. In this way, Citibank obtained several hundred
desirable locations. Once these locations were secured, Citibank pursued a two-
pronged strategy in Japan.

First, Citibank's ATM machines were innovative, usable twelve-plus hours per
day, with access to the bank's on-line, real-time database. This was in contrast to the
most Japanese banks, whose ATMs were only available eight hours a day and whose
static data bases were refreshed nightly. The Citibank functionality permitted the
introduction of new products, such as foreign exchange (FX) transactions, which
others could not match.

A second piece of Citibank's strategy was to leverage Japan's ubiquitous ISDN-
to-the-home telephone network and offer powerful financial service products to the
consumers through that channel. Many of these were supported through a sophisticated call center which in turn linked into global Citibank services. With this combination, relatively high net worth Japanese customers could benefit from Citibank's
economies of scale and scope.

These two moves allowed Citibank to achieve a distinctive position by offering
better products, more conveniently. They thus were able to break into a highly profitable part of the Japanese retail market.

The Citibank Japan story is more complex and multi-faceted than this brief
anecdote can convey. It is clear, however, that Citibank Japan's innovations were
only possible because of computers and communications technology, coupled with
services that were attractive to customers.

General Electric

GE as a corporation was a relative latecomer to the effective use of digital technologies (Lowe 2001, chapter 7). Ironically, GE had an early lead in electronic data
interchange (EDI) systems. This was a cumbersome technology, however, that
required adopters to make expensive, rigid changes to their internal systems for
purchasing and other functions. Though EDI proved successful under some limited
conditions, it never really took off.

The advent of the Internet and the Web dramatically changed the rules. GE eventually did change course and seize this opportunity (Venkatraman and Henderson 1998; Bylinsky 1997; Woolley 1997) by developing a successful Web-based purchasing portal, the GE Trading Process Network. The effort went through four phases:

- Internet-based internal consolidation of purchasing and RFQ's for certain items
- Expansion of internal system to include "all items" purchased by GE with participation in electronic markets
- Expansion to include GE suppliers and buyers
- Opening up of GE internal purchasing portal to anyone

GE's experience demonstrated the significant efficiencies that can result from taking a basic required core back-office function, purchasing, and completely rethinking it. The result is dramatically more efficient—faster, with less error, fewer people, less inventory and more effective use of resources. Importantly, this basic change to a back-office process had beneficial ripple effects. It led to involving suppliers more closely with the design of GE products and to the propagation of other IT-enabled changes involving customers and product designers.

It is important to note, however, that this propagation is slow, as it involves shifts in deeply ingrained work habits and requires investment in new skills and new systems. It has thus not had noticeable impact yet on GE's overall organization structure or on many other major processes.

Lithonia

The Lithonia innovation story began in the 1970s with the remaking of their organization through implementation of a central database and an internal communications network, all accomplished with IBM's active help. The major result was to put the independent agent at the center of Lithonia, a controversial and risky step. The effectiveness of the new structure and the new IT tools that everyone could use to do their job resulted in a firm that not only had lower cost but also was easy to do business with (Davenport and Nohria 1994).

As customers and lighting technology became more sophisticated, Lithonia was later able to exploit the Internet, new database technologies, and software tools such as expert systems to build a system with enhanced functionality, always aimed at solving a customer's problem quickly and easily.

One highly simplified example of this is a situation where lighting fixtures are needed for a multi-use skyscraper in New York. Lithonia systems permit the architects to work with interactive design tools to ensure the lighting specifications meet the user needs. If Lithonia does not make the appropriate fixture, its systems identify the manufacturer who does. In addition, when appropriate, the system can order the part electronically. Once all the thousands of fixtures are specified, from several different Lithonia factories and dozens of other suppliers, the Lithonia systems can consolidate these by floor and in sequence on the floor. The net result is that large trucks arrive at the construction site at times specified by the builder with the correct fixtures for a given floor and location.

Lithonia has moved over the years from making lighting fixtures, to selling lighting systems to providing lighting solutions. Each step in this move progression has required working closely with the customer, plus changing Lithonia's internal organizational structure and skill mix and constantly evolving Lithonia's IT infrastructure to cut elapsed times and increase asset utilization.

7-Eleven Japan

7-Eleven Japan remains a profitable and growing chain of convenience stores and is the largest operation of its type in Japan and perhaps the world.[2] 7-Eleven has evolved an extremely flexible network of profitable, high-turnover small retail outlets in high traffic areas. The stores are networked and record every transaction as it occurs. This on-line, real-time environment allows 7-Eleven to stay on top of customer preferences, keep extremely low inventories and yet rarely run out of products (Toigo 1994). Mutually reinforcing practices are in place throughout the whole company. The distribution network manages to replenish stores three or four times a day, even in gridlocked Tokyo traffic. Incentive systems and employee training focus on understanding customers and customer service. The IT system, which is the enabling backbone of the entire operation, is constantly evolving as needs change and opportunities emerge.

There is a high degree of compatibility between 7-Eleven's tightly focused strategy of meeting consumers' daily convenience needs; the company's organizational structure, which is very flat, with clusters of six or seven stores and highly efficient centralized key functions such as logistics, purchasing, and training; sharp, clear processes that provide the quality data needed to make decisions and an interactive communication network to move data quickly to wherever it is needed; an emphasis on well-trained people with values that match the bright, well-lit, attractive stores; and technology focused on serving customers rapidly with exactly what they need and like.

These five inter-related sets of factors appear from the outside to have meshed together particularly well in the case of 7-Eleven Japan. They are mutually reinforcing (Kotabe 1995) and provide another example that supports earlier theoretical and empirical work undertaken as part a prior MIT research program, "Management in the 1990s" (Scott Morton 1991, Allen and Scott Morton 1994). Although the theory and principles are clear, their conscious translation to practice is rare. 7-Eleven Japan appears to be one of the very few cases of a public company where such an integrated approach is thoroughly embedded in the fabric of the organization.

USAA Insurance

USAA is a group founded by ex-military personnel who had the idea of providing life insurance to members of the military. Initially, only members of the military and their direct family members were eligible to be insured. This was a homogeneous group and the risk profile of its members could be understood well. That in turn allowed for very competitive rates that could still result in a profitable operation, as costs were kept low. Growth was dependent on product features and service. Since military personnel move frequently, it was important to be able to follow an individual across states within the U.S. and between countries outside the U.S., all while providing non-stop insurance coverage.

USAA became particularly good at serving its customer base, and subsequently expanded from the original life insurance product to add other forms of personal insurance, such as homeowner's and automobile coverage. Through a sophisticated mix of computer software and call centers, plus a detailed understanding of its customers, USAA built up an effective, complex, web of products and services tailored uniquely to the marketplace it served. Once successful, it was then able to expand its customer base to include relatives of military personnel. The key to success once again was a focus on customers' needs, a clearly articulated strategy and investment in an evolving set of systems and procedures that provided customer value while enabling profitable growth (Mack 1988; Brophy 1989).

Thermo Electron

Thermo Electron was started by an MIT professor, George Hatsopolous, with an interest in thermodynamics. After the company enjoyed several years of successful growth, senior management noticed that several promising younger employees were leaving to start their own firms. The senior team investigated and discovered that in several cases the young employees were leaving in frustration because their direct supervisors would not support their emerging ideas. Hatsopolous, as CEO, decided that while only some of these innovative ideas would be likely to succeed, it would still behoove Thermo to nurture inventors and their ideas to see which ones might end up meeting a market need.[3]

As Hatsopolous implemented this plan, the process of nurturing inventors' ideas came to have three phases. The first was to give the inventor a small budget and a time horizon in which to report progress. If this phase was passed, a virtual company was formed and given some capital. At this stage, the inventor was expected to find customers who would pay to use the product. If this second phase was successful, venture capital firms were brought in, one was chosen, and an IPO was undertaken. Thermo Electron retained a percentage, though not always a majority, of the newly issued shares. Some were held by the inventor, other members of his team, and the VC, and the rest were sold to the public. Some of these "spin-out" firms eventually became large enough in their own right that they repeated the cycle and spun out new firms themselves.

During the 1970s and 1980s, this process resulted in Thermo creating more than a dozen such companies with a market capitalization in the mid-1990s of more than $5 billion (Anslinger *et al.* 1997). More importantly this process created a virtuous circle. Thermo, as the company came to be known, developed a reputation among engineers, particularly at MIT, of being a place that rewarded and backed creativity. As a result, Thermo had its pick of the very best engineering applicants who were also excited by the idea of inventing and developing something new.

Thermo had a strategy focused on a particular segment of science and engineering, thermodynamics, and developed products from that base. Its inventors then searched until they found a customer with an appropriate need and modified the product until there was a match. They hired creative, talented people and put in place an organizational structure that could evolve to maximize particular business opportunities. The strategy, people, organizational structure, and management processes nicely reinforced of the science and engineering technology base.

As this effective system moved through time, it grew from one to more than a dozen independently traded new companies, each with its own legal, administrative, personnel, and marketing functions to perform. Thermo's headquarters tried to perform many of these functions centrally to benefit from economies of scale and provide clear accounting control. But as the number of companies expanded, this became an increasingly complex and expensive task. Added to this complexity was the fact that some of the new business opportunities required new kinds of engineering, science, and product expertise. During this organic expansion, Thermo also made some fifteen small acquisitions in order to obtain clusters of relevant expertise. These acquisitions brought with them questions of administrative, cultural, and systems fit, all of which took management time and attention. These acquisitions were all fairly small, however, so the process, while expensive and cumbersome, still worked fairly well.

A major shift in strategy came in 1988, when Thermo decided to make a major acquisition and no longer rely just on the internal idea development and spin-out path. This acquisition was massive, relative to Thermo's size, and effectively spelled the end of the company's remarkable success.

There appeared to be two reasons. One is that the acquisition was so large and in such a different business that it was extremely difficult to integrate into the existing Thermo culture and structure. The second reason predated the acquisition. Thermo never put in place the kind of seamless, timely information flow and related processes required for management to keep in touch with what was happening with the underlying customer and business processes. Thermo's use of IT to support backbone core processes, front-end customer linkages, and central databases that encourage synergy appears to have been woefully limited.

In other words, the IT component that was one of the enabling factors in an effective late 20th century organization appeared to have been almost totally lacking. Perhaps even if there had been an effective electronic support for how work was implemented and managed, the shift in strategy may have put Thermo in line for a setback anyway. Certainly, the lack of IT-enabled coordination mechanisms was a contributing factor in Thermo's downturn.

External Forces and Internal Dimensions of Organization

One of the primary challenges any organization faces is to maintain its economic vitality. As the external environment changes, the nature of what the organization does and how it does it may also have to be modified. One result of MIT's Management in the 1990s research program was to provide evidence and a conceptual framework that helps to explain this central evolutionary task.

Two important and widely influential scholars originated the core idea of figure 7.1. The first idea, already referred to, was that of the business historian, Alfred Chandler. When he was on the faculty at MIT in the 1950s, he wrote a seminal book, *Strategy and Structure*. In this he traced the history of four then-leading firms: Du Pont, General Motors, Standard Oil of New Jersey, and Sears Roebuck. Chandler showed how, as the firms grew from their origins in the 1880s, they had modified their organization structure to match their evolving strategy. Chandler was the first to show a causal, two-way link between an organization's strategy and its structure.

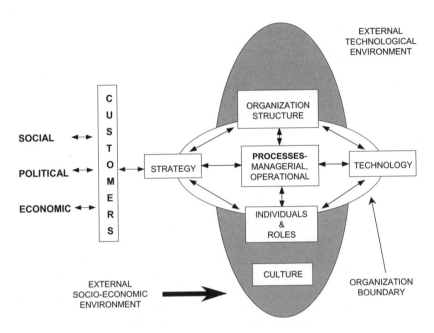

Figure 7.1
Dynamic Tension between External Forces and Internal Dimensions of the Organization (adapted from Scott Morton 1995)

At the same time, totally independently, an organizational behavior professor, Harold Leavit, then at Carnegie-Mellon University, showed that a large element of what is important to managers and organizations is captured by four forces: task, technology, people, and organizational structure. These four are dynamically and mutually interdependent. The sum of the tasks being worked in an organization at any moment in time represents its enacted strategy, so it is logically consistent with Leavit's ideas to substitute the word "strategy" for "tasks" in his diagram.

Figure 7.1 takes Chandler and Leavit's work and makes three additions. In reading their original work in light of the concepts and vocabulary of the 1990s, it became clear that both Chandler and Leavit spent considerable time describing and discussing dimensions of what we would now call "processes." These can be thought of as the set of activities that keep the organization together and moving toward its goal and objectives. Hence in figure 7.1, processes have been made another of the key dimensions of an organization.

A second addition has been to draw on Ed Schein's (1984) work that established the central role of corporate culture in shaping what an organization is in practice.

By "culture," Schein means the shared values of the organization. People in organizations build up a set of shared values that help determine how processes will operate and what the organization structure will mean in practice.

The third addition is to put Chandler and Leavit's view of the organization in a slightly wider context. In particular, strategy must ultimately be focused on a set of customers if the firm is to have any meaning at all. These customers are inevitably and inextricably part of the external environment in which firms live and work. Both the customers and the larger social, political, and economic environment set the context for the firm, so they are raised explicitly in figure 7.1.

Figure 7.1 then helps to frame the discussion so far in terms of the changing external environment, the discontinuities in technology and the new kinds of organizations that are emerging. No one of these forces dominates. It is the dynamic interplay among them that determines the outcome over time. The Management in the 1990s research program showed how the failure to invest in the central ellipse (people and their skills, management processes and incentives, operational processes and their re-engineering, and appropriate organizational structures) has blocked effective change in many organizations. As figure 7.1 shows, the strategy cannot be changed to match the customers and the technology unless changes are made to some combination of organizational structures, processes, and human skills and incentives.

The central argument is that the new expanded and evolving forms of IT can, if used creatively and embedded in the organization, radically affect production of goods and services and communication between all parts of an organization. This is very likely to affect which product is cost-effective to create, what work needs to be done to create it, and where and when such work should be done. These factors all become subject to change. Such sweeping change in where and when work is done will very frequently, perhaps inevitably, result in a very different organization. Finding an effective way to recombine these new productive forces is part of what drives the seven organizations above and is certainly the central message from the most interesting example that emerged from the Interesting Organizations project—Schneider National.

Schneider enjoyed the advantage of starting small, and therefore had minimal embedded legacy practices to overcome. Schneider was further helped by being privately held by a creative and dynamic owner. There are, however, many companies that meet these two conditions. Schneider is one of the very few to have succeeded in a way that suggests it will last.

The Schneider story is one of the "digitalization" of a company coupled with the creation of a culture and supporting practices. The term "digitalization" is *not* about computers and the back office or about supply chains or customer systems or any other of the myriad technology "solutions" that fill the business press. Rather, it is about completely re-making a business, and eventually an industry, and delivering a wholly different level of service far more efficiently and effectively in ways that benefit all participants, including the final consumer.

This example comes from what some would see as a boring industry: long-distance full truck-load transportation. Schneider has been able to transform traditional trucking into a highly-skilled, value-adding premium service. It evolved from simply moving a freight from A to B into moving the freight plus guaranteeing levels of quality, timeliness, and cost unobtainable before. This has resulted in an entirely new standard of performance for the industry.

Schneider National[4]

Schneider National Inc. today is the largest "truck load" transportation company in the U.S. In the late 1990s, Schneider's annual revenues were approximately $3 billion, and it had 20,000 employees.

Schneider's Beginnings

Schneider began in 1935 when A. J. "Al" Schneider sold the family car to buy his first truck. The company grew steadily and began acquiring other trucking companies to increase the depth and range of its operations. Don Schneider, Al's son, became CEO in 1973 and restructured Schneider into a holding company with diverse trucking-related units.

Deregulation and Lean Manufacturing Bring Change

The Motor Carrier Act of 1980 deregulated the U.S. trucking industry, bringing new opportunities and threats for industry participants. Trucking companies gained much greater leeway in what services they could provide, how they could price them and where they could operate. This led to a tripling of the number of trucking companies. But brutal competition saw 12,000 of these companies go bankrupt.

In the 1980s and 1990s, manufacturers adopted just-in-time (JIT) manufacturing techniques, which had unexpected effects on the trucking industry. Trucking firms now had to provide fast, reliable deliveries of smaller loads. With JIT, a botched pickup or a late-running truck had worse consequences for the receiving company.

Thus, manufacturers started rating trucking companies on their quality of service, especially on-time delivery. Yet tighter delivery schedules of smaller loads meant less revenue per trip and more "deadhead trips" (trips with an empty truck). Because the costs to operate a lightly-loaded (or empty) truck are almost as high as those of operating a full one, carriers saw increased costs per item delivered. In the early years of JIT manufacturing, customers grudgingly paid the costs of deadhead return trips and less-than-full truckload service, but they were constantly pressuring trucking companies to trim such costs.

Thus, deregulation and new manufacturing methods created new demands on trucking companies both to reduce their costs and improve their service. Schneider National chose to pursue a technological route to creating competitive advantage. Don Schneider was already using the power of IT to improve back-office chores such as billing and payroll. Then, a personal visit from Irwin Jacobs, president of QualComm, alerted Schneider to technology that would change the way his firm dealt with customers, drivers and trucks. Don Schneider saw that every part of the company might have to change if the technology was to truly be effective. In coming years, he oversaw the installation of sophisticated new IT systems, which became the basis for a new way of competing.

Schneider's IT Architecture

There are three major elements of Schneider's portfolio of technology to support the architecture depicted in figure 7.2.

SUMIT (Schneider Utility Managing Integrated Transportation) is a common real-time system for customers, carriers and Schneider management. It features: automation for orders (entry, management, and billing); load management to consolidate less-than-truckload (LTL) shipments; mode optimization to select the optimal carrier (surface, rail, water or air); real-time status and alerts.

EDI (Electronic Data Interchange) provides paperless linkages to many of Schneider's customers and handles more than 70 percent of the firm's invoices.

Satellite Communications Technology links Schneider's central control system in Green Bay, Wisc., to all the company's trucks throughout North America and, now, Europe. Costing $3,500 per truck and about .05 cents per mile, this system provides driver-to-control-center communication and location data to within 30 yards. This permits precise scheduling of departures, pick-ups and deliveries. The system greatly reduces drivers' non-productive time and increases asset utilization.

Schneider was the first in the trucking industry to invest in QualComm's OmniTRACS satellite system, starting in 1988. Schneider is now installing the technology on trailers as well as tractors and is again the industry pioneer. The system will let Schneider better manage its trailer assets by linking critical trailer

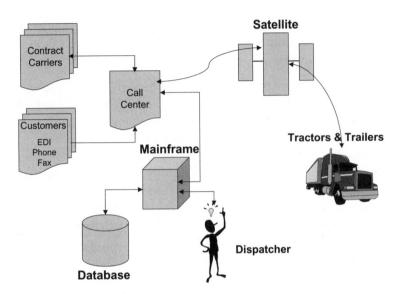

Figure 7.2
Schneider National's Technology Architecture

location and status directly into the company's fleet management and logistics systems.

Although Schneider has chose to invest heavily in technology, the investments represented a means to an end, as Don Schneider's comment reveals:

When we first put a satellite in, I was telling one of our major customers, an automotive company, how good this communication would be. They said "Look Schneider, I don't care if you use carrier pigeons to talk to your drivers. All I care about is that your price does not go up and that you deliver on time, any way that you know how."

Impact of Technology at Schneider

A technology-intensive strategy both reduced costs and improved service levels. Costs dropped from $1 per mile in 1980 to $0.60 per mile in 1998, which more than paid for Schneider's hefty investments in IT. The fraction of late deliveries dropped by more than a factor of ten, even as delivery deadlines have tightened. Automated information systems reduced errors and improved responsiveness to customers. Decision support helped Schneider price its services and only accept profitable shipments. As a result, Schneider National has been called "an information system masquerading as a trucking line."

Although technology enabled efficient, high-quality operations, it did not, by itself, make Schneider successful. Concomitant changes in people's jobs and associated business processes were needed.

Changes for the Drivers   Drivers are crucial to Schneider because they are the face of Schneider at customers' loading docks and because drivers account for some 40 percent of shipping cost. However, driver loyalty is low in the industry, as few drivers stay with any company, or with the profession, for very long.

When Schneider introduced the satellite communications system, the company worried that drivers would leave because of the "big brother" tracking features and complex equipment. But the drivers quickly learned and liked the system, a fact that illustrates the difficulty of predicting the effects of technology. Drivers liked the system because it boosted their productivity, mainly by reducing tedious paperwork and eliminating time wasted pulling off of the road to find a phone, call Schneider, get put on hold, etc. Because drivers are paid for miles driven, they especially value the opportunity to stay on the road.

Beyond the productivity improvements, Schneider's technology helped improve working conditions. Technology helps minimize the problem of drivers' time away from families. For example, drivers' families can send emergency messages at any time, which reduces drivers' fears of being unreachable while on the road. Technology also tracks the dates of birthdays and anniversaries to help drivers get their driving done and keep commitments to family.

Changes for the Customer Service Representatives   Schneider's new technologies had a major impact on the customer service representatives (CSRs) that handle most of Schneider's day-to-day interactions with customers. Before digitalization initiatives like EDI, SUMIT, and satellite communications, customer service was a thankless job that involved handling routine requests and making frustrating attempts to contact drivers.

With satellite communications, CSRs can now pinpoint the location and status of shipments. Customers' changes to schedules can be confirmed quickly and confidently. But more importantly, technology reduced the number of routine calls because customers can check order status themselves via the Web. CSRs now have more interesting jobs tackling high-value customer needs, and they have the technological tools to meet these needs.

Changes for the Service Team Leaders   Schneider's service team leaders provide management and support functions to drivers such as helping drivers get the load they need, making sure they get home on time, and tracking driver performance.

Before digitalization, the job of a Schneider service team leader was a paper-intensive process of managing driver logs, internal documentation on who carried which load, exception reports regarding problems, and a range of internal performance reports.

In creating a paperless system, Schneider largely automated time-consuming reporting functions. Now, team leaders handle 40 drivers each, up from 25 each. With less time spent on routine paperwork, service team leaders can now talk to each driver daily. Daily communication is vital to Schneider, because driver hiring and retention is a major constraint on growth. Ensuring that drivers get the miles they need to earn a living—and make it home on days they want to be with their families—improves driver loyalty and retention.

Changes for the Transportation Planners (Dispatchers)   Transportation planners coordinate the movement of drivers, trucks, and loads. They try to minimize driving distance, minimize driver waiting times and equalize the availability of equipment nationwide, all within the constraints of scheduling demands and drivers' days off. Planners also face the vagaries of weather, road construction, and capricious customers.

In the past, planners did not know drivers' availability for the next load because they had to wait for the driver to call in. The frustrated planners typically generated long lists of tentative assignments and gambled on whether drivers would call for an assignment within the allotted window of time.

With satellite communications, transportation planners have more reliable estimates of truck locations and driver availability, and can send dispatch instructions and receive driver confirmation in minutes. Planners now coordinate activities more tightly to reduce waiting time for drivers, shorten deadhead trips, and prevent service problems.

Decision support software also changed the nature of transportation planners' jobs. In the past, Schneider relied on the experience and judgment of planners for all decisions. Since then, Schneider has embedded much of the analysis and decision-making process into software that can automatically balance the panoply of probabilities and contingencies required to assign drivers to loads. But the software supports—rather than replaces—transportation planners. Experienced planners can override the software's match-up of drivers and loads to cover complex exceptions related to the special needs of customers, drivers and the situation. Overall, planners override the system in only 20 percent of cases.

The preceding subsections illustrate how the work of all Schneider employees has changed. These changes have required everyone in the company to develop new skills and take on new responsibilities.

From Basic Trucking to Solving Customers' Problems

The transformation of Schneider National mirrors the changes in the larger economy. But while other older companies have risen, fallen, and been replaced by newer companies, Schneider has continuously transformed itself. Early on, Schneider was a classic trucking company—a unionized blue-collar firm, offering simple, well-delineated, undifferentiated trucking. In its present form, Schneider is a more knowledge-intensive, non-union, diversified services company that blurs traditional provider-customer and provider-competitor boundaries.

Current Structure of Schneider

Schneider National is a holding company with a set of eight internally-grown subsidiaries that are listed below. Three of the eight subsidiaries look like traditional trucking companies:

• *Schneider Van*—Traditional low-cost trucking with 13,000 drivers, 12,000 tractors, and 35,000 trailers

• *Schneider Bulk*—Shipment of liquids and chemicals with 700 tanker trailers

• *Schneider Specialized*—Shipment of overweight, oversized, and fragile items.

The other five subsidiaries are units that provide new services Schneider has created during the 1980s and 1990s in response to customers:

• *Schneider Dedicated*—Takes over the ownership and operations of private fleets

• *Schneider Finance*—Full-service truck and trailer dealer, sales and leasing

• *Schneider Intermodal*—Manages shipments that combine trucking with rail and water-borne shipping

• *Schneider Brokerage*—Matches loads to trucks drawn from a network of over 1,000 pre-qualified carriers (including competitors as well as Schneider)

• *Schneider Logistics*—Analyzes, designs, implements, and manages logistics systems for customers.

Schneider's New Relationships with Customers and Competitors

Schneider's transformation has blurred the traditional boundary separating a service provider from its customers and from its competitors. In the past, most shipping transactions were arm's-length—Company A put a load on a truck from Company B for movement to Company C. Now, Schneider enters into complex relationships and combinations of services that defy such traditional arm's-length

SCHNEIDER NATIONAL

RELATIONSHIPS - CUSTOMERS AND COMPETITORS

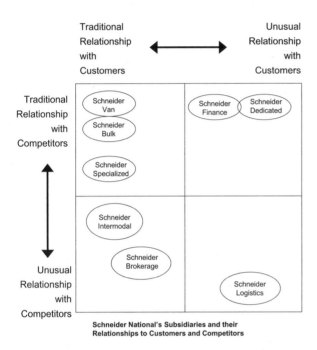

Schneider National's Subsidiaries and their
Relationships to Customers and Competitors

Figure 7.3
Schneider National's Subsidiaries and their Relationship to Customers and Competitors

arrangements. Many of these services would seem to divert revenues from Schneider to competitors or forgo them with customers.

Figure 7.3 arranges the eight subsidiaries of Schneider along two axes. The horizontal axis denotes the nature of the relationship of Schneider to its customers with the left-to-right axis moving from traditional to non-traditional relationships with customers. The vertical axis denotes the nature of the relationship of Schneider to its competitors, moving top-to-bottom from traditional to non-traditional relationships with competitors. At the extremes are the very traditional Schneider Van (which competes with other trucking companies for freight hauling jobs) and the most unusual Schneider Logistics (which does high-level consulting, logistics system design, and unbiased analyses of which carriers to use).

Although inconsistent with the strategy of a pure trucking company, Schneider's behavior is consistent with A. J. Schneider's 60-year-old mission statement: "We have only one thing to sell, and that is service." In fulfilling this mission statement, Schneider has improved its traditional trucking operations and repackaged them to create new services and new subsidiaries. The following sections show how these new businesses work.

Schneider Dedicated: Blurring the Traditional Provider-Customer Line

Schneider Dedicated is an outsourcing service that takes over a customer company's private fleet. Rather than just adding the customer's loads to Schneider Van's workload, these arrangements blur the line between Schneider and the customer. For example:

• the trucks are on Schneider's books but are painted in the customer's colors and only used for the customer's loads

• the drivers are Schneider employees but wear the customer's livery and only drive the customer's loads

• the managers use Schneider's software, but modify it to meet the customer's needs.

As John Lanigan, General Manager of the Dedicated division, describes it, "We really create a new trucking company for each new customer." Schneider's operations research Ph.D.s and experienced IT personnel work with the customer to meld customer and Schneider IT systems together. The outcome is less of a cookie-cutter outsourcing service contract and more like a complex intertwining of Schneider and the customer company. Digitalization lets Schneider embed hard-won logistics knowledge into scalable, flexible IT systems and to track the complex interplay of assets, personnel and processes that each new Schneider Dedicated contract entails.

Schneider Finance: Blurring the Traditional Provider-Customer Line

Schneider Finance helps companies get their own new trucks and trailers, using Schneider's economies of scale to get good prices. Schneider Finance is essentially a full-service truck sales and leasing company—actively marketing a complete range of trucks, engines, and trailers.

Although one might think that this strategy could lead to a loss of long-term recurring revenue from shipping contracts, Schneider has a myriad of other opportunities to serve customers who buy or lease trucks through Schneider Finance. These include:

- taking over or managing the customer's private fleet (Schneider Dedicated)
- creating or managing the customer's logistics systems (Schneider Logistics)
- providing supplementary shipping capacity (Schneider Van and Schneider Brokerage)

As an important side benefit, Schneider also obtains better price discounts on its own purchases because of the increased volume of trucks bought. Thus, Schneider Finance is another example of Schneider using a non-traditional, counterintuitive strategy to improve its competitive position.

Schneider Intermodal: Blurring the Traditional Company-Competitor Line

Schneider Intermodal handles shipments via rail and water, when such modes make the most sense. Rather than spurn these competing modes of transport, Schneider sees them as just one more way to provide good service to its customers.

The subsidiary uses Schneider's well-developed IT systems and processes to make intermodal shipments transparent to the customer. Schneider can pick up the load; truck the shipment to the rail yard or port; have it shipped by rail or water; pick up the trailer at the other end; and deliver it to the destination. The customer pays Schneider and Schneider pays the other carrier. The customer gets a lower total cost of shipping, no additional hassle, only sacrificing a little speed of delivery.

Schneider Brokerage: Blurring the Traditional Company-Competitor Line

Schneider Brokerage is matchmaking service that connects loads—which Schneider cannot or does not want to carry itself—with available trucks from a network of qualified trucking companies, all of whom are competitors. For Schneider's customers, the brokerage service is entirely transparent because of Schneider's IT systems. The customer tells Schneider about the load and Schneider makes sure it gets shipped. The customer does not have to worry about the details of finding and qualifying a carrier.

For Schneider, the benefits of putting loads on competitors' trucks are threefold. First, Schneider gets a transaction fee for brokerage service. Second, Schneider can accept many more shipping contracts than it might otherwise, and thus can say "yes" to more customers in more situations. Third, Schneider can off-load less profitable shipments, (e.g., ones for which it might have no truck nearby).

Schneider Logistics: Blurring All the Traditional Lines

Schneider Logistics blurs both the lines between Schneider-to-customers and between Schneider-to-competitors. A customer company can outsource the entire logistics function to Schneider Logistics. This includes a wide range of analysis, design and management services with solutions for warehousing, distribution and inventory management. Schneider Logistics builds onto Schneider's core technological base with in-house IT that creates decision support and optimization tools for logistics. In such situations, Schneider Logistics personnel reside at customer sites and often manage carriers that are competitors to Schneider's traditional shipping lines.

Schneider Logistics' relationship with competitors is so unusual that there is a "Chinese wall" between it and the rest of Schneider. This is because Schneider Logistics provides services like carrier selection, has access to confidential data on Schneider's competitors and is tasked with making impartial selection decisions about competitors. If Schneider Logistics is to succeed, both its customers and Schneider's competitors must view the subsidiary as an impartial provider of logistics services.

Growth by Meeting Emerging Customer Needs

Over the last two decades, the result of Schneider's pursuit of new opportunities is that the non-traditional divisions (Schneider Logistics, Dedicated, Brokerage, Intermodal, and Finance) now dominate the company. Schneider Dedicated and Schneider Logistics are the largest and second largest divisions of Schneider, respectively. In aggregate, the non-traditional divisions generate more than twice the revenues of the traditional shipping divisions (Schneider Van, Bulk, and Specialized). The rise to prominence in the firm of these new units is all the more impressive, given that Schneider's overall revenues doubled during the 1990s.

At the core of Schneider's ability to change is the company's willingness to accept and then leverage customers' challenges. When 3M wanted to outsource logistics in 1983, a decade before anyone else, Schneider agreed and created what became Schneider Logistics. When Case Corporation wanted logistics help in Europe in early 1998, Schneider said "yes" and formed its first international division, Schneider Logistics Europe. Accepting new challenges not only ensures that customers stay with Schneider, but also means that Schneider stays close to its customers as their needs evolve in a changing world.

Schneider's response to customer requests is not simply a "satisfy the customer at all costs" approach. Digitalization—in the form of information systems, extensive models, and reams of data on past shipments—helps Schneider to determine objectively what it can and cannot do. If a customer wants an overly aggressive shipping schedule on a route, then Schneider will negotiate a more feasible schedule or decline the job. The key is that Schneider has cultivated an ability to offer a wide range of services and to understand what it can do profitably without creating rules that limit flexibility.

Schneider's strategy of doing more for its customers is not just a matter of self-less devotion, nor is it a simple reactive strategy. Schneider could not effectively respond to novel customer requests without its investments in people, processes, and technology. Indeed, Schneider's most important and most hidden asset is its ability to learn the customer's situation and create a tailored solution in record time. This is especially important at Schneider Dedicated and Schneider Logistics, where solutions must meld Schneider's technology and processes with those of the client. Schneider's seemingly expensive asset base lets it take on new challenges that create new businesses, sustaining growth in an otherwise uncertain environment.

Culture and Values Support Digitalization

Schneider's values and culture underpin its transformation. The firm's explicitly-articulated and consistently-stressed set of values emphasize integrity (respect, trust, honesty, and self-esteem) and performance (achievement, enthusiasm, compensation, entrepreneurship). Schneider's identity statement characterizes its culture: "*The Orange On-Time Machine*: Safe, Courteous, Hustling Associates Creating Solutions That Excite Our Customers." Transportation planning leader David Dietrich noted that "Orange isn't just a color, it's a way of life." Schneider's culture has helped digitalization take hold.

Creating and maintaining this culture starts in the hiring process. "We look for a rounded skill set and alignment with our values, which include learning throughout your career," said Tim Fliss, Vice President of Human Resources. "We look for people who are comfortable with technology. We do hiring in the operating centers, so when you come for an interview, you see people with PCs on their desk and headsets—it's obvious the role technology will play in your job." Thus, the selection process prunes candidates who don't relate well to technology.

Once hired, all non-driver employees spend at least two days in training, while managers spend four days. Employees learn about the industry and the company, with Don Schneider himself leading the sessions that describe the company's core values. "He talks to every new drivers' class, explains the company's values, and makes everyone aware of their importance to the company's goals," said one Schneider customer. "Everyone in that operation knows that their job is serving the customer."

Although Schneider National is a private company, Don Schneider took the remarkable step of creating an independent board of directors with the power to fire him. In an interview, Don explained his rationale:

Humans need a tension to be effective. With my goals and the way I think about my values, I want to keep the company private—public companies have too short-term an outlook. But in order to stay private, I needed the same tension, so I formed an outside board and took all the voting stock and put in it a trust fund that's run by the board. That made it pure— they have total responsibility. They could fire me. I have to go through a yearly evaluation, and they could determine that it's best for the 20,000 employees if they fire me.

Schneider's culture helps it win new contracts. Ed Root, former Director of Transportation for Libbey-Owens-Ford, interviewed drivers when assessing a long-term dedicated carriage partnership with Schneider. The drivers' genuine regard for their employer was a key factor in his company choosing Schneider.

Conclusion

Inevitably, there is no enduring competitive advantage from technology. Today, 280,000 trucks in the industry use the satellite communication system first used at Schneider. Other firms will copy and improve what the leader initiates.

As the Schneider story indicates, however, investing in constant adaptation can move the technology forward in new ways. Firms that are close to their customers and marketplaces are more likely to have insights that lead to investments with high payoffs. And firms that have complementary investments in the broader network of skills, structure, and processes will likely achieve a kind of advantage that is hard to duplicate.

New technologies gave Schneider the chance to learn how to build a complementary web of activities that shows every sign of being lasting. This web is a complex network of factors—strategy and structure, process, people and culture–that must continually be balanced as the organization evolves to meet ever-changing external pressures.

Figure 7.4 summarizes how Schneider made careful moves in strategy, technology, organizational structure, operational and management processes, and support for its people. The net result is an effective, growing organization whose customers and employees work together to thrive in a changing world.

The ability to grow and evolve such an organization is rare, but we would submit that the ability to maintain this holistic balance will distinguish successful organizations in the decades ahead. One can certainly see in Schneider how technology

STRUCTURE

- Highly motivated, semi-
  autonomous , very flat

EXTERNAL	STRATEGY	PROCESS	TECHNOLOGY
Deregulation	- Led by customers	- Decisions at front line with full information	- Embedded in operations (trucks)
Lean Customers	- Information is central, not only physical assets	- Real ownership of results	- Always experimenting (wireless)
Bigger Competitors	- Leverage knowledge		

PEOPLE

- Highly motivated

- Trusted

Figure 7.4
Model of External Forces and Internal Organizational Dimensions at Schneider National

was both an enabler and a creator in "digitalizing" the corporation. The genius of Don Schneider and his team, however, was to build the necessary related web of complementary dimensions that will let their creation evolve through time.

Acknowledgements

Other MIT faculty, researchers and students who worked on the Interesting Organizations project were Martha Broad, Frank Feist, Robert Halperin, Robert Laubacher, Thomas Malone, Roanne Neuwirth, Wanda Orlikowski, and Jeanne Ross. Special thanks go to Andrea Meyer of Working Knowledge, who was project manager and lead researcher for the Interesting Organizations Database and who assisted in the preparation of this manuscript.

Notes

1. Citibank Japan account based on interviews.

2. Seven-11 account based on interviews.

3. Thermo Electron account based on interviews with George Hatsopolous, founder and chairman; John Hatsopolous, CFO; Robert Howard, executive vice president; Walter Bornhorst, CEO of Thermo Process Systems; John Wood, CEO of Thermedics.

4. The material on Schneider is drawn from a series of cases prepared by Andrea Meyer and Michael S. Scott Morton with the generous help of Schneider employees in 2000 and 2001.

References

Allen, Thomas J., and Michael S. Scott Morton, eds. 1994. *Information Technology and the Corporation of the 1990s: Research Studies*. New York and Oxford: Oxford University Press.

Alter, Allan E. 1994. Jack be Agile, Jack be Quick. *Industry Week*, January 17, 61.

Anslinger, Patricia, Dennis Carey, Kristin Fink, and Chris Gagnon. 1997. Equity carve-outs: A new spin on the corporate structure. *McKinsey Quarterly* (1): 165–172.

Bylinsky, Gene. 1997. Sales are Clicking on Manufacturing's Internet Mart. *Fortune*, July 7.

Brophy, Beth. 1989. You're in the Office of the Future Now. *U.S. News and World Report*, April 17: 50–52.

Chandler, Alfred D., Jr. 1962. *Strategy and Structure: Chapters in the History of the Industrial Enterprise*. Cambridge, Mass.: MIT Press.

Davenport, Thomas H. and Nitin Nohria. 1994. Case management and the integration of labor. *Sloan Management Review* 35 (Winter): 11–24.

Galbraith, Jay. 1973. *Designing Complex Organizations*. Reading, Mass.: Addison-Wesley.

Galbraith, Jay. 2000. *Designing the Global Corporation*. San Francisco: Jossey-Bass.

Hock, Dee. 1999. *The Birth of the Chaordic Age*. San Francisco: Berrett Koehler.

Information Week. 1997. The Net Pays Off. January 27.

Kotabe, Masaa. 1995. The return of 7-Eleven from Japan: The vanguard program. *Columbia Journal of World Business*, December 22.

Lanza, Julie. 1993. Thermo's Children find a friendly environment. *Boston Business Journal*, February 26, 10.

Lissack, Michael R. 1996. Chaos and Complexity—What does it have to do with knowledge management? Complexity, Science, and Liberty Conference, Quebec, June.

Lowe, Janet. 2001. *Welch: An American Icon*. New York: John Wiley & Sons.

Mack, Toni. 1988. They have faith in us. *Forbes*, July 25.

Mahajan, Rakesh. 1995. Building the Virtual Enterprise. 4th Annual Agility Forum Conference, Atlanta, March.

Quinn, James Brian. 1992. *Intelligent Enterprise: A Knowledge and Service Paradigm for Industry*. New York: Free Press.

Sabbagh, Karl. 1998. *21st Century Jet: The Making of the Boeing 777*. New York: Scribner.

Schein, Edgar H. 1984. Coming to a New Awareness of Organizational Culture. Sloan Management Review 25 (Winter): 3–16.

Scott Morton, Michael S., ed. 1991. *The Corporation of the 1990s: Information Technology and Organizational Transformation*. New York and Oxford: Oxford University Press.

Scott Morton, Michael S. 1995. Emerging Organizational Forms: Work and Organization in the 21st Century. *European Management Journal* 13 (December): 339–345.

Semler, Ricardo. 1989. Managing without Managers. *Harvard Business Review* 67 (September–October): 76–84.

Semler, Ricardo. 1994. *Maverick: The Success Story Behind the World's Most Unusual Workplace*. London: Arrow.

Semler, Ricardo. 1995. Why My Former Employees Still Work for Me. *Harvard Business Review* 72 (January–February): 64–74.

Sheridan, John H. 1996. Re-engineering isn't enough. 5th Annual Agility Forum Conference, Boston, March 5–7.

Toigo, Jon William. 1994. Minimizing risk with data warehousing. *Enterprise Systems Journal*, September 1, S16.

Venkatraman, N., and John Henderson. 1998. Real Strategies for Virtual Organizing. *Sloan Management Review* 40 (Fall): 33–48.

Woolley, Scott. 1997. Double Click for Resin: Large-scale Commerce on the Internet? *Forbes*, March 10.

III WHAT CAN YOU DO ABOUT IT?

The changes that swept through the business world in the 1980s and 1990s opened up a wide range of new organizational possibilities. This section examines some of these possibilities, from both strategic and organizational perspectives.

Inventing New Strategies

We start with a subsection focused on how strategy has evolved since the days of the traditional hierarchical firm. This subsection—Inventing New Strategies—addresses new approaches to achieving competitive advantage that have emerged with the reconfiguring of organizations in recent years.

Strategy in the heyday of the multidivisional corporation was about turning industrial organization economics—which was born out of the trust-busting ethos of the early twentieth century—on its head. Corporate strategists used the principles of industrial organization to find ways to extract, and maintain, monopoly rents. Thus the main questions were: What is the structure of our industry? and How is our firm positioned? The primary strategic levers were entry and exit, and once a firm decided to compete, the primary choice was between striving for low cost or differentiating its products (Ghemawat 2002).

As the post-World War II corporate order came under pressure in the 1980s and 1990s, there was growing recognition that old forms of structural advantage were increasingly less sustainable in volatile sectors (Coyne and Subramanian 1996). New strategic opportunities were emerging, which involved not so much positioning an individual firm as a stand-alone actor, but instead, exploiting ties between firms. Of particular importance were ties with both customers and suppliers. Each relationship implied an alternative to the old cost vs. product differentiation tradeoff. Both articles in the first subsection address the strategic opportunities afforded by the newly emerging business framework.

In the first article, Arnoldo Hax and Dean Wilde contend that in addition to the old cost/differentiation choice, which they term competition based on product economics, today's connected business environment now offers two additional strategic opportunities. One is competition based on customer economics, in which a firm solves a customer's problem with its product or service offering. The other is competition based on system economics, in which a firm locks in a technical standard and attracts complementors to develop products based on it (see Hax & Wilde 2001).

Competing based on customer economics requires firms to have close ties with customers, so they can develop offerings that solve customer problems. The first mass-produced products often represented only a very gross fit with customer preferences, but in that era, even a rough approximation with actual needs led to an overall increase in consumer utility because of the far lower cost. Product differentiation, which came later, represented an incremental move beyond mass standardization and provided a better fit between product offering and customer preferences. In recent years, several new approaches have enabled a far closer fit between customer needs and the product characteristics. One is mass customization, enabled by the use of product platforms and modular designs. The other is providing solutions, combinations of products and services tailored to meet customers' specific needs. Both these approaches can be seen as a kind of super product differentiation. But the differences between them and traditional product differentiation—a focus on individual customers, as opposed to broad customer segments; rich communications links to enable direct customer-firm interaction vs. one-to-many mass marketing; close collaboration with outside firms that provide subsystems of the solution—are great enough that the new approaches are truly different in kind.

Competing based on system economics requires that a firm be able to manage its product innovation effectively enough to become a leader whose technical standard is widely accepted in the industry. It also requires that the firm encourage a myriad of other companies within its industry ecosystem to develop complementary products based on its standard.

Hax and Wilde lay out the firm and industry characteristics required for each of the three competitive stances—product, customer and system-based competition—to be viable. They then go on to show how increasingly close relationships—what they call "bonding"—are required as a firm moves from competing on the basis of a standardized product and works toward achieving customer lock-in; and then moves further toward locking in a technology standard, which requires close interconnections with both customers and the suppliers and partners who produce complementary products. They end by noting processes and priorities that allow execution of the three strategies and the performance metrics appropriate to each.

Charles Fine's article is a distillation of his extensive research on supply chains in a broad range of industries (see Fine 1999). The article starts by introducing the concept of clockspeed—the pace of key industry variables like product development cycle time and the life-span of factory equipment. Fine has compared fast clockspeed industries—Internet services, computers, media—to sectors that operate at a slower pace—for instance, autos and aircraft. He found that all industries exhibit similar dynamics; in fast clockspeed sectors, things just play out more quickly. The fast clockspeed industries—what Fine calls industrial fruit flies—thus have lessons to provide to more leisurely sectors. And as the pace of business overall picks up, these lessons must be absorbed increasingly quickly.

Fine found one key dynamic that is important in many sectors: a tendency for industries to oscillate between vertical structures—where an integrated product designed and produced by a single vendor dominates (for example, IBM in the 1960s)—and horizontal structures—where suppliers of modular components tend to dominate (for example, the personal computer industry in the 1980s). This oscillation creates increasing opportunity—and risk—for firms in both the single vendor and component supplier positions. Among the strategic implications are that single vendors who dominate when a vertical structure prevails must beware of decisions that allow suppliers to supplant their position—as IBM allowed Microsoft and Intel to do in the personal computer industry.

Fine emphasizes that in today's volatile business environment, there is no such thing as lasting competitive advantage. Given this reality, he sees the critical core competency to be an ability to incorporate supply chain considerations in the innovation process. He calls this capacity three-dimensional concurrent engineering: the ability to take into account, at the same time, design of the product, the manufacturing process, and the supply chain.

Inventing New Organizations

Organizational innovation—the ability to invent, and reinvent, organizations on a real-time, ongoing basis—will be an important characteristic of successful firms in the twenty-first century. This will not simply be a matter of traditional organizational redesign as known in the age of the hierarchical corporation.

When considering twenty-first century organizational invention, it is useful to recall the themes outlined in this volume's first section on how the business world is changing—volatility and uncertainty in the environment, organizational decentralization, and IT-enabled connectivity both inside and between firms. The five articles in the next sub-section—Inventing New Organizations—address how these factors will shape the work of inventing twenty-first century organizations.

The article on the Process Handbook by Malone *et al.* presents a way of thinking—and a software tool—that can enable organizational invention in an ever-changing environment. A world of fluid firm boundaries and rapid change will require continual organizational reconfiguration, with supplier, partner, and customer relationships constantly being adjusted. It will also require an ability to reshape internal processes on an ongoing basis. To do this effectively involves going beyond static concepts like organization charts and headcounts, and instead adopting a more dynamic view of modular, interchangeable processes. As the chapter puts it, the Process Handbook views organizations not by looking at the nouns—the organizational units or individuals within them—but by looking at the verbs—the living processes that are enacted on an ongoing basis within those units by those people. This means seeing organizations—and entire value chains—not as squares on the chart but as a series of interconnected, mix-and-match processes that can be taken apart and reassembled in a variety of unexpected ways.

By mapping processes and providing a framework for understanding their deep structure, the Process Handbook gives organizational inventors new capabilities in undertaking their work. If they are revamping internal processes, they can get ideas for alternative approaches—in some cases from surprising places—by searching in the handbook's repository of business knowledge. If they are piecing together processes across firms, the handbook can provide insight into how those processes might be combined. Widespread use of such a tool could ultimately allow twenty-first century business people to rapidly reconfigure inter-connectable processes, the way they cut and paste information between applications on their computer desktops today (see Malone, Crowston, and Herman 2003).

The next chapter, by Nina Krushwitz and George Roth, shows an early version of this kind of organizational invention in action. It is an excerpt from a learning history that documented one of the 21st Century Initiative's special projects. The project was a joint effort between the Sloan School's Process Handbook team; the consulting firm, A. T. Kearney, a major sponsor of the Initiative; and one of A. T. Kearney's clients, a large financial services firm. The project involved the redesign of some hiring processes at the financial services firm. The article describes how the special project diverged from traditional process re-engineering methods. Using the handbook as a process mapping and creativity tool led the team to take a novel approach. Krushwitz and Roth show how the university-industry collaboration generated a new set of ideas about how to manage the hiring process and also developed a general navigational tool, the Process Compass, that allows users to navigate conceptually through a large database of business processes.

The next chapter, by Wanda Orlikowski and Debra Hofman, is based on field-work at the help desk of a software firm and addresses the subject of organizational change in decentralized, information-rich settings. The twenty-first century can be expected to feature extended enterprises where numerous interconnected entities collaborate—both inside and across corporate boundaries—with each organizational node possessing significant autonomy. This sort of structure can't be run from the top by command-and-control fiat; it instead requires giving local actors the information they need and trusting them to make decisions based on their better view from the front lines. It also requires an experimental approach, an ability to run trials and then quickly read results and adapt, with quick feedback loops, an approach the nimblest players in the high tech sector tout as "do it, fix it." A hallmark of the twenty-first century organization thus will be an ability to gather feedback and adjust course. At the same time, the information accessible to local actors in real time will lead them to launch novel, unanticipated initiatives. Twenty-first century managers must thus be able to take in stride—even take advantage of—the unexpected. As Orlikowski and Hofman put it, they need to be adept at working with "improvisational change."

The chapter on "X-teams" by Deborah Ancona, Henrik Bresman, and Katrin Kaeufer, is based on recent research at a number of large firms and describes the characteristics of successful teams operating in complex, uncertain settings. The team has emerged as a key unit of the new organizational order, supplanting the bureaucratic pyramid as the archetypal work group. Though being able to function well internally is a prerequisite for effectiveness, Ancona, Bresman, and Kauefer show that another key characteristic of successful teams is they are highly connected—to constituencies inside their own firm and to important outside actors—partners, suppliers, and customers—as well. This external orientation allows X-teams to be more in touch with cues from the environment and to adjust rapidly to change—shifts in customer preferences, emerging technical developments, and reorientation of their own company's strategic priorities.

To achieve a combination of team focus, while still maintaining wide external ties, X-teams have evolved a complex structure. They have several types of members: a core group, the ones with "skin in the game," who assume leadership roles; operational members who do the work; and others who comprise an "outer net," who bring key expertise or resources and typically join on a part-time basis. Membership is also fluid, with people rotating in and out over the lifetime of the team. X-teams rely on a set of broadly agreed-upon tools and practices—meetings, formal decision-making procedures, deadlines and schedules—to coordinate their internal activity. The larger cross-team organizational context is important as well. It serves to establish and reinforce internal team practices and provides a broad information infrastructure and learning culture that allows the culling of "lessons learned" from past stumbles—and successes.

X-teams represent one vision of the kind of organizations that will meet the needs of the volatile 21st century environment—small groups, with fluid membership and so able to expand or contract as needed, operating autonomously to meet a particular objective, but heavily linked to external groups, and making use of some standardized practices within a broader cultural context. X-teams, as described in this chapter, are a product of large, decentralized firms; but teams exhibiting similar characteristics could also operate in other contexts—in collaborations among partners in supply chains or among e-lancers working together on a project basis over the Internet.

A strong technology backbone will be a key enabler of twenty-first century business, as shown in the next article on the information system (IS) organization, by John Rockart, Michael Earl, and Jeanne Ross. Based on a study done in the mid-1990s, this chapter contains lessons that are just as applicable today. Among other things, Rockart, Earl, and Ross describe one of the promising alternatives for organizing in a decentralized environment: a *federal* structure. In a federal IS organization, a central group runs the common infrastructure and provides a standardized set of desktop functions to everyone in the firm. Local IS groups, housed inside operational units and working closely with them, develop the specialized IT functionality—usually in the form of custom-written software—to meet particular business needs.

A federal structure allows achievement of scale economies and global connectivity—through low-cost operation of the common infrastructure—and a large measure of autonomy in meeting business-specific IS needs, through the workings of the local IS units. It allows organizations to operate in a highly decentralized manner, granting decision-making authority to the front lines, while at the same time providing communication links that allow for cross-unit information sharing and collaboration.

The five articles in this subsection on Inventing New Organizations present not so much descriptions of how twenty-first century organizations are likely to look, but rather, a set of perspectives and tools that will allow the organizational inventors of the future to go about their work. The concepts presented in the articles—mix-and-match processes; improvisational change; focused, highly connected teams operating within a supportive institutional framework; networked, flexible information systems—are components from which next generation organizations will be built.

References

Coyne, Kevin P. and Somu Subramaniam. 1996. Bringing discipline to strategy. *McKinsey Quarterly* (4): 14–25.

Fine, Charles H. 1999. *Clockspeed: Winning Industry Control in the Age of Temporary Advantage.* Reading, Mass.: Perseus Books.

Ghemawat, Pankaj. 2002. Competition and Business Strategy in Historical Perspective. *Business History Review* 76 (Spring): 37–74.

Hax, Arnoldo C., and Dean L. Wilde. 2001. *The Delta Project: Discovering New Sources of Profitability in a Networked Economy*. New York: St. Martins Press.

Malone, Thomas W., Kevin G. Crowston, and George Herman. 2003. *Toward a Global Repository for Organizing Business Knowledge: The MIT Process Handbook*. Cambridge, Mass.: MIT Press.

Inventing New Strategies

8 The Delta Model: Adaptive Management for a Changing World

Arnoldo C. Hax and Dean L. Wilde II

The most influential contemporary strategic framework, espoused by Michael Porter, is based on two exclusive ways to compete: low cost or differentiation.[1] A company can achieve low cost by aggressively reducing costs or differentiate by creating something that is perceived industrywide as unique. Although low cost and differentiation call for fairly distinct strategies, both center on product economics or on delivering the "best product." Customers are attracted by a low price or by the differentiating product characteristics that go beyond price.

Although the best-product strategy continues to be relevant, our research shows that it does not describe all the ways companies compete in the current environment. Two companies illustrate this point:

• Microsoft has been a phenomenal success, perhaps the model for a modern business in a complex environment. By 1998, Microsoft had created $270 billion of market value in excess of debt and equity. Did it do this by having the best product? Microsoft does not have a 90 percent share of the market for personal computer operating systems because of low price. While it may have an effective cost infrastructure, its position is not based on being the low-cost provider. On the other hand, its operating system and, most certainly, the MS-DOS product that fueled its dominance, has never had the best features or been the easiest to use. In fact, many would argue that Apple had the best set of differentiated features. Nonetheless, Microsoft is unambiguously the market leader. The source of its success is a distinctive competitive position that is not best product, but rather one supported by the economics of the system as a whole, which we label "system lock-in."

• Jack Welch, General Electric's legendary CEO, gets upset if someone describes GE as a conglomerate. GE's tremendous strength in financial services has made it unique among its peers in its ability to provide sophisticated financing options to customers and support to businesses in its portfolio. Beyond financial services, GE has actively extended from selling products to providing after-market services for many of its core businesses. In the aircraft business, for example, where GE effectively splits the market 50/50 with Pratt & Whitney, the commercial airlines have traditionally maintained their own engines. GE is now offering to maintain their engines, and can present a fairly compelling offer to the airlines, owing to their technical expertise and their ability to capture a higher volume of business than any one carrier. GE signed a ten year, $2.3 billion contract with British Airways in March 2000 under which GE will carry out 85 percent of the engine maintenance work on BA's entire fleet—including engines made by rivals Rolls-Royce and Pratt &

The Delta Project

Three years ago, we initiated a dialogue among some senior executives and faculty members at the MIT Sloan School of Management to identify the issues and challenges that managers were facing. The senior managers participating were Skip LeFauve, CEO of Saturn; Gerhard Schulmeyer, then CEO of Asea Brown Boveri America; Iain Anderson, CEO of Chemical Coordination at Unilever; Judy Lewent, CFO of Merck; and Bert Morris, chief executive of operations at National Westminster Bank. The faculty members were Charles Fine, Arnoldo Hax, Henry Jacoby, Thomas Magnanti, Robert McKersie, Stewart Myers, John Rockart, Edgar Schein, Michael Scott Morton, and John Van Maanen. We explored in depth the forces confronting business worldwide to determine whether current frameworks responded to modern issues.

What resulted from the discussions was a coherent picture of a world that defies clear definition. The only common denominator is continuous, inexorable change. Conventional theories and business practices are not providing the necessary guidance and support for decision making.

The Delta Project discussions were the foundation for our own reflections on how to respond effectively to these challenges and led to a new framework we call the "Delta model." It is anchored in a different business model and offers adaptive processes that can help managers deal with the new challenges of complexity, uncertainty, and change.

Whitney. Today, GE is busy transforming the carrier's maintenance practices. It is moving BA to a just-in-time inventory system for parts, and instituting self-directed teams and other advanced management practices from its own plants. David J. Kilonback, who oversees the deal for BA, says the shift saved the carrier money and management time, in addition to providing speedier engine turnaround. Building on the BA deal, GE inked a $1 billion, multiyear contract in September 2000 to service US Air's GE engines. A closer examination of GE thus reveals a well-conceived strategic approach, which we label "customer solutions."

Clearly, existing management frameworks do not address the challenges managers face today (see the sidebar). Based on our research on more than 100 companies, we have developed the Delta model, which makes four major contributions. First, it defines strategic positions that reflect fundamentally new sources of profitability. Second, it aligns these strategic options with a firm's activities and thus provides congruency between strategic direction and execution. Third, it introduces adaptive processes with the capability to continually respond to an uncertain environment. And, finally, it shows that granular metrics are the drivers of performance in complex industries.

The Triangle: Three Strategic Options

Our research gave rise to a new business model, the "triangle," that better reflects the many ways to compete in the current economy (see figure 8.1). The new model

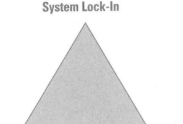

Competition Based on System Economics:
Complementor lock-in, competitor lock-out,
proprietary standard

System Lock-In

Customer Solutions   **Best Product**

Competition Based on   **Competition Based on**
Customer Economics: **Product Economics:**
Reducing customer costs or   Low cost or differentiated position
increasing profits

Figure 8.1
The Triangle: Three Distinct Strategic Options

fills a significant void in the development of strategic thinking by offering *three*
potential options: best product, customer solutions, and system lock-in.

The *best-product* strategic option is built on the classic forms of competition
through low cost or differentiation. Its relevant economic drivers are centered on a
product or service. A company can achieve cost leadership by aggressively pursuing economies of scale, product and process simplification, and significant product
market share that allow it to exploit experience and learning effects. A company
can differentiate by enhancing product attributes in a way that adds value for the
customer. It can achieve this differentiation through technology, brand image, additional features, or special services. Every strategic option searches for a way to bond
with the customer, which is reflected in a significant switching cost. Through the best-
product option, companies bond with customers through the intrinsic superiority of
their product or service. Important aids for this purpose are introducing products
rapidly, being first to market, and establishing a so-called dominant design.[2]

The *customer solutions* strategic option is based on a wider offering of products
and services that satisfies most if not all the customer's needs. The focus here is on

the customer's economics, rather than the product's economics. A company might offer a broad bundle of products and services that is targeted and customized to a specific customer's needs. In that respect, the most relevant performance measurement of this option is customer market share. Customer bonding, obtained through close proximity to the client, allows a company to anticipate needs and work jointly to develop new products. Bonding is enhanced by learning and customization. Learning has a dual effect: The investment the customer makes in learning how to use a product or service can constitute a significant switching cost, while learning about customer needs will increase the company's ability to satisfy his or her requirements. Both have a positive impact in the final bonding relationship. Often this strategic option calls for the development of partnerships and alliances, which could include other suppliers, competitors, and customers linked by their ability to complement a customer offering.

The *system lock-in* strategic option has the widest possible scope. Instead of narrowly focusing on the product or the customer, the company considers all the meaningful players in the system that contribute to the creation of economic value. In this strategic position, bonding plays its most influential role. The company is particularly concerned with nurturing, attracting, and retaining so-called "complementors,"[3] along with the normal industry participants. (A complementor is not a competitor but a provider of products and services that enhance a company's offering.) Typical examples include computer hardware and software producers; high-fidelity equipment manufacturers and CD providers; TV set, video recorder, and videocassette makers; and producers of telephone handsets and telecom networks. The critical issue here is looking at the overall architecture of the system: How can a company gain complementors' share in order to lock out competitors and lock in customers? The epitome of this position is achieving the *de facto* proprietary standard.

Although, in reality, these options are not mutually exclusive, and a business could decide on a blended strategy, it is useful to consider the three alternatives as distinct ways of competing, with different scope, scale, and bonding (see figure 8.2). The scope significantly increases as we move from best product to system lock-in. At the extreme end of the best-product position, where a company often opts for low cost, the scope is trimmed to a minimum. The scope expands to include product features as a company moves to a differentiated best-product position. It further expands beyond the product to include the customer's activities in the case of customer solutions. The company finally reaches the broadest possible scope as a system lock-in company when it includes complementors.

	Best Product	Customer Solutions	System Lock-In
Scope	Defeatured ⟷ Fully featured • Low cost • Differentiated	Broad Product Range: • Bundling • Joint development • Outsourcing	Nurturing Complementors: • Variety and number • Open architecture
Scale	Product: • Market share	Customer: • Customer share	System: • Complementor share
Bonding	Link to Product: • First to market • Dominant design	Link to Customers: • Customer lock-in • Learning • Customization	Link to System: • Competitor lock-out • Proprietary standards

Figure 8.2
Characteristics of Three Options for Strategic Positioning

Scale is a critical strategic factor typically measured as product market share, which is appropriate when evaluating a best-product position. In the case of customer solutions, a company must consider its share of a customer's purchases. For a system lock-in position, complementor share is the most crucial consideration.

Ultimately, bonding deals with the forces that link the product or service with the customer. In the best-product option, this is done through the characteristics of the product itself. The customer solutions position achieves this through learning and customization. In the system lock-in position, the utmost bonding mechanism is the proprietary standard, which is a fundamental force in driving profitability and sustainability.

Understanding the Strategic Positions

We can see the distinct nature of the three strategic positions by examining some companies that share the same outstanding business success but have achieved their high performance through strikingly different strategies and draw on fundamentally different sources of profitability (see figure 8.3).

Best-Product Position

Nucor Corporation is the fourth largest steel producer in the United States and the largest minimill producer. The objective of its classic best-product strategy is to be the lowest-cost producer in the steel industry. Its costs are $40 to $50 per ton less than those in the modern, fully integrated mills. Its sales per employee are $560,000

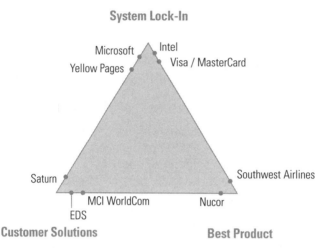

Figure 8.3
Options for Strategic Positioning

per year, compared to an average $240,000 for the industry. It has achieved this performance through a single-minded focus on product economics. Nucor's CEO John Correnti attributes 80 percent of its low-cost performance to a low-cost culture and only 20 percent to technology. In fact, during Nucor's boom years, between 1975 and 1986, twenty-five of its minimill competitors were closed or sold. Metrics reinforce this low-cost culture. Throughout the corporation, there is a strong alignment between the objectives and metrics critical to the strategy, namely, to be low-cost, and to the measurements and incentives for teams and individuals.

Nucor's financial performance resulting from this strategy is extraordinary. Before new management took over Nucor in 1966, the company was worth $13 million in market value. Thirty-two years later, this management and the processes it employed took Nucor to $5 billion in market value or 35 percent compounded growth—a spectacular result in the steel industry.

Southwest Airlines is another example of phenomenal performance through a best-product strategy. It relentlessly focuses on product economics and drives to cut product costs, sometimes reducing the scope and eliminating features from its service in the process. For example, it does not offer baggage handling, passenger ticketing, advance reservations, or hot food.

The activities that Southwest continues to perform it does differently. It emphasizes shuttle flights that efficiently utilize an aircraft on repeated trips between two airports, rather than using the hubs and spokes of the full-service carriers. It concentrates on the smaller and less congested airports surrounding large cities. It exclusively uses the Boeing 737, rather than the diverse fleets of the established carriers, thus reducing the costs of maintenance and training.

New companies may have an advantage over existing firms in originating radically new strategic positions founded on low cost because they may find it easier to redefine activities. Existing firms have embedded systems, processes, and procedures that are often obstacles to change and normally carry a heavy cost infrastructure. Many successful small companies have penetrated well-established industries and promptly reached a position of cost leadership in a more narrowly defined product segment, as in the cases of Nucor and Southwest, Dell and Gateway in personal computers, and WilTel in telecommunications. All these companies have had the same pattern: They narrowed the scope of their offering relative to the incumbents, they eliminated some features of the product, and they collapsed the activities of the value chain by eliminating some and outsourcing others. They perform the remaining activities differently, for either cost or product differentiation.

Customer Solutions Position

This competitive position reflects a shift in strategic attention from product to customer—from product economics to customer economics and the customer's experience.

Electronic Data Systems (EDS) is a clear example of a customer solutions provider. EDS has achieved prominence in the data processing industry by singularly positioning itself as a firm that has no interest in individual hardware or software companies. Its role is to provide the best solutions to cover total information needs, regardless of the components' origins. In the process, it has built a highly respected record by delivering cost-effective and tailor-made solutions to each customer. EDS has completely changed the perception of how to manage IT resources. While once IT was regarded as the brain of the company and every firm developed its own strong, internal IT group, now IT outsourcing is commonplace and even expected.

As a customer solutions provider, EDS measures its success by how much it improves the customer's bottom line or how it enhances the customer's economics. Typically, it goes into an organization that is currently spending hundreds of millions of dollars annually and delivers significant savings while, at the same time, enhancing the firm's current IT capabilities. This achievement is important in an industry that is cost-sensitive, rapidly changing, and extremely complex and sophisticated. EDS achieves these gains by extending the scope of its services to include activities previously performed by the customer. By focusing on IT, operations scale, and experience relative to the customer, it can offer services at a lower cost and/or higher quality than the customers themselves can.

MCI WorldCom provides a contrasting example of a customer solutions position. Where EDS has built value by "vertically" expanding its service scope into activities previously performed by the customer, MCI WorldCom is an almost pure example of expanding "horizontally" across a range of related services for the targeted customer segment, or bundling. It bundles the services together to reduce complexity for the customer. The customer benefits from a single bill, one contact point for customer service and sales, and potentially a more integrated, highly utilized network, but the products are the same. MCI WorldCom benefits through higher revenue per customer and longer customer retention, because it is harder to change vendors, and through lower-cost customer service and sales. Clearly, MCI WorldCom is following a strategy that is changing the rules of competition in the telecom industry and drawing on new sources of profitability. It is shifting the dimension of competitive advantage from product share to customer share.

Saturn, another example of the customer solutions position, is one of the most creative managerial initiatives in the past ten years. It abandoned a focus on products and turned its attention to changing the customer's full life-cycle experience. Saturn deliberately decided to design a car that would produce a driving experience close to the Toyota Corolla or the Honda Civic. It satisfied owners of these Japanese cars and therefore wanted to make the transition as easy as possible. Inherently, Saturn abandoned the best-product strategy and decided to create a product that was no different from the leading competition.

Instead, Saturn redefined the terms of engagement with the customer at the dealership. As any American buyer knows, purchasing a car can be unpleasant, subject to all kinds of uncomfortable pressures. Saturn targeted its dealers from a list of the top 5 percent of dealers in the United States, regardless of the brands they represented. Saturn offered extraordinary terms, which required a major commitment from the dealers to learn the Saturn culture and to make multimillion-dollar investments in the dealership.

First, and not just symbolically, Saturn changed the name "dealer," with the implicit connotation of negotiation and haggling, to "retailer," which connotes loyalty and fairness. Next, it instituted a no-haggling policy. Every car, and every accessory in the car, had a fixed price throughout the United States. In fact, the dealers educated customers on the features and price of the car and how they compared to competitors. Saturn also established a complete rezoning and expansion of retailer areas, thus limiting competition and allowing for more effective use of a central warehouse that a circle of Saturn dealers could share to lower inventory and costs. Additionally, it broke with tradition in the auto industry by offering a remarkable deal: "Satisfaction guaranteed, or your money back, with no questions asked." Saturn also implemented, for the first time, a "full car" recall. It replaced the complete car, not simply a component, and issued the recall within two weeks of finding symptoms of the problem.

Not surprisingly, customer response was overwhelming, creating what has become a cult among Saturn owners and thus giving Saturn the highest customer satisfaction rating in the industry—a phenomenal accomplishment for a car that retails for about one-fourth the price of luxury cars. Saturn's most powerful advertising campaign became the "word of mouth" from pleased customers, proving that focusing on the customer can be as strong a force in achieving competitive advantage as focusing on the product.

System Lock-in Position

In the system lock-in position are companies that can claim to own *de facto* standards in their industry. These companies are the beneficiaries of the massive investments that other industry participants make to complement their product or service. Microsoft and Intel are prime examples. Eighty percent to 90 percent of the PC software applications are designed to work with Microsoft's personal computer operating system (e.g., Windows 98) and with Intel's microprocessor design (e.g., Pentium), the combination often referred to as Wintel. As a customer, if you want access to the majority of the applications, you have to buy a Microsoft Windows operating system; 90 percent do. As an applications software provider, if you want access to 90 percent of the market, you have to write your software to work with Microsoft Windows; most do.

This is a virtuous feedback loop that accelerates, independent of the product around which it is spinning. The same relationship supports the demand for Intel's microprocessors. Microsoft and Intel do not win on the basis of product cost, product differentiation, or a customer solution; they have system lock-in. Apple Computer has long had the reputation of having a better operating system or a better product. Motorola has frequently designed a faster microprocessor. Microsoft and Intel, nonetheless, have long held the lock on the industry.

Not every product or service can be a proprietary standard; there are opportunities only in certain parts of the industry architecture and only at certain times. Microsoft, Intel, and Cisco have a shrewd ability to spot this potential in their respective fields and then relentlessly pursue the attainment, consolidation, and extension of system lock-in. Some of the most spectacular value creation in recent history has resulted. By 1998, Microsoft had created $270 billion of market value in excess of the debt and equity investment in the company, Intel had created $160 billion, and Cisco had created $100 billion.

In a nontechnology area, the Yellow Pages is one of the most widely recognized directories and most strongly held proprietary standards in the United States. The business, which has massive 50 percent net margins, is a fundamentally simple business. The Regional Bell Operating Companies, including Bell Atlantic, Ameritech, Bell South, and so on, owned the business and outsourced many of its activities, such as sales and book production. In 1984, when the Yellow Pages market opened for competition, there were many new entrants, including the companies that had provided the outsourcing services. Experts predicted rapid loss of market share and declining margins. Afterward, the incumbent providers retained 85 percent of the market, and their margins were unchanged. How did this happen?

The Yellow Pages has tremendous system lock-in. Businesses want to place their ads in a book with the most readership, and consumers want to use the book that has the most ads. When new companies entered the market, they could distribute books to every household but could not guarantee usage. Even with the steep 50 percent to 70 percent discounts the new books offered, businesses could not afford to discontinue their ads in the incumbent book with proven usage. Despite enhancements like color maps and coupons, consumers found the new books with fewer and smaller ads to have more size advantage than utility and threw them out. The virtuous circle could not be broken, and the existing books sustained their market position.

Financial services is another industry in which standards have emerged and are a force in determining competitive success. The key players in the credit card system are merchants, cards, consumers, and banks. American Express was the dominant competitor early on, albeit with a charge card rather than a credit card. Its strategy was to serve high-end business people, particularly those traveling abroad. The well-known slogan, "Don't leave home without it," and a worldwide array of American Express offices helped Amex achieve something close to a customer solutions position. Securing a lot of merchants was not part of Amex's strategy.

In contrast, Visa and MasterCard designed an open system, available to all banks, and aggressively pursued all merchants, in part through lower merchant fees. They created a virtuous loop—consumers prefer the cards accepted by the majority of the merchants, and merchants prefer the card held by the majority of the customers. This strategy culminated in strong system lock-in and MasterCard and Visa's achievement of a proprietary standard. Visa and MasterCard now represent more than 80 percent of the cards in circulation. It is interesting to note that at this time, Microsoft, Intel, and Visa and MasterCard are all under threats of suits by the U.S.

Department of Justice. Excessive power can lead to alleged abuses that call the attention of regulatory agencies.

One should not necessarily conclude that the pursuit of one strategic position is always more attractive than the other. There are big winners and losers in every option. Apple failed at owning the dominant operating standard. Banyan failed at achieving a *de facto* standard in the local area network operating system market, relative to Novell. The right option for a firm depends on its particular circumstances.

Economic Perspectives of the Strategic Positions

The three strategic positions are focused on three distinct economic perspectives (see figure 8.4). The economic implications of the best-product position are shown in Part A of the figure. The average business performer reflects the average cost of the industry and the margin available to the average player. In contrast are the low-cost competitor and the differentiated competitor; these two positions are the basic trade-offs represented in classic strategic positioning.

The lowest-cost performer is able to obtain a higher margin while still competitively pricing the product. This is a strong competitive advantage because the efficiency of the cost structure allows pricing below the cost of the average competitor that, in the long run, might put the average performers out of business. This is why the alternative to low cost must be differentiation, offering unique product attributes that the customer values and will pay a premium for. The differentiated player could have a higher cost than the average performer while still enjoying a fairly high margin because of the inherent additional value of the product. While the graph is simplistic, it represents important economic hurdles. To have a genuine low-cost position, a company needs to demonstrate lower relative unit costs. To have the economic leverage of a differentiated product, a company needs to show clearly that the customer will pay more, and that this premium is more than the added costs.

By contrast, the customer solutions position (shown in Part B of figure 8.4) centers on how products and services will impact the customer economics, either by lowering the customer's internal costs or by allowing the customers to have higher revenue. The customer solutions provider may have higher costs, but these are far outweighed by the economic contributions to the customer. The economic hurdle here is to show measurable and positive impact on the customer's profit.

Finally, we can contrast the economics of the system lock-in position with the other alternatives by recognizing that the scope is further enlarged to encompass

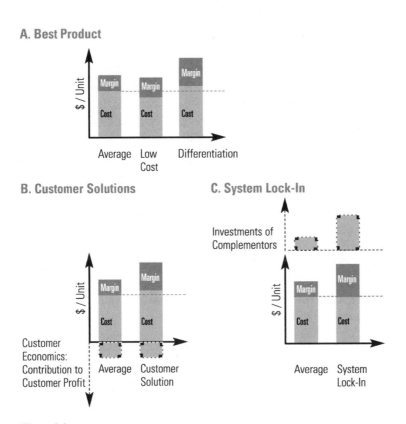

Figure 8.4
Economic Perspectives of the Strategic Positions

the total system of which products or services are part. The economic hurdle is both to create additional value to the system as a whole through the heavy investment by complementors, and then to be able to appropriate this value. Part C in figure 8.4 shows an average competitor whose complementors modestly add value to the overall system. In contrast, the owner of a proprietary standard has been able to get significant investments from its complementors, which adds value to its system. At the same time, its ability to appropriate this added value is evident in its higher margins.

The Bonding Continuum

Bonding is a primary element in each distinct strategic position and deserves closer examination. Bonding is a continuum that extends from the customer's first loyalty

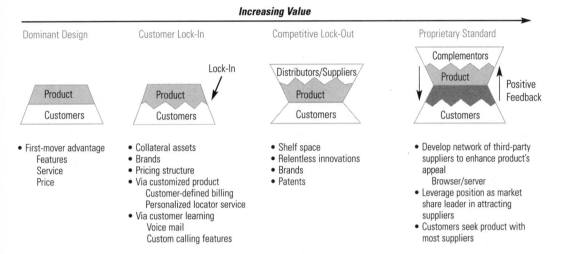

Figure 8.5
Bonding Continuum

to a product to full system lock-in with proprietary standards. We have identified four stages in bonding (see figure 8.5).

Establishing Dominant Design

In the first stage, dominant design, customers are attracted to a product because it uniquely excels in the dimensions they deeply care about. If the product positioning is one of low cost, then low price leads to loyalty. If the strategic positioning is differentiation, the features or services that accompany the product could attract and retain the customer.

In an embryonic industry that does not yet have a defined product design, various competitors do enormous experimentation. Product variety eventually consolidates to a common design that has the features and characteristics that customers expect from the product type. This emerging dominant design fills the requirements of many users for a particular product, although it may not exactly meet the requirements of any particular segment of the customer base. In that regard, the dominant design is generic and standardized as opposed to customized. The competitor generating this design captures the first element of loyalty from customers and has first-mover advantage.

For example, IBM benefited from a dominant design—the IBM PC. Its format included a monitor, a standard disk drive, the QWERTY keyboard, the Intel chip, open architecture, and the MS-DOS operating system. They came together to define the ideal PC for the market, which every other PC-compatible manufacturer would later have to emulate.

Locking In Customers

Beyond the stage of dominant design, there are clear opportunities to achieve higher, more tangible switching costs on the part of the customer. One such move is to enhance the product's inherent characteristics by offering additional support that makes it more accessible and attractive and thus harder to switch from, thereby locking in the customer. Collateral assets, which the firm owns and which complement the core product, can be effective in achieving this goal. Ownership of distribution channels, of specialized salesforces, and of technical support staff and, very importantly, a brand-supporting image can significantly increase product function, make it more appealing to the customer, and make the whole package more difficult to imitate. Brands as a collateral asset can reinforce lock-in when the product is unfamiliar and the functionality unknown, so that the assurance of support can dissipate doubts about product performance and encourage repeat purchase.

National Starch, a customer solutions company, provides an excellent example of customer lock-in. National Starch appears deeply rooted in rather mundane and pedestrian products, glue and starch. However, it has an unsurpassed history of long-term superior performance, not only in its industry, but also compared to most U.S. corporations. The source of its success is its extraordinary technological capabilities coupled with an intimate knowledge of all its key customers. R&D personnel, technical service staff, and marketing and sales managers have accumulated enormous knowledge on customer needs, the state of new product development, and ways to aid customers in revenue expansion and cost containment. The essence of National Starch's business is a joint working relationship with the customer.

One spectacular product that emerged from this relationship was a most sophisticated adhesive that eliminated welding airplane wings to an aircraft body. This product has two critical characteristics: One, the product contributes to the total quality of the final product, the airplane. Second, despite its great criticality, the product accounts for a negligible portion of the total cost of the airplane. With these two conditions, National Starch faces high profit potential. The moral here is that by creatively constructing a tight working relationship with the customer, a company can "decommoditize" a product. The bonds are strong because the company is not only providing a product but embracing the customer's own activities and enhancing its economics.

Price structure can influence bonding with customers as well. Two of the most innovative marketing programs in the 1980s were American Airlines' Frequent

Flyer program and MCI's "Friends and Family" promotion. Both programs were widely acclaimed because they created some lock-in for traditional commodity businesses.

Customized products and services can also lock in customers, through personalized services, customer care, and even billing. In the consumer market for the financial services industry, Merrill Lynch first introduced customer management accounts, but Fidelity, Schwab, and other institutions followed. The accounts are tailored to the user's circumstances; characteristics of bill payment, brokerage, mutual fund investments, IRA accounts, credit cards, and checking accounts are specific to and chosen by the customer. The effort to move this information to a new account creates a switching cost for the customer.

Another benefit of close customer proximity is that the customer and the supplier bond over time. A newcomer finds it hard to break into a relationship that has developed mutual investments and benefits. Additionally, a product can create its own learning experience. For example, once you learn how to use the Lotus 1-2-3 spreadsheet application, there is a significant additional effort to switch to Microsoft Excel.

Locking Out Competitors

There is a thin line between locking in customers and locking out competitors. First, once a company acquires a customer, it is hard for that customer to switch to an alternative. Second, significant barriers make it difficult for a competitor to imitate or to enter the business.

Four forces contribute to competitor lock-out. The first is based on the restrictions of distribution channels. Physical distribution channels, in particular, are limited in their ability to handle multiple product lines. At the extreme end of the spectrum are channels that carry only one product, such as soda fountains that serve only one brand of soda. If Coca-Cola captures the channel, Pepsi is preempted from that specific market and vice versa.

In this environment, brands can also generate competitor lock-out. They create customer demand that causes retailers to stock the branded product, at the expense of competitive products, given the physical constraints. In turn, shelf presence further enhances demand and the brand because people can buy only the products available. This reinforcing loop causes branding to be particularly effective for consolidating share and creating system lock-in when the industry structure includes physical distribution channels; this is in contrast to an industry that uses expandable channels such as telemarketing or direct mail.

Another way to lock out competitors is to establish a continuous stream of new products that can result in self-obsolescence and create enormous barriers to imitation or entry. Digital Equipment Corporation's origins in the 1950s provide a good example of competitor lock-out in an embryonic industry. DEC engineers had great freedom to both propose and follow through on their innovations. There was an unprecedented stream of new computers, with one breakthrough after another. DEC produced more than fifteen new versions in less than six years. As a result, competitors had difficulty passing a moving target. Furthermore, DEC users had to develop tailor-made software applications. Most importantly, all DEC computers were compatible with each other; therefore legacy software could run on the new equipment. The DEC architecture was not open; competitors thus not only had to match the technical features, but also had to be compatible with the existing software base. In ten years, DEC became the second largest computer company in the world.

Patents can lock competitors out, but also offer some challenges. In the pharmaceutical industry, a significant portion of a patent's length is often consumed before the product is released because of the time required for trials and FDA approval. Sometimes, half a patent's life expires before the product is introduced. This is compounded when patents are required in other countries, each with different requirements for documentation, languages, testing, legal compliance, and so on. In this situation, speed is key to competitive lock-out.

Sustaining Proprietary Standards

If a firm is able to reach and sustain proprietary standards, the rewards are immense. There are two requirements for this position. First, customer switching costs need to be high. Second, it has to be difficult or expensive for a competitor to copy the product. There are a number of ways to achieve system lock-in and to secure a proprietary standard. While one might presume that this would be the dominant of the three positions in our business model, it is not always possible to develop a standard in every market segment. Even if a standard can be developed, a single firm might not be able to appropriate it. And not all firms have the capabilities to achieve a proprietary standard.

Managers can ask several questions to assess whether their company can achieve a proprietary standard:

• Do we have an open architecture, or can we create one? An open architecture allows the attraction, development, and innovation of many complementors.

• Is there a potential for a large variety and number of complementors that can be enabled through a standard?

- Is the standard hard to copy? A complex interface that is rapidly evolving makes it difficult for competitors to imitate.
- Is the industry architecture being redefined?

Adaptive Processes to Link Strategy with Execution

By describing the three fundamental strategic positions, we have provided the mechanism to define the vision of a business—that elusive but indispensable requirement in successful management. The first challenge is to construct distinct business options that respond to the new realities of the current environment.

The next challenge is to link strategy with execution. More strategies fail because of ineffective execution than poor design. More often than not, a company's basic business processes are not aligned with the strategy. During the past few years, a proliferation of the so-called best business practices, including total quality management, business re-engineering, continuous improvement, benchmarking, time-based competition, and lean production, have been primarily directed at improving a firm's operational effectiveness. In theory and in application, these practices are decoupled from strategy. As a result, they contribute to creating a pattern of commoditization as companies imitate each other, thus preventing a truly differentiated strategic position.

The Delta model starts with the selection of a distinctive strategic position and then calls for the integration of the collective processes, not of one individual business process such as operational effectiveness. It is the *balance* of the fundamental processes that creates a unique and sustainable competitive position.

Complexity and uncertainty in the market create a problem in implementing any plan. The only assumption that remains valid over time is that the other assumptions will change. Strategy needs to adapt continuously, and therefore implementation itself needs to respond to market changes and to an improved understanding of the market. That understanding becomes apparent only during implementation.

In the Delta model, adaptive processes link strategy with execution by:

(1) defining the key business processes that are the repository of the primary operational tasks,

(2) aligning their role with the desired strategic position,

(3) seeking a coherent integration across these processes to produce unifying action, and

(4) incorporating responsive mechanisms as a core part of each process to ensure flexibility and change in an uncertain market.

Three Adaptive Processes

In the early 1990s, a powerfully simple idea developed: Businesses should be viewed not just in terms of functions, divisions, or products, but also as processes.[4] Processes should be the central focus when companies want to link strategy and execution. We have identified three fundamental processes that are always present and are the repository of key strategic tasks:

1. *Operational effectiveness*—the delivery of products and services to the customer. Conceived in its broadest sense, this process includes all the supply chain elements. Its primary focus is to produce the most effective cost and asset infrastructure to support the business's desired strategic position. It is the heart of the productive engine and the source of capacity and efficiency. Although it is relevant for all businesses, it becomes most important when a company chooses a strategic position of best product.

2. *Customer targeting*—the activities that attract, satisfy, and retain the customer. This process ensures that the customer relationships are managed most effectively. It identifies and selects attractive customers and enhances customer performance, either by reducing the customer's cost base or by increasing its revenue stream. At its heart, this process establishes the best revenue infrastructure for the business. While customer targeting is critical to all businesses, it is most important when the strategic position is that of total customer solutions.

3. *Innovation*—a continuous stream of new products and services to maintain the business's future viability. This process mobilizes all the firm's creative resources including technical, production, and marketing capabilities to develop an innovative infrastructure. The center of this process is the renewal of the business in order to sustain its competitive advantage and its superior financial performance. While preserving the innovative capabilities is critical to all businesses, it becomes central when the strategic position is that of system lock-in.

Alignment of Adaptive Processes with Strategy

The triangle we discussed earlier is the motor that drives the selection of strategic positioning, which, in turn, defines the role of each adaptive process. A firm's actions must be aligned with its strategic position, and the results must give feedback for adapting the strategy. This is the essence of adaptive management. Consistency, congruency, and feedback are the guiding principles. Not only does the role of each process need to adapt to each strategic option, but also the priorities with regard to each are affected. Next we examine the role of each adaptive process in supporting each strategic position of the business (see figure 8.6).

Operational Effectiveness

When operational effectiveness supports a best-product strategy, it is imperative to reduce the product costs by paying careful attention to the drivers of that cost. However, in the case of customer solutions, operational effectiveness is also concerned with the horizontal linkages between products in the bundled offer. The ultimate goal is to improve the customer's economics, even if that sometimes raises the product's costs. The relevant cost focus is the combined impact on the customer's business and the company's. In the system lock-in strategy, the product cost is perhaps the least relevant among all the positions. What is important is the value of the system through the creation of standards, the investments by the complementors, and their integration to improve overall performance.

For example, a data communications provider of private lines seeking a best-product position would focus on reducing maintenance costs to a minimum, given certain quality guidelines. A customer solutions provider would look closely at the customer's activities. It would reduce the customer's costs by adding equipment to diagnose a problem or perhaps by adding large-scale alternate back-up systems. In intranet services, in which a customer buys a highly secure private-line network using Internet protocols, a company might attempt a system lock-in position. Customers may find it increasingly expensive to switch or split vendors as they add applications and geographic locations to the same secure intranet. Establishing a low-cost infrastructure is less important than encouraging the customer to install more sites and to use more applications that run on an intranet platform.

Customer Targeting

When supporting a customer solutions position, companies seek to target key customers by offering a bundled solution, either alone or through alliances. This often requires targeting vertical markets and resorting to customized products as appropriate.

Channel ownership itself becomes an issue, in order to gain greater knowledge and access to the customer. For instance, in 1993, Merck, a leading research-based pharmaceutical company, acquired Medco, a premier distributor of generic drugs.

Strategic Positioning

Adaptive Process	Best Product	Customer Solutions	System Lock-In
Operational Effectiveness	Best Product Cost • Identify product cost drivers • Improve stand-alone product cost	Best Customer Value • Improve customer's economics • Improve horizontal linkages across components of the total solutions	Best System Performance • Improve system performance • Integrate complementors
Customer Targeting	Target Distribution Channels • Maximize coverage through multiple channels • Obtain low-cost distribution • Optimize channel mix and channel profitability	Target Customer Bundles • Enhance customer interfaces • Explore alliances to bundle solutions • Select key vertical markets • Examine channel ownership options	Target System Architecture • Identify leading complementors in the system • Enhance complementor interfaces • Harmonize system architecture • Expand number and variety of complementors

Innovation	Product Innovation
	• Develop family of products based on common platform
	• First to market, or follow rapidly — stream of products
		Customer Sourced Innovation
		• Identify and exploit joint development linked to the customer value chain
		• Expand your offer into the customer value chain to improve customer economics
		• Integrate and innovate customer care functions
		• Increase customer lock-in through customization and learning
			System Innovation
			• Emphasize features supporting lock-in
			• Proliferate complementors
			• Design proprietary standards within open architecture
			   Complex interfaces
			   Rapid evolution
			   Backward compatibility

Figure 8.6
Role of Adaptive Processes in Supporting Strategy

This allowed Merck to obtain the leading mail-order catalog, have access to unique distribution, and gain ownership of a customer database covering patients, physicians, and proprietary formulary.

When locking in a system, the key "customer" targets are the complementors, so the company can consolidate the lock-in position and neutralize competitor's actions. In short, the targeted customer is fundamentally different in these three options. At times, the final consumer or product user, although important, is not the critical strategic target. For example, we all know that its customers do not universally love Microsoft. The power of the owner of the systems standards gives the end user few choices.

In the software industry, software game providers typically adhere to a best-product strategic position and target customers as a way to get access to as many customers as possible. American Management Systems, which has a customer solutions position, implements customized software and thus targets vertical markets. Novell, which has a system lock-in position, has the proprietary standard for LAN operating systems and needs to put its premium effort into attracting and serving both application developers and the 30,000 value-added resellers that distribute and customize NetWare.

Innovation

When it comes to supporting a best-product strategy, renewal of the business is seen in terms of securing a continuous stream of products, often by sharing a common platform. If truly successful, that innovation will lead to establishment of a dominant design that represents the strongest base for competitive advantage with a best-product strategy. In the case of the customer solutions strategy, innovation plays an important role through the successful development of joint products with key customers. In this respect, this adaptive process is central not only for developing future customers, but for maintaining current ones. Furthermore, the customer is the primary source of innovation, not the conventional R&D labs.

The role of innovation in system lock-in is perhaps more critical than in any other strategic option. Often the technology is responsible for designing the architecture that will generate the system standard, that will allow the ownership of that standard, and that will preclude the standard from being copied or becoming obsolete. As we have indicated, it is more likely that a standard will be achieved if the architecture is based on open interfaces and characterized by rapid evolution with backward compatibility. In this instance, it is the innovation of the complementors that sustains the standard.

In the semiconductor industry, Hitachi and NEC are among the leading producers in dynamic random access memory (DRAM) semiconductors. This segment has been characterized by short product life cycles and declining prices. To succeed, every one to two years these companies develop new chips, which employ technology four times better than the previous generation, in facilities that cost more than $1 billion to construct. These two companies have chosen the best-product position and pursue innovation to support their competitive advantage.

Motorola's semiconductor business follows a customer solutions strategy that focuses on the automobile industry, among others. The BMW 740 has fifty microprocessors that control many aspects of its functionality and are critical to its differentiation. Motorola works with the manufacturers to develop these customized chips; the innovations are joint.

As a system lock-in provider, Intel depends on the rapid development of a complex standard. It developed five microprocessors, from the 8086 to the Pentium, from 1978 to 1996. This innovation is unique in at least two respects. First, it requires backward compatibility, which allows old complementors to work with the new product and ensures the continuation of the standard. Second, having secured the standard, it has the luxury of occasionally incorporating a larger part of the system into its standard to enhance its features and to further extend the interfaces with applications. There is a balancing act in grabbing additional functions from one complementor and in preserving the relationships and open architecture with other complementors, but a proven standard allows the freedom to do this.

Priorities of Each Adaptive Process

The concept of assigning priorities to the adaptive processes could be controversial. Some might insist on giving equal importance to each process and argue for the criticality of simultaneously having low cost, excellent customer targeting, and superior innovation. Choosing priorities does not dismiss one process or another but recognizes the intrinsic difference of each strategic position with its unavoidable, inherent trade-offs.

We've ranked the adaptive process priorities for each strategic option (see figure 8.7). The "consistency corridor" aligns the process of highest importance to each strategic position. Accordingly, the best-product position needs the lowest-cost infrastructure, which originates in the operational effectiveness process. Second, it requires the support of a stream of new products to prolong its current vitality into the future, the innovation process. Finally, the customer targeting process ensures the massive access to distribution channels.

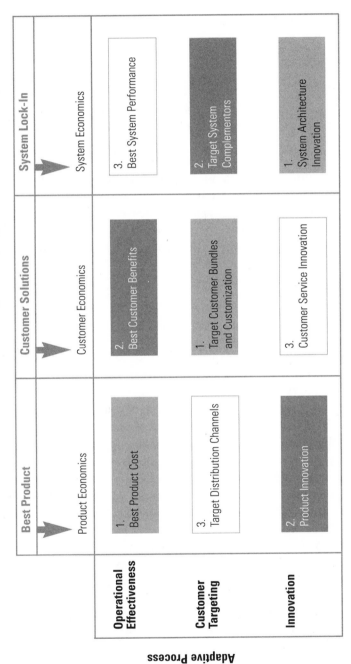

Strategic Positioning

Figure 8.7
Priorities of Adaptive Processes in Each Strategic Position

The customer solutions position has the effective targeting of the customer as its first priority. This is necessary to identify the required product bundles and to detect the needs for customization. Second, the operational effectiveness process ensures the delivery of the products and services to improve the customer economics. Innovation has the third ranking, not because it is unimportant for joint product development with the customer, but because the customer solutions position does not necessarily require leadership in new products, services, and features relative to that called for in the other strategic positions. Often the new product capabilities to support this strategy originate through alliances and the close collaboration with the customer.

The system lock-in position has innovation as its leading adaptive process. It contributes to the creation of the systems architecture that allows for standards to be conceived and owned. The next level of support comes from targeting the system's complementors to consolidate the lock-in position and, quite significantly, the lock-out of competitors. Finally, the operational effectiveness position is responsible for improving the system performance. While this process is important, the two previous adaptive processes are more relevant.

Feedback

Feedback is a core attribute of the Delta model and addresses the additional problem in linking strategy with execution mentioned earlier—growing market uncertainties and the requirement for an adaptive strategy. During implementation, managers need to monitor its performance and intended results and make corrections as needed. Closely related to feedback are learning and communication. As actions are tested and their merits or limitations become apparent, managers can understand more deeply the business issues they intend to solve.

Feedback is an integral part of the processes. For example, Capital One, a leader in the credit card industry, strongly emphasizes customer targeting. It has realized huge competitive advantage by recognizing that the credit card industry isn't one market, but millions. While the credit card may seem simple—money and interest rates—the potential variations are infinite. The challenge is to identify these segments before the competition. The linchpin of Capital One's customer targeting process is scientific trials, testing, and feedback. At the beginning of the process, Capital One managers brainstorm offers, drawing from a broad range of sources, including intuition and research. Next, they vary the core offer along the key dimensions—product, price, promotion, and channel—and identify a range of customer cells for test marketing. Then they screen the results to select the offers with the highest profit or net present value in view of the full customer life cycle.

In-depth metrics are critical in this screening. Capital One dissects profitability down to the smallest micro-segment, for example, types of customers, frequency of use, type of use (credit or transactions), bill paying, tenure, and costs of acquiring the customer. Having the right data is clearly important because acquisition costs have risen from $40 to more than $200 per customer during the past ten years.

If an offer passes the test, Capital One rolls it out to the whole target group. More importantly, information generated in the process yields hypotheses for other offers that may be more profitable. Capital One designs a family of offers with the understanding that they will not necessarily be successful, but that they provide seeds for future success. This approach contrasts starkly with the conventional "trial," in which a company launches a test of one product variation to a nonsegmented group of customers. When this fails, the company learns little in the process that can indicate a more successful variation.

Capital One's approach has enabled it to be the first to exploit innovations, such as balance transfers and secured cards. It is a competence that extends well beyond credit cards and is applicable to many other products, such as cellular phones, installment loans, auto loans, mortgages, life insurance, and mutual funds.

All three adaptive processes have common responsive mechanisms for obtaining feedback:

1. *Set hypotheses* in the context of the vision expressed by the Delta model and the role of each adaptive process based on the business strategic position.

2. *Identify variations* to reflect the drivers of cost, revenue, and profit for the business. Each adaptive process has its own set of drivers that change according to the role of the process as the company moves from best product to customer solutions to system lock-in.

3. *Admit that the future is unpredictable* by conducting trials and tests. In a basic sense, optimization represents an unreachable ideal that can be more destructive than helpful; instead we are committed to a continuous stream of experimentation.

4. *Measure and screen performance* to allow the company to separate success from failure and learn from both. In-depth measures are essential. High-level, aggregate indicators do not sort out the pockets of high profitability.

Granular Segmentation

Metrics are fundamental to the Delta model; they chart the course for implementing the desired strategic position and are at the heart of adaptation. Unfortunately, most businesses are limited in their ability to identify and track effective performance metrics, for two key reasons.

First, metrics have heavily depended on financial and accounting data, which explain how the business *has* performed but provide little insight on *future* performance. To anticipate the future, it is necessary to track performance against the adaptive processes, which are the initiatives enabling the strategy. Most importantly, the metrics need to clearly align with the strategic position.

Figure 8.8 shows distinctly different metrics for each strategic position, according to the adaptive process. Operational effectiveness goes well beyond the conventional role of ensuring a low-cost infrastructure for the delivery of products and services. In the case of customer solutions, it also allows inquiry into the best way to add value to the customer by quantifying the economics of the value chain and how alternative products affect it. Moreover, in a system lock-in strategy, it also examines the total potential of the product's system and how the system can contribute to product enhancement and profitability. Likewise, customer targeting goes beyond the stereotype of customer identification and prioritization to get to the roots of customer profitability and the ability to appropriate system profits. Finally, innovation is not simply a process of new product development but also a way to secure customer bonding and competitive lock-out.

Aggregation is the second reason that conventional metrics are inadequate. Most top executives have information based on broad aggregates and averages. However, our research shows that the inherent variability beneath the averages points to the root cause or fundamental drivers of cost, revenue, or profit. Managing by averages leads to below-average performance.

An example in the telecommunications industry illustrates the nature and value of granular metrics. The overall activities and cost chain for providing a local data circuit are shown in figure 8.9. Dissection of the cost into finer elements reveals wide variability. The highest-cost order was more than ten times the lowest-cost order. Also, these high costs were concentrated in a few orders; 20 percent of the orders generated 75 percent of the total costs in order fulfillment. It was not possible from the averages to know how well or poorly the company was fulfilling orders.

Other dimensions of this cost variability, such as location, explain the cost behavior. Among this telephone company's five locations, the unit cost was more than twice as high at some sites than at others. These differences were driven by structural factors, such as the scale of the facilities or the density of the service area, and managerial factors, such as training, incentives, or practices.

At one location, we dissected the interconnected activities such as order entry, design, facilities configuration, switch testing, and so on. In 70 percent of the orders,

	Best Product	Customer Solutions	System Lock-In

Operational Effectiveness (Cost Drivers)	• Cost performance
	  Unit cost
	  Life cycle cost
	  Variable and total cost
	• Cost drivers
	• Quality performance
	• Degree of differentiation
		• Customer value chain; total cost
		  Total revenue and profit
		• Customer economic drivers
		• Impact on customer profit due to service versus competitors
			• Description of system infrastructure
			• Total system costs/revenues
			• Complementor's investments and profits
			• Complementor's costs of adhering to standard
			• System performance drivers

Customer Targeting (Profit Drivers)	• Product market share
	• Channel cost
	• Product profit
	  By product type
	  By offer, by channel
	• Profit drivers
		• Customer share
		• Customer retention
		• Profitability by customer, individual, and segment
		• Customer bonding, switching costs
			• System market share
			• Share of complementors
			  Percentage of investment tied to proprietary standard
			• Profit by complementor

Innovation (Renewal Drivers)	• Rate of product introduction
	• Time to market
	• Percentage of sales from new products
	• Cost of product development
	• R&D as percentage of sales
		• Relative involvement in customer value chain
		• Percentage of product development
		  From joint development
		  Customized
		• Degree of product scope
		  Current versus potential bundling
			• Switching costs for complementors and customers
			• Rate of product development
			• Cost for competitors to imitate standard

Figure 8.8
Key Performance Metrics for Different Strategic Positions

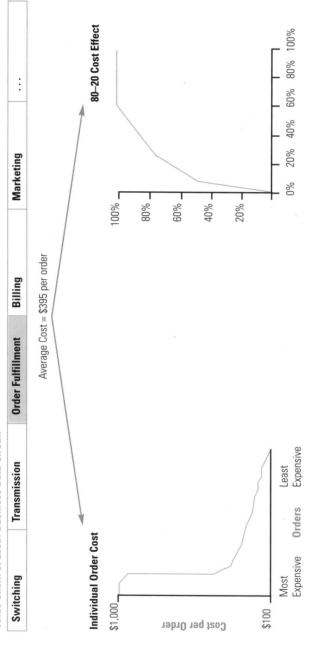

Figure 8.9
Cost Behavior in the Telecommunications Industry

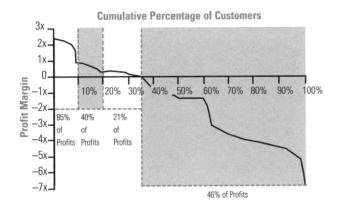

Figure 8.10
Credit Card Customers' Profit Margin Contribution. Source: Dean & Company analysis

each step proceeded flawlessly and resulted in on-time, low-cost delivery. In the other 30 percent, the order failed in one or more steps and required expensive, time-consuming remedial attention. The high-cost order path was ten times the cost of the low-cost path. Some of the high costs were caused by the people involved and some by the particular facility. Some groups consistently operated at three to five times the cost or speed of others. By comparing the groups and their different work practices, training, experience, or incentives, we began to formulate specific, focused efforts to address the high pockets of cost.

This pattern of economic behavior is the rule, not the exception. In our research, the concentrations of cost became more pronounced and the solutions more focused. Granular segmentation allows a company to focus, to measure, to learn, and to innovate.

The same pattern was evident in profit performance. Figure 8.10 shows a huge variation in profit margin by individual credit-card customers. The customers were ranked from most to least profitable. The top 10 percent of the customers contributed 99 percent of the business profits, the next 10 percent accounted for 43 percent of additional profits, and the next 16 percent of the customers added 25 percent more. Only 36 percent of the customers contributed to profitability and collectively accounted for 167 percent of the business profits. Unfortunately, the remaining 64 percent of the customers produced losses equivalent to 67 percent of the total profits.

While many companies tend to dwell on one measure of customer attractiveness, we found that no one factor adequately explains the variation in customer profitability. A high-usage customer can be unprofitable due to low outstanding balances. Given high acquisition costs, a long-time customer can make a low-balance customer profitable. The combination of all these factors, which seem to grow with the complexity of the business, leads to greater profit concentrations.

Business has become a complex interaction of many employees, customers, suppliers, teams, procedures, and processes, with each unit operating according to straightforward rules. When combined into a system, however, certain accelerating or stagnating patterns emerge—in demand, revenue, or cost. Companies that can adaptively capture the unpredictable explosions in market growth, while arresting the eruptions in cost, will generate massive market value. A company needs to segment at granular levels, but retain a strategic perspective within a unified framework.

Conclusion

The Delta model answers current challenges by significantly expanding the spectrum of available strategic positions. It recognizes customer-focused options and the emergence of proprietary standards to create an unassailable competitive advantage.

A firm's day-to-day activities need to change to realize the different strategies described by aligning the adaptive processes with the strategic positions. Inherent in the adaptive processes are trade-offs and different priorities critical for intelligent implementation. Feedback is central to the adaptative capabilities for competing in a radically changing and uncertain world. Granular segmentation is necessary to the effectiveness of the adaptive processes.

As complexity permeates the business environment, it is dangerous to give simple answers to complex questions. The Delta model deals with complexity by providing a rich overall framework that integrates a firm's options and activities without running the risk of oversimplifying the context in which it makes decisions.

Acknowledgments

This chapter is reprinted with permission from *Sloan Management Review* 40, no. 2 (Winter 1999), 11–28.

Notes

1. Porter 1980.
2. Utterback 1994.

3. For the concept of complementors, see Brandenburger and B. J. Nalebuff (1996).

4. The chief proponents of this thinking were Hammer and Champy; see Hammer and Champy (1993).

References

Brandenburger, A. M., and B. J. Nalebuff. 1996. *Co-opetition*. New York: Doubleday.

Hammer, M., and J. Champy. 1993. *Reengineering the Corporation*. New York: Harper.

Porter, M. E. 1980. *Competitive Strategy*. New York: Free Press.

Utterback, J. M. 1994. *Mastering the Dynamics of Innovation*. Boston: Harvard Business School Press.

9 Clockspeed-based Strategies for Supply Chain Design

Charles H. Fine

Biologists study fruit flies because their fast rates of evolution permit rapid learning that can then be applied to understanding the genetics of slower-clockspeed species—like humans (Lawrence 1992, Gladwell 1996). During the past decade, I have been studying the supply chains of the *industrial* equivalent of fruit flies—fast-clockspeed industries, such as Internet services, personal computers, and multimedia entertainment—in search of robust principles for supply chain design. The most important lesson from the industrial fruit flies is one that should prove heartening to the supply chain community. I phrase it as follows: The ultimate core competency of an organization is "supply chain design," which I define as choosing what capabilities along the value chain to invest in and develop internally and which to allocate for development by suppliers. In a fast-clockspeed world, that means designing and redesigning the firm's chain of capabilities for a series of competitive advantages (often quite temporary) in a rapidly evolving world.

Beware of Intel Inside

Consider the evolution of one of the information-rich fruit flies of the late twentieth century—the computer industry. In the early 1980s, when IBM launched its first personal computer (PC), the company pretty much was the entire computer industry. IBM was a technologically deep organization that designed and produced its super-sophisticated mainframe products almost exclusively with internal capabilities. But the PC presented IBM with a special "three-dimensional concurrent engineering" challenge: The company needed to create a new product, a new process to manufacture it, and a new supply chain to feed that process and distribute the product.

To keep costs low and increase speed to market, IBM chose a modular product design with a modular supply chain design, built around major components furnished by two virtually unknown companies: Intel and Microsoft. By 1998, the fast-evolving personal computer had gone through seven microprocessor generations: 8088, 286, 386, 486, and Pentium I, II, and III. Still a powerful, profitable, and influential company by the standards of the computer industry, IBM had nonetheless been far outdistanced by its two hand-picked suppliers, who had taken the lion's share of the profits and industry clout that flowed from IBM's standard-setting product. IBM's suppliers also won the allegiance of millions of customers who came to care far more about the supplier's logo—"Intel Inside" or "Windows 95"—than about the brand name of the company that assembled the components and shipped the final product. The power in the chain had shifted, as had the financial rewards (Baldwin and Clark 1999, Grove 1996).

The IBM-Intel-Microsoft saga provides a rich set of lessons from the fruit flies: When designing your supply chain, whatever your industry, beware of the phenomenon of "Intel Inside." Furthermore, understand that make-vs.-buy decisions should not be made primarily on which supply option is a little bit cheaper or a little bit faster to market. Rather, supply chain design needs to be recognized as a strategic activity that can determine the fates of companies and industries—and of profits and power. Finally, we observe that the element of the supply chain that controls the chain can shift over time: In computers, it was first the OEM and later the component makers who wielded the most clout in the chain.

These lessons apply equally well to slower clockspeed industries such as automobiles. The role of electronics subsystems in cars, for example, has evolved dramatically since the 1960s, when little more than a vehicle's lights, radio, windshield wipers, and starter motor were electrically controlled. Today, the dollar value of a car's electronics is overtaking the value of its steel body, for example, and the electronic system rivals the steel body as one of the most important subsystems. In fact, virtually all the features that affect customers' perceptions of a vehicle are—or soon will be—mediated by electronics. Those features include acceleration, braking, steering, handling, and seating, as well as the communication, information, and entertainment systems (Womack *et al.* 1990).

Of course, the evolution of the importance of electronics in the car has profound implications for the relative power and value of various players in the automotive value chain. The relatively slow clockspeed of the automotive landscape gives industry players some time for deliberation and choice. But there may come a day when customers choose automobiles based on whether it sports a logo saying "Denso Inside," "Delphi Inside," or "Bosch Inside" rather than by the name of the company that stamped and welded the sheet metal.

Supply Chain Structural Dynamics Along the Double Helix

Another set of insights from the computer industry helps us to understand the patterns of evolution in supply chain structures. In the 1970s and the early 1980s the computer industry's structure was decidedly vertical (Grove 1996). The three largest companies, IBM, Digital Equipment Corporation (DEC), and Hewlett-Packard, were highly integrated, as was the second tier of computer makers. Companies tended to provide most of the key elements of their own computer systems, from the operating system and applications software to the peripherals and electronic hardware, rather than sourcing bundles of subsystem modules acquired from third parties.

In this era, products and systems typically exhibited closed, integral architectures. That is, there was little or no interchangeability across different companies' systems. DEC peripherals and software, for example, did not work in IBM machines, and vice versa—so each company maintained technological competencies across many elements in the chain.

IBM had significant market power during that time and was very profitable. By holding to its closed product architecture, the company kept existing customers hostage—any competing machine they bought would be incompatible with their IBMs (Baldwin and Clark 1999). At the same time, Big Blue emphasized the value of its overall systems-and-service package, determined to stave off competitors who might offer better performance on one or another piece of the package.

In the late 1970s, IBM faced a challenge from upstart Apple Computer. IBM's competitive response, the PC, catalyzed a dramatic change throughout the industry, which quickly moved from a vertical to a horizontal structure. The dominant product was no longer the IBM computer, but the IBM-compatible computer. The modular architecture encouraged companies large and small to enter the fray and supply subsystems for the industry: semiconductors, circuit boards, applications software, peripherals, network services, and PC design and assembly.

A single product/supply chain decision (by a dominant producer) triggered a momentous structural shift—from a vertical/integral industry structure to a horizontal/modular one (Grove 1996, 40). The universal availability of the Intel and Microsoft subsystems led dozens of entrepreneurs to enter the personal computer business with IBM-compatibles. The modular (mix-and-match) architecture created significant competition within each segment of the horizontally structured industry.

In this industry, so recently organized along monolithic, vertical lines, there now appeared a spate of separate sub-industries—not only for microprocessors and operating systems, but for peripherals, software, network services, and so on. Within each of the categories, new businesses emerged, making it easier and easier for a computer maker to shop around for just the right combination of subsystems.

On balance, this spread of competition was a healthy development for the industry and for computer buyers, but certainly not for IBM shareholders, who saw their company lose about $100 billion in market value between 1986 and 1992 (Baldwin and Clark 1999). Some observers have speculated that this model of horizontal/modular competition, which also evolved in telecommunications during the 1990s, might be the new (and permanent) industrial structure for many industries. However, further examination suggests that the horizontal/modular structure may also prove to be quite unstable—as unstable as the vertical/integral structures that give birth to them.

Why might the horizontal/modular supply chain structure be short-lived? Let's look again at the fruit flies in the PC industry.

Modular industry and supply chain structures tend to create fierce, commodity-like competition within individual niches. Such competition keeps the players highly focused on their survival. However, over time, a shakeout typically occurs, and stronger players—those that manage to develop an edge in costs, quality, technology, or service, for example—drive out weaker ones. Once a firm is large enough to exert some market power in its segment, it sees the opportunity to expand vertically as well. Microsoft and Intel, each of which came to dominate its respective segment, have exhibited this behavior. Intel expanded from microprocessors to design and assembly of motherboard modules, making significant inroads into an arena typically controlled by the systems assemblers such as Compaq, Dell, and IBM. In addition, with each new microprocessor generation, Intel added more functions on the chip (functions that applications software suppliers traditionally offered), thereby making incursions into the software applications segment as well (Joglekar 1996).

In the case of Microsoft, dominance in PC operating systems has led to the company's entry into applications software, network services, Web browsers, server operating systems, and multi-media content development and delivery. In short, Microsoft looks a little bit more each day like the old IBM—attempting to dominate increasingly large slices of the overall industry and earning monopoly-like profits in the process. Microsoft's ability to integrate across the segments is particularly vivid (to both competitors and regulators) because its market share is so large and information technology is so flexible.

The computer industry of the 1980s and 1990s therefore illustrates an entire cycle of supply chain structure evolution (figure 9.1). Consider the dynamic forces at work: When the industry structure is vertical and the product architecture is integral, the forces of disintegration push toward a horizontal and modular configuration. These forces include:

1. The relentless entry of niche competitors hoping to pick off discrete industry segments.

2. The challenge of keeping ahead of the competition across the many dimensions of technology and markets required by an integral system.

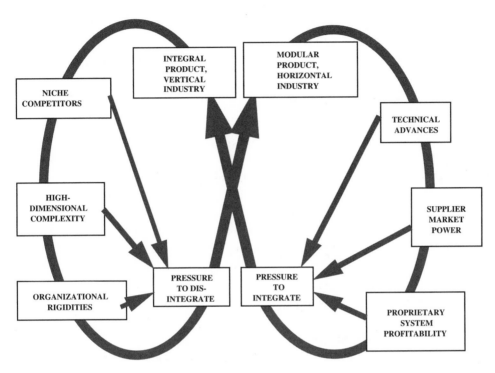

Figure 9.1
The Double Helix Illustrates the Oscillation in Supply Chain Structure between Vertical/integral and Horizontal/modular (Fine and Whitney 1996)

3. The bureaucratic and organizational rigidities that often settle upon large, established companies (Fine *et al.* 1998).

These forces typically weaken the vertical giant and create pressure toward disintegration to a more horizontal, modular structure. IBM, it might be argued, had all these forces lined up against it: Constant pressure from niche entrants, particularly in software and peripherals; competitors who took the lead in some technological segments (Intel's invention of the microprocessor, for example); and the many layers of bureaucracy that grew up as IBM expanded its headcount to almost a half million employees at its peak in the 1980s.

On the other hand, when an industry supply chain has a horizontal/modular structure, another set of forces push toward more vertical integration and integral product architectures. These forces include:

1. Technical advances in one subsystem can make that the scarce commodity in the chain, giving market power to its owner.

2. Market power in one subsystem encourages bundling with other subsystems to increase control and add more value.

3. Market power in one subsystem encourages engineering integration with other subsystems to develop proprietary integral solutions.

We therefore learn another important lesson about the evolution of supply chain structures: They should not be expected to be stable. Instead one should expect supply chain structures to cycle between integral/vertical and horizontal/modular forms. Furthermore, the speed with which the structures cycle is influenced by the clockspeed of the industry. In the computer industry, less than two decades transpired before a full cycle had come to completion. In the auto industry, however, the current modularization trends are closing a cycle begun in the first decade of this century.

Clockspeed Drivers and Outsourcing for Speed

Studying the evolution of fruit fly industries provides other insights into supply chains. For example, many in the supply chain community are familiar with the bullwhip principle (i.e., the "first law of supply chain dynamics"), which states that the magnitude of demand volatility a company faces increases the farther upstream it resides in the supply chain (Forrester 1958, Sterman 1989). Thus, personal computer manufacturers experience less demand volatility than semiconductor manufacturers, who, in turn, experience less demand volatility than their semiconductor equipment suppliers.

Study of clockspeeds in the fruit fly industries has led me to posit what I call clockspeed amplification—"the second law of supply chain dynamics" (Joglekar and Fine 1998). This hypothesis states that the industry clockspeed a company faces increases the farther downstream it is located in the supply chain. Thus, personal computer manufacturers experience faster clockspeeds (e.g., shorter product life cycles) than semiconductor manufacturers, who, in turn, experience faster clockspeeds than the semiconductor equipment suppliers.

This insight helps us understand the unprecedented clockspeeds experienced in our economy in the 1990s and helps us peer into the future as well. In particular, when some core technology far upstream in the value chain experiences a fast clockspeed, the rapid rates of change experienced there accelerate as they cascade down the supply chain. So the "killer technology" rates (Fine and Kimerling 1997) experienced this decade in semiconductors and fiber optic cable, as examples, have driven hyper-fast clockspeeds in the information and communication industries, which, in turn, contribute to the supply chains of virtually every other industry on the globe.

If rapid rates of technological innovation are clockspeed accelerators, what are the decelerators? One key clockspeed damper is system complexity. Dell is able to come out with new computer models much more frequently than Lockheed-Martin turns out new fighter jets because a fighter jet is a far more complex system than a PC is. Modularizing a product's architecture breaks it down into simpler subsystems and often enables a faster development pace.

Within the defense industry, for example, complex computer systems for signal and image processing on aircraft, surface ships, and submarines have been modularized from the other subsystems and successfully outsourced to Mercury Computer Systems. The Aegis naval defense systems, recently in the news with the potential Taiwanese export order, the unmanned spy planes flying over Bosnia and Kosovo, and the sonar systems in much of the Navy's submarine fleet, are all equipped with Mercury's specialized computers.

Such modularization and outsourcing not only significantly reduces product development times for the defense suppliers, but eases the way for frequent and profitable upgrades as more powerful imaging technology is developed. As another example, makers of complex medical imaging systems such as General Electric, Marconi, Philips, and Siemens, have also outsourced imaging computer systems to Mercury Computer to speed their development cycles and improve the performance of their machines. Magnetic Resonance Imaging (MRI) and Computed Tomography (CT) systems have advanced as rapidly as almost any technology in the medical field, leading to on-the-spot diagnoses in many hospitals. By outsourcing Mercury's advanced technology, these suppliers have cut their time to market and stolen a march on some less resourceful competitors.

Finally, in the telecommunications domain, wireless service providers such as Ericsson, Lucent, Motorola, and Nortel may soon find that outsourcing opportunities such as inserting Mercury Computer's signal processing technology may double or triple base station capacity and provide the higher data rates needed by the advancing Internet-based applications. Having wireless wideband early is likely to determine the leaders in this rapidly developing field and outsourcing the technology could be the answer for many of today's suppliers. OEM firms will have to weigh the merits of speed and technology innovation from outsourcing. In the highly competitive environments of the Internet age, victory often goes to the fleetest of execution.

Implementation: Three-Dimensional Concurrent Engineering

Stimulated by the success of superior Japanese manufacturing methods, many Western manufacturers in the 1980s worked overtime to benchmark remarkable companies such as Toyota and Sony. By the early 1990s, many had achieved a huge breakthrough in their understanding of competitive advantage through manufacturing. A large portion of the learning came under the heading of concurrent engineering, or CE, or design for manufacturing, known as DFM (Nevins and Whitney 1989, Ulrich and Eppinger 1994, Fleischer and Liker 1997). Managers realized that they could not achieve improved manufacturing performance solely, or even primarily, by concentrating on the factory; rather, they had to focus on concurrently designing the product and the manufacturing process—that is, designing the product for manufacturability.

Three-dimensional concurrent engineering (3-DCE) extends this concept from products and manufacturing to the concurrent design and development of capabilities chains. In particular, once one recognizes the strategic nature of supply chain design, one feels almost compelled to integrate it with product and process development.

The good news is that the implementation of 3-DCE does not require radical surgery in organizational processes. This news should come as a relief for the many who have re-engineered and have been re-engineered by managers who insist they must blow up their existing organizations in order to create necessary change.

Instead of such a radical solution, even as an antidote to it, I advocate leveraging one basic organizational methodology, variously referred to as concurrent engineering, the product development process design-build teams, or integrated product teams (IPTs), as the core of the implementation process for three-dimensional concurrent engineering.

Figure 9.2 illustrates several interactions across product, process, and supply chain development activities. Where the three ovals overlap we locate those activities that need to be undertaken concurrently, either bilaterally or collectively, among the three functions. This diagram further illustrates that not all of the activities undertaken within any of the three functions need to be performed in conjunction with members of the other groups. That is, not all work must take place in integrated product teams. Rather, IPTs would concern themselves only with tasks where activities of two or all three functions overlap.

Figure 9.2 attempts to capture visually many of the ideas of 3-DCE. One can consider how architecture decisions are made through discussions within and across the product, process, and supply chain organizations. A further refinement of the over-

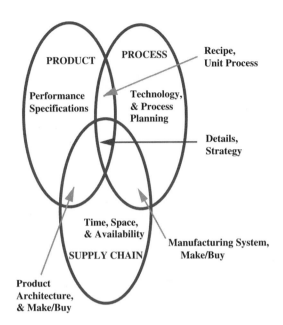

Figure 9.2
Overlapping Responsibilities across Product, Process, and Supply Chain Development Activities

lapping areas of concurrency across product, process, and supply chain development appears in figure 9.3, which also highlights the imperative of concurrency.

This figure divides each of the three developmental areas—product, process, and supply chain—into two sub-activities:

• *Product development* is subdivided into activities of architectural choices (for example, integrality vs. modularity decisions) and detailed design choices (for example, performance and functional specifications for the detailed product design).

• *Process development* is divided into the development of unit processes (that is, the process technologies and equipment to be used) and manufacturing systems development—decisions about plant and operations systems design and layout (for instance, process/job shop focus vs. product/cellular focus).

• *Supply chain development* is divided into the supply chain architecture decisions and logistics/coordination system decisions. Supply chain architecture decisions include decisions on whether to make or buy a component, sourcing decisions (for example, choosing which companies to include in the supply chain), and contracting decisions (such as structuring the relationships among the supply chain

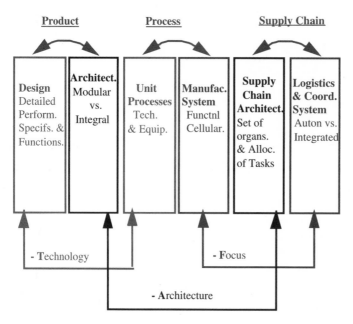

Figure 9.3
The 3-DCE Concurrency Model

members). Logistics and coordination decisions include the inventory, delivery, and information systems to support ongoing operation of the supply chain.

The next two cases, from Intel and Chrysler, further illustrate these ideas.

Intel

In an era and industry of unprecedented clockspeed acceleration, Intel Corporation has risen about as quickly as any corporation in history as a major manufacturer. Most of Intel's growth to a $30+ billion corporation occurred over less than a decade, a period during which the company built highly capital-intensive factories and introduced new products at a blistering pace. Much of its success in keeping competitors at bay during the period of explosive growth resulted from the ability to execute new product and process development with many new suppliers at break-neck speed. In short, Intel proved to be a master of fast-clockspeed 3-DCE.

Given the complexity of the underlying technologies, we can gain a valuable understanding of how Intel simplified the daunting 3-DCE challenges it faced. Its approach offers lessons for any company contemplating a shift to three-dimensional concurrent engineering. Intel's microprocessor product families—popularly known as the 286, 386, 486, and Pentium processors—resulted from a massive product development process, involving hundreds of engineers and scientists working over multiple sites and multiple years (Osborne 1993).

Historically in the semiconductor industry DRAM (dynamic random access memory) products absorbed the lion's share of new process technology investment. Each new generation of product—64 Kb RAM, 256 Kb RAM, 1 Mb RAM, and so forth—was launched on an all-new generation of manufacturing process (typically denoted by the smallest line-width on the integrated circuits). Thus, for a DRAM manufacturer, launching a new product meant simultaneously launching a new process—always a complex affair. Through most of the 1980s, the Japanese semiconductor companies concentrated on DRAM design and production, exploiting their skills in precision clean manufacturing. The Japanese tended to be the process technology leaders into each new smaller line-width process generation.

By the early 1990s, however, Intel found itself in the position of needing new processes (for example, more metallization layers) in advance of the DRAM industry's needs or its willingness to invest in such processes. As a result, the DRAM makers no longer unequivocally drove process development. Having emerged as the 800-pound gorilla of the industry in the early 1990s, Intel had to learn to be a process technology leader and to develop systems whereby it could continue to improve process technology while accelerating its pace of product development.

Intel crafted a brilliant 3-DCE strategy that used product/process modularity to reduce significantly the complexity of the company's technical challenge: Throughout the 1990s, the company launched each new microprocessor generation on the "platform" of an old (line-width) process. Alternately, each new process generation was launched with an "old" product technology. For instance, Intel introduced its i486 chip on the one-micron process developed for the i386 chip, a process that had already been debugged. Following the success of this process, Intel created the .8-micron process, which was first tried on the now-proven i486 chip. Next, it launched the Pentium chip on the proven .8-micron process before moving it over to the new .6-micron process. Leveraging this system of alternating product and process launches, Intel created almost perfect modularity between product and process, a marriage that reduced dramatically the complexity of any given launch. Reducing the complexity of concurrent engineering has, of course, been one of the keys to Intel's success in its hyperfast-clockspeed industry.

When viewed through the lens of the third dimension, however, Intel's link between process and supply chain is much more integral. That is, process development goes hand in glove with supply chain development. Especially by the mid-1990s, when Intel needed to drive new process technologies rather than adapt technologies that had already been pretty much debugged by the DRAM manufacturers, Intel found itself nurturing start-up companies that were just developing the advanced technologies necessary for the next-generation processes Intel needed. As a result, Intel fostered integral development of new processes and new suppliers to support those processes.

Chrysler

In some ways, Chrysler of the 1990s could be likened to Compaq of the 1980s. Through a modular product and supply chain strategy, each company managed to upset the advantages of much larger rivals and to trigger a chain reaction of events that altered dramatically the structure of the entire industry (Dyer 1996).

Through the lens of 3-DCE, we can see both the strengths and potential weaknesses of Chrysler's strategy more clearly (Whitney 1998). By outsourcing the development and integration of numerous automotive subsystems, Chrysler cut dramatically the total time and cost required to develop and launch a new vehicle. The company has effectively exploited the opportunities from this approach, as described earlier.

Because Chrysler, in contrast to many of its competitors, is so quick from concept to car, the company has enjoyed a high rating with consumers on the most desirable designs and features. Such designs allowed Chrysler to charge premium prices with minimal rebating throughout much of the 1990s.

Conclusion

I believe that the increased interest in supply chain design as a strategic precursor to supply chain management will only increase in the decade to come as industry clockspeeds continue to accelerate, and the half-lives of many capabilities in our existing supply chains need replacement and/or upgrading. Furthermore, I believe that analyzing the dynamics of supply chains in the fast-clockspeed fruit fly industries can provide insights to companies in all industries for assessing strategic options in a rapidly evolving industrial world.

Acknowledgments

This chapter is reprinted with permission from *Production and Operations Management* 9, no. 3 (Fall 2000): 213–221. Parts of it are based on chapters in Charles

H. Fine, *Clockspeed: Winning Control in the Age of Temporary Advantage*, Reading, Mass.: Perseus, 1998.

The author is indebted to Randy Bollig, Intel's director of corporate capital acquisition in the late 1990s, for these insights into Intel's supplier development system.

References

Baldwin, Carliss, and Kim Clark. 1999. *Design Rules: The Power of Modularity*. Cambridge, Mass.: MIT Press.

Dyer, Jeffrey. 1996. How Chrysler Created an American Keiretsu. *Harvard Business Review* 74 (July–August): 42–56.

Fine, Charles H., and Daniel E. Whitney. 1996. Is the Make/Buy Decision Process a Core Competency? MIT Center for Technology, Policy and Industrial Development Working Paper.

Fine, Charles, and Lionel Kimerling. 1997. Biography of a Killer Technology: Optoelectronics Drives Industrial Growth with the Speed of Light. Special Report for the Optoelectronics Industry Development Association, June.

Fine, Charles, Mila Getmansky, Paulo Goncalves, and Nelson Repenning. 1998. Industry and Product Structure Dynamics: From Integration to Disintegration and Back. MIT Sloan School of Management Working Paper.

Fleischer, Mitchell, and Jeffrey Liker. 1997. *Concurrent Engineering Effectiveness*. Cincinnati: Hansen Gardner.

Forrester, Jay W. 1958. Industrial Dynamics: A Major Breakthrough for Decision Makers. *Harvard Business Review* 36 (July–August): 37–66.

Gladwell, Malcolm. 1996. The New Age of Man. *The New Yorker*, September 30.

Grove, Andrew S. 1996. *Only the Paranoid Survive*. New York: Currency Doubleday.

Joglekar, Nitindra. 1996. The Technology Treadmill: Managing Product Performance and Production Ramp-Up in Fast-Paced Industries. Unpublished doctoral dissertation, MIT Sloan School of Management.

Joglekar, Nitindra, and Charles Fine. 1998. Decomposition of Clockspeed within Technology Supply Chains. MIT Working Paper.

Lawrence, Peter A. 1992. *The Making of a Fly: The Genetics of Animal Design*. Cambridge: Blackwell Science Ltd.

Nevins, James, and Daniel Whitney. 1989. *Concurrent Design of Products and Processes: A Strategy for the Next Generation in Manufacturing*. New York: McGraw-Hill.

Osborne, Sean. 1993. Product Development Cycle Time Characterization Through Modeling of Process Iteration, MS thesis, MIT-Leaders for Manufacturing program.

Sterman, John. 1989. Modeling Managerial Behavior: Misperceptions of Feedback in a Dynamic Decision Making Experiment. *Management Science* 35 (3): 321–339.

Ulrich, K., and S. Eppinger. 1994. *Product Design and Development*. New York: McGraw-Hill.

Whitney, Daniel. 1998. Identifying Integration Risk during Concept Design. Presentation to MIT Symposium on Supply Chains, May 13.

Womack, Jim, Daniel Jones, and Daniel Roos. 1990. *The Machine that Changed the World*. New York: Rawson Associates.

Inventing New Organizations

10 Tools for Inventing Organizations: Toward a Handbook of Organizational Processes

Thomas W. Malone, Kevin Crowston, Jintae Lee, Brian Pentland, Chrysanthos Dellarocas, George Wyner, John Quimby, Abraham Bernstein, George Herman, Mark Klein, Charles S. Osborn, and Elisa O'Donnell

Introduction

In recent years, we have seen striking examples of process innovations that have transformed the way organizations work. Although initially uncommon and perceived as radical, ideas like just-in-time inventory control and concurrent engineering have become accepted as "best practice" (Carter & Baker, 1991). These innovative practices have clearly been beneficial, but most organizations remain in need of improvement, as suggested by the on going popularity of "total quality management," "business process redesign," and "the learning organization." These slogans summarize ideas with real value, but they provide too little guidance about what the improved organization might look like in particular situations. They hold out the promise of innovation, but lack the details needed to accomplish it.

The gap between the need to innovate and the tools for doing so leaves us with a problem: How can we move beyond the practices of today to invent the best practices of tomorrow? And where will we keep getting new ideas for organizational processes to adapt to a continually changing world? For instance, how can we understand and exploit the new organizational possibilities enabled by the continuing, dramatic improvements in information technology? Given time, managers and employees of companies will certainly develop new ways of working that take advantage of these new opportunities. For quicker progress on these problems, however, our best hope is to develop a more systematic theoretical and empirical foundation for understanding organizational processes. If we are to understand successful organizational practices, we must be able to recognize and represent the organizational practices we see. And to improve organizational practice in a particular situation, we must also be able to imagine alternative ways of accomplishing the same things. Finally, we need some way of judging which alternatives are likely to be useful or desirable in which situations.

This paper reports on the first five years of work in a project to address these problems by

(1) developing methodologies and software tools for representing and codifying organizational processes at varying levels of abstraction, and

(2) collecting, organizing, and analyzing numerous examples of how different groups and companies perform similar functions.

The result of this work is an on-line Process Handbook which can be used to help people:

(1) redesign existing business processes,

(2) invent new processes (especially those that take advantage of information technology), and

(3) organize and share knowledge about organizational practices.

We also expect this Process Handbook to be useful in automatically (or semiautomatically) generating software to support or analyze business processes, but that is not the focus of this paper (see Dellarocas, 1996, 1997a, 1997b).

The goal of compiling a complete handbook of business processes is, of course, a never-ending task. Our goal in this research project is more modest: to provide a "proof of concept" that limited versions of such a handbook are both technically feasible and managerially useful. Though this project is not yet complete, the initial goal of demonstrating the basic technical feasibility of this approach has been achieved, and that is the primary focus of this paper. We have also conducted field tests that demonstrate the potential managerial usefulness of such handbooks and we include a description of one such test.

The Key Intellectual Challenge: How to Represent Organizational Processes?

In order to develop a system that could be used in the ways listed above, the key theoretical challenge is to develop techniques for representing processes. Fortunately, the last several decades of research in computer science and other disciplines have resulted in a number of well-developed approaches to representing processes, such as flow charts and data-flow diagrams (e.g., Yourdon, 1989), state transition diagrams (e.g., Lewis & Papadimitriou, 1981; Winograd and Flores, 1986), Petri nets (e.g., Peterson, 1977; Holt, 1988; Singh and Rein, 1992), and goal-based models (e.g., Yu, 1992). These approaches have been used by many organizations to map their own specific processes, and some have used them to represent widely-used generic processes (e.g., Scheer, 1994; Maull, Childe, Bennett, Weaver, and Smart, 1995; Winograd and Flores, 1986; Carlson, 1979). For example, a number of consulting firms and other organizations have already developed "best practice" databases that include verbal descriptions, key concepts, and sometimes detailed process maps for a variety of generic processes such as logistics, marketing, and manufacturing (e.g., Peters, 1992, pp. 387–390; *CIO Magazine*, 1992). It is clear, therefore, that it is technically feasible to assemble a large set of process descriptions collected from many

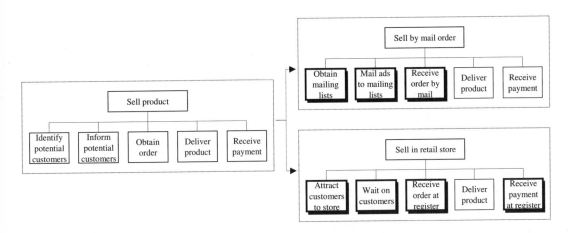

Figure 10.1
Sample Representations of Three Different Sales Processes
"Sell by mail order" and "Sell in retail store" are specializations of the generic sales process "Sell something." Subactivities that are changed are shadowed.

different organizations. It is also clear that such libraries of process descriptions can be useful to managers and consultants. The research question, then, is not whether it is possible to have a useful repository of knowledge about business processes. These databases already demonstrate that it is. Instead, the question is "How can we do better than these early databases?"

To answer this question, we have developed a new approach to analyzing and representing organizational processes that explicitly represents the similarities (and the differences) among a collection of related processes. Our representation exploits two sources of intellectual leverage: (1) notions of *specialization of processes* based on ideas about inheritance from object-oriented programming, and (2) concepts about *managing dependencies* from coordination theory.

Specialization of Processes

Most process mapping techniques analyze business processes using only one primary dimension: breaking a process into its different *parts*. Our representation adds a second dimension: differentiating a process into its different *types*. Figure 10.1 illustrates the difference between these two dimensions. In this figure, the generic activity called "Sell product" is broken apart into parts (or *subactivities*) like "Identify potential customers" and "Inform potential customers." The generic activity is also differentiated into types (or *specializations*) like "Sell by mail order" and "Sell in retail store".

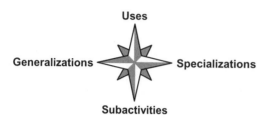

Figure 10.2
The Process Compass
The Process Compass illustrates two dimensions for analyzing business processes. The vertical dimension distinguishes different of a process; The horizontal dimension distinguishes different *types* of a process.

As in object-oriented programming (e.g., Stefik and Bobrow, 1986; Wegner, 1987; Brachman and Levesque, 1985), the specialized processes automatically inherit properties of their more generic "parents," except where they explicitly add or change a property. For instance, in "Sell by mail order," the subactivities of "delivering a product" and "receiving payment" are inherited without modification, but "Identifying prospects" is replaced by the more specialized activity of "Obtaining mailing lists."

Using this approach, any number of activities can be arranged in a richly interconnected two-dimensional network. Each of the subactivities shown in Figure 10.1, for instance, can be further broken down into more detailed subactivities (e.g., "Type mailing list name into computer") or more specialized types (e.g., "Sell hamburgers at McDonald's retail restaurant #493") to any level desired. In general, we use the term "activity" for all business processes, including all their subparts and subtypes at all levels.

We have found the Process Compass shown in figure 10.2 to be a useful way of summarizing the two dimensions. The vertical dimension represents the conventional way of analyzing processes: according to their different *parts*. The horizontal dimension is the novel one: analyzing processes according to their different *types*. From any activity in the Process Handbook, you can go in four different directions: (1) *down* to the different parts of the activity (its "subactivities"), (2) *up* to the larger activities of which this one is a part (its "uses"), (3) *right* to the different types of this activity (its "specializations") and (4) *left* to the different activities of which this one is a type (its "generalizations").

Comparison with Object-Oriented Programming   To readers familiar with conventional object-oriented programming techniques, it is worth commenting on the difference between our approach and conventional object-oriented programming. The difference is a subtle, but important, shift of perspective from specializing *objects* to specializing *processes* (see Stefik, 1981; Friedland, 1979; Thomsen, 1987; Madsen, Moller-Pedersen, and Nygard, 1993; Wyner and Lee, 1995; and other references in the section below on related work in computer science).

In a sense, this approach is a kind of "dual" of the traditional object-oriented approach. Traditional object-oriented programming includes a hierarchy of increasingly specialized *objects*, which may have associated with them *actions* (or "methods"). Our approach, by contrast, includes a hierarchy of increasingly specialized *actions* (or "processes") which may have associated with them *objects*. Loosely speaking, then, traditional object-oriented programming involves inheriting down a hierarchy of *nouns*; our approach involves inheriting down a hierarchy of *verbs*.

In a sense, of course, these two approaches are formally equivalent. Anything that can be done in one could be done in the other. The two approaches can also, quite usefully, coexist in the same system. The process-oriented approach we are describing, however, appears to be particularly appropriate for the analysis and design of business processes.

Bundles and Tradeoff Tables   In developing tools to support specialization, we have found it useful to combine specializations into what we call "bundles" of related alternatives. These bundles do not have a direct parallel in traditional object-oriented languages; however, they are comparable to "facets" in information science (Rowley, 1992). For instance, figure 10.3 shows part of the specialization hierarchy for sales processes. In this example, one bundle of specializations for "Sell something" is related to *how* the sale is made: direct mail, retail storefront, or direct sales force. Another bundle of specializations has to do with *what* is being sold: beer, automotive components, or financial services.

Comparing alternative specializations is usually meaningful only *within* a bundle of related alternatives. For example, comparing "retail store front sales" to "direct mail sales" is sensible, but comparing "retail store front sales" to "selling automotive components" is not. Where there are related alternative specializations in a bundle, our handbook can include comparisons of the alternatives on multiple dimensions, thus making explicit the tradeoff between these dimensions. For example, figure 10.4 shows a "tradeoff matrix" that compares alternatives in terms of their ratings on various criteria; different specializations are the rows and different characteristics are the columns. As in the Sibyl system (Lee and Lai, 1991), items in the cells of this matrix can be associated with detailed justifications for the various

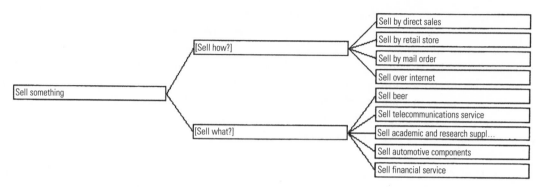

Figure 10.3
Summary Display Showing Specializations of the Activity "Sell Something"
Items in brackets (such as "[Sell how?]") are "bundles" which group together sets of related specializations. Items in bold have further specializations. The screen images used in this and subsequent figures
were created with the software tools described below.

ratings. For very generic processes such as those shown here, the cells would usually
contain rough qualitative comparisons (such as "High," "Medium," and "Low");
for specific process examples, they may contain detailed quantitative performance
metrics for time, cost, job satisfaction, or other factors. In some cases, these comparisons may be the result of systematic studies; in others, they may be simply rough
guesses by knowledgeable managers or consultants (with appropriate indications of
their preliminary nature); and, of course, in some cases, there may not be enough
information to include any comparisons at all.

Dependencies and coordination

The second key concept we are using is the notion from coordination theory
(e.g., Malone and Crowston, 1994) that *coordination* can be defined as *managing
dependencies among activities*. From this perspective, we can characterize different
kinds of *dependencies* and the alternative *coordination processes* that can manage
them. Such coordination processes are both ubiquitous (i.e., the same mechanisms
are found in many different processes) and variable (i.e., there are many different
mechanisms that can be used to manage a particular dependency). Therefore,
identifying dependencies and coordination mechanisms offers special leverage for
redesigning processes. The power of analyzing processes in terms of dependencies
and coordination mechanisms is greatly increased by access to a rich library of alternative coordination mechanisms for different kinds of dependencies. Therefore, a
critical component of the Process Handbook is a library of generic coordination
mechanisms.

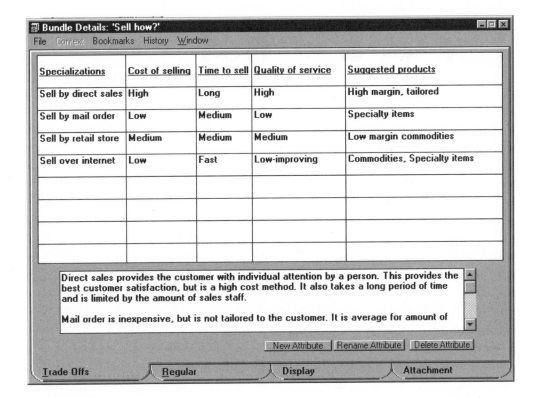

Figure 10.4
Tradeoff Matrix
A tradeoff matrix showing typical advantages and disadvantages of different specializations for the generic sales process. Note that the values in this version of the matrix are not intended to be definitive, merely suggestive.

Figure 10.5 suggests the beginnings of such an analysis (see Crowston, 1991; Zlotkin, 1995). The figure shows three basic kinds of dependencies: *flow, sharing,* and *fit.* These three types of dependencies arise from resources that are related to multiple activities. *Flow dependencies* arise whenever one activity produces a resource that is used by another activity. This kind of dependency occurs all the time in almost all processes and is the focus of most existing process mapping techniques (such as flow charts). *Sharing dependencies* occur whenever multiple activities all use the same resource. For example, this kind of dependency arises when two activities need to be done by the same person, when they need to use the same machine on a factory floor, or when they both use money from the same budget. Even though this kind of dependency between activities is usually omitted from flow charts,

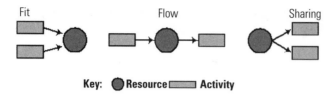

Figure 10.5
Three Basic Types of Dependencies Among Activities
(Adapted from Zlotkin, 1995).

Table 10.1
Examples of Elementary Dependencies between Activities and Alternative Coordination Mechanisms
for Managing Them

Dependency	Examples of coordination mechanisms for managing dependency
Flow	
Prerequisite ("right time")	• Make to order vs. make to inventory ("pull" vs. "push"). • Place orders using "economic order quantity," "Just In Time" (kanban system), or detailed advanced planning.
Accessibility ("right place")	Ship by various transportation modes or make at point of use
Usability ("right thing")	Use standards or ask individual users (e.g., by having customer agree to purchase and/or by using participatory design)
Sharing	"First come/first serve," priority order, budgets, managerial decision, market-like bidding
Fit	Boeing's total simulation vs. Microsoft's daily build

allocating shared resources is clearly a critical aspect of many management activities. Finally, *fit dependencies* arise when multiple activities collectively produce a single resource. For example, when several different engineers are designing different parts of a car (such as the engine, the transmission, and the body) there is a dependency between their activities that results from the fact that the pieces they are each designing need to fit together in the completed car.

Table 10.1 extends this analysis by showing how the different kinds of dependencies can be associated with a set of alternative coordination processes for managing them. For example, the table shows that "sharing" dependencies (shared resource constraints) can be managed by a variety of coordination mechanisms such as "first come/first serve," priority order, budgets, managerial decision, and market-like bidding. If three job shop workers need to use the same machine, for instance, they could use a simple "first come/first serve" mechanism. Alternatively, they could use a form of budgeting with each worker having pre-assigned time slots, or a manager could explicitly decide what to do whenever two workers wanted to use the machine at the same time. In some cases, the owner might even want to sell time on the machine and the person willing to pay the most would get it. In this way, new processes can be generated by considering alternative coordination mechanisms for a given dependency.

While the dependencies shown in table 10.1 are certainly not the only ones possible, our current working hypothesis is that all other dependencies can be usefully analyzed as specializations or combinations of those shown in the table. Similarly, even though there are many other possible coordination processes, the table illustrates how a library of generic coordination processes can be organized according to the dependencies they manage.

Specialization and Decomposition of Dependencies   Some dependencies can be viewed as specializations of others. For instance, *task assignment* can be seen as a special case of sharing, where the "resource" being shared is the time of people who can do the tasks. This implies that the coordination mechanisms for sharing in general can be specialized to apply to task assignment. In other cases, some dependencies can be seen as being composed of others. For instance, *flow dependencies* can be viewed as a combination of three other kinds of dependencies: *prerequisite* constraints (an item must be produced before it can be used), *accessibility* constraints (an item that is produced must be made available for use), and *usability* constraints, (an item that is produced should be "usable" by the activity that uses it). Loosely speaking, managing these three dependencies amounts to having the right thing (usability), in the right place (accessibility), at the right time (prerequisite). Each of these different kinds of dependencies, in turn, may have different processes for managing it; for example, the prerequisite dependency might be managed by keeping an inventory of the resource making it to order when it is needed, while usability may be managed through a product design process.

Related Work in Organization Theory and Design

In some respects, this work represents another step on what Sanchez (1993, p. 73) calls "the long and thorny way to an organizational taxonomy." Because our work draws heavily on the concept of specialization (and therefore classification), it is related to other taxonomies of organizations (e.g., Woodward, 1965; Thompson, 1967; Pugh, Hickson, and Hinings, 1968; Mintzberg, 1979; Ulrich and McKelvey, 1990; Salancik and Leblebici, 1988). The main difference is that except for Salancik and Leblebici (1988), most work in this area has classified whole organizations (or parts of organizations). Instead, we classify processes. McKelvey (1982) argues that the study of organizations is at a "pre-Linnaean" stage, awaiting a more systematic taxonomy to enable further scientific progress. By focusing on processes, the perspective introduced here extends previous work and provides a significant new alternative in this important problem area.

For example, our work not only provides a framework for classification, but also a framework for identifying possible alternatives and improvements. Previously, Salancik and Leblebici (1988) introduced a grammatical approach to analyzing specific organizational processes that enabled the generation of new processes by the constrained rearrangement of component activities. Our representation extends this approach, adding specialization and inheritance of activities as well as explicit representation of various kinds of dependencies. Specialization enables us to generate new processes by using alternative sets of more primitive actions. Explicit representation of dependencies allows us to generate many possible coordination processes for managing these dependencies. For example, Salancik and Leblebici's alternative orderings can all be generated as alternative ways of coordinating the basic flow and other dependencies among the activities.

Our framework also emphasizes the importance of coordination in organizational design. Our concept of dependencies, for instance, elaborates on and refines the traditional concept of interdependence from organization theory (Thompson, 1967). As Thompson makes clear, interdependence between organizational subunits is a result of the way workflows are organized between them. Thompson identified three kinds of interdependence: pooled, sequential, and reciprocal. For each of these, he identified typical coordination strategies, such as standardization, planning, and mutual adjustment. As these concepts have been applied over the years, however, the concept of interdependence has come to describe relationships between organizational subunits. In a sense, therefore, our approach reasserts Thompson's original insight by emphasizing that dependencies arise between activities in a process, not between departments *per se*. We extend Thompson's work by identifying a much finer-grained set of dependencies and a much richer set of coordination mechanisms for managing them.

We are able to explicitly relate dependencies and coordination mechanisms in this manner because our typology of dependencies is based on the pattern of use of common resources that creates the dependency, rather than on the topology of the relationship between the actors, as in Thompson's three categories. This approach makes it clearer which coordination mechanisms should be considered as alternatives, namely those that address the same kinds and uses of resources.

In representing processes computationally, our work is also similar to other computational organizational models (e.g., Cohen, March, and Olsen, 1972; Carley *et al.*, 1992; Levitt *et al.*, 1994; Gasser and Majchrzak, 1994; Baligh, Burton, and Obel, 1990;

Masuch and LaPotin, 1989). One major difference from most of this work, however, is that we focus on *organizing knowledge,* not on *simulating performance.* We can, of course, include simulation models and their results in the knowledge we organize, but our focus is on useful ways of organizing this knowledge, not on generating it.

For instance, Carley *et al.* (1992) developed Plural Soar, a simulation of a team of actors retrieving items from a warehouse. They used this simulation to study the effect of communications between actors and of individual memory on the performance of the group. In our system, the basic processes followed by the group could be stored and specialized to include or omit communication and memory. We could also include the performance of each variation as found from the simulation.

The Process Interchange Format (PIF), described below, is intended to simplify the task of translating process descriptions between a wide variety of such systems.

Related Work in Computer Science

The idea of generic processes (or "scripts" or "plans") has a long history in the field of artificial intelligence (e.g., Schank and Abelson, 1977; Schank, 1982; Chandrasekaran, 1983; Clancey, 1983; Tenenberg, 1986; Bhandaru and Croft, 1990; Lefkowitz and Croft, 1990; Chandrasekaran *et al.*, 1992; Marques *et al.*, 1992). Of particular relevance to our work is the work on "skeletal plans" (Stefik, 1981; Friedland, 1979; Friedland and Iwakasi, 1985), where an abstract plan is successively elaborated (and "specialized") for a given task. The Process Handbook can also be viewed as a case-based reasoner (Kolodner, 1993) since many of the processes represented in the Handbook are case examples from specific organizations.

Unlike these AI systems, however, the Process Handbook uses both process specialization and dependencies with coordination mechanisms to generate and organize a large number of examples and generalizations about them. For example, unlike a conventional case-based reasoner with only a library of previous cases, the Process Handbook can also contain an extensive (human-generated) network of generic processes that summarize and organize the existing cases and that also help generate and evaluate new possibilities.

Outside the area of artificial intelligence, the notion of specializing processes has also been used occasionally in other parts of computer science. For example, a few programming languages (e.g., Thomsen, 1987; Madsen, Moller-Pedersen, and Nygard, 1993) include mechanisms for defining specialization hierarchies of processes and combining actions from different levels in various ways at run-time. However, even in the parts of computer science where this work has been done, the potential power of systematically inheriting patterns of activities, dependencies, and other properties though networks of increasingly specialized processes does not seem to be widely appreciated.

In recent years, the idea of explicitly representing the processes associated with connections between activities has begun to receive some attention (e.g., Stovsky and Weide, 1988). For example, several recent architectural description languages (ADLs) are used to describe software systems in terms of components and connectors, where both components and connectors are first-class entities (Allen and Garlan, 1994; Shaw *et al.*, 1995; Shaw and Garlan, 1996). Components are analogous to our activities, while connectors correspond to our coordination processes. However, in these ADLs connectors are implementation-level abstractions (such as a pipe, or a client/server protocol). In contrast, the Process Handbook notion of dependencies also supports hierarchies of specification-level abstractions for interconnection relationships.

A key difference between our work and most previous work in all these areas of computer science comes from the difference in goals. The previous work in artificial intelligence and programming languages was primarily focused on building computer systems that, themselves, design or carry out processes. Our primary goal, on the other hand, is to build computer systems that help people design or carry out processes.

Because we have focused on *supporting* human decision-makers—not replacing them—there is no requirement that all our process descriptions be detailed or formalized enough to be executable by automated systems. Instead, it is up to the users of the Handbook to describe different processes at different levels of detail depending on their needs and the costs and benefits of going to more detailed levels. Therefore, unlike some of the well-known attempts to create comprehensive ontologies of actions (e.g. Lenat, 1995; Schank and Abelson, 1977), users of the Process Handbook do not have to wait for the resolution of difficult knowledge representation issues nor invest a large amount of effort in formalizing knowledge that is not immediately useful.

For domains in which the processes are formalized in enough detail, however, the Handbook can greatly facilitate the re-use of previously defined models such as simulations, workflow systems, transaction processing systems, or other software modules (e.g., Dellarocas, 1996, 1997a, 1997b).

Results

The combination of approaches described above should make it practical to store large numbers of processes, and, more importantly, enable users to generate a rich set of possible alternative processes. To test the feasibility of our approaches, we developed a series of prototype versions of a Process Handbook. The primary results of this work have been a set of *software tools* for viewing and manipulating process descriptions and a body of *information content* about business processes. In addition to these primary results, this section also includes brief descriptions of our *methodologies* for analyzing and organizing process descriptions and a *field test* of our approach.

Software Tools: The Process Handbook System

To date, the most visible product of our project is a set of software tools for storing and manipulating process descriptions. The core system manages the database of process descriptions and displays and edits selected entries. Our current system is implemented under the Microsoft Windows operating system using Microsoft's Visual Basic programming language and numerous third-party modules for that environment (i.e., VBXs). The process descriptions are stored in a relational database (currently Microsoft Access) with an interface layer above the database that represents processes using the concepts described above (Ahmed, 1995; Bernstein, Dellarocas, Malone, and Quimby, 1995). This interface allows users to retrieve, view, and edit process descriptions, including adding new subactivities and specializations.

The user interface includes:

(1) *templates for describing activities*, including standard fields (like name, description, and author) and custom fields for specialized information about particular kinds of activities

(2) *links between activities*, including standard links (like generalizations, specializations, and subactivities), as well as arbitrary "navigational links" with which users can group activities in any way they want, and

(3) *summary views of specializations and decompositions*, which allow direct manipulation of the database, including operations such as adding, changing, deleting, or moving entries.

The system also provides:

(4) *automated support for inheritance*, so that changes in an activity are automatically made in all its specializations that have not over-ridden them, and

(5) *automated support for dependencies*, so that users can specify the kind of dependency that exists between two or more activities and then search the space of possible coordination mechanisms for that dependency to identify a coordination mechanism (Elly, 1996).

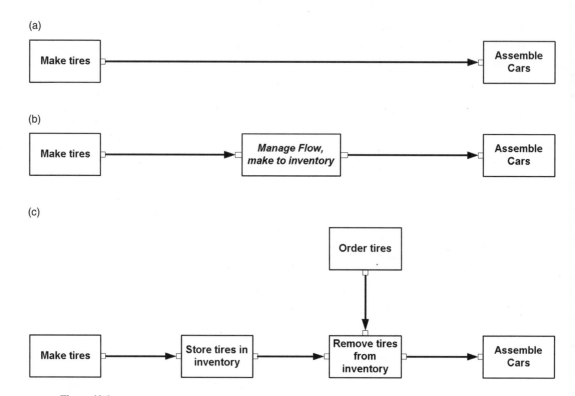

Figure 10.6
Alternative Views of the Same Sample Process
The first view (a) shows a "flow" dependency between two activities. The second view (b) shows the flow dependency replaced by the coordination process that manages it. The third view (c) shows the subactivities of the coordination process and the respective dependencies among them. Users can easily switch back and forth among these different views of the same process.

With this last feature, users can easily switch back and forth between viewing the dependency or the coordination mechanism that manages the dependency (see figure 10.6). By successively replacing dependencies with coordination mechanisms and activities with their specializations, users can easily see many different views of the same process, from the most abstract to the most detailed.

Web Interface   We have also developed a World Wide Web interface to the system that allows users to view (but not to change) the contents of the Process Handbook from anywhere on the Internet. Using a standard Web browser, users can see information structured with templates, links, and inheritance, and they can contribute to on-line discussions about each of the activities.

Process Interchange Format   While we believe the tool described above has several unique advantages, there are many other process tools available for tasks such as flowcharting, simulation, workflow, and Computer-Aided Software Engineering (CASE). To increase the potential sources and uses for process descriptions in the handbook, we wanted to be able to move processes back and forth between these different tools. To help make this possibility more likely, we organized a working group, including people from our project and from several other university research groups and companies sponsoring our research. This group has developed a Process Interchange Format (PIF) for moving process descriptions between systems that use diverse representations (Lee *et al.*, 1994; Lee *et al.*, 1996). Via PIF, a process in one system (e.g. a process modeller) can be used by another (say, a simulator), whose result in turn can be used by yet another system. Each system uses as much as possible of the process descriptions and passes on information it cannot "understand" to other systems (Lee and Malone, 1990; Chan, 1995).

Information Content: The Process Handbook Database

To test the feasibility of our approach it was critical to enter a significant number of process descriptions into the system. As table 10.2 summarizes, the handbook currently contains more than 3,400 activities, some from specific organizations and some generic processes. This information content is the second major result of our work to date.

Examples from Specific Organizations   In addition to using secondary sources of data (such as published descriptions of innovative business practices), we have focused our primary data collection on the domain of "supply chain management"— the process by which an organization (or group of organizations) manages the acquisition of inputs, the successive transformations of these inputs into products, and the distribution of these products to customers. For example, the handbook includes results from several MIT masters' thesis studies of supply chain processes ranging from a Mexican beer factory to a university purchasing process (Geisler, 1995; Leavitt, 1995; Lyon, 1995; Ruelas Gossi, 1995). The entries also include a number of examples drawn from the "Interesting Organizations Database" collected from published sources and student projects as part of an MIT research initiative on Inventing the Organizations of the 21st Century.

Generic Business Processes   To take advantage of inheritance and to help find useful process analogies, we need to integrate specific process examples into a more general framework. To develop such a framework of generic processes, we first reviewed generic business process models from a variety of published sources (e.g.,

Table 10.2
Summary of Current Contents of the Process Handbook Database (as of 10/1/97)

Kind of activity	Approx. no. of specific organizations represented	Approx. no. of activities	Maximum no. of levels of specialization	Maximum no. of levels of decomposition	Sample activity names
Examples from specific organizations					
Manufacturing	3	325	2	6	Brew beer
Other "supply chain" processes	4	235	4	5	Build walls
Others	143	240	4	2	Select human resources
Generic processes					
Generic business processes	N/A	200	3	4	Sell something
Generic coordination processes	N/A	200	7	2	Manage accessibility by collocation
Other generic activities	N/A	2200	20	10	Acquire human resources
Total	150	3400	20	10	

Davenport, 1993). Based on this work, we defined the broadest *organizational* process in the Process Handbook as "Produce something." This term is intended to include both manufacturing organizations (which produce products) and service organizations (which produce services). We intend that every activity that occurs in an organization should fit somewhere in one of the five subactivities of this all-encompassing process:

(1) design,

(2) purchasing and inbound logistics,

(3) production,

(4) sales and outbound logistics, and

(5) general management and administrative functions.

Drawing on our general knowledge of business and a variety of published sources, including textbooks in marketing (Kotler, 1997) and product design (Ulrich and Eppinger, 1995), we have developed several levels of more detailed subactivities for these generic business activities.

However, the Process Handbook does not force a single perspective on these activities. For example, several of the generic business process models we reviewed are now included in the handbook as alternative specializations of "Produce something." These different models provide different *views* of how a business can be decomposed into subactivities. When several different specializations of an activity all include the same lower-level subactivities, but group them in different ways, we define the different specializations as alternative "views." Many such views are possible, and they are all functionally equivalent, so it would not make sense to claim that any particular set of generic business processes is definitive or intrinsically superior. Instead, users can pick the views they find most useful or appealing.

Other Generic Activities In addition to the high-level generic business processes and generic coordination mechanisms described above, many other kinds of activities occur as basic building blocks of business processes. For example, activities like making a decision or approving an application are parts of many organizational processes. In order to take advantage of process inheritance and maximize the generativity of our framework, all activities need to be placed somewhere in the specialization hierarchy.

We have explored several alternatives for how to organize the specialization hierarchy that makes this possible. The most promising approach we have found so far (which we currently use in the handbook) is illustrated in figure 10.7. The basic idea is to create a high-level framework of a small number of very generic activities, and then to classify all other activities as specializations of these high-level activities.

In the current version of this taxonomy, the top level consists of very general activities like Create, Destroy, Modify, and Preserve. These most general processes can occur for any kind of object. As the table illustrates, these generic processes are further specialized down to the lowest level of activity in the handbook. We have found it useful in many cases to group specializations into bundles based on questions about who, what, where, why, when, and how. For example, the bundles under the generic "Get" activity, include "Get what?" and "Get how?" As with the other areas of the Process Handbook, the further development of this part of the process taxonomy is an active part of our ongoing research. The taxonomy we have developed so far demonstrates the basic feasibility of organizing large numbers of activities in a unified specialization hierarchy.

Methodologies

For this approach to be feasible for large-scale use, we need to be able to systematically analyze processes and integrate them into the Process Handbook. In

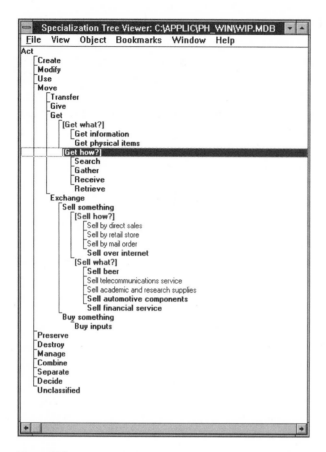

Figure 10.7
An Outline View of the First Two Levels of the Specialization Hierarchy and Selected Further Special-izations of the Generic Activity "Move" (as of 11/1/96)

addition to developing methods for analyzing processes (with or without the Pro-cess Handbook repository), we are also refining methods for editing and integrat-ing information about processes into the handbook database. For instance, a "top-down" approach to analyzing a new process for the handbook is to start with similar examples already in the handbook, create a new specialization, and then modify the specialization as needed to describe the new process. An alternative "bottom-up" approach is to start by entering a description of the new process and then connecting it to existing processes in the handbook that are generaliza-tions of the whole process or its subactivities. In the course of adding these new specializations to existing processes, the existing processes may be modified to include generalizations of elements in the new processes.

In many cases, we believe the best approach is a combination of both these approaches: working both top-down and bottom-up to successively refine both old and new process descriptions and maximizing the insights along the way. Our experiences with these methodologies are now being formalized (e.g., Crowston and Osborn, 1996; Pentland *et al.*, 1994) and integrated into teaching materials.

Field Testing the Process Handbook: A Case Study

In a sense, each new process description entered into the handbook is a field test of the framework, because it raises the question: Can this process be adequately represented? But the more important question is: What can we get back from the handbook? What kinds of activities can this representation support? To answer this question, we have begun to field test the handbook in real organizations that are engaged in process improvement efforts. While not in any sense controlled experiments, these field studies provide concrete illustrations of the potential managerial usefulness of the Process Handbook concepts. One such study is summarized here (see Herman *et al.*, 1997; and Roth, 1997 for additional details). This study was done in collaboration with one of our corporate research sponsors, the A. T. Kearney consulting firm, and one of their clients which we call "Firm A" to preserve the client's anonymity.

Firm A was experiencing increasing problems with its hiring process. It was growing rapidly in a tightening labor market, and it had a culture of independent, competitive business units. Together, these factors led to increases in the time and cost to hire people and to increasingly frequent instances of business units "hoarding" candidates or bidding against each other for the same candidate.

In an effort to improve the hiring process, the organization had invested a great deal of time and energy into "as is" process analysis using conventional techniques such as flowcharting. But its leaders also wanted some way to come up with highly innovative ideas about how to improve their process. In this spirit, they agreed to participate in a field test of the Process Handbook system and concepts. A study team of about 8 people was formed consisting of members from MIT, A. T. Kearney, and Firm A.

The team's first step was simply to see how the hiring process was represented in the Process Handbook. Several of the steps in the Handbook activity called "Hire human resources" were similar to those already identified by the "as is" analysis (e.g., identify need, determine source, select, and make offer). One immediate insight, however, resulted from the fact that the Process Handbook representation of hiring included a step of "pay employee" which had not been included in the "as is" analysis. Even though they hadn't previously thought of it in this way, the team members from Firm A found it surprising and useful to realize that the employee receiving a first paycheck is, in a sense, the logical culmination of the hiring process. Receiving a (correct) paycheck, for instance, confirms that the hiring information has been entered correctly in the relevant administrative systems.

Using the Concepts of Specialization   To generate further insights and alternatives, the team looked in the Process Handbook at specializations of the overall hiring process and then at the specializations of each of its subactivities. In terms of the Process Compass mentioned above, the team looked first to the right, then down and to the right. In doing so, they came across examples such as Marriott Hotels, where an automated telephone system asks job candidates a series of questions about their qualifications and salary requirements. At the end of the call, callers are immediately told if they're qualified for the position and invited to schedule an interview through the system's automated scheduling feature. Although most appropriate for lower-level personnel, this example was very thought-provoking for the project team.

The team found numerous other similarly intriguing examples in the handbook. For example, they found descriptions of

(1) BMW using a simulated assembly line to help select assembly line workers,

(2) Whirlpool having a corporate-wide "human capital war room" with databases of projected skill needs and capacities,

(3) Doubletree, which seeks to systematically identify dimensions of employee success in its organization and then hire candidates with similar traits.

This use of the Process Handbook is similar to the traditional "benchmarking" or "best practice" approach of learning from other examples of the same process. Even here, however, the use of specialization in the handbook allows much richer ways of indexing large numbers of examples than any other "best practices" database of which we are aware.

In an effort to expand their horizons even further, the team's next step was to look in the handbook for more distant analogies (or "cousins") of the hiring process. That is, they looked first at generalizations ("ancestors") of the hiring process and then at other specializations ("descendants") of these generalizations. (In terms of the Process Compass, they moved left and then right again.)

For example, "hiring" is classified in the handbook as a specialization of "buying," so a handbook user who looks at the generalizations of "hiring" will encounter "buying." In retrospect, this connection may seem obvious (hiring is a form of buying someone's time), but this analogy had not been obvious to the project team, and it proved to be a very stimulating source of insights. In exploring other specializations of buying, for instance, the team encountered examples like (1) Motorola's extensive quality audits and rating systems for its suppliers, (2) Acer's different sourcing strategies for different kinds of materials, and (3) General Electric's Internet-based system through which purchasing agents can find and compare suppliers. Each of these examples stimulated specific ideas about possible improvements in the hiring process for Firm A: (1) quality ratings for recruiters, (2) creating different hiring processes for different kinds of positions, and (3) identifying candidates using the Internet, respectively.

Using the Concepts of Coordination   After exploring a number of such distant analogies, the team then began to systematically explore and compare many different possible combinations of specializations and coordination processes for hiring. One of the most interesting insights from this part of the process came from focusing on the shared resource dependency for recruiter time. Firm A used a variety of internal and external recruiters, and the time of these recruiters had to be somehow shared across all the positions being filled at any given time. The coordination process Firm A currently used for managing this dependency was to have recruiting managers for each business unit assign each new search to a specific recruiter.

When analyzing this process from a coordination point of view, the team quickly identified a variety of other possible ways to manage this dependency, including all the coordination processes listed for sharing dependencies in table 10.1. The team was particularly intrigued by the idea of using market-like bidding systems for this purpose. In one scenario the team developed, for instance, recruiters would "bid" on the opportunity to fill a new position by specifying how long they estimated it would take them to fill the position. Later, when the position had actually been filled, the recruiter's fee would be adjusted for significant over- or under-performance relative to the original bid.

One compelling advantage of this scheme is that it could more easily exploit information that is often ignored completely in the current system. For instance, a recruiter who had just filled one position for a C++ programmer, but who knew that three other highly qualified candidates identified in the same search were still available, could take this information into account in making a low bid on a new search for a C++ programmer in another business unit.

Our project ended before Firm A had implemented any of the ideas generated in this phase of the project, and no quantitative evaluation of the idea-generating phase of the project was done. However, in the meeting where the final project results were presented, the executive vice-president of human resources in Firm A eloquently articulated our aspirations in the project by saying that he felt he had "passed through a doorway where all sorts of things he had never imagined before now seemed possible."

Discussion

This case illustrates a number of advantages of using a specialization hierarchy in combination with the explicit representation of coordination and dependencies. First, this field test showed that specialization can substantially reduce the amount of work necessary to analyze a new process. By simply identifying a process as a "hiring process," for example, a great deal of information can be automatically inherited. Then, only the changes that matter for the purpose at hand need to be explicitly entered. This helps support a rapid assessment of the basic features of a process, rather than laborious detailing (what Hammer and Champy, 1993, refer to as "analysis paralysis"). For example in the field test, the team chose to ignore nearly all of the "as is" analysis that had previously been done by Firm A and focus on a very simple, abstract view of the hiring process and its first-level subactivities. This level of detail, alone, was sufficient to generate all the insights described above.

Second, the specialization hierarchy provided a powerful framework for generating new process ideas. For example, some of today's "best practice" databases support cross-fertilization across industries within the same business function, but we do not know of any others that would support the kind of cross-fertilization across business functions (from purchasing to human resources) described above.

Since coordination processes are often those most susceptible to being changed by information technology, a particularly important use of this approach is to use generic knowledge about alternative coordination mechanisms to generate new process ideas. For instance, the ideas about using bidding to allocate recruiter time were stimulated by very generic knowledge about coordination, and would presumably be more feasible because of the cheaper communication made possible by information technologies (see Crowston, 1997, for other similar examples).

Another feature of our approach that makes it particularly useful for generating new process ideas is that we focus attention on processes as distinct entities that can be described independently of organizational structures or the roles of particular people or groups. This "process-oriented" approach to business seems particularly useful, in (a) identifying new ways of doing old tasks, even if the new ways involve very different actors and (b) managing connected processes that span organizational boundaries, either across groups in a single firm or across firms in "networked" and "virtual" organizations.

In addition to these advantages, our process-oriented approach has limitations, too. For instance, any static process representation can give the impression that the process is more stable and routine than most business processes actually are. In contrast to most other process representations, however, our approach helps us explicitly deal with this issue by representing the stable—or typical—aspects of a process at the generic level and then also representing as many specialized variations as is useful.

Another risk of having libraries of explicit process representations like ours is that people will interpret them too rigidly. While it is sometimes appropriate to collect prescriptive rules or procedures in a handbook like ours, we think that in most situations a Process Handbook will be most useful as a *resource* to help people figure out what to do, rather than as a *prescription* of what they should do.

The Editorial Challenge   One of the most important ways in which our approach differs from many other computational approaches to similar problems is that we do not rely primarily on intelligent computer systems to analyze, reason about, or simulate business processes. Instead, we place substantial importance on the role of intelligent human "editors" to select, refine, and structure the knowledge represented in the handbook. This approach has both strengths and weaknesses.

On the one hand, it allows us to take advantage of human abilities to analyze, organize, and communicate knowledge in ways that go far beyond the capabilities of today's computers. For example, the task of developing good generic models for the marketing and sales process is similar, in many ways, to writing a good textbook or developing comprehensive theories about marketing and sales. Human abilities to do tasks like these will almost certainly exceed those of computers for the foreseeable future.

On the other hand, relying on human effort in this way means that the success of our approach depends significantly on the quality and amount of human intelligence applied to the problem of generating and organizing knowledge in the system. For example, a complex and confusing network of poorly organized process categories may be even worse than no categories at all.

In general, as process descriptions are added to the handbook, we will face a problem that is analogous to that faced by researchers in many fields: how to ensure that results cumulate in a meaningful way. Since we foresee a wide variety of potential users and contributors, it would be unrealistic to expect equal rigor from all of them. Rather than attempting to enforce uniform standards, we plan to allow a wide variety of data from diverse sources, but to require that the specific sources, methods, and significance of that data be described in enough detail to allow users of the handbook to judge whether it is valid and reliable enough for their own purposes. In this respect, the handbook has an advantage over more formal approaches because it allows many alternatives to co-exist in the system. At the same time, this openness contributes to the editorial problem of ensuring that the entries are consistently and usefully classified. We believe that adopting solutions analogous to those that have already been found successful in other domains is a promising approach. For example, we have found it useful to think about roles like authors, editors, and reviewers for groups of entries in the Process Handbook.

It is also encouraging to note that the specialization structure of the handbook provides a potentially powerful advantage that has not been widely available to any knowledge-generating communities before: Well-organized and accurate process knowledge at the "left" of the specialization network is automatically inherited throughout the other parts of the network where it applies. In this sense, then, the system amplifies the effort of intelligent humans by automatically linking their work to a variety of contexts where it may be useful.

Conclusion

There is, of course, much more work to be done to develop and test the ideas described here. For example, better tools for process analysis and editing need to be created, more information content needs to be added to the Process Handbook, and systematic tests of how the ideas can be applied in different kinds of situations need to be performed. However, we believe that our work so far has demonstrated the basic feasibility and contribution of the approach and its potential for significant further progress. We hope, for example, that this research will provide a set of intellectual tools and an extensive database to help people learn about organizations, invent new kinds of organizations, and improve existing processes. Perhaps most importantly, we hope this research will help us understand the possibilities for creating new kinds of organizations that are not only more effective, but also, more fulfilling for their members.

Acknowledgments

This chapter is reprinted with permission from *Management Science* 45, no. 3 (March 1999), 425–443. © 1999, the Institute for Operations Research and the Management Sciences, 901 Elkridge Landing Road, Suite 400, Linthicum, MD 21090.

Parts of this paper appeared previously in Malone, Crowston, Lee, and Pentland (1993).

This work was supported, in part, by the National Science Foundation (Grant Nos. IRI-8903034, IRI-9224093, and DMI-9628949) and the Defense Advanced Research Projects Agency (DARPA). It was also supported by the following corporate sponsors: British Telecom, Daimler Benz, Digital Equipment Corporation, Electronic Data Systems (EDS), Fuji Xerox, Matsushita, National Westminster Bank, Statoil, Telia, Union Bank of Switzerland, Unilever, and other sponsors of the MIT Center for Coordination Science and the MIT Initiative on Inventing the Organizations of the 21st Century. The software described in this paper is the subject of pending patent applications by MIT.

We would like to thank Marc Gerstein, Fred Luconi, and Gilad Zlotkin for their long-term contributions to many aspects of this project. We would like to thank John Gerhart for his significant early contributions to the content of the database and Martha Broad, Bob Halperin, Ed Heresniak, and Roanne Neuwirth for their contributions to the management of the project. We would also like to specifically thank the following students for their contributions to the development of the software tools described here: Erfan Ahmed, Frank Chan, Yassir Elley, Umar Farooq, Phil Grabner, Naved Khan, Vuong Nguyen, Greg Pal, Narasimha Rao, and Calvin Yuen. In addition, we would like to thank the dozens of students and others who contributed content to the database or who used the concepts developed in this project to analyze business processes. In particular, we would like to thank the following students whose work is specifically included in the current database: Gary Cheng, Martha Geisler, Paul Gutwald, Clarissa Hidalgo, Jeff Huang, Wilder Leavitt, William Lyon, Alejandro Ruelas Gossi, and Jin Xia. Finally, we would like to thank the members of the Process Handbook advisory board: Michael Cohen, John McDermott, and the late Gerald Salancik.

References

Allen, R., and G. Garlan. 1994. Formalizing Architectural Connection. In Proceedings of the 16th International Conference on Software Engineering, 71–80, Sorrento, Italy, March.

Ahmed, Erfanuddin. 1995. *A Data Abstraction with Inheritance in the Process Handbook.* Unpublished M.S. thesis, Department of Electrical Engineering and Computer Science, MIT.

Baligh, H. H., R. M. Burton, and B. Obel. 1990. Devising expert systems in organization theory: The Organizational Consultant. In *Organization, Management, and Expert Systems*, edited by M. Masuch. Berlin: Walter de Gruyter, 35–57.

Bernstein, A., C. Dellarocas, T. W. Malone, and J. Quimby. 1995. Software tools for a Process Handbook. *IEEE Bulletin on Data Engineering* 18 (March): 41–47.

Bhandaru, N., and W. B. Croft. 1990. An architecture for supporting goal-based cooperative work. In *Multi-User Interfaces and Applications*, edited by S. Gibbs and A. A. Verrijin-Stuart. Amsterdam: Elsevier, 337–354.

Brachman, R. J., and H. J. Levesque, eds. 1985. *Readings in Knowledge Representation*. Los Altos, Calif.: Morgan Kaufmann.

Carley, K., J. Kjaer-Hansen, A. Newell, and M. Prietula. 1992. Plural-Soar: Capabilities and coordination of multiple agents. In *Artificial Intelligence in organization and management theory: Models of distributed intelligence*, edited by M. Masuch and M. Warglien. New York: Elsevier Science, 87–118.

Carlson, W. M. 1979. Business Information Analysis and Integration Technique (BIAIT)—The new horizon. *Database* (Spring): 3–9.

Carter, D. E., and B. S. Baker. 1991. *Concurrent Engineering: The Product Development Environment for the 1990s*. Reading, Mass.: Addison-Wesley.

Chan, Frank Y. 1995. *The Round Trip Problem: A Solution for the Process Handbook*. Unpublished M.S. thesis, Department of Electrical Engineering and Computer Science, MIT.

Chandrasekaran, B. 1983. Towards a taxonomy of problem solving types. *AI Magazine*, 4 (1): 9–17.

Chandrasekaran, B., T. R. Johnson, and J. W. Smith. 1992. Task-structure analysis for knowledge modeling. *Communications of the ACM*, 35 (9), 124–137.

CIO Magazine. 1992. Back Support for Benchmarkers, *CIO*, June 1, 16. (Note: This article gives a brief description of the activities of the International Benchmarking Clearinghouse. More detail is available from the following site on the World Wide Web: http://www.apqc.org/)

Clancey, W. J. 1983. The epistemology of a rule-based expert system—A framework for explanation. *Artificial Intelligence*, 20 (3), 215–251.

Cohen, M., J. G. March, and J. P. Olsen. 1972. A garbage can model of organizational choice. *Administrative Science Quarterly* 17:1.

Crowston, K. 1991. *Towards a Coordination Cookbook: Recipes for Multi-Agent Action*. Ph.D. dissertation, MIT Sloan School of Management.

Crowston, K. 1997. A coordination theory approach to organizational process design. *Organization Science*, 8 (2), 157–175.

Crowston, K., and C. Osborn, C. 1996. A coordination theory approach to process documentation and redesign. MIT Center for Coordination Science Working Paper.

Davenport, T. 1993. *Process Innovation: Reengineering Work through Information Technology*. Boston, Mass: Harvard Business School Press.

Dellarocas, C. 1996. *A Coordination Perspective on Software Architecture: Towards a Design Handbook for Integrating Software Components*. Ph.D. dissertation, MIT Department of Electrical Engineering and Computer Science.

Dellarocas, C. 1997a. Towards A Design Handbook for Integrating Software Components. *Proceedings of the 5th International Symposium on Assessment of Software Tools* (SAST'97), Pittsburgh, June 2–5.

Dellarocas, C. 1997b. The SYNTHESIS Environment for Component-Based Software Development. *Proceedings of the 8th International Workshop on Software Technology and Engineering Practice* (STEP'97), London, July 14–18.

Dellarocas, C., J. Lee, T. W. Malone, K. Crowston, and B. Pentland. 1994. Using a process handbook to design organizational processes. *Proceedings of the AAAI '94 Stanford Spring Symposium on Computational Organization Design*. Stanford, Calif.

Elley, Yassir. 1996. *A Flexible Process Editor for the Process Handbook*. Master's thesis, MIT Department of Electrical Engineering and Computer Science.

Friedland, P. E. 1979. Knowledge-based Experiment Design in Molecular Genetics. Technical Report. No. 79–771, Ph.D. dissertation, Computer Science Department, Stanford University.

Friedland, P. E., and Y. Iwasaki. 1985. The concept and implementation of skeletal plans. *Journal of Automated Reasoning, 1* (2).

Gasser, L., and A. Majchrzak. 1994. ACTION Integrates Manufacturing Strategy, Design, and Planning. In *Ergonomics of Hybrid Automated Systems IV*, edited by P. Kidd and W. Karwowski. Netherlands: IOS Press.

Geisler, Martha A. 1995. *The Evolving Health Care Delivery Systems: Applying the Process Handbook Methodology to Gain a Vision of the Future*. Unpublished M.S. thesis, MIT Sloan School of Management.

Hammer, M., and J. Champy. 1993. *Reengineering the Corporation.* New York: Harper Business.

Herman, G., M. Klein, T. W. Malone, and E. O'Donnell. 1997. A Template Based Methodology for Process Redesign. MIT Center for Coordination Science, unpublished working paper.

Holt, A. W. 1988. Diplans: A new language for the study and implementation of coordination. *ACM Transactions on Office Information Systems* 6 (2): 109–125.

Kolodner, J. 1993. *Case-based Reasoning*. San Mateo, CA: Morgan Kaufmann.

Kotler, Philip. 1997. *Marketing management*, 9th ed. New Jersey: Prentice Hall.

Leavitt, Wilder. 1995. *Health Care Delivery Systems: Using the MIT CCS Handbook to Create Organizations for the 21st Century*. Unpublished M.S. thesis, MIT Sloan School of Management.

Lee, J., and K.-Y. Lai. 1991. What's in design rationale? *Human-Computer Interaction*, 6 (3–4): 251–280.

Lee, J., and T. W. Malone. 1990. Partially shared views: A scheme for communicating among groups that use different type hierarchies. *ACM Transactions on Information Systems* 8 (1): 1–26.

Lee, J., G. Yost, and the PIF Working Group. 1994. *The PIF Process Interchange Format and Framework*. MIT CCS Working Report #180.

Lee, Jintae, Michel Grunninger, Yan Jin, Thomas Malone, Austin Tate, Gregg Yost, and other members of the PIF Working Group. 1996. The PiF Process Interchange Format and Framework Version 1.1, *Proceedings of Workshop on Ontological Engineering*, ECAI '96. Budapest, Hungary. (Also available as MIT Center for Coordination Science, Working Paper #194 and on the World Wide Web at http://ccs.mit.edu/pif.)

Lefkowitz, L. S., and W. B. Croft. 1990. Interactive planning for knowledge-based task management. Technical Report, Collaborative Systems Laboratory, Department of Computer and Information Science, University of Massachusetts, Amherst.

Lenat, D. B. 1995. CYC: A Large-Scale Investment in Knowledge Infrastructure. *Communications of the ACM* 38 (11), 33–38.

Levitt, R. E., G. Cohen, J. C. Kunz, C. I. Nass, T. Christiansen, and Y. Jin. 1994. The Virtual Design Team: Simulating how organizations' structure and information processing tools affect team performance. In Computational Organization Theory, K. M. Carley and M. J. Prietula, eds. Hillsdale, N.J.: Erlbaum.

Lewis, H. R., and C. H. Papadimitriou. 1981. *Elements of the Theory of Computation*. New York: Prentice-Hall.

Lyon, William K. 1995. *The Process Handbook Supply Chain Re-engineering*. Unpublished M.S. thesis, MIT Sloan School of Management.

Madsen, O. L., B. Moller-Pedersen, and K. Nygaard, K. 1993. *Object-Oriented Programming in the Beta Programming Language,* Reading, Mass.: Addison-Wesley.

Malone, T. W. and K. Crowston. 1994. The interdisciplinary study of coordination, *ACM Computing Surveys*, 26 (1), 87–119.

Malone, T. W., K. Crowston, J. Lee, and B. Pentland. 1993. Tools for inventing organizations: Toward a handbook of organizational processes. *Proceedings of the 2nd IEEE Workshop on Enabling Technologies Infrastructure for Collaborative Enterprises*. Morgantown, W. Va., April 20–22.

Marques, D., G. Dallemagne, G. Klinker, J. McDermott, and D. Tung. 1992. Easy programming: Empowering people to build their own applications. *IEEE Expert*, 7 (June): 16–29.

Masuch, M., and P. LaPotin, P. 1989. Beyond Garbage Cans: An AI Model of Organizational Choice. *Administrative Science Quarterly*, 34: 38–67.

Maull, R., S. Childe, J. Bennett, A. Weaver, and A. Smart. 1995. Different types of manufacturing processes and IDEF0 models describing standard business processes. Working paper WP/GR/J9501 , School of Computing, University of Plymouth, Plymouth, Devon, U.K.

McKelvey, B. 1982. *Organizational Systematics—Taxonomy, Evolution, Classification.* Berkeley: University of California Press.

Mintzberg, H. 1979. *The Structuring of Organizations.* Englewood Cliffs, N.J.: Prentice-Hall.

Pentland, B. T., C. Osborne, G. Wyner, and F. Luconi. 1994. Useful descriptions of organizational processes: Collecting data for the Process Handbook. Unpublished working paper, Center for Coordination Science, MIT.

Peters, T. 1992. *Liberation Management.* New York: Knopf.

Peterson, J. L. 1977. Petri nets. *ACM Computing Surveys,* 9 (3): 223–252.

Pugh, D.S., D. J. Hickson, and C. R. Hinings. 1968. An empirical taxonomy of work organizations, Administrative Science Quarterly 14: 115–126.

Roth, G. 1997. Uniting theory and practice: An illustrative case for bridging knowledge and action. Unpublished working paper, MIT Initiative on Inventing the Organizations of the 21st Century.

Rowley, J. 1992. *Organizing Knowledge,* 2d ed. Brookfield, Vt.: Ashgate.

Ruelas Gossi, Alejandro. 1995. *Inventing Organizations for the 21st Century in Mexico: Supply Chain Management in a Brewery.* Unpublished M.S. thesis, MIT Sloan School of Management.

Salancik, G. R., and H. Leblebici. 1988. Variety and form in organizing transactions: A generative grammer of organizations. In *Research in the Sociology of Organizations,* N. DiTomaso and S. B. Bacharach, eds. Greenwich, Conn.: JAI Press.

Sanchez, Julio C. 1993. The Long and Thorny Way to an Organizational Taxonomy. *Organization Studies* 14 (1): 73–92.

Schank, R. C. 1982. *Dynamic Memory: A theory of reminding and learning in computers and people.* New York: Cambridge University Press.

Schank, R. C., and R. P. Abelson. 1977. *Scripts, Plans, Goals, and Understanding: An Inquiry into Human Knowledge.* Hillsdale, N.J.: Erlbaum.

Scheer, A.-W. 1994. *Business Process Re-engineering: Reference Models for Industrial Enterprises,* 2d ed. New York: Springer-Verlag.

Shaw, M. *et al.* 1995. Abstractions for Software Architecture and Tools to Support Them. IEEE Transactions on Software Engineering (April): 314–335.

Shaw, M., and D. Garlan. 1996. Software Architecture: Perspectives on An Emerging Discipline. Upper Saddle River, N.J.: Prentice-Hall.

Singh, B., and G. L. Rein. 1992. *Role Interaction Nets (RIN): A process description formalism.* Technical Report No. CT-083–92. Austin, Texas: MCC.

Stefik, M. 1981. Planning with constraints (MOLGEN: Part 1). *Artificial Intelligence,* 16 (2): 111–139.

Stefik, M., and D. G. Bobrow. 1986. Object-oriented programming: Themes and variations. *AI Magazine* 6 (Winter): 40–62.

Stovsky, M. P., and B. W. Weide. 1988. Building Interprocess Communication Models Using STILE. *Proceedings of the 21st Annual Hawaii International Conference On System Sciences,* vol. 2, 639–647.

Tenenberg, J. 1986. Planning with abstraction. In *Proceedings of AAAI-86, Fifth National Conference on Artificial Intelligence.* Philadelphia.

Thompson, J. D. 1967. *Organizations in Action: Social Science Bases of Administrative Theory.* New York: McGraw-Hill.

Thomsen, K. S. 1987. Inheritance on processes, exemplified on distributed termination detection. *International Journal of Parallel Programming,* 16 (1): 17–53.

Ulrich, K. T., and S. D. Eppinger. 1995. *Product design and development.* New York: McGraw-Hill.

Ulrich, D. O., and B. McKelvey. 1990. General Organizational Classification: an empirical test using the United States and Japanese electronics industries. *Organization Science* 1: 99–118.

Wegner, P. 1987. Dimensions of object-based language design. In *Proceedings of the Conference on Object-Oriented Systems, Languages, and Applications (OOPSLA '87),* Orlando, 168–182.

Winograd, T., and F. Flores. 1986. *Understanding computers and cognition: A new foundation for design.* Norwood, N.J.: Ablex.

Woodward, J. 1965. *Industrial organizations: Theory and practice.* London, New York: Oxford University Press.

Wyner, G., and J. Lee. 1995. Applying Specialization to Process Models. In *Proceedings of the Conference on Organizational Computing Systems.* Milpitas, Calif., August.

Yourdon, E. 1989. *Modern Structured Analysis.* Englewood Cliffs, N.J.: Yourdon.

Yu, E. S. K. 1992. Modeling organizations for information systems requirements engineering. *Proceedings IEEE.*

Zlotkin, G. 1995. Coordinating Resource Based Depedencies. MIT Center for Coordination Science Unpublished working paper.

11 Inventing Organizations with the Process Handbook: Excerpts from a Learning History

Nina Kruschwitz and George Roth

Introduction

A learning history is an account of events that took place in an organization, or a group of organizations, told through the differing perspectives of the many people involved. Its purpose is to help the participants, as well as other both inside and outside the organization, to learn from what occurred. This chapter is comprised of excerpts from a learning history about a research project undertaken as part of MIT's Initiative on Inventing the Organizations of the 21st Century. The excerpts here focus on events that led to some of the most important results of the project. Other parts of the original learning history focus on the benefits, and challenges, of partnerships involving university researchers and corporate sponsors (Krushwitz and Roth 1999).

Background on the 21st Century Initiative Special Project

The research project that served as the basis of the learning history was a collaboration between three organizations: the Center for Coordination Science, a research center at MIT's Sloan School of Management; a process consulting firm that was a major sponsor of the 21st Century Initiative (known in the learning history as Process Consulting Company, or PCC); and a financial services company that was a client of PCC (known in the learning history as Finserv). The project came about through an intersection of the interests of the three organizations.

In its Process Handbook project, CCS had been developing a body of theory and tools that the CCS research team believed could help business organizations to manage processes more effectively. A test of the Process Handbook in a real company setting would be an opportunity to validate the concepts and tools.

As a sponsor of the 21st Century Initiative, PCC had come to be familiar with the Process Handbook. Several consultants at PCC were intrigued by potential the Process Handbook presented for developing new, innovative approaches for undertaking process consulting work.

FinServ was in the midst of an enterprise-wide redesign of its hiring process. Several members of the internal team working on the hiring process redesign were former colleagues of the PCC consultant who was the liaison to the 21st Century Initiative.

Learning Histories

Learning histories are a methodology designed to reflect upon, capture, and diffuse learning from project initiatives across organizations (Roth and Kleiner, 1995, Roth, 1996). The learning history is a document planned and researched by an insider/outsider team, organized around significant business accomplishments and emergent themes related to learning. The materials are presented as a jointly told tale using participants' narrative (from interview transcripts) in a two-column format to distinguish researchers' perspectives from participants' experience. For more information, refer to *http://ccs.mit.edu/lh.*

A learning history describes what happens in the voice of participants. It not only documents the "hard" facts and events, but what people thought about those events, and how they perceived their own and others' actions. The learning history unveils the differences in people's perceptions.

Several different styles of text exist in this "jointly-told" tale. Text running across the width of the full page provides the context and background for each part of the story and leads into the narrative in the two-column format.

In the minor column, you will see critical observations and key questions from the "learning historians." These comments tell why the major column text was chosen, and ask questions to prompt reflection and application to your own situation.

The major column contains the primary narrative. You will see each paragraph in the major column credited to a particular individual, who tells his or her part of the story.

In a series of conversations held in the fall of 1996, people at CCS, PCC, and FinServ discussed the possibility of a collaboration. The idea was to undertake a project in which a joint team would use ideas and tools developed in the Process Handbook work as a component of the hiring process redesign effort at FinServ. In early December, managers at FinServ approved the idea, formally engaging PCC to undertake a large process redesign engagement, with the Process Handbook effort as one part.

The project began with a kick-off meeting, attended by representatives of all three organizations, in mid-December. The project carried on through the winter and into the spring of 1996–1997, concluding with a series of presentations at MIT, FinServ, and PCC.

Leading Actors

In the learning history prepared on this project, none of the individual participants is identified by name, but only by title. The participants who appear in these excerpts are:

MIT Director	Faculty member and tenured professor at MIT's Sloan School of Management.
MIT Researcher	Research Associate directly involved in the special project. Previously worked for a large computer company.
MIT Project Manager	Member of the CCS staff who was project manager for the special project. Came from an industry background.
MIT Affiliates	Research scientists at MIT and professors at other universities who worked on developing the Process Handbook.
MIT Students	Graduate students at MIT's Sloan School of Management who took part in special project meetings.
PCC Consultant	Consultant responsible for establishing and managing the special project. She was based in PCC's Boston office.
PCC Adjuncts	Two consultants who were peripherally involved in the special project but closely involved with the consulting work at FinServ.
FinServ Designer	Business process analyst and designer who was actively involved with the special project at MIT. He had worked at PCC prior to joining FinServ.

Bagging Insights: An Exciting Beginning

When the special project team started meeting, enthusiasm was high, and everyone was ready to "dive in." The group kept track of interesting ideas or insights as they happened. These insights occurred as the team used the PH database to point it to hiring process examples and alternatives in the 21st Century Initiatives Interesting Organizations database. Capturing ideas that would be relevant for FinServ was called "insight bagging." In the course of a few weekly meetings a list of 42 insights was generated (see "Examples of Insights"). These insights were a validation of the PH's usefulness, and important in the project's progress.

> *MIT Director* We tried to have two people in pre-set roles at every meeting. Anyone should feel free to point out an insight they thought was interesting, but one person was specifically charged with the role of "insight spotter"— observing out loud when an insight occurred. The other role was an "insight bagger," who was to record the insight. This

methodology produces a lot of mini insights. There is no guarantee that you will get any major insight, but almost every time you use the PH you get micro insights. It was too easy not to notice them. You could go away from the meeting with the feeling that some interesting things happened but not quite remember what they were.

Some team members said that some of these insights were irrelevant and impossible to evaluate.

FinServ Designer   We came up with examples, some from the database, of how things could work, like "bidding." They had some feasibility. They weren't totally pie-in-the-sky, and I thought at some point they could be evaluated in terms of how they might work.

MIT Project Manager   The actual meeting activity was a combination of PH processes, common sense, and brainstorming. We didn't learn much detail about FinServ's problems or what possible solutions might be. [FinServ Designer] was having a good enough time coming—this was his two hours a week where he could think creatively—he was okay with that, even though there might not have been direct applicability between some of the brainstorming suggestions and the real problems back at FinServ. It was hard to know. I remember when I started working here at MIT I was amazed and happy to be in an atmosphere where people were so bright and interesting. I think [FinServ Designer] was experiencing that too. There was some concern early on that he would have to justify spending time here, and that was part of why we needed results.

The PCC Consultant said her quietness in meetings, interpreted by the MIT Project Manager as happiness, was her strategy to get the FinServ Designer engaged.

I got the sense that not only was he feeling that he was seeing some useful stuff, but he was also thinking and talking openly about how he could use this: "Not only is this interesting, but I would actually use this to give a presentation to my boss, and this could enhance my ability to work at FinServ." And since [FinServ Designer] was happy, I think [PCC Consultant] was happy, too.

Since people were having a good time, it made issues about expectations fall by the wayside. If it was hard for me to describe the meetings to other people here at MIT, it must have been even harder for him.

A New Focus for Consulting

The way the Process Handbook was used in the special project meetings suggested a new approach for conducting business process redesign to PCC. The team could

Examples of Insights

Insights generated from special project meetings totaled 60, with most of these occurring in the first few weeks of meeting. The following are examples of insights that occurred in the early meetings.

1. Insight for the future process re-engineering efforts: Do process re-engineering consulting in two parallel teams. The first team, made up of people knowledgeable about process details, can supply the second team, made up of high-level visionaries, with enough information about costing yet leave the high-level visionaries free to develop far-reaching analysis.

2. High-level hiring candidates (e.g., Oracle database analysts) can be viewed as having perishable availability. In addition, they become ripe again a few years later and therefore one strategy may be to cultivate them throughout their careers. On the other hand, entry-level candidates can be regarded as commodities with a certain set of attributes.

3. One way for FinServ to develop selection criteria might be to do an analysis of past hires and to determine "what did successful people look like at the time they were hired?" One could look at outcome measures (e.g., annual performance evaluation ratings) to determine success.

4. The characteristics of the people you want to hire are systematizable to a greater degree with "commodity-type" jobs (e.g., customer service reps, etc.). The more senior the position, the less you can systematize job requirements.

5. Creativity techniques could be added to the PH where the user would be prompted to help brainstorm; for instance, "If you're interested in sourcing, here are some structured questions to ask."

6. FinServ budgets are driven in part by the current state of the financial markets. The managing process used for job requisitions should match the flexibility inherent in this market.

7. Job requisitions state what we want the employee to do, but we describe the ideal candidate by how they are, e.g., hard-working, self-motivated, responsible.

8. Consider the hiring process as a "buying options on a futures market" process.

9. The "closed-door" thought model helps when thinking about dependencies between two processes. Imagine two parties in windowless rooms: What would they need to communicate? This analysis could be simplified by focusing on the "most promising" ways to manage the dependency.

move quickly from an understanding of how work was done to developing and evaluating alternatives. Generating alternative process designs early was substantially different from typical re-engineering efforts, where significant time and effort is taken up in documenting and costing "as is" processes.

Focusing on alternatives early on in the redesign process generated more enthusiasm and a creative focus for those engaged in redesign activities—much as the special project team itself was experiencing. A detailed "as is" analysis could come later, on a much more focused basis, when the processes and the ways in which they would change were identified. In a consulting project, a Process Handbook approach would save clients' time and money in the analysis phase, with the added benefit that this approach would also develop the support needed to implement proposed changes.

The combined experience of all the special project team participants was important in seeing the usefulness of a PH approach.

PCC Adjunct Consultant   A lot of documentation of the "as-is" is really unproductive. It just makes projects go longer and is expensive. The idea of cutting down on that and going straight to design is really interesting and very applicable. You could skim enough knowledge to understand just what you need to change and then do the redesign work. People always find that more interesting, and you can get momentum and enthusiasm going.

MIT Director   I have explicitly studied creativity techniques, and am sort of an implicit practitioner of those techniques. In a certain sense a lot of this work is creativity techniques applied to process invention. Instead of having to make up everything from scratch, a lot of the structure and content is already there. The alternatives can be automatically generated and you just have to evaluate them.

PCC Consultant   When you go through visioning and do creativity sessions, you hope you'll get ideas. What the PH was actually doing for us was defining, in a much more structured way, the transition from looking at the "as is" to some kind of a new state. When we saw that, it became clear that this was interesting, this was useful.

MIT Student   Left to their own devices, PCC would have spent a lot of time measuring the efficiency of different parts of the existing process. Typical business process re-engineering. What was neat was that the specialization hierarchy really did bring them up to a different level to look at the process in a completely different way. It was interesting to see the Process Handbook used as a brainstorming facilitation tool. I hadn't looked at it that way before.

I was impressed by its power to help consultants get out of their box. I thought it could also help people who might not be very knowledgeable do re-engineering. In a lot of projects, consultants get so focused on the nitty-gritty details of the efficiency of a particular process, and then lose sight of the forest for the trees.

To what extent might the use of the PH have been determined by the skills and experiences of the PCC consultant, who was known for her skills in bringing creativity into process redesign consulting engagements?

MIT Researcher   I'd always considered "as is" documentation of questionable worth myself. At [previous employer] we had been implementing a major new software package, and I had been the project manager for its installation. I had wanted to spend two weeks looking at "as-is" and six weeks looking at the way we wanted it to be. I was overruled by a senior manager: "No, we want to spend time looking at the as-is." That eventually took ten weeks with a separate consulting firm, spending hundreds of thousands of dollars, and producing four inches of documentation, before we even started thinking of the way we wanted things to be. The people who had been involved, who actually understood the as-is, didn't have to have it on paper in order to do it better. They could have gone right to design.

From Insights to Understanding: Making the Miracle Visible

After the first month of special project meetings, the special project team meetings had produced almost 60 different insights about the hire process. At this stage, the PCC and FinServ team members faced the challenge of communicating these findings—and the method that had generated them—back to their organizations.

What would it take to make knowledge that was implicit in the minds of the PH researchers—how to use the handbook—explicit for others to see and understand? How could what they had done as a team itself be clarified, organized, and presented to others?

The MIT Researcher, responding to PCC's and FinServ's requests, developed a way of showing how to generate alternative processes. He created a systematic way to consider a set of alternatives to take into account when redesigning a business process. This framework, which became known as the Cafeteria Menu, yielded 72 alternatives for considering the basic choices in a process.

This is only one way of using the Cafeteria Menu approach. It can be used with any combination of dimensions and alternatives the participants in the process think will be useful. For more details and examples, see Malone, Crowston, and Herman (2003) and Malone (2003).

Much of the special project team's research work was based on delving into the complex details of an analytical process. It had been hard for the non-academics, like the PCC Consultant and the FinServ Designer, to completely follow what the researchers were doing. It was even harder for them to figure out how they could tell others what they did.

Working one-on-one with the researchers, the PCC Consultant looked for a simple way of describing how to use the PH. The researchers each had their own slightly different ways of explaining and using it. The PCC Consultant sought a description that encompassed all of their methods.

> *PCC Consultant* [MIT Director] and I worked very closely, and I also kept going back to [MIT Affiliated Researcher] at [another university]. I'd have a meeting with [MIT Researcher] and then say, "I think this is what he is really saying. Now, would [MIT Affiliated Researcher] view this in this way?" I'd bring what we had come up with to [MIT Affiliated Researcher] and get his perspective and then I'd go back that night and digest it and say, "Let's try and think of the framework that unifies these different views."
>
> I actually ended up being a broker for people who had used the tool, coming up with a framework that we could all buy into. Those were the people that needed to be connected, that hadn' been connected before. All I did was internalize it in a way that I could understand it and spit it back out. There had been no mechanism for that. Not having been involved in true research before, I'd never been in a situation where you just went along a path and saw where it led. I did not expect to have to pull all this together. I thought MIT would be saying, "This is how we use it." Even though [MIT Director] had told me all along it was research, I didn't think it would be as loosey-goosey as it was, or that it would be up to the sponsor to create the framework. [MIT Director] and [MIT Researcher] probably always had this in their minds, but we were pulling it out and making it explicit so that we and our client could understand it. That is what ended up happening. It was just a question of getting it out of their heads and putting it down on paper.

At different points, team members attributed the creation of the Process Compass to different members. Retrospectively, people have agreed that the MIT Researcher was its creator. The PCC Consultant, however, created the conditions for its development.

These ideas for using the PH came to be called the Process Compass. Like a navigational compass, the Process Compass is a device to help orient users as to where they are—in this case, the choices they have in developing alternative processes. It was based on a visual icon that helped people decide what "direction" to move in (see Sidebar: The Process Compass).

This kind of "translation" was something that 21C sponsors had wanted for some time, but were unable to develop themselves. It was the drive of the PCC Consultant, not the structure of the special project nor initiative of the researchers, that reconciled and synthesized the various views from which the Process Compass was created.

The Cafeteria Menu

The Process Handbook helps people redesigning business process make choices in their new process designs. Considering and evaluating a large number of choices, particularly when you want to be sure that you have considered all reasonable options, can be a daunting task. The name, a "cafeteria-style" menu, was developed to describe the possible choices. The Cafeteria Menu provided a systematic way to consider possible design choices. Using a Cafeteria Menu, a process designer chooses among options for each subactivity to generate process alternatives in a manner similar to choosing courses from menu choices in a cafeteria.

Using this framework generates a total number of 72 (4 by 3 by 6) possible choices. Activities are considered based on the who, how, and why (3 dimensions) and the when, where, what and how much (4 dimensions) of a process. The range of possible alternatives form a 3 by 4 matrix. The matrix is expanded by considering six possible coordinating actions that can be taken—create, destroy, modify, preserve, combine, and separate. For each subactivity all 72 alternatives may not be appropriate for consideration, nor worthy of extensive evaluation. The figure below illustrates this point in that it shows fewer than ten choices for each subactivity.

Cafeteria Style Menu of Options: Commodity Hires

Identify Need	*Determine Source*	*Select (by whom)*	*Select (how)*	*Offer*	*Install*

• Standards
• Committee
• Manager
• Computer Agent
	• Internet
	• Self ID
	• Network
	• Organization
	• Journal
	• Advertising
	• Mailing List
	• Catalog
	• Search Firms
	• Database
	• Job Fairs
		• External Agency:
		  - Prof. Agency
		  - Computer Agent
		• Internal:
		  - Managers
		  - Employees
		  - HR
		• - Computer Agent
			• Aptitude or other Success Dimensions
			• Interview:
			  - on line
			  - group
			  - screen
			  - individual
			• Trial:
			  -Internship
			  -Probation
			• Qualification:
			  - certification
			  - education
			• Reference Check
				• Purchasing
				• Electronic Requisition
				• Electronic Catalog
				• Blanket Order
					• Standards
					• Customized

Trade Off Matrix

	Speed of Reaching Candidate	Breadth of Access	Cost	Quality of Candidates
Internet	**+**	**-**	**+**	**-**
Job Fair	**-**	**-**	**-**	**+**
Advertising	**+**	**+**	**-**	**-**

Key
+ = positive
- = negative
-/+ = neutral

Figure 11.1

The Process Compass idea had different values for different people. That value seemed to depend upon the depth of PH understanding that a person already had.

> *MIT Student* We talked about the compass and the directions for maybe ten minutes in the beginning of the meeting, and then for the rest of the meeting everyone referred to "northwest" or "south." As a metaphor it took hold quite quickly.

> *FinServ HR Planner* [PCC Consultant] really helped give a language to [MIT Researcher] and [MIT Director] about how to describe the handbook. There was a real logic to the compass that I found quite useful. We did not use it when we were working, but once she came up with it, everything seemed a lot clearer in retrospect.

Metaphors still need to be "embedded" to be useful. Those who were familiar with the Handbook now needed to replace the "lattice" metaphor with the "compass."

> *MIT Student* In the last meeting, we were talking and sort of conceptualizing what direction we could move in, and somebody said, "Well, that would be in the northwest direction." I thought, "Oh, okay." But you still had to have this mental image firmly in your head for that to make sense. To me, it wasn't that new. It was something that [MIT Director] always talked about as "the lattice," and it basically just represented the dimensions of the lattice.[1]

> *MIT Director* Using the Process Compass you could cycle around in almost any order. You could get a quick, even an intuitive, sense of what the deep structure was. Then immediately jump to, "Between these three things we thought of, which is best?" Then go back, and think a little more deeply about what the real essence was, identify some more alternatives, be more systematic in combinations, and keep cycling around at many different levels. It was very much like a brainstorming or creativity technique. In fact, one way of thinking about the whole thing is to say it is exactly a creativity technique applied to business processes.

The creation of the compass was an important step in the process of making the "miracle" of process redesign visible. It described the way researchers used the Process Handbook and provided a way for the PCC Consultant to communicate what had been learned to FinServ and PCC.

The Process Compass

The Process Compass provides a clear and concise way to communicate the PH approach to redesigning business processes. The compass uses innovation and the generation of novel ideas as the starting point for re-engineering. By shifting time and attention away from detailed analysis of existing processes ("as-is" analysis) to innovation, the focus shifts to generating new process-alternative ideas. Those new ideas then become the focus for evaluating process improvements over processes the organization is presently using.

The Process Compass implements the PH concepts, representing them with a graphic that is easy for people to conceptualize and use as the basis for choosing among alternative redesign activities. It proposes starting with existing processes and moving in one of the following directions to generate alternative views of a business process:

1) **North** is more abstract by aggregating activities into their parent activities.

2) **South** is more specific by decomposing activities into components.
   (The north-south dimension concerns the parts of an activity, and represents the *detail* at which a process is examined; what has traditionally been referred to as functional decomposition.)

3) **East** is more specific and examines alternative types of coordination mechanisms and activities.

4) **West** is more abstract and represents the process and its purpose.
   (The west-east dimension concerns types of an activity, and represents the *abstraction* at which information-flow-based and decision-making activities in a process are examined.)

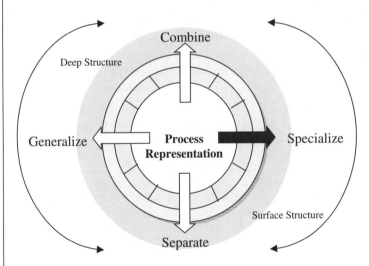

Figure 11.2
The Process Compass

The Process Compass helps people use the PH by suggesting that they move north and west to find the essential "deep structure" of a process, and move south and east to generate a palette of candidate surface structures from which a new process design can be selected. At any point in the redesign process, people can use the Process Compass to help them choose the "direction" of their examination based on their intended emphasis—generating alternatives or specifying optimal choices.

Conclusion: The Art and Science of Change

Most approaches to redesigning processes are very analytical. This analytical, or "scientific," approach can alienate and exclude the people who are being asked to change how they do their work. It is usually left to experts, with specialized knowledge for capturing and analyzing data, to propose how processes should be changed. This approach creates the impression that there is a "science of change." Yet, those close to the people and the implementation of re-engineering know that human-system change is not that precise, and there is an art to achieving expected outcome. The "art of change" recognizes that evoking greater efficiency and new behaviors is not as simple or causal as traditional re-engineering assumes.

The Process Handbook, while based on coordination theory and an analytical scientific approach, was used as a creativity tool that approached change as an art, or at least recognized the intuition and artist's sensibilities needed for effective change. Developments like the Process Compass and the Cafeteria Menu allowed people with less experience to become users of the Process Handbook. Perhaps the ultimate users of process change—those who are expected to change as their work and tasks are altered—could one day themselves redesign their own processes using the Process Handbook.

FinServ HR Planner The whole organization change process—how you get people enrolled and accepting of why a change needs to be made and how it's going to be executed—is very difficult. The complexity of that part of the process is always underestimated. Everyone knows it's the key thing, but it's still a challenge to do it.

MIT Director One of the important things we did in the course of this project was to get more explicit about the methodology for thinking about applying the PH to process change. For instance, there is a matter of art and judgment and intuition about where the likely payoffs are—where you should spend your biggest effort, and what kind of things you

Involving large numbers of people may ultimately result in much more successful redesigns—precisely because those who will be affected will be able to influence and "own" the new processes.

could just think cursorily about as opposed to exhaustively analyzing every single possibility. Just being more explicit about that was a big contribution.

The most important thing for us to do was to make it as easy as possible to communicate the concepts. To the degree that you can use simple terms and graphical devices as opposed to complex, esoteric, and academic sounding terms—you make it easier to communicate the ideas.

It makes less of an "in group/out group," and breaks the barrier to understanding and applying all of those things which are necessary if you want to have 2,000 people doing the design, as opposed to 2.

As with most tools, the Process Handbook can be used in many ways. The Process Handbook was so named deliberately, to avoid the connotation of the tool as an "expert"—but rather as a tool intended to complement people, not substitute them.

One of the opportunities foreseen in developing the concept of the Process Handbook was its role in designing future organizations. What will be the core work of future organizations, and what role will people have in those firms? Peter Drucker has for some time proposed that knowledge is "the only meaningful economic resource." This statement implies that the critical resource in any organization is its people, or "knowledge workers." Can the Process Handbook be used to engage these people in designing processes for applying their knowledge? The learning time required to understand and use the PH is significant. New approaches, like the Process Compass, seem essential to the MIT team's vision of how a Process Handbook could help create organizations of the 21st century.

Acknowledgments

This chapter is comprised of excerpts from Nina Kruschwitz and George Roth, Inventing Organizations of the 21st Century: Producing knowledge through collaboration, MIT 21st Century Initiative Working Paper #031, March 1999. The full text of the original working paper is available on the World Wide Web at http://ccs.mit.edu/papers/pdf/wp207and031.pdf.

Note

1. The "lattice of abstraction" which the MIT Director refers to is an extension of the "ladder of inference" described by Chris Argyris (1990, pp. 88–89) in two dimensions.

References

Argyris, Chris. 1990. *Overcoming Organizational Defenses*. Needham, Mass.: Allyn and Bacon.

Kruschwitz, Nina, and George Roth. 1999. Inventing Organizations of the 21st Century: Producing knowledge through collaboration, MIT 21st Century Initiative Working Paper #031, March.

Roth, George L. 1996. Learning Histories: Using documentation to assess and facilitate organizational learning. MIT Organizational Learning Center Working Paper.

Roth, George, and Art Kleiner. 1995. Learning about Organizational Learning—Creating a Learning History. MIT Organizational Learning Center Working Paper.

12 An Improvisational Model for Change Management: The Case of Groupware Technologies

Wanda J. Orlikowski and J. Debra Hofman

In her discussion of technology design, Suchman refers to two different approaches to open sea navigation—the European and the Trukese:

> The European navigator begins with a plan—a course—which he has charted according to certain universal principles, and he carries out his voyage by relating his every move to that plan. His effort throughout his voyage is directed to remaining "on course." If unexpected events occur, he must first alter the plan, then respond accordingly. The Trukese navigator begins with an objective rather than a plan. He sets off toward the objective and responds to conditions as they arise in an *ad hoc* fashion. He utilizes information provided by the wind, the waves, the tide and current, the fauna, the stars, the clouds, the sound of the water on the side of the boat, and he steers accordingly. His effort is directed to doing whatever is necessary to reach the objective.[1]

Like Suchman, we too find this contrast in approaches instructive and use it here to motivate our discussion of managing technological change. In particular, we suggest that how people think about managing change in organizations most often resembles the European approach to navigation. That is, they believe they need to start with a plan for the change, charted according to certain general organizational principles, and that they need to relate their actions to that plan, ensuring throughout that the change remains on course.

However, when we examine how change occurs in practice, we find that it much more closely resembles the voyage of the Trukese. That is, people end up responding to conditions as they arise, often in an *ad hoc* fashion, doing whatever is necessary to implement change. In a manner similar to Argyris and Schön's contrast between espoused theories and theories-in-use, we suggest that there is a discrepancy between how people think about technological change and how they implement it.[2] Moreover, we suggest that this discrepancy significantly contributes to the difficulties and challenges that contemporary organizations face as they attempt to introduce and effectively implement technology-based change.

Traditional ways of thinking about technological change have their roots in Lewin's three-stage change model of "unfreezing," "change," and "refreezing."[3] According to this model, the organization prepares for change, implements the change, and then strives to regain stability as soon as possible. Such a model, which treats change as an event to be managed during a specified period,[4] may have been appropriate for organizations that were relatively stable and bounded and whose functionality was sufficiently fixed to allow for detailed specification. Today, however, given more turbulent, flexible, and uncertain organizational and environmental conditions, such a model is becoming less appropriate—hence, the discrepancy.

This discrepancy is particularly pronounced when the technology being implemented is open-ended and customizable, as in the case of the new information technologies that are known as groupware.[5] Groupware technologies provide electronic networks that support communication, coordination, and collaboration through facilities such as information exchange, shared repositories, discussion forums, and messaging. Such technologies are typically designed with an open architecture that is adaptable by end users, allowing them to customize existing features and create new applications.[6] Rather than automating a predefined sequence of operations and transactions, these technologies tend to be general-purpose tools that are used in different ways across various organizational activities and contexts. Organizations need the experience of using groupware technologies in particular ways and in particular contexts to better understand how they may be most useful in practice. In such a technological context, the traditional change model is thus particularly discrepant.

The discrepancy is also evident when organizations use information technologies to attempt unprecedented, complex changes such as global integration or distributed knowledge management. A primary example is the attempt by many companies to redefine and integrate global value chain activities that were previously managed independently. While there is typically some understanding up-front of the magnitude of such a change, the depth and complexity of the interactions among these activities is fully understood only as the changes are implemented. For many organizations, such initiatives represent a new ball game, not only because they haven't played the game before but because most of the rules are still evolving. In a world with uncertain rules, the traditional model for devising and executing a game plan is very difficult to enact. And, as recent strategy research has suggested, planning in such circumstances is more effective as an ongoing endeavor, reflecting the changing, unfolding environments with which organizations interact.[7]

In many situations, therefore, predefining the technological changes to be implemented and accurately predicting their organizational impact is infeasible. Hence, the models of planned change that often inform implementation of new technologies are less than effective. We suggest that what would be more appropriate is a way of thinking about change that reflects the unprecedented, uncertain, open-ended, complex, and flexible nature of the technologies and organizational initiatives involved. Such a model would enable organizations to systematically absorb, respond to, and even leverage unexpected events, evolving technological capabilities, emerging practices, and unanticipated outcomes. Such a model for managing change would accommodate—indeed, encourage—ongoing and iterative experimentation, use, and learning. Such a model sees change management more as an ongoing improvisation than a staged event. Here we propose such an alternative model and describe a case study of groupware implementation in a customer support organization to illustrate the value of the model in practice. We conclude by discussing the conditions under which such an improvisational model may be a powerful way to manage the implementation and use of new technologies.

An Improvisational Model for Managing Change

The improvisational model for managing technological change is based on research we have done on the implementation and use of open-ended information technologies. The model rests on two major assumptions that differentiate it from traditional models of change: First, the changes associated with technology implementations constitute an ongoing process rather than an event with an end point after which the organization can expect to return to a reasonably steady state. Second, all the technological and organizational changes made during the ongoing process cannot, by definition, be anticipated ahead of time.

Given these assumptions, our improvisational change model recognizes three different types of change: anticipated, emergent, and opportunity-based. These change types are elaborations on Mintzberg's distinction between deliberate and emergent strategies.[8] Here, we distinguish between *anticipated* changes—changes that are planned ahead of time and occur as intended—and *emergent* changes—changes that arise spontaneously from local innovation and that are not originally anticipated or intended. An example of an anticipated change is the implementation of e-mail software that accomplishes its intended aim to facilitate increased, quicker communication among organizational members. An example of an emergent change is the use of the e-mail network as an informal grapevine disseminating rumors throughout an organization. This use of e-mail is typically not planned or anticipated when the network is implemented but often emerges tacitly over time in particular organizational contexts.

We further differentiate these two types of changes from *opportunity-based* changes—changes that are not anticipated ahead of time but are introduced purposefully and intentionally during the change process in response to an unexpected opportunity, event, or breakdown. For example, as companies gain experience with the World Wide Web, they are finding opportunities to apply and leverage its capabilities in ways that they did not anticipate or plan before the introduction of the

Figure 12.1
An Improvisational Model of Change Management over Time

Web. Both anticipated and opportunity-based changes involve deliberate action, in contrast to emergent changes that arise spontaneously and usually tacitly from people's practices with the technology over time.[9]

The three types of change build on each other iteratively over time (see figure 12.1). While there is no predefined sequence in which the different types of change occur, the deployment of new technology often entails an initial anticipated organizational change associated with the installation of the new hardware and software. Over time, however, use of the new technology will typically involve a series of opportunity-based, emergent, and further anticipated changes, the order of which cannot be determined in advance because the changes interact with each other in response to outcomes, events, and conditions arising through experimentation and use.

One way of thinking about this model of change is to consider the analogy of a jazz band. While members of a jazz band, unlike members of a symphony orchestra, do not decide in advance exactly what notes each is going to play, they do decide ahead of time what musical composition will form the basis of their performance. Once the performance begins, each player is free to explore and innovate, departing from the original composition. Yet the performance works because all members are playing within the same rhythmic structure and have a shared understanding of the rules of this musical genre. What they are doing is improvising—enacting an ongoing series of local innovations that embellish the original structure, respond to spontaneous departures and unexpected opportunities, and iterate and build on each other over time. Using our earlier terminology, the jazz musicians are engaging in anticipated, opportunity-based, and emergent action during the course of their performance to create an effective, creative response to local conditions.

Similarly, an improvisational model for managing technological change in organizations is not a predefined program of change charted by management ahead of time. Rather, it recognizes that technological change is an iterative series of different changes, many unpredictable at the start, that evolve from practical experience with the new technologies. Using such a model to manage change requires a set of processes and mechanisms to recognize the different types of change as they occur and to respond effectively to them. The illustrative case we present next suggests that when an organization is open to the capabilities offered by a new technological platform and willing to embrace an improvisational change model, it can achieve innovative organizational changes.

The Case of Zeta

Zeta is one of the top fifty software companies in the United States, with $100 million in revenues and about 1,000 employees. It produces and sells a range of powerful software products that provide capabilities such as decision support, executive information, and marketing analysis. Zeta is headquartered in the Midwest, with sales and client-service field offices throughout the world.

Specialists in the customer service department (CSD) at Zeta provide technical support via telephone to clients, consultants, value-added resellers, Zeta client-service representatives in the field, and other Zeta employees who use the products. This technical support is often quite complex. Specialists typically devote several hours of research to each problem, often searching through reference material, attempting to replicate the problem, and reviewing program source code. Some incidents require interaction with members of other departments such as quality assurance, documentation, and product development. The CSD employs approximately fifty specialists and is headed by a director and two managers.

In 1992, the CSD purchased the Lotus Notes groupware technology within which it developed a new incident tracking support system (ITSS) to help it log customer calls and keep a history of progress toward resolving customers' problems. Following a successful pilot of the new system, the CSD decided to commit to the Notes platform and to deploy ITSS throughout its department. The acquisition of new technology to facilitate customer call tracking was motivated by a number of factors. The existing tracking system was a homegrown system that had been developed when the department was much smaller and Zeta's product portfolio much narrower. The system was not real-time, entry of calls was haphazard, information accuracy was a concern, and performance was slow and unreliable. It provided little assistance for reusing prior solutions and no support for the management of resources in the department. The volume and complexity of calls to the CSD had increased in recent years due to the introduction of new products, the expanded sophistication of existing products, and the extended range of operating platforms supported. Such shifts had made replacement of the tracking system a priority, as the CSD managers were particularly concerned that the homegrown system provided no ability to track calls, query the status of particular calls, understand the workload, balance resources, identify issues and problems before they became crises, and obtain up-to-date and accurate documentation on work in progress and work completed. In addition, calls would occasionally be lost, as the slips of paper on which they were recorded would get mislaid or inadvertently thrown away.

Introduction of ITSS

The initial introduction of the new ITSS system was accompanied by anticipated changes in the nature of both the specialists' and managers' work. In contrast to the previous system, which had been designed to capture only a brief description of the problem and its final resolution, ITSS was designed to allow specialists to document every step they took in resolving a particular incident. That is, it was designed to enable the capture of the full history of an incident. As specialists began to use ITSS this way, the focus of their work shifted from primarily research—solving problems—to both research and documentation—solving problems and documenting work in progress.

The ITSS database quickly began to grow as each specialist documented his or her resolution process in detail. While documenting calls took time, it also saved time by providing a rich database of information that could be searched for potential resolutions. Moreover, this new database of information served as an unexpected, informal learning mechanism by giving the specialists exposure to a wide range of problems and solutions. As one specialist noted: "If it is quiet, I will check on my fellow colleagues to see what . . . kind of calls they get, so I might learn something from them . . . just in case something might ring a bell when someone else calls." At the same time, however, using the ITSS database as a sole source of information did pose some risk because there were no guarantees of the accuracy of the information. To minimize this risk, the specialists tacitly developed informal quality indicators to help them distinguish between reliable and unreliable data. For example, resolutions that were comprehensively documented, documented by certain individuals, or verified by the customer were considered reliable sources of information.

In addition to these changes in specialists' work, the CSD managers' use of the new system improved their ability to control the department's resources. Specialists' use of ITSS to document calls provided managers with detailed workload information, which was used to justify increased headcount and adjust work schedules and shift assignments on a dynamic and as-needed basis. ITSS also supplied managers with more accurate information on specialists' work process, for example, the particular steps followed to research and resolve a problem, the areas in which specialists sought advice or were stalled, and the quality of their resolutions. As managers began to rely on the ITSS data to evaluate specialists' performance, they expanded the criteria they used to do this evaluation. For example, quality of work-in-progress documentation was included as an explicit evaluation criterion, and documentation skills became a factor in the hiring process.

Structural Changes

As the CSD gained experience with and better understood the capabilities of the groupware technology, the managers introduced a change in the structure of the department to further leverage these capabilities. This change had not been planned prior to the implementation of ITSS, but the growing reliance on ITSS and an appreciation of the capabilities of the groupware technology created an opportunity for the CSD to redistribute call loads. In particular, the CSD established "first line" and "second line" support levels, with junior specialists assigned to the first line, and senior specialists to the second line. The CSD created partnerships between the less experienced junior specialists and the more experienced senior specialists. Frontline specialists now took all incoming calls, resolved as many as they could, and then electronically transferred calls to their second-line partners when they were overloaded or had especially difficult calls. In addition to handling calls transferred to them, senior specialists were expected to proactively monitor their frontline partners' progress on calls and to provide assistance.

While this partnership idea was conceptually sound, it regularly broke down in practice. Junior specialists were often reluctant to hand off calls, fearing that such transfers would reflect poorly on their competence or that they would be overloading their more senior partners. Senior specialists, in turn, were usually too busy resolving complex incidents to spend much time monitoring their junior partners' call status or progress. In response to this unanticipated breakdown in the partnership idea, the CSD managers introduced another opportunity-based structural change. They created a new intermediary role that was filled by a senior specialist who mediated between the first and second lines, regularly monitored junior specialists' call loads and work in progress, and dynamically reassigned calls as appropriate. The new intermediary role served as a buffer between the junior and senior specialists, facilitating the transfer of calls and relieving senior specialists of the responsibility to constantly monitor their frontline partners. With these structural changes, the CSD in effect changed the prior undifferentiated, fixed division of labor within the department to a dynamic distribution of work reflecting different levels of experience, various areas of expertise, and shifting workloads. In response to the new distribution of work, managers adjusted their evaluation criteria to reflect the changed responsibilities and roles within the CSD.

Another change that emerged over time was a shift in the nature of collaboration within the CSD from a primarily reactive mode to a more proactive one. Because all specialists now had access to the database of calls in the department, they began to go through each others' calls to see which ones they could help with, rather than waiting to be asked if they had a solution to a particular problem (which is how they had solicited and received help in the past). This shift from solicited to unsolicited assistance was facilitated by the capabilities of the groupware technology, the complex nature of the work, existing evaluation criteria that stressed teamwork, and the long-standing cooperative and collegial culture in the CSD. Several specialists commented: "Everyone realizes that we all have a certain piece of the puzzle. . . . I may have one critical piece, and Jenny may have another piece. . . . If we all work separately, we're never going to get the puzzle together. But by everybody working together, we have the entire puzzle"; "Here I don't care who grabs credit for my work. . . . This support department does well because we're a team, not because we're all individuals."[10] Managers responded to this shift in work practices by adjusting specialists' evaluation criteria to specifically consider unsolicited help. As one manager explained: "When I'm looking at incidents, I'll see what help other people have offered, and that does give me another indication of how well they're working as a team."

Later Changes

After approximately one year of using ITSS, the CSD implemented two further organizational changes around the groupware technology. Both had been anticipated in the initial planning for ITSS, although the exact timing for their implementation had been left unspecified. First, the ITSS application was installed in three overseas support offices, with copies of all the ITSS databases replicated regularly across the four support sites (United States, United Kingdom, Australia, and Europe). This provided all support specialists with a more extensive knowledge base on which to search for possibly helpful resolutions. The use of ITSS in all the support offices further allowed specialists to transfer calls across offices, essentially enacting a global support department within Zeta.

Second, the CSD initiated and funded the development of a number of bug-tracking systems that were implemented within groupware and deployed in Zeta's departments of product development, product management, and quality assurance.

These bug-tracking applications were linked into ITSS and enabled specialists to enter any bugs they had discovered in their problem resolution activities directly into the relevant product's bug-tracking system. Specialists could now also directly query the status of particular bugs and even change their priority if customer calls indicated that such an escalation was needed. Specialists in particular found this change invaluable. For the other departments, the link with ITSS allowed users such as product managers and developers to access the ITSS records and trace the particular incidents that had uncovered certain bugs or specific use problems. Only the developers had some reservations about the introduction of the bug-tracking application—reservations that were associated with the severe time constraints under which they worked to produce new releases of Zeta products.

In addition to the improved coordination and integration achieved with other departments and offices, the CSD also realized further opportunity-based innovations and emergent changes within its own practices. For example, as the number of incidents in ITSS grew, some senior specialists began to realize that they could use the information in the system to help train newcomers. By extracting certain records from the ITSS database, the specialists created a training database of sample problems with which newly hired specialists could work. Using the communication capabilities of the groupware technology, these senior specialists could monitor their trainees' progress through the sample database and intervene to educate when necessary. As one senior specialist noted: "We can kind of keep up to the minute on their progress. . . . If they're on the wrong track, we can intercept them and say, 'Go check this, go look at that.' But it's not like we have to actually sit with them and review things. It's sort of an on-line, interactive thing." As a result of this new training mechanism, the time for new specialists to begin taking customer calls was reduced from eight weeks to about five.

Another change was related to access control. An ongoing issue for the CSD was who (if anybody) outside the CSD should have access to the ITSS database with its customer call information and specialists' work-in-progress documentation. This issue was not anticipated before the acquisition of the technology. While the managers were worried about how to respond to the increasing demand for access to ITSS as the database became more valuable and word about its content spread throughout the company, they continued to handle each access request as it came up. Over time, they used a variety of control mechanisms ranging from giving limited access to some "trusted" individuals, generating summary reports of selected ITSS information for others, and refusing any access to still others. As one manager explained, only after some time did they realize that their various *ad hoc* responses to different access requests amounted to, in essence, a set of rules and procedures

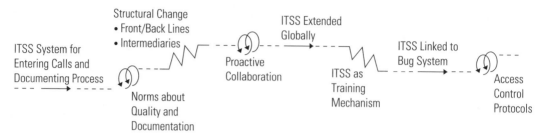

Figure 12.2
Zeta's Improvisational Management of Change over Time

about access control. By responding locally to various requests and situations over time, an implicit access control policy for the use of ITSS evolved and emerged.

Zeta's Change Model

Along with the introduction of the new technology and the development of the ITSS application, the CSD first implemented some planned organizational changes, expanding the specialists' work to include work-in-progress documentation and adjusting the managers' work to take advantage of the real-time access to workload information. (Figure 12.2 represents the change model around the groupware technology that Zeta followed in its CSD.) The changes were anticipated before introducing the new technology. As specialists and managers began to work in new ways with the technology, a number of changes emerged in practice, such as the specialists developing norms to determine the quality and value of prior resolutions, and managers paying attention to documentation skills in hiring and evaluation decisions.

Building on these anticipated and emergent changes, the CSD introduced a set of opportunity-based changes, creating junior-senior specialist partnerships to take advantage of the shared database and communication capabilities of the technology and then adding the new intermediary role in response to the unexpected problems with partnership and work reassignment. The CSD did not anticipate these changes at the start, nor did the changes emerge spontaneously in working with the new technology. Rather, the CSD conceived of and implemented the changes *in situ* and in response to the opportunities and issues that arose as it gained experience and better understood the new technology and their particular use of it. This change process around the groupware technology continued through the second year at Zeta when some anticipated organizational changes were followed by both emergent and opportunity-based changes associated with unfolding events and the learn-ing and experience gained by using the new technology in practice.

Overall, what we see here is an iterative and ongoing series of anticipated, emer-gent, and opportunity-based changes that allowed Zeta to learn from practical experience, respond to unexpected outcomes and capabilities, and adapt both the technology and the organization as appropriate. In effect, Zeta's change model cycles through anticipated, emergent, and opportunity-based organizational changes over time. It is a change model that explicitly recognizes the inevitability, legitimacy, and value of ongoing learning and change in practice.

Enabling Conditions

Clearly, there were certain aspects of the Zeta organization that enabled it to effec-tively adopt an improvisational change model to implement and use the groupware technology. Our research at Zeta and other companies suggests that at least two sets of enabling conditions are critical: aligning key dimensions of the change process and dedicating resources to provide ongoing support for the change process. We consider each in turn.

Aligning Key Change Dimensions

An important influence on the effectiveness of any change process is the interde-pendent relationship among three dimensions: the technology, the organizational context (including culture, structure, roles, and responsibilities), and the change model used to manage change (see figure 12.3). Ideally, the interaction among these three dimensions is compatible or, at a minimum, not in opposition.

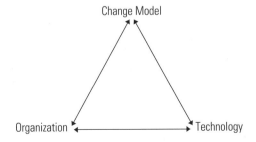

Figure 12.3
Aligning the Change Model, the Technology, and the Organization

First, consider the relation of the change model and the technology being implemented. When the technology has been designed to operate like a "black box," allowing little adaptation by users, an improvisational approach may not be more effective than the traditional approach to technology implementation. Similarly, when the technology is well established and its impacts are reasonably well understood, a traditional planned change approach may be effective. However, when the technology being implemented is new and unprecedented and, additionally, is open-ended and customizable, an improvisational model providing the flexibility for organizations to adapt and learn through use becomes more appropriate. Such is the case, we believe, with the groupware technologies available today.

Second, the relation of the change model to organizational context is also relevant. A flexible change model, while likely to be problematic in a rigid, control-oriented, or bureaucratic culture, is well suited to an informal, cooperative culture such as the one at the CSD. In another study, we examined the MidCo organization's successful adoption and implementation of CASE (computer-aided software engineering) tools within its information systems organization.[11] While MidCo, a multinational chemical products company with revenues of more than $1.5 billion, was a relatively traditional organization in many ways, key aspects of its culture— a commitment to total quality management, a focus on organizational learning and employee empowerment, as well as a long-term outlook—were particularly compatible with the improvisational model it used to manage ongoing organizational changes around the new software development technology.

Finally, there is the important relationship between the technology and the organizational context. At Zeta, the CSD's cooperative, team-oriented culture was compatible with the collaborative nature of the new groupware technology. Indeed, the CSD's existing culture allowed it to take advantage of the opportunity for improved collaboration that the groupware technology afforded. Moreover, when existing roles, responsibilities, and evaluation criteria became less salient, the CSD managers expanded or adjusted them to reflect new uses of the technology.

Compare these change efforts to those of Alpha, a professional services firm that introduced the Notes groupware technology to leverage knowledge sharing and to coordinate distributed activities.[12] While the physical deployment of groupware grew very rapidly, anticipated benefits were realized much more slowly. Key to the reluctance to use groupware for knowledge sharing was a perceived incompatibility between the collaborative nature of the technology and the individualistic and competitive nature of the organization. As in many professional services firms, Alpha rewarded individual rather than team performance and promoted employees based on "up or out" evaluation criteria. In such an environment, knowledge sharing via a global Notes network was seen to threaten status, distinctive competence, and power. In contrast to Zeta, managers at Alpha did not adjust policies, roles, incentives, and evaluation criteria to better align their organization with the intended use and capabilities of the technology they had invested in.

Dedicating Resources for Ongoing Support

An ongoing change process requires dedicated support over time to adapt both the organization and the technology to changing organizational conditions, use practices, and technological capabilities. Opportunity-based change, in particular, depends on the ability of the organization to notice and recognize opportunities, issues, breakdowns, and unexpected outcomes as they arise. This requires attention on the part of appropriate individuals in the organization to track technology use over time and to initiate organizational and technological adjustments that will mitigate or take advantage of the identified problems and opportunities.

At Zeta, the managers and technologists played this role, incorporating it into their other responsibilities. So, for example, the managers adjusted the structure of their department by introducing first-line/second-line partnerships to facilitate a dynamic division of labor and then made further adaptations by introducing an intermediary role to overcome some unanticipated difficulties associated with the initial change. Similarly, the technologists working with the CSD incorporated enhancements to the ITSS system as they realized ways to improve ease of use and access time. The CSD's commitment to noticing and responding to appropriate changes did not end after the implementation of the technology. The managers clearly realized that the change process they had embarked on with the use of groupware was ongoing, as one manager noted: "We've had ITSS for two years. I'm surprised that the enthusiasm hasn't gone away. . . . I think it's because it's been changed on a regular basis. . . . Knowing that [the changes are going to get implemented] keeps you wanting to think about it and keep going."

Ongoing change in the use of groupware technology also requires ongoing adjustments to the technology itself as users learn and gain experience with the new technology's capabilities over time. Without dedicated technology support to implement these adaptations and innovations, the continued experimentation and learning in use central to an improvisational change model may be stalled or thwarted. At Zeta, a dedicated technology group supported the CSD's use of groupware and ITSS. Initially consisting of one developer, this group grew over time as groupware use expanded. After two years, the group included four full-time technologists who provided technology support for the various systems that had been deployed within Zeta via the Notes platform. The group also maintained strong ties with all its users through regular meetings and communications. This dedicated, ongoing technical support ensured that the technology would continue to be updated, adjusted, and expanded as appropriate.

The value of ongoing support to enable ongoing organizational and technological change was similarly important in another organization we studied, the R&D division of a large Japanese manufacturing firm.[13] A newly formed product development team within the R&D division installed a groupware technology, the Usenet news system (a computer conferencing system). Similar to the CSD at Zeta, the team's use of this new technology also iterated among anticipated, emergent, and opportunity-based changes over time. Here, a small group of users who had previously used the groupware technology took on the responsibility to manage and support its ongoing use for themselves and their colleagues. They tracked technology usage and project events as they unfolded, responded as appropriate with adjustments to communication policies and technology functionality, and proactively made changes to the team's use of the conferencing system to leverage opportunities as they arose.

Conclusion

Global, responsive, team-based, networked—these are the watchwords for organizations of the nineties. As managers redesign and reinvent organizations in a new image, many are turning to information technologies to enable more flexible processes, greater knowledge sharing, and global integration. At the same time, effectively implementing the organizational changes associated with these technologies remains difficult in a turbulent, complex, and uncertain environment. We believe that a significant factor contributing to these challenges is the growing discrepancy between the way people think about technological change and the way they actually implement it.

We propose that people's assumptions about technology-based change and the way it is supposed to happen are based on models that are no longer appropriate. Traditional models for managing technology-based change treat change as a sequential series of predefined steps that are bounded within a specified time. With these models as a guide, it makes sense to define—as the European navigator does—a plan of action in advance of the change and track events against the plan, striving throughout the change to remain on track. Deviations from the intended course—the anticipated versus the actual—then require explanation, the subtle (and sometimes not-so-subtle) implication being that there has been some failure, some inadequacy in planning, that has led to this deviation. Indeed, many organizational mechanisms such as budgeting and resource planning are based on these notions. The problem is that change as it actually occurs today more closely resembles the voyage of the Trukese navigator, and the models and mechanisms most commonly used to think about and manage change do not effectively support this experience of change.

We have offered here an improvisational change model as a different way of thinking about managing the introduction and ongoing use of information technologies to support the more flexible, complex, and integrated structures and processes demanded in organizations today. In contrast to traditional models of technological change, this improvisational model recognizes that change is typically an ongoing process made up of opportunities and challenges that are not necessarily predictable at the start. It defines a process that iterates among three types of change—anticipated, emergent, and opportunity-based—and that allows the organization to experiment and learn as it uses the technology over time. Most importantly, it offers a systematic approach with which to understand and better manage the realities of technology-based change in today's organizations.

Because such a model requires a tolerance for flexibility and uncertainty, adopting it implies that managers relinquish what is often an implicit paradigm of "command and control."[14] An improvisational model, however, is not anarchy, and neither is it a matter of "muddling through." We are not implying that planning is unnecessary or should be abandoned. We are suggesting, instead, that a plan is a guide rather than a blueprint and that deviations from the plan, rather than being seen as a symptom of failure, are to be expected and actively managed.[15]

Rather than predefining each step and then controlling events to fit the plan, management creates an environment that facilitates improvisation. In such an environment, management provides, supports, and nurtures the expectations, norms, and resources that guide the ongoing change process. Malone refers to such a style of managing as "cultivation."[16] Consider again the jazz band. While each band member is free to improvise during the performance, the result is typically not discordant. Rather, it is harmonious because each player operates within an overall framework, conforms to a shared set of values and norms, and has access to a known repertoire of rules and resources. Similarly, while many changes at Zeta's CSD were not planned, they were compatible with the overall objectives and intentions of the department's members, their shared norms and team orientation, and the designs and capabilities of the technology.

Effectively executing an improvisational change model also requires aligning the technology and the organizational context with the change model. Such alignment does not happen automatically. It requires explicit, ongoing examination and adjustment, where and when necessary, of the technology and the organization. As such, mechanisms and resources allocated to ongoing support of the change process are critical. Tracking and noticing events and issues as they unfold is a responsibility that appropriate members of the organization need to own. Along with the responsibility, these organizational members require the authority, credibility, influence, and resources to implement the ongoing changes. Creating the environment; aligning the technology, context, and change model; and distributing the appropriate responsibility and resources are critically important in the effective use of an improvisational model, particularly as they represent a significant (and therefore challenging) departure from the standard practice in effect in many organizations.

An improvisational model of change, however, does not apply to all situations. As we have noted, it is most appropriate for open-ended, customizable technologies or for complex, unprecedented change. In addition, as one reviewer noted, "Jazz is not everyone's 'cup of tea.' . . . Some people are incapable of playing jazz, much less able to listen to what they consider to be 'noise.'" We noted above that some cultures do not support experimentation and learning. As a result, they are probably not receptive to an improvisational model and are less likely to succeed with it. As these organizations attempt to implement new organizational forms, however, they too may find an improvisational model to be a particularly valuable approach to managing technological change in the twenty-first century.

Acknowledgments

This chapter is reprinted with permission from *Sloan Management Review* 38, no. 2 (Winter 1997): 11–22. The authors would like to thank the editor and reviewers for their helpful comments on an earlier version of this manuscript. We gratefully appreciate the research support of MIT's Center for Coordination Science and Center for Information Systems Research.

Notes

1. G. Berreman (1966) cited in Suchman (1987).

2. Argyris and Schön 1978.

3. Lewin 1952, Kwon and Zmud 1987.

4. Pettigrew 1985.

5. Not all groupware technologies are flexible and customizable (e.g., fixed-function e-mail systems). We are interested here only in those that are (e.g., Lotus Notes).

6. DeJean and DeJean 1991, Malone, Lai, and Fry 1992.

7. Mintzberg 1994, McGrath and MacMillan 1995.

8. Mintzberg 1987.

9. Orlikowski 1996.

10. Orlikowski 1995.

11. Gallivan, Hofman, and Orlikowski 1994.

12. Orlikowski 1992.

13. Orlikowski, Yates, Okamura, and Fujimoto 1995.

14. Zuboff 1988.

15. Suchman 1987.

16. Informal conversation with T.W. Malone, 1996.

References

Argyris, C., and D. A. Schön. 1978. *Organizational Learning*. Reading, Mass.: Addison-Wesley.

DeJean, D., and S. B. DeJean. 1991. *Lotus Notes at Work*. New York: Lotus Books.

Gallivan, M. J., J. D. Hofman, and W. J. Orlikowski. 1994. Implementing Radical Change: Gradual Versus Rapid Pace. Proceedings of the Fifteenth International Conference on Information Systems. Vancouver, December, 14–17.

Kwon, T. K., and R. W. Zmud. 1987. Unifying the Fragmented Models of Information Systems Implementation. In *Critical Issues in Information Systems Research*, edited by R. J. Boland Jr. and R. A. Hirschheim. New York: John Wiley.

Lewin, K. 1952. Group Decision and Social Change. In *Readings in Social Psychology*, edited by E. Newcombe and R. Harley. New York: Henry Holt.

Malone, T. W., K. Y. Lai, and C. Fry. 1992. Experiments with OVAL: A Radically Tailorable Tool for Cooperative Work. Proceedings of the Third Conference on Computer-Supported Cooperative Work. Toronto, November.

Malone, T. W. 1996. Informal conversation with author.

McGrath, R. G., and I. C. MacMillan. 1995. Discovery-Driven Planning. *Harvard Business Review* 73 (July–August): 44–54.

Mintzberg, H. 1987. Crafting Strategy. *Harvard Business Review* 65 (July–August): 66–75.

Mintzberg, H. 1994. The Fall and Rise of Strategic Planning. *Harvard Business Review* 73 (January–February): 107–114.

Orlikowski, W. J. 1992. Learning from Notes: Organizational Issues in Groupware Implementation. Proceedings of the Third Conference on Computer-Supported Cooperative Work. Toronto, November.

Orlikowski, W. J. 1995. Evolving with Notes: Organizational Change around Groupware Technology. MIT Sloan School of Management working paper 3823.

Orlikowski, W. J., J. Yates, K. Okamura, and M. Fujimoto. 1995. Shaping Electronic Communication: The Metastructuring of Technology in Use. *Organization Science* 6 (July–August): 423–444.

Orlikowski, W. J. 1996. Improvising Organizational Transformation over Time: A Situated Change Perspective. *Information Systems Research* 7 (March): 63–92.

Pettigrew, A. M. 1985. *The Awakening Giant*. Oxford: Blackwell Publishers.

Suchman, L. 1987. *Plans and Situated Actions: The Problem of Human Machine Communication*. Cambridge: Cambridge University Press.

Zuboff, S. 1988. *In the Age of the Smart Machine*. New York: Basic Books.

13 The Comparative Advantage of X-Teams

Deborah Ancona, Henrik Bresman, and Katrin Kaeufer

The current environment demands a new brand of team—one that emphasizes outreach to stakeholders and adapts easily to flatter organizational structures, changing information, and increasing complexity. Often teams that seem to be doing everything right—establishing clear roles and responsibilities, building trust among members, defining goals—nevertheless see their projects fail or get axed. We know one such team that had a highly promising product. But because team members failed to get buy-in from division managers, they saw their project starve for lack of resources. Another group worked well as a team but didn't gather important competitive information; its product was obsolete before launch.

Why do bad things happen to good teams? Our research suggests that they are too inwardly focused and lacking in flexibility. Successful teams emphasize outreach to stakeholders both inside and outside their companies. Their entrepreneurial focus helps them respond more nimbly than traditional teams to the rapidly changing characteristics of work, technology and customer demands.

These new, externally oriented, adaptive teams, which we call *X-teams*, are seeing positive results across a wide variety of functions and industries. One such team in the oil business has done an exceptional job of disseminating an innovative method of oil exploration throughout the organization. Sales teams have brought in more revenue. Drug-development teams have been more adept at getting external technology into their companies. Product-development teams have been more innovative—and have been more often on time and on budget.

The current environment—with its flatter organizational structures, interdependence of tasks and teams, constantly revised information, and increasing complexity—requires a networked approach. X-teams have emerged to meet that need. In some cases, they appear spontaneously. In other cases, forward-looking companies have established specific organizational incentives to support X-teams and their high performance levels.

Our studies all support the notion that the rules handed down by best-selling books on high-performing teams need to be revised. (See "About the Research.") Teams that succeed today don't merely work well around a conference table or create team spirit. In fact, too much focus inside the team can be fatal. Instead, teams must be able to adapt to the new competitive landscape, as X-teams do. X-teams manage across boundaries—lobbying for resources, connecting to new change initiatives, seeking up-to-date information, and linking to other groups inside and outside the company. Research shows that X-teams often outperform their traditional counterparts.[1]

About the Research

Our research occurred over many years and with many types of teams and industries. The bottom line is that certain team characteristics coincided with better performance. We call the high-performing teams X-teams.

When we asked some managers with responsibility for consulting teams to rate teams with X-team characteristics, they ranked them high—1 or 2 on a 5-point scale, with 1 being the best performer. But they ranked more-traditional teams 3, 4, or 5.* In another study, 37 percent of X-team customers said that the teams were meeting customer needs better than in the past, compared with 23 percent of more-traditional teams' customers.[†]

Teams in two companies we call Zeus and Pharma Inc. are of particular interest.

Zeus. Swallow is a product-development team at Zeus, a multidivisional company developing proprietary hardware and software products. It is especially illustrative of X-team activity. Zeus has since been acquired by one of the world's largest computer makers.

Pharma Inc. Pharma is a large international pharmaceuticals enterprise. At the time of our research, it had experienced a string of mergers and acquisitions that resulted in drugs being developed by different organizational units, each of which had a distinctly different management approach. The unit with the best-performing teams illustrates organizational characteristics conducive to X-team behavior.

Table 13.1
Studies that Served as Basis for X-teams Research

Type of Company	Number of Teams	Length of Time Studied	Methodology
One telecommunications company	100	4 months	Interviews, survey
One educational-consulting company	5	1 year	Interviews, surveys, logs, observation
Five high-tech, product-development companies	45	2 years	Interviews, surveys, logs, observation
One multinational, integrated oil company	2	Life of the teams	Project reports
One computer manufacturer	5	2 years	Interviews, observation
One large pharmaceuticals company, 3 units	12	2 years	Interviews, survey, observation, project reports

* Ancona 1990.
[†] For the product-development teams, using X-team characteristics as predictors of adherence to budget and schedule—and innovation, as rated by managers—yielded statistically significant results at greater than .01.

Five Components That Make X-Teams Successful

X-teams are set apart from traditional teams by five hallmarks: external activity, extensive ties, expandable structures, flexible membership, and internal mechanisms for execution. (See figure 13.1.)

External Activity

The first hallmark of the X-team is members' external activity.[2] Members manage across boundaries, reaching into the political, informational and task-specific structures around them. In some cases, the team leader takes on the outreach; in other cases, it is shared by everyone. High levels of external activity are key, but effectiveness depends on knowing when to use the particular kind called for: ambassadorship, scouting, or task coordination.

It doesn't matter how technically competent a team is if the most relevant competency is the ability to lobby for resources with top management. And even resources mean little without an ability to reach outsiders who have the knowledge and information to help team members apply the resources effectively. Thus at any given time, any X-team member may be conducting one or more of the three external activities.

Ambassadorial Activity   Ambassadorial activity is aimed at managing upward— that is, marketing the project and the team to the company power structure, maintaining the team's reputation, lobbying for resources, and keeping track of allies and competitors. Ambassadorial activity helps the team link its work to key strategic initiatives; and it alerts team members to shifting organizational strategies and political upheaval so that potential threats can be identified and the damage limited.

For example, the leader of what we call the Swallow team wanted to manufacture a new computer using a revolutionary design. The company's operating committee, however, wanted only a product upgrade. The team leader worked with a key decision maker on the operating committee to portray the benefits of the product to the organization—and eventually got permission for the design. He continued to provide updates on the team's progress, while keeping tabs on the committee's key resource-allocation decisions.

Scouting   Scouting activity helps a team gather information located throughout the company and the industry. It involves lateral and downward searches through the organization to understand who has knowledge and expertise. It also means investigating markets, new technologies, and competitor activities. Team members in our

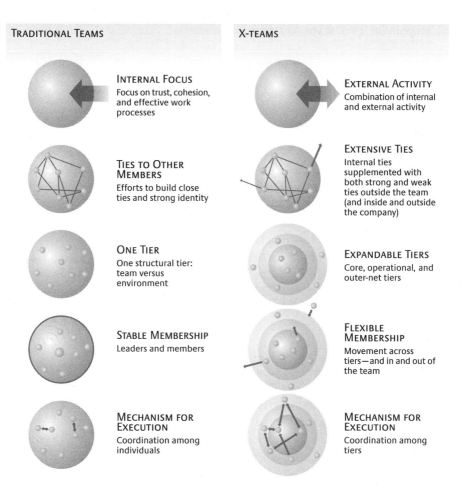

Figure 13.1
X-Teams Versus Traditional Teams: Five Components

studies used many different modes of scouting, from the ambitious and expensive (hiring consultants) to the quick and cheap (having a cup of coffee with an old college professor or spending an hour surfing the Internet).

Effective teams monitor how much information they need—for some, extensive scouting early on to get the lay of the land is all that's needed. For others, scouting continues throughout the life of the team. In particular, teams working with technologies created by outsiders can never relax their scouting activities.

Task Coordination Task-coordinator activity is much more focused than scouting. It's for managing the lateral connections across functions and the interdependencies with other units. Team members negotiate with other groups, trade their services and get feedback on how well their work meets expectations. Task-coordinator activity involves cajoling and pushing other groups to follow through on commitments so that the team can meet its deadlines and keep work flowing. When the Swallow team needed to check some new components quickly and learned that the testing machine was booked, team members explored swapping times with another team, using the machine at night, or using machines elsewhere—whatever it took to keep the work on track.

Extensive Ties

In order to engage in such external activity, team members need to have extensive ties with outsiders. Ties that academic researchers call *weak ties* are good for certain purposes—for example, when teams need to round up handy knowledge and expertise within the company. One team we studied gave a senior position to a new hire straight out of graduate school because of his ties to important experts at prestigious academic institutions. The ties were weak but extensive and contributed immensely to the success of the team's project.

Strong ties, however, facilitate higher levels of cooperation and the transfer of complex knowledge. Strong ties are most likely to be forged when relationships are critical to both sides and built over long periods of time.[3] In the case of Swallow, the team leader's prior relationship with the operating-committee member helped snare funding for the revolutionary computer design. And the three team members from manufacturing had ties that smoothed the transition from design to production.

Expandable Tiers

But how to structure a large, complex team? How to combine the identity and separateness of a team with the dense ties and external interactions needed to accomplish today's work? Our research shows that X-teams operate through three distinct tiers that create differentiated types of team membership—the core tier, operational tier, and outer-net tier—and that members may perform duties within more than one tier.

Core Members   The core of the X-team is often, but not always, present at the start of the team. Core members carry the team's history and identity. While simultaneously coordinating the multiple parts of the team, they create the team strategy and make key decisions. They understand why early decisions were made and can offer a rationale for current decisions and structures. The core is not a management level, however. Core members frequently work beside other members of equal or higher rank, and serve on other X-teams as operational or outer-net members.

The first core member of the Swallow team was the leader; then two senior engineers joined and helped to create the original product design and to choose more members. The core members were committed to the revolutionary computer concept and accepted its risks. They understood how quickly they had to act in order to make an impact on the market. The core members chose more engineers for the team, helped coordinate the work across subgroups, and kept in touch with the company's operating committee and other groups. They decided when to get feedback from outsiders, and they set up a process to make the critical decisions about how compatible with industry standards to make the design. They organized team social events—and when members had to work long hours to make a deadline, they even brought in beds.

Having multiple people in the core helps keep the team going when one or two core members leave, and it allows a core member who gets involved with operational work to hand off core tasks. Teams that lose all their core members at once take many months to get back on track.

Operational Members   The team's operational members do the ongoing work. Whether that's designing a computer, creating an academic course, or deciding where to drill for oil, the operational members get the job done. They often are tightly connected to one another and to the core (and may include some core members). In the Swallow group, 15 engineers were brought into the operational layer to work on the preliminary design. They made key technical decisions, but each focused on one part of the design and left oversight of the whole to the core.

Outer-Net Members   Outer-net members often join the team to handle some task that is separable from ongoing work. They may be part-time or part-cycle members, tied barely at all to one another but strongly to the operational or core members. Outer-net members bring specialized expertise, and different individuals may participate in the outer net as the task of the team changes.

For example, when the Swallow team wanted to ensure its initial design made sense to others, it brought in outer-net people from other parts of R&D. For two weeks, the enlarged team met to discuss the design, its potential problems, ideas for changes, and solutions for problems that operational members had identified. Then those new members left. Meanwhile, designated members of the core group met weekly with different outer-net members—people from purchasing, diagnostics, and marketing—for information sharing, feedback, and smoothing the flow of work across groups. Some X-teams' outer nets also include people from other companies.

The three-tier structure is currently in use at a small, entrepreneurial startup we know—except that the employees there say "pigs," "chickens," and "cows" to refer to core, operational, and outer-net team members. Think about a bacon-and-eggs breakfast. The pig is committed (he's given his life), the chicken is involved, and the cow provides milk that enhances the meal. The startup's terms are handy for discussing roles and responsibilities. A person might say, "You don't need to do that; you're only a chicken" or "We need this cow to graze here for at least two weeks."

Flexible Membership

X-team membership is fluid.[4] People may move in and out of the team during its life or move across layers. In a product-development team similar to Swallow, there was a manufacturing member who shifted from outer-net member to operational member to core member. At first, he was an adviser about components; next he worked on the actual product; then he organized the whole team when it needed to move the product into manufacturing. He became team leader and managed the transition of team members back into engineering as more manufacturing members were brought in.

Mechanisms for Execution

An increasing focus on the external context does not mean that the internal team processes are unimportant. In fact, traditional coordination mechanisms such as clear roles and goals may be even more important when team members are communicating externally, membership is changing, and there are different versions of membership. The trick is to avoid getting so internally focused and tied to other team members that external outreach is ignored. X-teams find three different coordination mechanisms especially useful: integrative meetings, transparent decision making, and scheduling tools such as shared timelines.

First, through integrative meetings, team members share the external information each has obtained. That helps keep everyone informed and increases the information's value by making it widely available. The meetings ensure that decisions are based on real-time data from combinations of task-coordinator, scouting, and ambassadorial activity.

Second, transparent decision making, which keeps people informed about the reasons behind choices, is good for nudging everyone in the same direction and for maintaining motivation. Even when team members are frustrated that a component they have worked on has been dropped, they appreciate knowing about the change and why it has been made.

Finally, measures such as clearly communicated but flexible deadlines allow members to pace themselves and to coordinate work with others. The just-in-time flexibility allows for deadline shifts and adjustment. If external circumstances change, then work changes and new deadlines are established.

Putting the Pieces Together

X-team components form a self-reinforcing system. To engage in high levels of external activity, team members bring to the table outside ties forged in past professional experience. To be responsive to new information and new coordination needs, X-teams have flexible membership and a structure featuring multiple tiers and roles. To handle information and multiple activities, they have coordination mechanisms and a strong core. The five components cannot work in isolation. They complement one another. Although small or new teams may not have all five components, fully developed X-teams usually do.

Supporting X-Teams

The more dependent a team is on knowledge and resources in its external environment, the more critical is the organizational context. Companies that want high-performing X-teams can create a supportive organizational context—with three-tier structures mandated for teams, explicit decision rules, accessible information, and a learning culture. Within a company, it's generally the organizational unit that sets those parameters, provides resources, and lays down rules. (See figure 13.2.)

A large pharmaceuticals company that we call Pharma Inc. illustrates the importance of such support. One of the authors was asked to investigate a dramatic performance variation among drug-development teams that were working on molecules from external sources. (Such projects are known as in-licensing projects.) A performance assessment showed that the teams of one unit were doing well, the teams of a second unit showed varying results, and the teams of a third unit were

STAFFING THE TEAM

- Before staffing the team, understand the external context
- Change team members as needed
- Treat a team member's connections as a key competency

BUILDING THE TEAM

- Map the external domain, including key stakeholders
- Create mechanisms for internal *and* external communication
- Set team goals, knowing what external constituencies want

CREATE A SUPPORTIVE ORGANIZATIONAL ENVIRONMENT

- Design and support a three-tier team structure
- Formulate decision rules for an unambiguous yet flexible process
- Maintain a rich information infrastructure
- Establish a learning culture

X-TEAM

Figure 13.2
Creating an X-Team

doing poorly. To probe the differences, we picked a chronological sequence of three teams at the best-performing site (the Alpha site) and three teams at the worst-performing site (the Omega site) for a careful study.

The story that emerged seemed almost implausibly black-and-white: All the central steps the three Alpha teams took seemed to contribute to positive performance, whereas the opposite was true for the Omega teams. It appeared that despite fluctuating external circumstances, the Omega teams were sticking to a traditional approach that had served them well enough when they worked on internally developed molecules. The Alpha teams, however, were adapting to the changing environment by using an X-team approach, although they didn't call it that. In the wake of the molecular biology revolution, which has led to increased use of in-licensed molecules, they saw the importance of external activity and extensive ties, and they adapted.

Three-Tier Structure

Organizational structure has a profound effect on team behavior. All Alpha-unit teams used a mandated three-tier structure that gave core members oversight of the activities of operational and outer-net team members. Importantly, the roles were not a reflection of organizational hierarchy. Often a core-team member was junior in the organizational structure to an outer-net member.

Having the core team tied to the outer net was particularly helpful when much external technical knowledge was needed quickly. With links already established, a core member could get information from an outer-net member at short notice. The brief time commitment for serving on the outer net gave X-teams access to some of the company's most sought-after and overbooked functional experts.

The Omega-unit teams, however, used a traditional one-tier structure. In X-team terminology, the Omega teams had only core members. Although that worked well for coordination, it hampered team members' ability to adapt to changing external demands.

Explicit Decision Rules

X-teams favor decision rules that adapt to new circumstances. The Alpha unit's X-teams, like most product-development teams, used traditional flow charts, but they constantly updated them. Also, they complemented flow charts with decision rules that allowed the charts to become evolving tools rather than constraints. One such rule was that, all things being equal, the search for solid information was more important than speed. It wasn't that the teams tolerated slackers. In fact, at times speed had to take precedence over information, but it was the team leader's responsibility to identify when that should occur.

Another rule mandated that whenever important expertise was not available in the time allotted, a team member would be free to bring in additional outer-net members. Such rules allowed for flexibility but spared team members any ambiguity about what to do at important crossroads. Furthermore, the rules gave them the confidence to act on their own and to raise issues needing discussion. For example, it was never wrong for a team member to suggest that a process be stopped because of a lack of important information in that member's area. Even if the team overruled the request, speaking up on the basis of an explicit decision rule was definitely appropriate.

The Omega unit's teams, by contrast, used process flow charts quite rigidly and without complementary decision rules. Team members had to stick to the planned process and were allowed little latitude for tweaking the process even when they saw the need. There was no mechanism for making adjustments.

Accessible Information

Access to valid, up-to-date information is always critical, but when knowledge is widely dispersed, the information infrastructure becomes even more important. The Alpha unit had processes that supported teams' need for accessible data. After every project, a report was written detailing important issues and the lessons learned. The store of reports increased over time. In addition, the Alpha unit maintained a "know-who" database, which provided names of experts in various fields and explained the unit's historical relationship with those experts.

Unfortunately, at Omega, project reports were written only occasionally and contained mainly the results of internal lab tests. And Omega did not have a know-who database at all.

A Learning Culture

A useful information infrastructure cannot be established instantly. It has to be nurtured. That's why Alpha insisted on project reports whether or not the project was considered a success and regardless of time pressures on team members. Alpha also saw to it that past team members conferred with ongoing teams.

Strong recognition from top management at the Alpha unit reinforced the information infrastructure. The relentlessly communicated learning culture not only generated positive performance for any given team, but helped make every team perform better than the previous one.

The Omega unit had no such practices. As a consequence, new teams in that unit generally had to reinvent the wheel.

Is the X-Team for Your Company?

X-teams are particularly valuable in today's world (many companies already deploy X-teams without calling them that), but they are not for every situation. Their very nature as tools for responding to change makes them hard to manage. The membership of the X-team, the size of the team, the goals, and so on keep fluctuating.

In a traditional team, coordination is mostly internal to the team. It involves a clear task and the interaction of a limited number of members. In an X-team, coordination requirements are multiplied severalfold. The X-team's internal co-ordination involves more members, more information, and more diversity. On top of that are the external-coordination concerns. Executives considering X-teams must be sure the potential benefits are great enough for them to justify the extra challenges.

The IDEO product-development consulting firm thinks they are. IDEO, based in Palo Alto, Calif., is an example of a company that depends on the innovativeness and agility of its teams. During brainstorming, experts from multiple industries serve as outer-net members soliciting unique information. Team members go forth as "anthropologists" to observe how customers use their products and how the products might be improved. Employees at IDEO also have been busy creating a knowledge-distribution system they call Tool Box, which uses lively demonstrations to communicate learned knowledge and expertise.[5]

We recommend using an X-team when one or more of three conditions hold true. X-teams are appropriate, first, when organizational structures are flat, spread-out systems with numerous alliances rather than multilevel, centralized hierarchies. Flat organizations force teams to become more entrepreneurial in getting resources and in seeking and maintaining buy-in from stakeholders.[6]

Second, X-teams are advised when teams are dependent on information that is complex, externally dispersed, and rapidly changing. In such cases, it is critical to base decisions on real-time data.[7]

Third, use X-teams when a team's task is interwoven with tasks undertaken outside the team. For example, if every new product that a team works on is part of a family of products that others are working on too, teams need to coordinate their activities with what is going on around them.[8]

Increasingly, modern society is moving in a direction in which all three conditions are routinely true. That's why we believe that, ready or not, more organizations will have to adopt the X-team as their modus operandi.

Acknowledgments

This chapter is reprinted with permission from *Sloan Management Review* 43, no. 3 (Spring 2002): 33–40.

Notes

1. Gladstein 1984, Ancona and Caldwell 1992a, Ancona and Caldwell 1992b, Ancona 1990, Ancona and Caldwell 2000, Ancona and Kaeufer 2001, Bresman 2001.

2. Ancona 1992.

3. Granovetter 1973, Krackhardt 1992, Hansen 1999.

4. Ancona and Caldwell 1998.

5. Sutton and Hargadon 1996.

6. For a recent interpretation of power dynamics in organizations, see Yukl (2000).

7. Consistent with this logic, John Austin convincingly demonstrated how team members' knowledge of the location of distributed information has a positive impact on performance; see Austin (2000).

8. For an insightful account of how different tasks require different models of team management, see Eisenhardt and Tabrizi (1995).

References

Ancona, D. G. 1990. Outward Bound: Strategies for Team Survival in an Organization. *Academy of Management Journal* 33 (June): 334–365.

Ancona, D. G., and D. F. Caldwell. 1992a. Demography and Design: Predictors of New Product Team Performance. *Organization Science* 33 (August): 321–341.

Ancona, D. G., and D. F. Caldwell. 1992b. Bridging the Boundary: External Activity and Performance in Organizational Teams. *Administrative Science Quarterly* 37 (December): 634–665.

Ancona, D. G., and D. F. Caldwell. 1998. Rethinking Team Composition From the Outside In. In *Research on Managing Groups and Teams,* edited by D. H. Gruenfeld. Stamford, Conn.: JAI Press.

Ancona, D. G., and D. F. Caldwell. 2000. Compose Teams to Assure Successful Boundary Activity. In *The Blackwell Handbook of Principles of Organizational Behavior*, edited by E. A. Locke. Oxford: Blackwell.

Ancona, D. G., and K. Kaeufer, 2001. The Outer-Net Team. Sloan School of Management Working Paper.

Austin, J. R. 2000. Knowing What and Whom Other People Know: Linking Transactive Memory with External Connections in Organizational Groups. Academy of Management Best Paper Proceedings, Toronto, August.

Bresman, H. M. 2001. External Sourcing of Core Technologies and the Architectural Dependency of Teams. MIT Sloan School of Management Working Paper 4215-01.

Eisenhardt, K. M., and B. Tabrizi. 1995. Accelerating Adaptive Processes: Product Innovation in the Global Computer Industry. *Administrative Science Quarterly* 40 (March): 84–110.

Gladstein, D. L. 1984. Groups in Context: A Model of Task Group Effectiveness. *Administrative Science Quarterly* 29 (December): 499–517.

Granovetter, M. S. 1973. The Strength of Weak Ties. *American Journal of Sociology* 78 (1973): 360–380.

Hansen, M. T. 1999. The Search-Transfer Problem: The Role of Weak Ties in Sharing Knowledge Across Organization Subunits. *Administrative Science Quarterly* 44 (March): 82–111.

Krackhardt, D. 1992. The Strength of Strong Ties: The Importance of Philos in Organizations. In *Networks and Organizations: Structure, Form and Action*, edited by N. Nohria and R. G. Eccles. Boston: Harvard Business School Press.

Sutton, R., and A. B. Hargadon, 1996. Brainstorming Groups in Context: Effectiveness in a Product Design Firm. *Administrative Science Quarterly* 41 (December): 685–718.

Yukl, G. 2000. Use Power Effectively. In *The Blackwell Handbook of Principles of Organization Behavior,* edited by E. A. Locke. Oxford: Blackwell.

14 Eight Imperatives for the New IT Organization

John F. Rockart, Michael J. Earl, and Jeanne W. Ross

Change has become the trademark of the business world in the 1990s. The pace of change is so frenetic that organizational theorists view change management as a critical competency—in some cases, *the* critical competency—for successful organizations in the future. New customer demands and technological capabilities are causing organizations to undergo transformations that involve redefining their very mission. Not surprisingly, subunits within those organizations, particularly the information technology (IT) function, are also rethinking their roles. The growing importance of information, coupled with the increased distribution of the technology to knowledgeable users, has both IT professionals and business managers reexamining the role of the IT unit. Some wonder whether there will even be a role for the IT function. This article presents our perspective on the future of the IT organization, based on three years of research on IT's changing role.

Our conclusions are partially drawn from a study of new IT management practices in fifty firms and a comparative study of IT organizations in four countries.[1] As part of the latter project, we interviewed IS executives at four large U.S. corporations and twelve European and Japanese companies. Their views on the future of IT organizations in general and, more particularly, their plans and change programs for their organizations, form the basis for our thinking. These CIOs and other IS managers with whom we have discussed the future role of IT offered diverse views of their environments. Most had unique plans for their particular units, but many common themes emerged.

We review these themes first by exploring changes in business and technology that are driving changes in the role and structure of IT units. We then define and discuss eight "imperatives" for IT organizations in responding to these changes. Finally, we suggest the responsibilities that will become core activities of the IT unit and emphasize a major factor necessary to its future success: line management's assumption of a joint leadership role for IT.

Business Change

Not surprisingly, the CIOs we interviewed said their firms were experiencing an increasingly volatile business environment, driven by greatly intensified global competition, which has major implications for firms. There is less slack time, both in developing new products and in delivering customer orders. Customer satisfaction no longer means just prompt, courteous service; it also means designing products and services to meet individual customer needs. Equally important, costs must continuously go down, not up. Finally, firms increasingly must give multinational customers a consistent product and simplified order and payment processes across their dispersed divisions.

The global competitive environment has, in turn, led to four major changes in how organizations operate and are managed. All involve major *process* change. All heavily involve IT. And all are necessary to compete in the new environment.

Re-engineering Operational Processes

The combined demands of decreased cycle times, increased customer service, and decreased costs have led to the phenomenon currently called "business process redesign." The aim is to improve business performance by taking a process view of the functions and activities in the firm's operational value chain. In essence, firms are redesigning each process by creating cross-functional linkages, eliminating steps that do not add value from the customer's perspective, and focusing on the horizontal information flows needed to support the process. Although many process redesign experiments have failed, companies like Xerox, J. C. Penney, and Texas Instruments, among others, have demonstrated that redesigning across the value chain can reduce inventories, lower head counts, shorten lead times, increase customer satisfaction, and increase profits.

Re-engineering Support Processes

Similarly, firms are re-engineering administrative and support processes that have often been inefficient in both cost and service. Some early exemplars of business process redesign were in the "back office." For example, Ford and Baxter Healthcare applied automation to remove redundant steps from administrative activities and applied rationalization to create shared service organizations. This drive to improve support processes continues and has evolved to include, for example, the outsourcing of accounting functions at British Petroleum and the creation of service units for internal and external businesses as in the mortgage processing at Guardian Royal Exchange.

Rethinking Managerial Information Flows

Companies are reorganizing to obtain the advantages of both centralization and decentralization. Formerly decentralized companies (e.g., Johnson & Johnson and Citibank) are centralizing some functions, such as purchasing and logistics man-

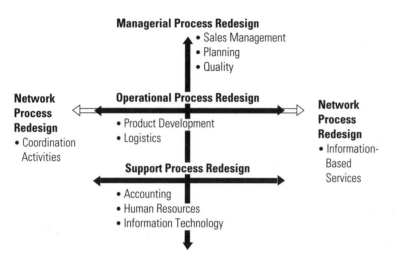

Figure 14.1
Four Types of Process Redesign

agement, to take advantage of their size and access to worldwide information and to respond to customer demands for one-stop shopping. Formerly centralized companies (e.g., Frito-Lay and Miller Brewing) are putting more decision-making power lower in the organization to better use both sales information and existing local knowledge about customers and to provide more effective customer service. These companies are moving toward a "federal" organization model that combines elements of both centralized and decentralized structures and processes.[2]

This increasingly understood need to have both the advantages of global resource management and responsiveness to local market conditions has led organizations to rethink more than just the horizontal (across the value chain) systems. It has also encouraged them to rethink their vertical processes—that is, their key managerial processes such as the planning process, the quality process, the sales managerial process, and so on.[3] Managerial processes, which, with the exception of financial management, were rarely designed at all in the past, can now, with IT, be designed to deliver appropriate operational, customer, and competitive information. Companies like Frito-Lay, Miller Brewing, and Xerox have redesigned many managerial processes specifically to deliver information lower in the hierarchy to teams closer to the customers, where decisions can be made with the latest detailed information. We call this "managerial process redesign" (see figure 14.1).

Redesigning Network Processes

A fourth type of process redesign under way involves a firm's external customers and suppliers (see figure 14.1). With the advent of more cost-effective communications technology, there is also a need to emphasize the design of improved approaches to what Forrester Research terms "the customer connection."[4] This also often extends in the reverse direction to supply chain integration, as illustrated by the Efficient Consumer Response initiative in the U.S. food industry.

Redesigning processes to serve customers is not new; it has been more than a decade since Federal Express added information to its service. In the 1980s, many organizations provided increased customer contact by giving customers access to their order-entry systems, and some, like Baxter Healthcare, went further by taking over related services for their clients.[5] But the magnitude of such opportunities offered by cheaper, broadband communications is now more apparent. United Airlines is moving to a ticketless approach for serving customers. State Street Bank has placed information formerly held in its mainframe files at customer premises in client/server form to facilitate improved, simpler analysis by customer personnel. The tide of customer-oriented process change is just beginning to swell. The opportunities and perils presented by the Internet and various private networks for companies with established brand names (banks, insurance companies, pharmaceuticals, and so on) are increasingly evident. In the last half of this decade, we will see major attention to such customer-oriented redesign initiatives.

Equally, the movements of quick response and efficient consumer response have seized on the technologies of electronic data interchange (EDI), shared databases, and collaborative systems to take time, inventory, and quality slack out of the supply chain. Wal-Mart's integration with Procter & Gamble in the United States, 7-Eleven's fast replenishment system in Japan, and Marks & Spencer's contract management system in the United Kingdom are examples. We call this integration of processes with customers and suppliers (plus allies) "network process redesign."

These four major efforts at process redesign are having a major impact on IT organizations. Although pressure for the business changes started in the manufacturing sector, the needs to reduce costs and increase services have spread to *all* sectors (including service, health, and education), and all IT organizations are affected. On the one hand, information technology enables most effective process change, so the load on IT organizations is becoming much heavier. On the other hand, IT units must reduce costs, raise quality, reduce lead times, and improve customer service. *The challenge for IT units is thus to do more with fewer resources.* As a result, some top IT executives are heavily engaged in thinking through the re-engineering of IT.

Technology Change

The technology environment has undergone a complete change in the past few years. Instead of a fairly stable, benign mainframe environment, IT now has to deal with a user-centered workstation environment supported primarily by server-based storage and processing. New development methodologies, integrated package suites, and exploding technologies create a situation in which IT units must interface with as many as 50 to 100 suppliers (not the previous 5 to 10 major ones) to meet their needs. And the IT industry is complex, uncertain, and ever changing. The key technological issues are:

• *Distributed Computing Environment.* Current users are well trained and more demanding as they install PCs and portables throughout the organization, often with nonstandard software. Power users abound and frequently are more knowledgeable about PCs than core IT personnel are. They are frequently the application innovators in an organization but often fail to understand what is necessary to provide secure, industrial-strength systems, so the IS staff must reverse-engineer applications they have developed. Unfortunately, even in 1996, client/server environments remain difficult to implement and support. Inadequate software, multiple suppliers, and new languages make the transition from thirty years of mainframe-based COBOL a challenge, and the "legacy systems" still have to be maintained.

• *New Development Methods.* Software development is moving slowly from COBOL on mainframes to object languages on server platforms. Meanwhile, management's dissatisfaction with previously costly and slow development, coupled with a sense that basic transaction processing has little competitive advantage, has led to the increased use of integrated packages like SAP. In most companies, IT is not prepared for this revolution. Many COBOL programmers and mainframe operators have difficulty making the transition to more complicated, uncertain technologies. Some CIOs describe new development methods and technologies as "black holes." Those firms that invest in training IT staff in new tools find that training costs are high and the payback sometimes slow. In addition, there are growing personnel losses as other firms look for people trained in the new development approaches.

• *Exploding Technology.* While IT staff people are already struggling to implement existing technologies, more technology changes loom. Object orientation, image processing, wireless communication, pen and voice processing, and multimedia are all becoming more useful. Most important are the emerging information highway capabilities, evidenced by the Internet, the World Wide Web, the emerging Microsoft Network, and services like CompuServe and America Online. They are changing the way that business is done and demand new skills and capabilities from the IT organization.

• *A New Industry.* Less than a decade ago, a few companies, led by IBM, dominated the computer industry and could supply most of the required technologies and services. Today, the many-layered industry includes hundreds of players.[6] Not only are there hardware, software, and communications suppliers, but systems integrators, facilities managers, information brokers, and so on. Almost daily, there are new entrants, new alliances, and new product announcements. The old certainties, along with many once successful products and vendors, are gone.

• *Availability of Outside Suppliers.* The outsourcing industry, once confined to a few firms such as EDS and a number of contract systems developers, has burgeoned. Outsourcing is on the mind of every senior executive who wants to cut costs or shrink (or reduce the perceived or real trouble connected with) the IT organization. While only a few firms, such as British Petroleum, ITT, and Kodak, have outsourced major portions of the IT function, most IT units have identified specific tasks that could be better served by companies specializing in IT services. Learning how to identify tasks that are candidates for outsourcing, negotiating an appropriate outsourcing contract, and managing the outsourcing agreement effectively are major new challenges IT executives face.

Eight Imperatives for IT

What do all these business and technological changes mean for the IT organization? The oft-cited metaphor of "changing an airplane engine in mid-flight" comes readily to mind. The business changes alone are daunting. However, major changes in systems development, in hardware and software, and in the rapidly changing, vastly increasing options for both computing and communications make the technology issues particularly challenging. These challenges are often coupled, however, with inadequate technical and business training in IT units and are compounded by IT spending patterns that disperse IT investment planning throughout firms. *In sum, the load on IT organizations is heavier than ever before, and the management of IT is more complex.*

Table 14.1
Eight Imperatives for the IT Organization

1. Achieve two-way strategic alignment.
2. Develop effective relationships with line management.
3. Deliver and implement new systems.
4. Build and manage infrastructure.
5. Reskill the IT organization.
6. Manage vendor partnerships.
7. Build high performance.
8. Redesign and manage the federal IT organization.

Given this environment, we see eight imperatives for the IT organizations of the late 1990s. To be truly successful, an IT organization must excel in each (see table 14.1).

Imperative 1: Achieve Two-Way Strategic Alignment

The first imperative is to align IT strategy with the organization's business strategy. With more than 50 percent of capital equipment investment in the United States now being devoted to information technology, IT has clearly become a major resource for management in carrying out its strategic initiatives. To ensure that investments in IT are targeted at strategic priorities, IT management must be knowledgeable about senior management's strategic and tactical thinking. The CIO must become either a formal or informal member of the top management team, and other senior IT executives must become members of key task forces. IT people must be present when business strategies are debated.

Alignment, however, is two-way. As firms consider their future in an information era of superhighways, multimedia, and information richness, IT executives should contribute more positively to management thinking by identifying the business threats and opportunities that IT poses. It is evident that technology influences strategy as well as vice versa.

Many firms ensure strategic alignment with more than just a new appreciation for the CIO's role. They also emphasize senior line management's ability to understand opportunities available through IT. Formal and informal senior management education about IT is under way in many firms that are conducting technology and strategy workshops. Leading-edge organizations have revived IT steering committees that are very different from those of the 1970s and 1980s, when each member argued vociferously for funding for his or her particular function or suborganization. Today's committees are formally charged with two primary objectives: (1) to ensure that appropriate education is provided for, and absorbed by, all members to enable them to make effective business decisions about information technology; and (2) to require members to take an organizationwide perspective in decisions on IT resources. These new committees reflect the need to support the processes noted in figure 14.1 and the increased importance of allocating scarce IT resources effectively.

Imperative 2: Develop Effective Relationships with Line Management

The key people using information technology in any organization are its functional, product, and geographical line managers. They provide the strategic and tactical direction and the commitment to implementation that converts visions of new systems into improved organizational processes. Thus IT personnel at all levels must develop strong, ongoing partnerships with line managers. Only through these relationships can the necessary communication occur to ensure that both business and technology capabilities are integrated into effective solutions for each level of the business. In an effective relationship, IT professionals and line managers work together to understand business opportunities, determine needed functionality, choose among technology options, and decide when urgent business needs demand sacrificing technical excellence for immediate, albeit incomplete, solutions. Beath, Goodhue, and Ross note that effective IT-business relationships are one of the three major resources (along with IT human resources and the technology infrastructure) that IT executives must manage well in order to deliver value to a firm.[7] These relationships demand that both IT and line managers accept accountability for systems projects, which is achievable only when both parties share their unique expertise.

IT organizations have made major efforts to move toward more effective relationships. In many companies, IT education now includes interpersonal skill-building, such as active listening, negotiation skills, or team-building. Many IT executives are assigning high-level "account managers," chosen for their knowledge of the business and technical capability, to focus specifically on IT-business communication and understanding. In addition, IT staff are strengthening contacts with the power users in each organization, not only to manage what they do, but also to learn from them.

In an article on CIO effectiveness, Earl and Feeny identified the IT-business relationship as critical to an IT organization's ability to add value to the business.[8] They observed that building the IT-business relationship overlaps with six other factors to enable a CIO to provide business value. We have adapted Earl and Feeny's frame-

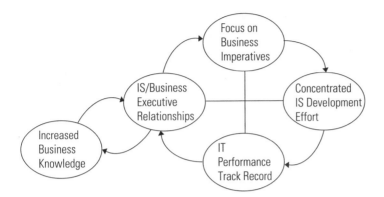

Figure 14.2
Key Attributes of Effective CIOs. Source: Adapted from M. J. Earl and D. J. Feeny, "Is your CIO Adding Value?," *Sloan Management Review*, volume 35, Spring 1994, pp. 11–20

work by concentrating on the relationship variable and three others: focusing on business imperatives, concentrating development efforts on strategically important initiatives, and establishing a credible IS performance track record. We have added another variable, increased business knowledge (see figure 14.2), which often underpins the efforts by some companies, such as British Petroleum, to turn systems professionals into business consultants.

These five strategies combine in a feedback loop that leads to ongoing IT success. IT managers utilize in-depth business knowledge to build strong executive relationships, which allow them to focus on business imperatives and then concentrate IT development efforts on those imperatives. Successful systems built for priorities then enhance IT's track record, which, in turn, improves business relationships at all levels. Successful systems and improved relationships in turn add to greater business knowledge, and the cycle continues to build. Earl and Feeny's targeting of relationships as a critical imperative for IT management is certainly appropriate.

Imperative 3: Deliver and Implement New Systems

Although the primary function of the IT department has been the development and operation of systems, today's approach to system development is radically different from the past. The task has changed from developing mainframe-based transaction-processing systems that support a single function to delivering desktop systems that address the integrated data needs of knowledge workers supporting redesigned processes. The environment has also changed, as internal clients have lost patience with long development times, inflexible interfaces, and cost overruns.

IT executives are responding to these challenges with a variety of strategies. Some have introduced time-box approaches, which require the delivery of usable system components at regular intervals. Time boxes force developers and their business partners to focus on functionality, thus avoiding overengineered solutions and unnecessary delays. Another way to avoid delays and target critical functionality, as noted above, is to recognize that high-level line managers must be the ultimate project leaders, thus ensuring that the business people who will use the system take responsibility for its implementation.

But faster cycle times and the need for data integration and sophisticated interfaces have led to more revolutionary changes as well, particularly in the extent to which firms rely on outside sources. For example, more IT units enlist the help of contractors, especially in areas where their tools and technologies are needed. Two prime examples are client/server systems and Internet applications. Some subcontract all specialist application development to niche third parties. Others use externally developed templates, i.e., CASE-based tools that they customize to meet their specific needs.

Firms are increasingly recognizing that they do not have the time, money, expertise, or inclination to develop large integrated systems in-house and are relying on integrated packages. As noted earlier, they are purchasing software from firms like SSA, SAP, Baan, and others to address their needs for integrated systems. Package implementation is decidedly different from in-house development. IT staff people must understand the system, adapt it to the platforms it can utilize, and troubleshoot code or table-driven procedures that were written outside the firm. More importantly, because packages inevitably require changes in business processes, IT must work even more closely with functional managers who are responsible for making the systems work in practice. Integrated systems projects require near equal staffing of technical and functional personnel.

Thus systems delivery often involves procurement and requires the experience and skills of an informed buyer. Purchased software provides a solution for organizational processes that offer no particular competitive advantage (or, where competitive advantage accrues, it does from use, not ownership). However, firms are still identifying applications that offer unique competitive features, in particular those that improve customer connections, and thus they are still developing software internally.

In sum, systems delivery now includes not only systems development but also procurement and integration. The total systems delivery load in most firms has increased greatly and shows no signs of slowing down, mostly because of the business and technology changes we have identified.

Imperative 4: Build and Manage Infrastructure

IT is currently charged with creating an "IT infrastructure" of telecommunications, computers, software, and data that is integrated and interconnected so that all types of information can be expeditiously—and effortlessly, from the users' viewpoint— routed through the network and redesigned processes. Because it involves fewer manual or complex computer-based interventions, a "seamless" infrastructure is cheaper to operate than independent, divisional infrastructures. In addition, an effective infrastructure is a prerequisite for doing business globally, where the sharing of information and knowledge throughout the organization is increasingly vital.

IT units must address four challenges in developing and supporting their firms' IT infrastructure. First, they must develop an *architecture* that defines the planned "shape" of the infrastructure. While hardware and software capabilities are obviously part of that architecture, the treatment of data (what is to be standardized, where it is to be located, and so on) and the treatment of applications—in particular, decisions on the embedding of applications into the infrastructure itself (e.g., office suites, e-mail)—are more important. Interestingly, some European companies in our study included the information processing skills required of users in their conceptualization of infrastructure.

Second, IT units must establish technology *standards* for implementing the architecture. This requires constant screening and testing to determine which technologies meet organizational needs for integration and support. The rapid pace of change in information technologies means that IT units must develop the ability to establish, support, re-evaluate, and, as appropriate, change technology standards. What is extremely clear is a movement toward increased emphasis on standards for improved cost and effectiveness. The time, energy, and expertise needed for making appropriate selections is slowly driving every major company to have a headquarters group, often in conjunction with a committee of IT personnel from local organizations, select a small set of corporate standards.

Third, IT executives must understand and communicate the *value* of the infrastructure. In most decentralized, federal organizations, local management is taxed for infrastructure support, so it becomes important that the value of the infrastructure is as apparent as the cost. The value of any infrastructure, however, depends on management's strategic vision for its use. Consequently, the infrastructure design and the money invested in it, and the infrastructure services that IT provides, have become senior management business decisions.[9]

Finally, IT units must *operate* an increasingly complex infrastructure. The user with a problem cares not at all about whether the error is located in telecommunications, mainframes, servers, routers, a database, or the application itself. He or she needs help. While there are currently no capabilities to look seamlessly through all aspects of the network, the responsibility for building and operating a full network will increasingly become the role of a new "super operations manager"—a chief network officer (CNO). Reporting to the CIO, this person will have end-to-end responsibility for one of the organization's critical assets. In effect, the CNO will be the IT chief operating officer, while the CIO handles the externally related activities such as vision, relationship, education, and consulting.

Imperative 5: Reskill the IT Organization

For almost two decades, the basic approach to systems development did not change. COBOL was the major language, and the mainframe was the major platform on which systems were developed. Today, by far the largest number of systems is being built for client/server use. Developers in this environment must regularly learn new programming languages, operating systems, and communications protocols. Support personnel are similarly challenged. And network operators find systems and network management to be particularly challenging as they migrate from hierarchical network environments to peer-to-peer networks. These changes have resulted in large gaps in the IT staff's technical skills.

Equally important, as IT becomes ubiquitous in all organizations and a critical element of new business strategies and tactics, most IT leaders have found that their staff people are woefully lacking in business knowledge and skills. If the necessary relationships are to be built (as noted in Imperative 2), IT reskilling must go beyond technology skills to business skills. None of these skills will be easy to develop among the current ranks. There are estimates that up to 50 percent of existing IT personnel will not be able to make the technical transition, much less be able to learn the appropriate business skills.

There is, as yet, no consensus on how to make the skill transition. Some companies, such as Morgan Stanley in New York City, are funding an extensive education program to reskill existing staff. Some are working with "new" client/server software companies, such as Cambridge Technology Partners, to both build systems and educate their people. Others are merely hiring people with the appropriate new skills and assigning existing staff primarily to the care and feeding of older systems. Whatever the approach, reskilling is under way in all IT organizations, at a very significant cost.

Imperative 6: Manage Vendor Partnerships

Outsourcing some IT responsibilities to computing services firms can compensate for skill shortages in IT units and relieve management of the need to oversee tasks that are not competitive strengths or core competencies. As a result of their economies of scale, many vendors in principle can provide more reliable, cost-effective support than in-house units, while allowing top IT management to focus on strategic priorities. However, making outsourcing work is a different proposition from deciding to outsource.[10] IT managers must be at least as skilled as the out-sourcer in each area, be informed buyers and prime negotiators, and derive satisfaction from seeing a job done well—not just from doing it. They are a different breed of IT manager, with the critical ability to recognize whether a vendor relationship is purely transactional and contractual or more strategic and joint.[11] Vendors and customers have suffered from confusion on this point.

Imperative 7: Build High Performance

In the 1990s, IT units, like all other functions in the firm, must strive to meet increasingly demanding performance goals and improve their economic and operational track record. In figure 14.2, we showed the importance of an IT track record in relationships with business management.

Affordability and cost efficiency have become vital issues as IT budgets continue to rise, especially when companies discover that more than 50 percent of expenditures is with the end user. Outsourcing and downsizing are two responses to this challenge. Companies are also installing new cost metrics to promote IT cost-consciousness, such as IT cost per unit of product or service, activity-based costing of IT services, and distribution cost analysis of IT-intensive operations.

Operational performance improvement has followed manufacturing trends. Companies have transferred TQM and customer service programs into the IT unit. For example, Motorola has introduced six-sigma performance goals in an IT quality program. Information-intensive service businesses are using customer surveys, simulated customer queries, and customer complaint analysis.

Finally, in manufacturing terminology again, "time to market" has become a primary issue. Systems can no longer constrain business development. A wait of two or more years for application development is unacceptable when markets are changing so fast. As mentioned earlier, new systems development methods, greater use of packages, and time-box projects are some approaches to shorten development time. Other approaches include prototyping, "80/20" requirements definitions, targeted deployment of end-user software tools, and Internet technologies.

These dimensions of IT performance not only affect the credibility of the IT unit but also show that IT is no different from other organizational units. IT must also perform effectively to enable the total competitiveness of any business.

Imperative 8: Redesign and Manage the Federal IT Organization

For the past three decades, IT organizations have struggled with the "centralization-decentralization" issue. The exact locus of all or part of IT decision-making power is critical, and getting the right distribution of managerial responsibilities is, thus, the eighth imperative.

Our research suggests that, increasingly, these responsibilities are distributed to *both* local organizations and the central IT unit, as Handy described.[12] Handy designated a "federal" organization that follows the political model of the division of power between a central authority and local governments (e.g., the federal government versus the states in the United States). His model allows for significant autonomy at the local level in business organizations but also the "scale" necessary for organizationwide planning, resource allocation, centralized purchasing, and other benefits.

Hodgkinson, in applying this theory to the IT organization, noted that both decentralized IT and centralized IT have real disadvantages (see figure 14.3).[13] Both, however, provide many advantages (see the central ellipse in the figure). Decentralization of some decisions fosters user control over IT priorities and business unit ownership of their systems, for example. On the other hand, economies of scale and control of standards can be gained only from centralized activities. Hodgkinson illustrates a federal organization that delegates some responsibilities to the center and much to the local organizations. What ties all this together is a well-thought-out IT vision, effective leadership, and groupwide IT strategy and architecture. These, in turn, enable the benefits of both centralization and decentralization and allow strategic control and synergy throughout the organization. Moving from the *status quo* to an effective federal organization, however, is not easy, especially in formerly decentralized organizations. Once a federal structure is in place, though, it can be easily modified as the requirements of the host organization change and technological learning evolves. It is thus a relatively stable structure.[14]

Past research on federal IS structures assumed a multidivisional context. However, single-line businesses are now also discovering the advantages of federalism. The model here is devolution of systems analysis and consultancy activities to departments, functions, or processes, and a unifying central responsibility for strategy and operations. In other words, federal structures help achieve alignment with the business, together with economy of scale and architectural integrity.

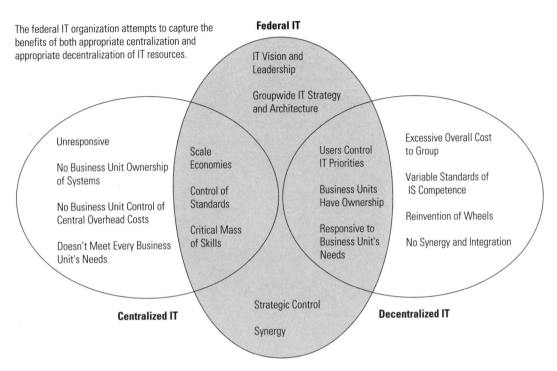

Figure 14.3
Federal IT. Source: S. L. Hodgkinson, "The Role of the Corporate IT Function in the Federal IT Organization," in M. J. Earl, ed., *Information Management: The Organizational Dimension* (Oxford: Oxford University Press, 1996)

The New Core IT Activities

While it is simple to describe the eight imperatives, putting everything in place to be effective in each area is *much* more difficult. Unfortunately, most IT organizations cannot succeed in all areas. Because of a lack of skills or just inadequate staff for all the IT-related efforts under way in most major organizations, outsourcing is increasing rapidly. In fact, most of the activities that the old IT organization once did—running the network, managing the utility, developing and maintaining systems, and managing workstations—can now move to an external vendor (see figure 14.4). What, if anything, are the current and future roles of the IT organization?

No matter how many or how few of the old organizational activities are outsourced, the IT organization itself has shifted from being primarily a "doing" function to a more business-centered, advisory, and management function. In large

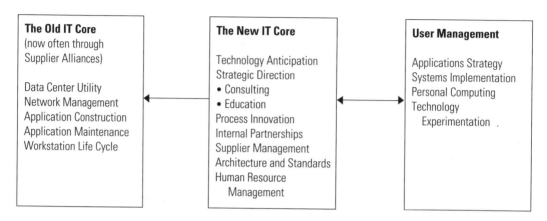

Figure 14.4
The New Core Activities for IT. Source: Adapted from J. Owens, "Transforming the Information Systems
Organization," CISR Endicott House XXIX Presentation, 2–3 December 1993

organizations, IT management will increasingly see its new primary roles as: (1)
ensuring that line managers at all levels understand IT's potential and how to use
the IT resource most effectively in carrying out their strategies; and (2) providing
advice and expertise to ensure effective implementation of the business strategies
and tactics. In other words, IT management will work with line management to
ensure that the business is doing the right things with information technology.

As a result, the IT organization's core responsibilities as we move toward the year
2000 will increasingly include understanding and interpreting technology trends;
working with line managers to help them develop IT-enhanced strategies; educat-
ing and consulting with line management to ensure that the strategic direction is
carried out; taking responsibility for, or supporting at the very least, effective process
innovation; developing relationships that permit useful internal partnerships; managing suppliers to whom parts of IT have been outsourced; and developing and managing the IT human resource (see central box in figure 14.4). The old core IT
activities, many of which are being subcontracted to the marketplace by outsourcing or joint ventures, are the "doing" activities; they may be retained in-house
(insourced) but are managed very much as a commodity (see left-hand box in the
figure). User-management responsibilities are both traditional—carrying ultimate
responsibility for applications strategy and for systems implementation—and new—
personal and local computing, and, increasingly, business-oriented experimentation
with new technologies (see right-hand box).

Given this division of activities, IT management not only is responsible for the
new IT core but also has to assist line and user management in managing IT activ-

ities. In addition, IT management has to ensure that the "old" tasks are efficiently and effectively carried out, either internally or externally. While both these concerns have always been part of the IT mission, too few organizations have successfully addressed the need for business-oriented IT personnel capable of building relationships necessary to work effectively with line managers and third parties. Today, this job is becoming the primary or "core" role of the IT organization.

Line Leadership

The success or failure of an organization's use of IT, however, is only partially dependent on the effectiveness of the IT organization. It is even more dependent on the capability of line managers at all levels to understand the capabilities of the IT resource and to use it effectively.

Information and information technology have become the fifth major resource available to executives for shaping an organization. Companies have managed four major resources for years: people, money, materials, and machines. But, today, information has become the source of product and process innovation and the wellspring of new businesses. IT is thus a major resource that—unlike single-purpose machines such as lathes, typewriters, and automobiles—can radically affect an organization's structure, the way it serves customers, and the way it communicates both internally and externally.

Only line managers are close enough to their business segments to see the most effective ways to utilize this resource. Only they possess the clout to embed IT into their strategies and to commit the necessary financial resources. Unless IT is included in line managers' strategy and tactics, and unless line managers can effectively understand and implement a process view of the world, the best IT organizations are almost powerless. For the past decade, we and others have pointed out that *line leadership is an absolute necessity*.[15] However, far too few organizations have delivered the appropriate education and training necessary for line managers to assume this responsibility.

In addition to effective planning for the use of the IT resource, line managers are also responsible for effective implementation of information technology. Although building good information systems is seldom easy, it is far easier than revamping the processes by which people work, their roles, their reward systems, the organization's accounting systems, or even the organization's structure or culture—all of which need to be altered to install today's process-based systems. About thirty years ago, Harold Leavitt emphasized that an organization's *strategy*, its *structure*, *people* and their roles, and its *technology* had to remain in balance (see figure 14.5). If any

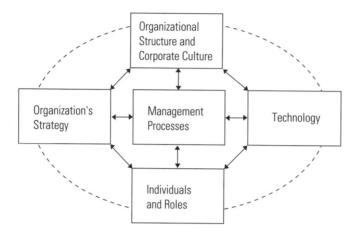

Figure 14.5
Leavitt's Balancing Act (adjusted). Source: H. J. Leavitt, "Applied Organizational Change in Industry,"
Handbook of Organizations (Chicago: Rand McNally, 1965), chapter 27, and J. F. Rockart and M. Scott
Morton, CISR, MIT Sloan School of Management, 1984

of the four variables changes, Leavitt noted, the others must also change to keep
the organization balanced.[16] A decade ago, Rockart and Scott Morton added a fifth
variable to the balancing act: organizational processes—not only horizontal and
vertical processes but also reward processes, accounting processes, and so on.[17]

With this diagram in mind, it becomes painfully obvious that to implement
systems successfully, line management must be heavily involved. IT management
can change only one variable, the *technology*, in accord with a strategic or tactical
change. The CIO has no power to effect the other necessary changes (in the center
section of the figure)—the changes in structure, culture, processes, and people's
roles—and therefore no power over the most crucial factors in an implementation
process aimed at vastly improving an organization's efficiency and effectiveness.
Only line management has the responsibility and power to effectively change these
variables. For an organization to successfully use IT today, IT management must
respond to the changing business and technology environment through effective
efforts in each of the eight imperatives. However, this alone is not enough. Line
management must also shoulder its twin roles of effective planning for the fifth
resource and for the implementation of new IT-based processes. If it does not, all
the herculean efforts that IT managers make to respond to the new environment
will be in vain.

Conclusion

The future IT organization must address the dual demands of improving the performance of its services while increasing the impact of those services on the firm's bottom line. In most firms, the IT unit will become smaller over time but will necessarily possess greater expertise in both technology and business processes. Most important, IT resources will be aimed at the organization's strategic needs.

The outsourcing of IT tasks seems likely to grow if IT management learns how to handle all the challenges. Then IT executives will focus their time and energies on the highest value-adding responsibilities, such as helping top management identify strategic opportunities and developing the blueprint for a solid IT infrastructure.

The IT unit of the future, even if smaller, will be more critical to its firm's operations. Effective IT units will help their firms apply IT to redesign processes and access needed information on a tight budget. Those who fail to address the eight imperatives, or who are unable to convince line management to undertake its leadership role in both IT-enabled strategy development and systems implementation, will be unable to support their organizations in a fast-changing, competitive world.

Acknowledgments

This chapter is reprinted with permission from *Sloan Management Review* 38, no. 1 (Fall 1996): 43–56. The authors gratefully acknowledge the support of the MIT Center for Information Systems Research, the IBM Institute for Electronic Government, the Centre for Research in Information Management at London Business School, and also Judith Quillard of MIT/CISR for her valuable suggestions.

Notes

1. See, for example, Ross, Beath, and Goodhue (1994), Ross, Beath, and Goodhue (1996). The comparative study, a joint research project between the MIT Center for Information Systems Research (CISR) and the Centre for Research in Information Management (CRIM) at London Business School, led by Michael Earl, examines similarities and differences in IT management in the United States, the United Kingdom, France, and Japan.

2. Handy 1990.

3. Applegate and Wishart 1989, Simons 1991.

4. Deutsch and McCarthy 1994.

5. Short and Venkatraman 1988.

6. The Computer Industry 1993.

7. Ross, Beath, and Goodhue 1996.

8. Earl and Feeny 1994.

9. Weill, Broadbent, and St. Clair 1994.

10. Earl 1996.

11. Henderson 1990.

12. Handy 1990.

13. Hodgkinson 1996.

14. Earl, Edwards, and Feeny 1996.

15. Rockart 1988, Boynton, Jacobs, and Zmud 1992.

16. Leavitt 1965.

17. Rockart and Scott Morton 1984.

References

Applegate, L. M., and N. A. Wishart. 1989. Frito-Lay, Inc.: A Strategic Transition (C). Harvard Business School Case 190–071.

Boynton, A. C., G. C. Jacobs, and R. W. Zmud. 1992. Whose Responsibility Is IT Management? *Sloan Management Review* 33 (Summer): 32–38.

Deutsch, H. W., and J. C. McCarthy. 1994. The New Customer Connection. Forrester Research, Computing Strategy Report, September.

Earl, M. J., and D. F. Feeny. 1994. Is Your CIO Adding Value? *Sloan Management Review* 35 (Spring): 11–20.

Earl, M. J. 1996. Limits to IT Outsourcing. *Sloan Management Review* 37 (Spring): 26–32.

Earl, M. J., B. R. Edwards, and D. F. Feeny. 1996. Configuring the IS Function in Complex Organizations. In *Information Management: The Organizational Dimension*, edited by Michael J. Earl. New York and Oxford: Oxford University Press, chapter 10.

Handy, C. 1990. *The Age of Unreason*. Boston: Harvard Business School Press.

Henderson, J. C. 1990. Plugging into Strategic Partnerships: The Critical IS Connection. *Sloan Management Review* 31 (Spring): 7–18.

Hodgkinson, S. L. 1996. The Role of the Corporate IT Function in the Federal IT Organization. In *Information Management: The Organizational Dimension*, edited by M. J. Earl. Oxford: Oxford University Press, chapter 12.

Leavitt, H. J. 1965. Applied Organizational Change in Industry. *Handbook of Organizations*. Chicago: Rand McNally.

Rockart, J. F., and M. S. Scott Morton. 1984. Implications of Changes in Information Technology for Corporate Strategy. *Interfaces* 14 (January-February): 84–85.

Rockart, J. F. 1998. The Line Takes the Leadership—IS Management in a Wired Society. *Sloan Management Review* 24 (Summer): 57–64.

Ross, J. W., C. M. Beath, and D. L. Goodhue. 1994. Reinventing the IS Organization: Evolution and Revolution in IT Management Practices. MIT Sloan School of Management, Center for Information Systems Research Working Paper 266.

Ross, J. W., C. M. Beath, and D. L. Goodhue. 1996. Develop Long-Term Competitiveness through IT Assets. *Sloan Management Review* 38 (Fall): 31–42.

Short, J. E., and N. Venkatraman. 1988. Baxter Healthcare Corporation: ASAP Express. Harvard Business School Case 188–080.

Simons, R. 1991. Strategic Orientation and Top Management Attention to Control Systems. *Strategic Management Journal* 12 (January): 49–62.

The Computer Industry. 1993. *Economist*, February 27, 3–18.

Weill, P., M. Broadbent, and D. St. Clair. 1994. Management by Maxim: The Formation of Information Technology Infrastructures. MIT Sloan School of Management, Center for Information Systems Research Working Paper 276.

IV WHAT DO YOU WANT IN THE FIRST PLACE?

If we are to invent the organizations of the twenty-first century, we must have some sense of what kind of organizations we want. The next section focuses on this issue by going beyond the purely economic calculus that has dominated the business world in recent years. These chapters reflect on what values are important to us and examine how our business organizations and our work in business can contribute to advancing those values.

The section begins with a "manifesto" prepared by a working group of Sloan faculty members titled, "What Do We Really Want?" This manifesto calls for future organizations to be sustainable across three key dimensions: social, personal, and environmental. It goes on to suggest that achieving such sustainability may require organizations to track a broader range of performance metrics than the bottom line and be responsive to a larger group of constituents than shareholders alone. The manifesto concludes with examples of new ideas developed by 21st Century Initiative researchers that have the potential to move future organizations closer to the envisioned sustainability. These include new kinds of "guilds" for temporary workers and independent contractors; accounting metrics that weigh the social value companies create; and efforts to integrate, as opposed to balance, work and personal life. The articles in the rest of this section explore several of these specific ideas in more detail.

The next two chapters focus on how to retain the economic efficiencies of the new organizational forms, while still providing some of the stability and security workers received under the mid-twentieth century corporate system. In the industrialized world, the adoption of information technology resulted in a growing demand for highly-skilled labor, a process that has exacerbated income inequality. And more volatile organizational patterns have eroded the traditional employment contract. So there is a keen need to create new institutional structures to ensure that twenty-first century business organizations are socially sustainable. The two chapters outline two related approaches to this problem.

The chapter by Thomas Kochan calls for rebuilding the kind of social contract that existed in the post-World War II era. Recognizing that the economic underpinnings of the old contract have eroded, he advocates building a new safety net to meet the economic realities of our time. Kochan envisions a role for the traditional workplace actors—employers, labor, and government. But he also sees an expanded role for what he calls "labor market intermediaries"—organizations that work across firms to provide placement, training and career development services. Many kinds of organizations are active in this realm—professional associations, branches of traditional unions, private temporary agencies and recruiting firms, regional consortia of employers, public training programs, Internet-based job and career information services. These intermediaries are especially well positioned to help workers navigate the more fluid careers that are likely to be prevalent in the twenty-first century.

Kochan also calls for innovative forms of employer-worker partnerships, including creative in-firm approaches to meeting workplace regulations. And he sees potential for government playing a constructive role in a variety of new ways—providing worker education and training; revamping employment law to enable more flexible forms of representation; and support for the creation of a new set of labor market institutions for the twenty-first century. Kochan concludes with an example of the kind of collaboration that will likely be required to reconstruct a viable social contract for workers in the future. He describes an innovative cooperative effort in the Boston area in which employers, unions, academics, and church leaders all came together to develop workplace guidelines and policy proposals to address work-family concerns (see Osterman, Kochan, Locke, and Piore 2001).

The next chapter, by Robert Laubacher and Thomas Malone, explores the potential of a new kind of labor market intermediary of the sort Kochan describes. This article focuses on the growing number of workers who operate outside the traditional employment relationship as independent contractors, self-employed workers, or temps. To address the potential insecurity and anomie such workers can face, Laubacher and Malone propose the creation of new kinds of independent organizations—what they call *guilds*—to assume some of the roles formerly played by long-term employers. Guilds can provide for their members many of the things workers formerly received from their employers—economic security, health insurance, pensions, training, access to career ladders, and a sense of identity and community.

Laubacher and Malone give examples of recent experiments by existing organizations—professional associations, unions, temporary agencies, community groups—to provide these kinds of benefits to their members. They also describe several innovative new organizations founded expressly to serve independent workers. They conclude by speculating on the possible future development of guilds and outlining implications for workers, employers, policy makers, and educators.

Kochan's and Laubacher and Malone's chapters focus on the U.S., but the organizational changes that have swept through American firms are also affecting rest of world. So questions about the social contract between workers and firms must be addressed in other regions as well, taking into account unique historical and cultural factors at play in each part of the world. Thus the perspectives offered in both these articles have relevance for non-U.S. settings.

In many parts of the world, an increase in work hours, the advent of two-career households, and a more demanding business environment have led to increasingly

urgent needs to integrate work and personal life in new ways. The next article, by
Lotte Bailyn, Joyce Fletcher, and Deborah Kolb, addresses this important issue.

Bailyn, Fletcher, and Kolb describe a series of experiments at a large American
firm, where senior management had pledged to find ways to help employees better
integrate work and their personal lives (see Rapoport, Fletcher, Pruitt, and Bailyn
2001). The experiments were carried out jointly by the researchers and employees
in the company. From the start, these efforts were predicated on a rejection of the
traditional notion that work and personal life were inherently in conflict. Rather
than seeing the situation as a zero-sum game, the people involved in these experiments asserted from the outset that it was possible to do both—to meet important
business goals and, at the same time, allow workers to have the time and freedom
to enjoy their personal lives.

The experiments were carried out in a variety of settings—a product development team, a call center, a sales and service unit. By moving out of the old either/or
mindset, all these groups were able to develop creative solutions that achieved
important business goals and also ended up providing workers with time and
flexibility to attend to their personal lives. In most cases, these solutions involved
simple interventions such as allowing call center workers to keep flexible schedules
or structuring engineers' workdays into periods of "interactive time" and "quiet
time" as a way to prevent the frequent interruptions that had been cutting their
productivity.

Putting business and personal concerns on an equal footing also helped to surface
some work patterns that were ineffective, but were not recognized as such until the
personal lens had been turned on them. For example, members of the product development team came to realize that engineers who staged heroic rushes to finish work
at the last minute had previously been seen as exhibiting exceptional commitment
and were praised and rewarded by their managers. But as the experiment went on,
and personal considerations came more to the fore, the team began to realize such
a pattern was inefficient, more a product of poor early-stage planning and execution than an indicator of dedication.

Perhaps most importantly, Bailyn, Fletcher, and Kolb discovered that the experiments involving joint pursuit of business and personal objectives were more successful than typical change initiatives inside the firm. These efforts affected workers
where they lived—in their personal lives—and so enjoyed much deeper support
than other initiatives, where workers did not have so large a stake.

The final article in this section, by Peter Senge and Goran Carstadt, addresses
the question of environmental sustainability. Senge and Carstadt contend that the
so-called "new economy" is not new at all, but simply an extension of the industrial

era's practices. A true new economy, in their eyes, would depart from the environmental profligacy of the industrial age and move toward natural sustainability.

The article shows that such a vision is not merely the province of activists at Greenpeace; it is now at top of the agenda of leading executives like John Browne of BP. These executives are driven by a belief that natural sustainability is not a burden to be evaded but a significant future business opportunity. Senge and Carsted go on to point out that achieving environmental sustainability will require a move away from the "take-make-waste" cycle that characterizes industrial production. In today's economy, only 10 percent of the matter extracted from the earth actually becomes a usable product; the remaining 90 percent is waste. And even the 10 percent made into products typically becomes waste when it is discarded. To move away from this cycle, Senge and Carsted suggest that we must look to the example of the natural world, with its pattern of produce-recycle-regenerate. A start would be reducing waste in three areas: during the production process itself; in the operation of products (for example, through design of cleaner-running cars); and recycling/remanufacturing after useful product life has ended.

Interestingly, Senge and Carsted note that achieving environmental sustainability will involve many of the organizational practices developed in recent years. In particular, firms must move from an emphasis on product sales to a focus on service-oriented solution provision. In addition, they must learn to view employees and value chain partners as part of larger social networks with a commitment to sustainability. There will also need to be new metrics to measure business success, such as the "triple-bottom-line" accounting—which measures a firm's economic, environmental, and social impact—now being used by Shell and other leading companies.

These articles don't provide all the final answers to the big challenges of inventing organizations that are socially, personally, and environmentally sustainable. But they each set such sustainability as their objective and together present creative ideas about how to reach that end. Perhaps most interestingly, many of them involve moving beyond the zero-sum approaches to these issues that were frequently employed in the past, and instead, explore new ways to achieve outcomes that benefit everyone involved.

References

Osterman, Paul, Thomas Kochan, Richard M. Locke, and Michael J. Piore. 2001. *Working in America: A Blueprint for the New Labor Market*. Cambridge, Mass.: MIT Press.

Rapoport, Rhona, Joyce K. Fletcher, Bettye H. Pruitt, and Lotte Bailyn, eds. 2001. *Beyond Work-Family Balance: Advancing Gender Equity and Workplace Performance*. San Francisco: Jossey-Bass.

15 What Do We Really Want? A Manifesto for the Organizations of the 21st Century

MIT 21st Century Initiative Manifesto Working Group
Deborah Ancona, Lotte Bailyn, Erik Brynjolfsson, John S. Carroll,
Thomas A. Kochan, Donald Lessard, Thomas W. Malone (chair),
Wanda J. Orlikowski, John F. Rockart, Michael S. Scott Morton,
Peter M. Senge, John D. Sterman, and JoAnne Yates

In many ways, today's organizations are working very well. But few institutions anywhere—be they educational, governmental, community, or business institutions—are serving societies' and individuals' needs as well as they could. In particular, business institutions, while arguably the healthiest of society's institutions, are operating far short of their potential to contribute broadly to societal well-being.

Today's firms are more technically capable and more economically efficient than ever before, and free market efficiencies are being realized in more and more countries around the world. In many cases, however, these highly efficient organizations are not achieving what we humans really want. The current organization of economic activity is intensifying economic inequity. It is eroding critical environmental systems. And it is generating unsustainable stresses on people, even those "succeeding" in the system. We believe that it is even growing increasingly dysfunctional from the vantage point of traditional economic effectiveness in a world where competitive advantage depends on generating and sharing knowledge and managing increasingly complex interdependencies and change.

For example, we believe that the increasing divergence between the "haves" and "have-nots" within countries and around the world cannot continue without morally troubling inequities and, perhaps, major social disruptions. We believe that the energy-intensive patterns of production and consumption fostered by the current organization of economic activity cannot be sustained without significant breakdowns in our natural environment. Finally, we believe that even the people who are most successful in these organizations often find their lives increasingly unsatisfying. For many, the conflicts between their work, their family, and the rest of their lives seem almost impossible to reconcile. Others find, as have many before them, that the material things they buy do not actually make them any happier.

In short, today's remarkably efficient organizations may be taking us, ever more rapidly, to a place where we don't really want to go. The solution to these problems, therefore, is not a purely technical one. It is, at its root, a question of values. We cannot hope to create better organizations without a sense of what we mean by "better," and we believe there is a strong need today for clear thinking about this question: What goals do we want our organizations to serve? In particular, we believe that business organizations—and the societal, economic, and other institutions within which they are embedded—should evaluate themselves by a broader set of criteria than the narrow economic criteria often used today.

At the same time, the problem is not purely one of values either. Even people with the same values may differ about how best to achieve them. We need, therefore, to learn as much as possible from today's novel organizational experiments and from existing theories about organizations and economic systems. Just as importantly, we need imagination to envision new possibilities for achieving our values. For example, by dramatically reducing the costs of communicating and coordinating, new information technologies make it economically feasible to organize human activities in ways that have never before been imagined.

In many countries around the world, today's political debates already include discussions of what values our organizations should achieve and how best to achieve them. The authors of this document have personal views that range widely across the political spectrum. We all believe, however, that it is important—and possible—to think about these issues at a level that goes beyond today's political debates. We hope that, by appealing to deep human values and imagining new possibilities, it will be possible to reframe today's political debates in important new ways.

We believe that the world of business and of organizations is now entering a period of significant changes—changes that many people believe will be as significant as those in the Industrial Revolution. We believe that this time of transition presents a historical window of opportunity—a time in which the choices we make will have a dramatic effect on the world in which we, our children, and our grandchildren will live.

We wish to set forth here, therefore, the reasons for our beliefs. We also wish to issue with this document a call to reflection about what we as individuals and societies really want, a call to imagination about radical new possibilities, and a call to action in making the choices that face us as wisely as possible.

What Isn't Working?

Toward Environmentally Sustainable Organizations

One of the most obvious examples of how today's industrial activities cannot be sustained indefinitely comes from the phenomenon of global warming. There has been significant disagreement for years about whether global warming is a reality. In 1995, however, the widely respected Inter-Governmental Panel on Climate Change (IPCC) published a report documenting a broad scientific consensus that global warming is, in fact, a reality. Even though there is still much uncertainty about the details of the phenomenon, the report concluded that human activities—such as the production of carbon dioxide—have led the average temperature of the earth's surface to rise over the last century, and if unchanged are likely to lead to continued temperature rises in the future.

One might expect large oil companies to be among the last to publicly agree that global warming is a problem. But John Browne, the CEO of British Petroleum, gave a recent speech in which he says that BP has reached the point where they take the potential dangers seriously and are actively beginning to address them:

We must now focus on what can and what should be done, not because we can be certain climate change is happening, but because the possibility can't be ignored. If we are all to take responsibility for the future of our planet, then it falls to us to begin to take precautionary action now.[1]

In another response to the same report, more than 2,500 economists including eight Nobel Laureates endorsed a statement agreeing with this conclusion and saying that:

The most efficient approach to slowing climate change is through market-based policies. In order for the world to achieve its climatic objectives at minimum cost, a cooperative approach among nations is required—such as an international emissions trading agreement.[2]

In this area, therefore, there is a clear need to invent new forms of production and new forms of organizations to use resources in ways that can preserve, rather than destroy, the physical environment of our planet.

Toward Socially Sustainable Organizations

In the U.S., the differences between high- and low-income segments of the population have increased significantly in the last two decades. In fact, some observers believe that these economies are becoming increasingly stratified into two tiers: a privileged economic elite of "haves" and a broad mass of economically disenfranchised "have-nots".

In global terms, too, the differences between "haves" and "have-nots" are becoming much more apparent. While the economic differences between emerging market countries and industrialized countries may be decreasing in real terms, the explosive growth of television, international travel, and other forms of communication have made people in the developing world much more aware of the differences than they were before.

Of course, these trends are not caused (and cannot be reversed) by the actions of individual organizations alone. They emerge from complex economic and social systems of which business organizations are only a part. However, many people believe that these trends cannot continue without morally troubling inequities and, perhaps, major social disruptions. There appears to be a clear need, therefore, to invent organizations—and social systems within which they operate—that can be both economically efficient and also widely perceived as equitable.

Toward Personally Sustainable Organizations

In the United States today, many people feel that their work lives and their personal lives are out of balance. In many jobs, for example, the average number of hours worked per week has increased, and in many families, both adults now have demanding jobs outside their home. The reasons for these changes are complex, but their result is that even many of the people who are most successful in their work organizations often find their lives increasingly unsatisfying.

What Do We Really Want?

In a sense, all the problems we've just described result from designing and operating organizations based on a narrow set of goals. For instance, many managers of today's publicly held companies believe that they are legally required to try to maximize the financial value of their current shareholders' investments, and to consider other goals only insofar as they ultimately affect this one.[3] We should not be surprised, therefore, to see organizations that are financially successful but whose actions have undesirable consequences for their societies, their employees, and their physical environment.

The basic problem here is that today's financial measures alone are not enough to reflect all the things we really think are important. But without explicit ways of recognizing other things that matter, it is very easy to forget (or underemphasize) them. In fact, as concepts like the Balanced Business Scorecard suggest, explicitly attending to a broader range of non-financial evaluation criteria may even lead to better financial performance, too.

To have any hope of creating better organizations, therefore, we need to think clearly about what goals we want our organizations to serve: What do we really want? One way to do this is to think first about who we mean by "we": Whose interests are being served? Business philosopher Charles Handy helps answer this question with his list of six kinds of "stakeholders" of an organization: (1) *customers*, (2) *employees*, (3) *investors*, (4) *suppliers*, (5) the *environment*, and (6) *society as a whole*.[4] By considering the interests of each of these different groups, we can identify—and make more explicit—the goals we would like our organizations to serve.

For example, how would companies operate differently if there were widely available measures of how well they created "good" jobs for people who would not otherwise have them, or of how well they prepared their workers for better jobs in the future? Or what if organizations designed work processes by considering from the beginning how employees could best *integrate* their work lives and their family lives instead of designing work processes first, and then trying to *balance* family needs afterwards?

A key need here is to find new ways of explicitly considering broader criteria of organizational success. In some cases, this will mean quantitatively measuring things not currently measured (such as the quality of jobs created). In other cases, it will mean bringing a new qualitative perspective to bear on evaluating and redesigning individual organizations (such as integrating work and family concerns in new ways).

Imagining New Possibilities

We are, of course, not the first to point out the importance of using broader, non-financial, criteria in evaluating businesses and other organizations. For example, there has been significant recent interest in Europe (especially in Britain) in the concept of "stakeholder capitalism," which explicitly takes into account the interests of the stakeholders listed above. In the U.S., there has also been recent interest in defining broader measures of economic well-being than simple Gross Domestic Product (GDP).[5]

Much of this previous work, however, has focused on what governments can do about the problems. While we believe that governments and laws will inevitably play an important role in solving (or exacerbating) these problems, we think it is also vital to consider what other people and organizations can do. We are particularly interested in what businesses and other organizations can do without explicit government intervention.

We also believe it is important to be both as reality-based and as creative as possible in imagining new kinds of organizations to better satisfy our real goals. To illustrate the kinds of thinking we believe are needed, we briefly describe in this section three examples of new organizational possibilities that have emerged in our work in the MIT Initiative on Inventing the Organizations of the 21st Century.

"Guilds" for Independent Contractors

If, as many observers believe, more and more people effectively become independent contractors in fluid project-based "virtual" organizations, where will they go to satisfy many of the human needs that are satisfied today by large organizations? Where will they go, for instance, for a sense of financial security, identity, companionship, and learning? We have developed a detailed scenario for one possible answer to this question:[6] They may join independent organizations that do not produce specific products but, instead, provide a stable "home" for their members. We call these organizations "guilds," evoking the crafts associations of the Middle Ages, and we assume that they could provide various forms of health and unemployment insurance, social networking, educational opportunities, and other services. We believe that there are a number of organizations today from which such guilds could grow: professional societies, unions, college alumni associations, temporary help agencies, religions, or neighborhoods.

Public Measures of Social Value Created by Companies

What if there were widely available measures of the value of "good" jobs a company created? Some organizations are already using surveys to rate companies in terms of how good they are as places to work. More elaborate financial measures could be created, for example, by comparing the income and benefits workers received in their current jobs to the income and other benefits they would receive in their next best alternative jobs.[7] How would such measures affect the behavior of workers and companies?

Some steps in this direction are being taken by companies, like Interface and Nike in the U.S. and Shell in Europe, that are exploring seriously what it would take to manage by a "triple bottom line" of economic, social, and environmental impact.

Integrating Work and Family Concerns, Not Balancing Them

We often assume that the needs of work and family are in conflict and that we must trade off one against the other. In a recent study at Xerox, however, an innovative project tried to help employees *integrate* their work lives and family lives, instead of designing work processes first and then trying to *balance* family needs afterwards. This approach led an engineering team, not only to have more time with their families, but also to complete their project sooner and with higher quality than comparable projects in their organization.[8]

What Can We Do?

Many people believe that the economic and social changes we are now undergoing are as important as any that have ever occurred in human history. Whether they are right or not, we all have opportunities to make choices about what our future will be like.

As nations and as societies, we constantly answer questions like: What values do we honor? What legislative policies will we enact? As organizations our choices include: What products will we sell? How will we organize ourselves to produce and sell these products? What kind of working environment will we provide? How will we interact with our social and physical environment? And as individuals we make choices like: What kind of work will we do? What kind of organizations will we work for? How will we treat our fellow humans, at work and elsewhere?

The choices we make today will create the world in which we, and all our children's children, will live tomorrow. We hope, with this document, to stimulate you to think about these choices as deeply, as creatively—and as wisely—as you possibly can.

Notes

1. Browne 1997.

2. See the following Web site maintained by a San Francisco based organization called "Redefining Progress," http://www.rprogress.org/.

3. Even in today's world, corporate directors have more latitude than they usually assume. In the U.S. for example, corporate officers are legally allowed to do what is in the best interests of their shareholders, broadly conceived, including the non-economic interests of current shareholders and the interests of potential future shareholders.

4. Handy 1994.

5. For example, see the following Web site for information about the Genuine Progress Indicator (GPI), http://www.rprogress.org

6. See the following papers: Malone and Laubacher 1998 (excerpts comprise chapter 6 of this volume; full text available at http://ccs.mit.edu/21c/21CWP001.html); Laubacher, Malone, and the MIT Scenario Working Group 1997 (available at http://ccs.mit.edu/21c/21CWP004.html).

7. This idea was suggested by Don Lessard.

8. Bailyn, Fletcher, and Kolb 1997.

References

Browne, John. 1997. Speech given at Stanford University Graduate School of Business, 19 May.

Handy, Charles. 1994. *The Age of Paradox*. Boston: Harvard Business School Press.

Malone, Thomas W., and Robert J. Laubacher. 1998. The Dawn of the E-lance Economy. *Harvard Business Review* 76 (September–October): 144–152.

Laubacher, Robert J., Thomas W. Malone, and the MIT Scenario Working Group. 1997. Two Scenarios for 21st Century Organizations: Shifting Networks of Small Firms or All-Encompassing "Virtual Countries"? MIT Initiative on Inventing the Organizations of the 21st Century, Working Paper No. 001 (available at http://ccs.mit.edu/21c/21CWP001.html).

Laubacher, Robert J., and Thomas W. Malone. 1997. *Flexible Work Arrangements and 21st Century Workers' Guilds*. MIT Initiative on "Inventing the Organizations of the 21st Century, Working Paper No. 004. (available at http://ccs.mit.edu/21c/21CWP004.html).

Bailyn, Lotte, Joyce K. Fletcher, and Deborah Kolb. Unexpected Connections: Considering Employees' Personal Lives Can Revitalize Your Business. *Sloan Management Review* 38 (Summer): 11–19.

16 Building a New Social Contract at Work: A Call to Action[1]

Thomas A. Kochan

A fundamental mismatch exists between today's workforce and workplace and the institutions and policies that support and govern them. As a consequence, both the workforce and economy are held back from reaching their full potentials and a gap is growing between the winners and losers in society. We therefore need to update these policies and institutions in ways that give workers and employers greater control over their destinies.

We have been talking and writing about these issues in many different forums during 1999. The main points emerging from these discussions are summarized below:

1. The old social contract grew out of the images of work and employment relations that were prevalent during the New Deal era: a long-term relationship between a large firm, competing mostly in an expanding domestic market, involving two types of employees—hourly wage earners and salaried managers—with a spouse at home attending to family and community matters.

2. The policies and institutions that evolved out of the New Deal were generally successful in producing a broadly shared prosperity and improved work quality for the majority of Americans. Wages and benefits improved in tandem with rising productivity and profits, and loyalty and good performance on the job were rewarded with increased security, dignity, opportunity, and savings for retirement. Collective bargaining, professional personnel/human resource management, and government regulations created a dynamic that resulted in incremental expansion and diffusion of comprehensive benefits, employment standards and protections, and systems for fair administration and enforcement of workplace policies.

3. Over time, the New Deal images of work became outmoded by globalization of markets, emerging technologies that created both new businesses and shifts in demand for labor and the organization of work, organizational restructuring that displaced senior and white-collar workers, variation in employment types and uncertainty in employment duration, increased diversity in the workforce, and increased interdependence between family and work responsibilities.

4. As a result, the old social contract has given way to a long period of stagnant real wages, increased inequality of income and wealth, falling health and pension coverage, increased job insecurity, decline in union coverage, increased litigation and conflict over government regulations and their enforcement, increased polarization

between business and labor on core values and issues, and a sustained impasse over labor policy.

5. There is also considerable good news to report. Innovations in how work is organized are spreading gradually to more workers; knowledge workers—those with high skills—are doing well in today's labor markets; the sustained macro-economic growth and tight labor markets are now producing modest improvements in real income and job opportunities for low-income workers; labor-management partnerships are helping some unions and companies adapt to their changing cir-cumstances; and flexible employment arrangements and practices are helping some families and employers integrate family and work responsibilities.

In what follows, I propose an institutional and policy framework for reconstruct-ing a social contract that allows working families and employers to regain control over their destinies at work. Many elements of a new policy and institutional frame-work can already be seen in the large number of innovative efforts under way in different settings around the country. If previous American traditions are true to form, the next generation of institutions and policies will emerge from these local experiments and innovations. But to date, these are still islands of innovation. To move them to a scale that benefits our overall society and economy requires lead-ership and support from national policy makers and professionals in all parts of our field.

I also challenge our profession and our national leaders to move from passive analysis to active advocacy for putting the future of work and the policies and insti-tutions governing employment at the top of the nation's agenda. To do so, we have to reframe our approach to these issues, bring new voices into the discussion, and offer new ideas capable of breaking the twenty-year stalemate America has endured over labor and employment policy issues.[2]

The Social Contract As a Metaphor

Throughout our discussions, I have used the social contract as a metaphor to reframe this debate. By the social contract, I mean "the expectations and obligations that workers, employers, and their communities and societies have for work and employ-ment relationships."[3] I believe this concept serves as a useful metaphor for our efforts because its philosophical underpinnings capture the central concern of workers and employers today and reflect the best values of our profession.

The key elements in this metaphor, borrowed from political philosophy, are summarized in table 16.1. Work and employment should be a voluntary relationship,

Table 16.1
Key Features of a Social Contract

Voluntary	Terms of employment are mutually agreed upon.
Consent of the governed	Processes ensure the parties can modify the contract's terms as conditions change.
Mutual responsibility	Each party is responsible to each other and to the broader society.
Enforceability	Each party can be held accountable for keeping its part of the understanding.
Subsidiarity and democracy	Parties closest to the workplace are able to control their own destinies.

Adapted from the published writings of Thomas Hobbes, John Locke, Jean-Jacques Rousseau, and John Rawls.

one mutually agreed upon and one that over time has processes and procedures that ensure continued consent of the governed. Each party to the employment relationship has responsibilities to each other and to society. Therefore, an employment relationship cannot be viewed, as it has come to be in today's winner-take-all economy, as solely a two-party instrumental exchange, focused on only narrow self-interest of the individual worker and his or her individual employer. Work and employment must contribute to a good society for all, however we define that term. For a social contract to be meaningful, it must also be enforceable in some sense, so that each party can be held accountable for keeping its part of the understanding.

Our uniquely American approach to the social contract reflects our highly decentralized traditions—we attempt to provide the parties closest to the workplace the rights, power, and capabilities needed to control their own destinies at work. This was the genius of the New Deal legislation providing for collective bargaining— what one of our distinguished predecessor presidents Milton Derber described as the American model of industrial democracy.[4] Labor legislation would establish the basics that should apply to all workers, and then collective bargaining would act as a tool for workers and employers to add to these basics in ways that fit each particular employment setting.

But we have allowed our unique American institutional approach to workplace relations to erode and atrophy. Indeed, collective bargaining is only a shadow of its original vision and stature, now covering less than one in seven workers in America. And the workplace is awash in specific workplace regulations, most of which are sensible and important in their own right; but some are not well suited to the variety of employment settings found in the economy, some conflict with each other, and some are out of the reach of enforcement to the average worker. We also have ceded responsibility for improving working conditions and living standards to the macro-economy. We can be thankful for the near-decade-long sustained prosperity that the American economy has enjoyed. The tight labor markets of the last several years have been successful in improving the lives of those near the bottom of the income and occupational ladder and those moving from welfare to work. In some respects, the macroeconomic policy makers have bailed out our profession. But we cannot assume the macroeconomic boom will do the job for us forever. At some point, we need to give parties in the workplace the tools to regain control over their destinies.

Starting Points: A Holistic View of Work and Its Role in Society

A new social contract must be grounded in a clear vision of what members of society expect from work. What must we achieve at work to contribute to a good society, and where does work fit into the larger set of institutions that constitute a modern, information-based, global economy? Figure 16.1 lays out a multidimensional, holistic view of work that can serve as a framework to evaluate the quality of the policies and institutions supporting and governing work.

If work has these multiple dimensions, then the institutions and policies that govern and support that work must be accountable for addressing each of them and their interrelationships. Too often our old institutions drew lines between these different aspects of work. Unions focused on improving the economic dimensions of work; employers took primary responsibility for shaping the workplace culture and designing and coordinating work to achieve maximum productivity and quality. Workers were expected to separate their families, communities, and citizenship responsibilities from their jobs through a division of labor within the family unit. If these dimensions are to become more interdependent today, all institutions at work must attend to these interdependencies.

The New Employment Institutions

Historically, our field has organized its analysis of the institutions governing employment relations around three key "actors"—employers, government, and labor, which is broadly defined to encompass both the workers themselves and the unions that may represent them. Today, however, we need to make two additional modifications to shape the employment institutions of the future: (1) add a fourth set of actors—the growing number of labor market intermediaries, community groups, and organizations that help structure labor markets and work and that address the interdependencies of work and family life today; (2) envision markets (labor, product, and financial) and technology not as external to the actors but as socially constructed parts of the institutional structure itself. To be sure, markets and technologies are influenced by many factors outside of work and employment. But it is precisely because we have allowed these forces to remain outside of our intellectual thinking and institutional design that we have lost control over our destinies at work. We need to think how changes in markets and technologies can be harnessed to achieve the full range of objectives the different parties bring to work and employment relationships. In what follows, I present the outlines of a theory of complementary employment institutions, each with distinctive functions but engaged constructively with each other to meet the needs of the contemporary workforce and economy. As we will see, each of these institutions needs to recast its role and image and its relationships with the others.

A Multiple-Stakeholder View of Firms

Since the New Deal, American firms have been assigned two competing responsibilities—to serve as agents for shareholders, by maximizing shareholder wealth, and to meet a series of (growing) responsibilities around which employment policies are built. These dual responsibilities have always been difficult to balance, and emphasis on each has risen and declined at different times. Paradoxically, just as pressures from shareholders have intensified, so too have human capital, knowledge, and learning come to be recognized as more critical strategic assets and organizational processes. And, to complicate matters further, these dual pressures come at a time when the boundary of the firm appears to be increasingly uncertain and blurred, as organizations restructure to find their "core competencies" and contract with other organizations in their value chain or networks for other necessary services and resources.

If the number of firms characterized by unstable organizational boundaries and uncertain tenure continues to grow, the locus of responsibility for employment policies may need to shift from the individual firm to the network of labor market institutions, across which employees are likely to move over the course of their careers. Individual firms then need to be more open to participating in a network of institutions that support and govern employment practices and opportunities, just as these same firms are now interacting with their networks of suppliers and vendors.

The range of interdependencies outlined suggests the need to shift political discourse and organizational analysis to conceive of firms as having multiple stakeholders, to whom they owe a fiduciary and social responsibility. This means accepting the view that employees who share residual risks by investing their individual and collective human capital should have a right to participate in the governance of the firm.[5] It also means accepting the reality that firms as employers will be held accountable for meeting the goals society sets for employment standards and human rights at work, and for working cooperatively with external labor market institutions. The task then is to design institutional forums and processes to allow these multiple stakeholders (in this case managers, employees, government agencies, and external labor market institutions) to work effectively together to achieve these multiple objectives. Given the uncertainties facing firms and their legitimate needs for flexibility and adaptability, these arrangements need to be decentralized and well informed of the needs of the different stakeholders that share an interest in these outcomes.

How might this be done? The labor policies of the New Deal envisioned collective bargaining as the central (essentially the sole) instrument for engaging and resolving worker and shareholder interests. While collective bargaining (and the threat of unions and collective bargaining on nonunion employers) performed well in structuring and adjusting a social contract that achieved a broadly shared prosperity from the 1940s through the 1960s, as a sole instrument it has not been able to cope with the changes encountered in markets, technologies, workforce demographics, and employer structures and practices since then. As a result, these last two decades have been a period of both tumultuous decline in collective bargaining coverage and significant innovation in firms and unions that are struggling to adapt to these changes.

The innovations largely take the form of more flexibility in work organization, employee participation in problem-solving at the workplace, and greater information sharing, consultation, or, in some instances, formal representation in strategic management decisions and corporate governance. In their most developed forms, we have tended to call these "labor-management partnerships." They certainly aren't perfect, nor are they a panacea, but they are the best ideas we have going at the moment. As our former IRRA president Lynn Williams put it, "the problem with labor-management partnerships is we just don't have enough of them." Therefore, we need to continue to study and practice how to make these partnerships work and to understand their limitations, while supporting and encouraging them in public policy, public discourse, and in our varying roles as professionals in this field.

These partnerships have proved most difficult to sustain in settings where the boundary of the firm is unstable, as it is in an increasing number of settings where technological changes and uncertain markets and emergence of new narrowly focused competitors make it difficult to assure employment security.[6] Because there are so few partnerships, and the basis for them is limited, we need to look for other institutional structures as well. The biggest challenge lies in how to substitute for the partnership model in nonunion or weakly unionized firms. Management culture (which abhors power sharing unless necessary), labor law (which limits such arrangements), and lack of employee power to influence strategic levels of decision making all rule out this option at the present time. There are no easy answers to this problem, and it may be the biggest institutional design challenge we will face in the upcoming years. In keeping with American tradition, we need to experiment with new options that bring the full range of voices into the process.

Experimentation is possible, and especially needed, to envision how government agencies and progressive firms might work together to achieve the goals embodied in workplace regulations. On the one hand, the increased variety of employment settings makes standard, uniform regulations inefficient and, from the standpoint of the individual firm, inflexible instruments for achieving the goals society has set for these policies. At the same time, many leading firms are implementing practices that go beyond minimum government standards. One option is to encourage firms, working together with their employees (and unions), to develop workplace institutions capable of internalizing responsibility for adapting and enforcing employment policies to fit their particular circumstances. In return, firms gain greater flexibility from government agencies over how they meet these policy objectives. Indeed, some government agencies are already experimenting with this type of approach.

In settings where the boundary of the firm is unstable and firms can no longer make a reasonable promise (tacit or real) of long-term employment security, the locus for employment policy and institution building needs to move from the work site and the individual firm to the labor market and the network of institutions that facilitate mobility. This implies that the individual firm is only one participant in a network of organizations and institutions that is capable of facilitating mobility, efficiently matching people to jobs, and sharing responsibility for investing in human capital and monitoring and improving employment standards.

This too requires significant institution building, but again, the process is already under way. The variety of labor market intermediaries, i.e., groups and organizations that operate outside the boundaries of individual firms, is expanding rapidly. I will discuss their roles in more detail later. The challenge is to build stronger alliances

and collaborative relationships among these institutions and among firms participating in these labor markets.

"Next Generation Unions"[7] and Professional Associations

Before discussing the role of unions in this new institutional framework, let's deal
with some basic issues. Unions are just as necessary and valuable today and in the
future as they have been in the past. This is a deep value shared not only by members
of this association but by the majority of the American public and by many leaders
in the business community as well.[8] Unions provide a critical service to a democratic
society as well as to their individual members. America is now paying the price for
allowing union representation to fall to such low levels. No task is more important
to our profession, and indeed to American society, than building the next generation of labor organizations. The good news is that there is an enormous amount of
innovation and internal debate taking place within the labor movement today over
how to achieve this objective. This bodes well, not just for the future of the labor
movement, but for American society as a whole.

Unfortunately, unions have an image problem and a strategic challenge. Workers,
employers, and the public in general, and indeed, many union leaders, see unions
as primarily defensive organizations to be called on for help only when a majority
of workers in a specific bargaining unit distrust the employer sufficiently to engage
in the high-risk, high-conflict battle needed to achieve union recognition and a
collective bargaining contract. To be sure, unions need to continue to provide
protection against arbitrary treatment at work. But the next generation unions must
address the full range of dimensions included in figure 16.1. They must focus on
enhancing dignity, voice, social interaction, economic security, productivity, and
family and community responsibilities. Serving this broader set of objectives
requires that unions have a positive vision of their roles. This positive vision must
become the central reason why employees join, participate in, and retain their
membership in the next generation unions, not whether or not they distrust their
present employer.

Figure 16.2 illustrates the multiple purposes that I believe the next generation
unions need to carry out for American workers and society. Space and time allow
only a brief listing here:

1. Collective bargaining will remain a bedrock role for unions. But it may be only
one of an increasing array of services provided, and it may be that not all union
members will want, need, or have access to collective bargaining as we know it today.

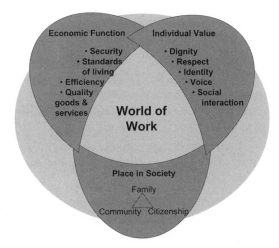

Figure 16.1
A Holistic View of Work

Figure 16.2
Multiple Purposes of the Next Generation Unions

To remain focused on defining unionism synonymous with gaining collective bargaining status, as it is structured today, is neither consistent with the historical traditions of American unions[9] nor responsive to the stated preferences of a majority of the unorganized workforce.[10] To do so will only lead to further union decline.

2. Given that over 70 percent of American workers want a direct voice at work,[11] the next-generation unions need to champion and support direct employee involvement and participation on the job to enhance worker learning; contribute to improved productivity, quality, and customer satisfaction; and to build a workplace culture that satisfies employees' expectations for voice, respect, and social interaction at work.

3. Unions need to engage corporate decision makers at the strategic level, where the real power resides and the critical choices are made that shape employment outcomes and long-term prospects. In some cases, this means forming partnerships with individual employers as previously discussed, such as Xerox, Levi Strauss, AT&T and its numerous offspring, Corning, Saturn, Kaiser Permanente, and others. But note, as this list suggests, these do not always last forever. In cases where the boundaries of the firm are uncertain (e.g., Levi's, AT&T's and its offspring's), unions need to rely on other devices, such as sharing information on working conditions in the full supply chain or building networks that cut across firm boundaries to coordinate efforts at a community or industry level. In still other cases, this requires amassing the knowledge and resources needed to engage the investor community or international financial agencies with capital investment and development strategies that work for the workforce as well as the investors. Given that the level at which capital allocations and other strategic choices are made is where the power lies, we cannot expect unions to do well in representing workers unless they too are active at this level. To do so requires new skills and knowledge as well as new strategies.

4. If the firm is declining in centrality, the local community and political affairs will grow in importance. The Webbs were right.[12] As they predicted more than one hundred years ago, government enactment and community participation are growing in importance for unions. If macroeconomic policies and, increasingly, international macrofinancial and trade policies are growing in importance, then unions need to strengthen their abilities to influence decisions and events at these levels. But equally important, if local community and labor market mobility are important, unions need to become more important actors at this level as well. This is what the living wage campaigns are all about. Unions need to continue working in coalition with community groups to make this role successful.

5. If job security is more uncertain, workers' abilities to move at low cost across employers become a more critical source of bargaining power and career security. For some workers, exit will be as important a source of bargaining power as voice inside the firm is for others. Unions of the future need to provide the full array of labor market mobility services—networks of contacts and job opportunities; portable pensions and benefits; education and skill accumulation and lifelong learning; and perhaps other personal legal and financial assistance as well. If the locus of social interaction and identity from work is shifting from the workplace to the occupation, unions need to once again become occupational community-building entities, much like the garment unions did in helping immigrants assimilate and make their way in a foreign environment during the early years of the twentieth century.

These different functions may not necessarily be performed by the same organizations. There might be specialization, core competencies, if you will. Some unions may choose to organize in traditional ways, relying on traditional employee motivations, while new organizations, professional associations, networks, etc., grow up that recruit, represent, and service members in new ways. I believe this would be a second-best solution. But if this is the case, then there must be active strategies for linking and cooperating across these different boundaries and mutual respect and support among the different organizations in the network—unions, professional organizations, others yet to be named or invented. Or we might see the labor movement as the hub of a wheel that coordinates the work of different groups.

For this vision of the next generation unions to become a reality, at least three things need to change. First, unions need to expand the ways they recruit and retain members. They need to recruit individuals and stay with them over the course of their careers rather than limit their organizing to the high-stakes, all-or-nothing, 50-percent majority it now takes to get one new member. The union-member relationship should be like that of a university student-alumni relationship—once a member, always a member. The fact is that there are nearly twice as many former union members in the labor force as there are current members.[13] Second, substantial change in labor law is needed to make it possible for unions to play these different roles effectively, a point to which I will return later. Third, American management culture needs to change significantly to accept the simple idea that workers should have the same freedom of association at work as they have in civil society.

If unions adopt this more positive vision and these varied approaches and are accepted as legitimate participants in labor market, workplace, and community affairs, America would be well on its way to ensuring that the next generation unions find their rightful place in the economy and society of the future.

Labor Market Intermediaries and Community Organizations

By the term "labor market intermediaries," we mean the full range of groups and organizations that operate outside the boundaries of individual firms. Their functions are to support the mobility of workers across jobs and the matching of workers to job opportunities, coordinate employers and/or labor-management joint efforts, provide training and educational services, or advocate for worker and/or family and community concerns. This is an illustrative, not exhaustive list, designed to make two simple points. The variety of intermediaries is expanding, and their importance as labor market institutions is growing, ranging from temporary help firms to recruiters in Silicon Valley and other tight labor markets, various family and work advisory services, cross-firm consortia, public and private training programs, and a host of Internet-based job placement services.

Equally impressive is the growth in the number and range of community groups and organizations engaged in promoting worker interests in community politics and worker advocacy activities. Here the boundary between "unions" and other groups gets increasingly blurred. The more than forty living-wage ordinances achieved through coalitions of labor organizations and community activists are a prime example.[14] Another example is the new roles that central labor councils are taking. For example, the one in Silicon Valley runs the gamut from being a temporary help service to a training and education center to a political mobilizing force. Indeed, a key challenge for unions and community organizations lies in developing sustained coalitions that both last beyond any single political campaign and that transition to ongoing sources of power and support inside employment relationships.

It may seem ironic to be arguing, as I am here, that in today's global world the local community and labor market will become a more important arena and institutional environment for shaping work in the future. But this is exactly the locus in which family and work responsibilities are joined, where most dual-career couples search for opportunities in tandem with their partners, where opportunities for life-long learning can be created and used most fully, and where the all-important social and professional networks are formed and sustained. Our history of policy and institutional innovation has strong local- and state-level roots. We would do well to learn from this history and invest heavily in building and supporting the local infrastructures needed to give future workers and employers greater control over their destinies.

Government As a Catalyst for Innovation and Flexibility

Government is sometimes viewed as a constraint on or an alternative to the market or private institutions. American political culture has always emphasized a limited role for government in private affairs, and especially, in private employment relationships. Therefore, the vision for government that grew out of the New Deal was for government to set minimum standards on a limited set of basic employment rights and then set the rules of the game for the parties' efforts to improve on these minimums and expand into new areas, as their interests and circumstances warranted.

This is a necessary, but not a sufficient, image or role for government as an actor in the labor market of the future. Instead, government and, most important, government leaders also need to have a clear vision and active strategy for building and supporting the innovative capacities of the complementary, private institutions discussed here.

The consensus starting point for government policy in working with both market forces and local institutions is to support education and training—lifelong learning opportunities for all workers.[15] Education, skills, and human capital are essential foundations for getting ahead in the labor market today.[16] Knowledge is both a critical asset for individual firms and for the overall economy and a source of power in the labor market. Government's unique responsibility is to provide the resources to support early childhood and basic education, and to work in tandem with other business and labor to encourage and support investment in lifelong learning for adult workers. If government leaders share the vision for the new institutional framework proposed here, they need to provide incentives and resources to workplace and labor market education and training programs, governed jointly by workers, employers, and relevant community representatives. This would ensure that scarce public resources are put to use in building general human capital, grounded in the skills needed in the local markets, while at the same time creating an incentive for these different stakeholders to work together on a collaborative basis.

A second role for government is also rather traditional, that of setting the basis for employment standards and enforcing the basic human rights that Americans expect at work. What rights to include in this list and at what level these standards should be set will continue to be key political issues, in the best sense of that term. But whatever standards are included and wherever the minimum standard is set, government must take a number of additional steps if it is to serve as a catalyst for innovation and a complement to what private actors are already doing to promote these objectives.

Government policy must be informed by what the best of private firms, unions, and other institutions are doing to address these objectives. This requires both an active research and analysis capability and active involvement of professionals, advising and consulting, to provide input to policy making and especially to its administration. This was the legacy of John R. Commons and his approach to employment policy administration.[17] It was the right approach then, and it is the right approach today.

As suggested earlier, government should look for opportunities to provide more flexibility to those employers and workplaces that have the institutional capacity in place to achieve labor policy objectives and that have a record of responsible behavior that justifies entrusting them with self-governance/enforcement responsibilities. Now comes the tough problem: Just what institutional capacity is necessary? Does it have to be limited to where a traditional union is present? If so, we limit the potential of this approach to a fraction of the labor force and reinforce the lines of demarcation across work groups that today's organization of work has rendered anachronistic. Moreover, it would freeze the institutional relations of the past, along with the embedded adversarial culture associated with formal union-management relations. But to simply extend it to any workplace that claims to have any form of employee participation would not be responsible and would lack the legitimacy and independence workers expect and indeed require. So America needs a new institutional form that has sufficient independence and expertise and power to carry out these functions, is representative of the full range of employees covered by the regulations, and is accepted by both employees and managers as a normal part of the workplace culture and process.[18]

Workplace safety and health provide the clearest opportunities for taking this approach, since there are established performance metrics against which workplaces can be judged, and the elements of a comprehensive system for managing and monitoring safety and health are widely known and generally accepted. A technically competent employee participation process is widely accepted as a critical element in this system. Finally, in unionized settings, the grievance procedure provides a channel for resolving disputes and claimed violations of worker rights. OSHA provides an appeal system for all workers, unionized or not. These same criteria could be used to extend self-governance systems to other employment standards' areas, wherever there are accepted verifiable performance metrics, knowledge of cause-and-effect practices that contribute to high performance, an effective, established system for employee participation, and a system for resolving disputes or claims involving individual rights. Without meaning to limit the possible areas for experimentation, I would suggest family and medical leave, wage and hour (particularly overtime and compensatory time) issues, and equal employment opportunity are especially well suited to different types of experimentation with this approach.

To make this approach work, significant expansions of the use of high-quality alternative dispute resolution systems will be needed. There is already significant experimentation under way in the use of alternative dispute resolution (ADR) (essentially mediation and arbitration) in resolving equal employment opportunity cases. Our field pioneered the development of these techniques in labor-management relations. But the stature enjoyed by mediation and arbitration in this domain did not occur overnight. Instead, mediators and arbitrators earned the respect of the parties and the courts the hard way—they learned how to make these processes work in different settings. We need to now do the same with respect to the use of ADR techniques in the broader area of employment rights' disputes. This might best proceed slowly and carefully, because there is tremendous potential for poorly designed systems or poorly trained neutrals to discredit ADR; to wit, the totally and unacceptable arbitration "system" used in the securities industry that gave rise to the Gilmer decision. In that model, neutrals are not mutually selected or chosen, and employees do not voluntarily choose to use arbitration. Instead, they must accept this proviso as a condition of employment. In short, the system is designed and controlled by the industry. We can do better and have, in the best traditions of our field, articulated a set of "due process protocols" that set minimum standards for these systems.[19] At least one state agency, the Massachusetts Commission Against Discrimination, has now gained nearly three years' experience using the principles embedded in the protocol, and the Equal Employment Opportunity Commission (EEOC) has likewise nearly a year of experience with a mediation program.[20] We need further experimentation with different approaches, and, most importantly, we need to monitor and evaluate these programs rigorously.

Finally, no updating of national labor and employment policies will be complete, and the new institutional structure and strategy outlined here will not be possible, unless we restore the right for workers to choose whether or not to be represented by a union or some other organization. American labor law and our inability to update it are nothing short of a national disgrace. Study after study has documented the failure of labor law to provide workers with the means to implement what the international community has (correctly) described as a fundamental human right, the right to join a union.[21] The issues that need to be addressed to fix the documented flaws are likewise clear. Delays in processing elections must be reduced; strong measures are needed to eliminate discharges for union organizing, and those that occur should be dealt with expeditiously and severely; and the ability to get a first contract, when a majority votes for union representation, must be ensured by arbitration if necessary. While I, along with many others, have specific views on how to address these and other problems with the law,[22] the specifics are clearly legitimate topics of debate. What should be unassailable is the need to address them.

Fixing the recognition process is only the beginning of comprehensive updating of our national labor relations policy. If we are to encourage and build on the new forms of employee voice and next generation unions suggested here, American labor law needs to support these alternative forms of participation and representation. If this is done on a contingent basis—i.e., new forms of participation would only be allowed in settings in which the employer fully respects workers' freedom of association rights (to be specific, where the firm does not have a past record of, or is not guilty of, unfair labor practices when workers attempt to organize)—we would create further incentives for employers to comply with this principle.[23]

While these are new and, I recognize, controversial ideas, I believe they can work and fit into the American traditions of decentralized, flexible, and ultimately pragmatic workplace cultures and institutions. Like the changes in the representation process called for previously, the specifics should be open to debate, but there should be no serious debate about the need to update this part of national labor policy. Workers want to participate in decisions affecting their work; employers depend on significant worker input to improve quality, productivity, and customer satisfaction. These issues cannot be separated from working conditions or other issues the law reserves for collective bargaining, and changes in the law are needed for public agencies to implement self-governance systems.

The final plank in a new role for government would be to promote building institutional capacity. The full arsenal of approaches needs to be employed, including grants to local committees and organizations to develop their infrastructures and professional skills, similar to the "New Directions" program used during the Carter administration, to support training of a cadre of industrial hygienists, tax incentives for joint training funds, and presidential leadership aimed at building a new culture of legitimacy and collaboration among employer, labor, and community group leaders.

The Need for Leadership

This last point—the need for presidential leadership—is especially important. If Franklin Roosevelt could provide the leadership needed to enact the New Deal labor policies, and Ronald Reagan could usher in an era of aggressive managerial actions against unions by firing air-traffic controllers, the next president can surely energize the country around an effort to support policies and institutions needed to build a new social contract based on the full range of human, economic, and social expectations and obligations we have for work today.

Neither we in the IRRA nor our national leaders can do this alone. We need to continue taking our ideas and message to the American public. Unless we engage a broad cross section of the public—young and old, women and men, entry-level and professional-managerial workers—our message will fall on deaf ears. And we must reach out to and include in these discussions the same wide web of groups and leaders from business, labor, community groups, family advocates, and others who share an interest in these issues. If we do our job well, then we can hold elected leaders' feet to the fire and insist they carry out their responsibilities by putting these issues front and center on the national agenda. As I said at the outset, the next generation of professionals in our field will judge us by how well we discharge this responsibility.

Acknowledgments

This chapter is an abridged version of the presidential address given at the 52nd annual meeting of the Industrial Relations Research Association, © 2000 Industrial Relations Research Association, Champaign IL. Reprinted with permission from the IRRA. The entire address is published in the *IRAA Proceedings of the 52nd Annual Meeting*, 1–25. Support for this work from the Edna McConnell Clark Foundation, the Alfred P. Sloan Foundation, the Ford Foundation, the Rockefeller Foundation, and the U.S. Department of Labor is gratefully acknowledged. Many of the ideas expressed here reflect the joint work with colleagues and students at MIT and the participants in the Task Force on Reconstructing America's Labor Market Institutions. The author is particularly indebted to Robert McKersie and fellow coordinators of this project, Paul Osterman, Michael Piore, and Richard Locke. The author remains responsible, however, for the views expressed here.

Notes

1. Full text of the address on which this chapter is based is available in the *Proceedings* of the Industrial Relations Research Association.

2. For a more complete discussion of these points, see IRRA (1999).

3. Thanks are due to the Task Force on Reconstructing America's Labor Market Institutions Working Group on the Social Contract and the Corporation for crafting this definition of the social contract.

4. Derber 1970.

5. See Blair (1994), Blair and Kochan (2000).

6. I am indebted to Richard Locke for emphasizing this point. See also Rubinstein and Heckscher (1999).

7. Credit is due to Amy Dean for first coining this term.

8. Gallup poll surveys and many other surveys continue to report that a majority of Americans continues to agree that unions are valuable institutions in society. For a statement on the importance of unions to a democratic society, jointly written by a group of leading business and labor leaders, see Collective Bargaining Forum (1999).

9. Cobble 2000.

10. Worker surveys and opinion polls have been consistent on this point for many years. For the most complete recent documentation and analysis of worker preferences for participation and representation on the job, see Freeman and Rogers (1999). See also the various polls conducted for the AFL-CIO by Peter Hart Associates.

11. See the data reported in Freeman and Rogers and the Peter Hart polls.

12. Webb and Webb 1897.

13. Peter Hart and Associates 1998 poll reports 28 percent of the nonunion workforce were union members at some prior point in their careers.

14. Giving Life to a Living Wage 1999. See also Uchitelle (1999).

15. See the emphasis placed on education and training in the Secretary of Labor's 1999 Labor Day report, *Futurework*, available at http://www.dol.gov/asp/programs/history/herman/reports/futurework/report.htm

16. For a recent review of the evidence showing increased returns to human capital, see Levy (1998).

17. Commons 1923.

18. For various proposals for how to implement this approach to monitoring and enforcing workplace regulations, see Levine (1997), Marshall (1997), Schneider (1997). For my own suggestions on how to do this, see Kochan (1998).

19. See Zack (1996).

20. For an evaluation of the Massachusetts experiment, see Kochan, Lautsch, and Bendersky (1999).

21. For a review of the evidence, see U.S. Departments of Commerce and Labor (1994).

22. These are laid out in more detail in Kochan (1998).

23. See Kochan (1998).

References

Blair, Margaret. 1994. *Ownership and Control*. Washington: Brookings Institution.

Blair, Margaret, and Thomas A. Kochan, eds. 2000. *The New Relationship: Human Capital in the Corporation*. Washington: Brookings Institution.

Cobble, Dorothy Sue. 2000. Historical Perspectives on Representing Non-Standard Workers. In *Non-Traditional Work Arrangements and the Changing Labor Market*, edited by Françoise Carré *et al.* Madison, Wisc.: Industrial Relations Research Association.

Collective Bargaining Forum. 1999. Principles for New Employment Relationships. *Perspectives on Work* 3 (1): 22–29.

Commons, John R. 1923. *Industrial Administration*. New York: Macmillan.

Derber, Milton. 1970. *The American Idea of Industrial Democracy, 1865–1965*. Urbana, Ill. University of Illinois Press.

Freeman, Richard B., and Joel Rogers. 1999. *What Do Workers Want?* Ithaca, N.Y.: Cornell University ILR Press.

Giving Life to a Living Wage. 1999. *Faith Works: Newsletter of the National Interfaith Committee for Worker Justice*. October/November.

IRRA. December 1999. First National Policy Forum. *Perspectives on Work* 3 (2).

Kochan, Thomas A. 1998. Labor Policy for the 21st Century. *University of Pennsylvania Journal of Labor and Employment Law* 1: 117–130.

Kochan, Thomas A., Brenda Lautsch, and Corinne Bendersky. 1999. Massachusetts Commission Against Discrimination Alternative Dispute Resolution Program Evaluation. MIT Institute for Work and Employment Research.

Levine, David. 1997. They Should Solve Their Own Problems: Reinventing Workplace Regulation. In *Government Regulation of the Employment Relationship: A Critical Appraisal,* edited by Bruce E. Kaufman. Madison, Wisc.: Industrial Relations Research Association.

Levy, Frank. 1998. *The New Dollars and Dreams*. New York: Russell Sage Foundation.

Marshall, Ray. 1997. The Role of Management and Competitiveness Strategies in Occupational Safety and Health Standards. In *Government Regulation of the Employment Relationship: A Critical Appraisal,* edited by Bruce E. Kaufman. Madison, Wisc.: Industrial Relations Research Association.

Rubinstein, Saul, and Charles Heckscher. 1999. Partnerships or Alliances: Alternatives or Complementary Models for Labor Management Relations? Rutgers University School of Management and Labor Relations.

Schneider, Thomas J. 1997. The Choice Is Simple: A Strong Independent Labor Movement or Federal Government Regulation. *In Government Regulation of the Employment Relationship: A Critical Appraisal*, edited by Bruce E. Kaufman. Madison, Wisc.: Industrial Relations Research Association.

Uchitelle, Louis. 1999. Minimum Wages, City by City. *New York Times*, November 19, Cl.

U.S. Departments of Commerce and Labor. 1994. *Fact-Finding Report of the Commission on the Future of Worker Management Relations*, chapter 3.

U.S. Department of Labor. 1999. *Futurework*. Available at http://www.dol.gov/asp/programs/history/herman/reports/futurework/report.htm

Webb, Beatrice, and Sidney Webb. 1897. *Industrial Democracy*. London: Longmans.

Zack, Arnold. 1996. Bringing Fairness and Due Process to Employment Arbitration. *Negotiations Journal* 12 (April): 163–169.

17 Retreat of the Firm and the Rise of Guilds: The Employment Relationship in an Age of Virtual Business

Robert Laubacher and Thomas W. Malone

Roy Lagemann is a technical writer who lives in California's Silicon Valley. Since the mid-1980s, he has worked primarily as a free lancer. He started his free lance career working nights and weekends while still holding an engineering job at a large Silicon Valley firm. Roy took courses at local universities, and through referrals and new assignments from past clients, quickly had enough work to quit his day job. A typical assignment took one to three months, and Roy usually juggled two or three at a time. His clients included big Silicon Valley companies like Hewlett Packard and Cisco, as well as startups. He built a tight network of other free lancers and relied on them when he needed someone to do extra writing or graphic design. Roy and his wife, who works with a small training business co-owned with her sister, cobbled together a semblance of the benefits package a large firm might offer. They obtained group rates on health insurance through Roy's wife's company, and every year, Roy took on a few assignments through a larger techical publications firm to take advantage of its subsidized 401K plan. Despite frequent offers from clients to work for them, he resisted, until the dot.com boom, when he was lured by stock options and signed on with a startup. But now, he says, the company's stock is "deep underwater . . . and I'm considering becoming an indie again to recover my lost freedom."

Upon returning from his honeymoon, Alan Singer was slated to start a new job on Wall Street. On the trip home, though, he felt unsettled. The new position in many ways represented Alan's ideal Wall Street job, but he wasn't excited about starting it. The frustrations of life inside big organizations had been building for a while; he wanted to go into business on his own. Encouraged by his self-employed wife, Alan turned down the position and set up shop as an advisor to small companies. Through a relative who worked in Silicon Alley, he got his first introductions to prospective clients. To make other contacts, he spoke at meetings of the New York Society of Security Analysts and Coop America, a group that promotes green businesses. Today, Alan works intensively with a small number of startups, some in high tech, some in traditional sectors, helping them to hone their business concepts and raise seed financing. "I've grown more in my time on my own," he says, "than in all the years I spent on Wall Street."

Jordan Dossett is a graphic designer based in the Washington, D.C. area. In early 2000, she posted a profile and samples of her work on elance.com, a Web site that matches "e-lancers" seeking work with buyers who need things done. In the three months after posting the profile, Jordan won 21 assignments to design logos, brochures and Web pages. She decided to quit her full-time job at a design firm and go out on her own, using elance and other Web sites to find work. One of the assignments Jordan completed through elance was for Jim Dale, the head of 100SF.com, an Internet portal for San Francisco-based non-profit organizations. Jim, on the West Coast, and Jordan, in DC, talked by phone and sent materials back and forth via the elance.com site. The assignment went smoothly, and both client and designer came away pleased. "I am really happy this all came together," says Jordan. "I got to know Jim a little and that's what I want. All of my services are based upon . . . personal attention." In this case, the personal attention was delivered electronically, via phone lines and Internet connections.

New Kinds of Companies, New Ways of Working

A generation ago, Roy Lagemann would likely have spent his career working for IBM, just as Alan Singer would probably never have left Wall Street. And Jordan Dossett's clients would have been exclusively based in the D.C. area. Roy, Alan, and Jordan's stories are unusual today, but they are by no means unique. These three are pioneers of a growing movement in the American workforce, a development that confounds many traditional assumptions about the rights and responsibilities of workers, employers and the government. In today's U.S. economy, information-age business organizations are leaving behind the industrial-age system of stable, long-term employment. As a result, most American workers feel a more tenuous attachment to their employers, and growing numbers are working outside the formal employment relationship altogether.

The traditional employment contract—the implicit agreement by which workers provided loyal service to their employers, and in exchange, received job security, health insurance and pensions, and a chance for career advancement—was a product of the mid-twentieth century and the business conditions prevailing then. Over the last quarter century, a very different world has emerged. Fiercer competition, startling advances in information and communications technologies, and new management techniques have caused large firms to become far more streamlined and have brought aggressive startup companies to the center of the American economy. These new practices are more efficient than the old, and can take at least some of the credit for the productivity gains in the U.S. economy that started in the mid-1990s.

In the new system, flexibility and responsiveness are the keys to success, and having a large cadre of dedicated workers attached to an organization is in many cases no longer an asset, but a significant liability. The symptoms of the change are readily apparent—downsizing, skill shortages, the "war" for high-end talent that broke out in the late 1990s—but these problems are frequently framed in the context of the old ways and diagnosed with solutions from an earlier time.

The cases of Roy, Alan, and Jordan illustrate a new way of thinking about the emerging realities. This approach no longer focuses only on the usual suspects of the industrial era—employers and government—to provide the benefits tradition-ally associated with a job. Instead, the new approach draws on a rich ecology of other organizations—what we call *guilds*—to provide a stable home and look after the long-term needs of today's mobile workers.

A variety of entities are stepping in to fill the guild role. In some cases existing organizations—professional associations, trade unions, staffing companies—are expanding their traditional charters. In other instances, new kinds of organizations—Web-based talent brokers or consortia involving community groups, employers, unions, and government agencies—are emerging. Guilds exhibit the characteristics of information age business organizations—grounded in particular local conditions, but able to forge partnerships and tap into networks to achieve national, even global reach. The rise of guilds overturns many old assumptions about the American workplace and represents a promising solution to the problems created by the decline of the old employment contract.

How We Got Here: Rise and Fall of the Traditional Employment Contract

The "traditional" U.S. employment system is actually a recent historical development. At the turn of the century, most American factory laborers worked in small crews under the authority of foremen, who could hire and fire at will and frequently resorted to violence to cajole their teams. Job security was low, and work rules and practices varied widely, even within the same factory. In the face of this arbitrary and often unjust system, labor activists, social reformers, and a new group of professionals inside corporations—personnel managers—attempted to introduce more uniform and equitable employment policies across firms and industries (Jacoby 1985, Cappelli 2000a).

Fitfully, over the course of the first half of the century, a new set of practices emerged. Firms hired entry-level workers, slotted them into clearly-defined positions, trained them in-house, and promoted those who performed well. Formal procedures governed the entire process. This system defined most work in America throughout the post-World War II era into the 1970s. While some Americans were left out, notably women and members of minority groups, the new employment system still represented a major improvement over the arbitrariness and uncertainty that characterized work life earlier in the century.

In the 1970s, this system began to unravel, a process that accelerated markedly in the 1980s and 1990s. Two major factors led to the erosion of the old employment system—competition became much more intense, and new information-driven ways of competing emerged. The effect of these developments was a change in the characteristics that gave firms a competitive edge—where scale and stability had been the keys to success before, speed and flexibility were now increasingly favored. Due to these changes, American business organizations of today are very different from their mid-century predecessors.[1]

One trend has been outsourcing, when tasks formerly done in-house at large firms are contracted out. The outsourcing movement began with support functions like housecleaning and catering, then extended into corporate staff activities like human resources, information technology, and finance. Today, even work formerly seen as central to any firm's mission, like product design and manufacturing, is commonly outsourced.

Another development has been the widespread restructuring of large firms. Nearly every big American corporation has restructured during the 1990s. This typically involves breaking up large divisions into numerous operating units that run more or less independently; the creation of autonomous work teams; and elimination of layers of supervisors and managers. The overall direction is toward giving greater responsibility to front-line workers and relying less on directives from the top.

Another development has been increasing reliance on temporary teams, when workers are brought together to work on a specific project and then are reassigned when the project is done. Such an approach has long been common in law, accounting, and consulting firms and is gaining increasing acceptance at big corporations.

The most radical new organizational form, the virtual corporation, involves small firms and free lancers, or even e-lancers—electronically connected free lancers, who post their qualifications and find assignments on the Internet (Malone and Laubacher 1998)—joining forces on a temporary basis, working together on a project, then disbanding when the work is completed. Virtual corporations of this sort have long characterized film production and construction and are increasingly prevalent in the most dynamic and fastest-growing sectors of the economy— computers and telecommunications, entertainment, biotechnology.

Flexible Employment Arrangements for Streamlined Organizations

The rise of these organizational approaches has led to increased reliance on flexible employment arrangements. Today, over 25 percent of American workers are part-timers, independent contractors, or temps. When contract and on-call work is included, the share of the nation's workforce operating outside the confines of the traditional, full-time job grows to nearly 30 percent.[2] In high-tech regions, these numbers can be significantly higher (Benner 1996). One recent survey revealed that only one in three employed Californians holds a permanent, full-time, day-shift job working on-site (Institute for Health Policy Studies, 1999).

This system has so far worked well for the most talented and highly skilled workers. People at the top end of labor force have seen their incomes grow rapidly in recent decades, and for the most part they enjoy greater flexibility and more interesting work. One result, though, has been that at the high end of the work force, many talented managers and professionals continue to hold traditional jobs but no longer view themselves as company men or women. Instead, they consider themselves free agents, akin to professional athletes or Hollywood actors, who must look out for their own careers first and foremost. They see their current position as ephemeral, mostly useful as a way to develop or maintain their skills and thereby stay attractive in the job market. One partner at a leading professional services firm made an explicit analogy between professional sports and the situation in his company and other professional service firms: "If you look at the NFL or NBA, you have a reduced loyalty to the team. . . . The same is true in the workplace. . . . There's no loyalty to the team, but loyalty to money, or career."

The new system is less friendly to workers with modest skills, who have faced stagnant or declining wages and greater uncertainty. Less skilled workers feel waning allegiance to employers, largely because employers have shown less allegiance to them. During the 1990s, average job tenure declined and the rates of what labor economists refer to as "worker dislocation"—in everyday terms, "firings"—increased, all during the longest economic boom in the nation's history. Layoffs, which formerly occurred only during bad times, routinely took place even as firms reported record earnings (Osterman 1999; Jacoby 1999a, 1999b; Cappelli 1999b).

Given these developments, the old black-and-white classification—which defined the full-time, 9-to-5 job as the norm, and deemed everything else as "nonstandard"—is no longer an appropriate lens for viewing employment arrangements. A more useful approach is to think of jobs as being classified along a spectrum, according to the duration of the relationship between the employer and worker and the means used to govern the relationship (figure 17.1).

At one extreme are jobs where the employer-worker tie may last for decades, even for the entirety of the worker's career. The traditional employment contract of the mid-twentieth century worked in this way. At the other end of the usual spectrum is free lance work, in which the relationship typically lasts for several weeks or months—though in some cases, it may only be a matter of a few days. In the middle are relationships that can be expected to last longer than a few months, but not for multiple decades. Many of today's jobs fit this category, based as they are on an understanding that the relationship will continue only as long as it is mutually beneficial to both the employer and worker. Interestingly, the spectrum is now being extended into "jobs" that are shorter in duration—hours or even minutes—by Internet sites like Hot Dispatch and guru.com, which allow people with specialized knowledge to offer expertise on a spot basis to customers seeking advice or answers to specific questions.

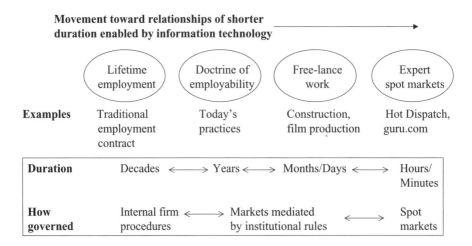

Figure 17.1
The Spectrum of Jobs

In general, information technology and greater reliance on market-based patterns has moved the American workforce toward employment relationships of shorter duration. This movement has been most pronounced in the IT sector itself, where the need for rapid innovation has placed a premium on organizational flexibility, and where there has been the greatest familiarity with the technologies that enable new organizational approaches.

The Challenge Posed by the New Employment Relationship

Given recent developments, large parts of the twenty-first century American economy can be expected to exhibit the characteristics seen today in the fastest moving sectors—innovation as the basis of competition, and as a result, a prevalence of flexible organizations ill-suited to supporting the old employment relationship. American society will face a major challenge in meeting the needs, of both firms and workers, formerly provided for by the traditional employment contract.

For firms, the old employment contract gave reliable access to a supply of workers with the right mix of skills. Many employers initially welcomed flexible work arrangements, because they led to reductions in fixed costs. But in the late 1990s, as the unemployment rate went down, many companies saw the flip side of the new system, as they faced increased competition for talent and had trouble filling key jobs.

For workers, the traditional employment contract provided a number of important things: economic security, through the promise of ongoing employment; benefits such as health insurance and pensions; prospects for career advancement, created by company training programs and opportunities for promotion up internal job ladders; a place for daily social interaction with co-workers; and a sense of identity and belonging. In a world where the traditional employment contract is increasingly scarce, many workers are understandably worried about how they will meet these important needs.

In addition to employers and workers, other institutions with a role in shaping workplace practices—in particular, government and schools—will also face the challenge of adopting to the new employment system. In the decades after World War II, the old employment system played an important role in diffusing prosperity and offering the prospect of upward mobility to millions. The crumbling of this important institution has left many Americans disillusioned and wary about the future (Sennett 1998).

The Traditional Approaches—and Their Shortcomings

Three approaches have traditionally been used to ensure firms an adequate supply of talent and to provide workers with security, careers and identity. The first was at the core of the old American employment system and involves firms taking primary responsibility for meeting these needs. The second has been prevalent throughout most of Europe, and involves government playing a major role. The third approach, which characterized American employment relations at the start of the twentieth century and increasingly characterizes them today, relies on employers and workers pursuing their own short-term interests. Each of these approaches has significant weaknesses in the current environment.

In the old American system, employers assumed responsibility for recruiting and developing a pool of workers with the right skills, through internal training and promotion and by providing insurance and pension plans. This scheme is incompatible with the flexibility required to compete in fast-moving, innovative sectors.

In Europe, the state plays a large role in job training and mandates that employers pay for government-administered social insurance. This approach has mitigated income inequality, but has also resulted in high unemployment, frustration among young people who cannot find work or launch careers, and slower rates of innovation. Most European countries and businesses are seeking ways to introduce more flexibility into their employment systems, while still maintaining a social safety net for their citizens.

With the unraveling of the old employment contract, the American workplace has increasingly become a place where it is every man, and woman, for him or herself. The same holds true for firms, who often find themselves engaged in a "war for talent." Meeting the needs of workers and firms in coming years is likely to require approaches that depart from earlier practices. Just as today's organizational practices represent a departure from the past to adapt to new competitive realities, so the new employment system will have to leave the past behind to adapt to the new organizational practices.

Some Recent Experiments

A number of initiatives have been launched to address the challenges posed by the new American workplace. Some are the work of long-established organizations, while in other cases, new organizations have been started to fill this role. These experiments are noteworthy because they sketch out the contours of solutions that could become more broadly applicable in the future. A look at a few is illustrative.

In 2001, the New York-based non-profit Working Today began offering a medical plan priced at a 30 to 50 percent discount against competing offerings to members of a consortium of professional groups, including the World Wide Web Artists Consortium, Webgrrls, the Graphic Artists Guild, and the Newspaper Guild. The effort primarily targets high-tech workers in Manhattan's Silicon Alley. This offering is the first step in a larger effort to build a delivery system that can provide services to the newly mobile workforce. Once the health plan is up and running, Working Today hopes to extend the model to different cities and among other groups, including lesser-skilled, lower-wage workers. After its delivery network is solidly in place, Working Today also hopes to introduce other services, such as training and career assistance.

"Personnel supply services"—the term used by the Bureau of Labor Statistics for temporary staffing agencies—had the fastest employment growth of any industry sector from 1988 to 1998. The number of positions filled by staffing companies expanded from 1.35 million to 3.23 million over that period (BLS 2000b). The range of jobs filled expanded along with the volume. Companies can now hire temporary executives, finance experts, and Web developers, in addition to the secretaries, technicians, and assembly-line workers that were long the industry's mainstay.

As more people have begun to work as temps, staffing companies increasingly offer health insurance, pensions, vacation and sick pay, and, in some cases, even stock options—the kind of benefits regular employees received under the traditional employment contract. With the spread of technology in the workplace, staffing firms have stepped up their training activities, with efforts including courses in computer-aided design for automotive engineers, Java workshops for mainframe programmers, and self-directed offerings that allow clerical staff to hone their PC skills.

Aquent Associates, a Boston-based staffing company, provides not only health, pension, and vacation benefits, but also extensive career assistance. Aquent calls this last service having "your own personal Jerry Maguire," an allusion to the Hollywood movie about an agent who represents professional athletes. A number of Web firms, such as elance.com, guru.com, and freeagent.com, offer not only project-matching but also career, health and pension plans, invoicing, and low-cost office supplies.

Jobs for Youth is a Boston-based organization that runs a 15-week program for workers trapped in low-wage, dead-end jobs. It provides training in computer skills and financial service industry back-office operations. Run in partnership with Boston-area employers like Mellon Bank, US Trust, and Brown Brothers Harriman, the Jobs for Youth program places trainees in jobs in sponsor firms. After they start working, graduates of the program can continue their education with classes at Suffolk University. The participating employers are pleased, reporting strong performance by trainees and attrition rates that are half the industry norm.

Guilds—Doing What the Employer Used to Do ... But Outside the Firm

As these examples show, many of the good things formerly associated with the employment contract can be provided by independent organizations. We call these independent organizations *guilds*, and we believe they represent one of the most promising approaches to solving the challenges posed by the new work arrangements. Guilds can provide tangible and intangible support for workers, and at the same time, be nimble enough to operate in an information economy where flexibility and the ability to adapt quickly are paramount. But unlike guilds of the Middle Ages or labor unions of the industrial era, these new organizations might not hold monopoly control over a profession or occupational group. Instead, in many cases, multiple guilds can be expected to compete to provide services to a given group of workers.

Three primary types of organizations are positioned to assume the guild role: occupationally-based worker associations; workforce brokers that match employers and workers; and regionally-based organizations with an interest in forwarding the interests of workers and firms in a particular geographic area.

Occupationally Based Groups

Occupationally based groups—professional associations like the World Wide Web Artists' Consortium and unions like the Communications Workers of America— have as their mission forwarding the interests of collections of workers active in the same industry or possessing similar workplace skills. These organizations are logical candidates to step in and assume some of the roles formerly played by firms.

Unions and professional associations already play these roles in film production and construction, two industries where free lancing is the norm. For example, members of the Screen Actor's Guild (SAG) need to earn only $6,000 in a calendar year to qualify for full health benefits for the entire subsequent year. In recognition of the short shelf-life of many actors' careers, the Guild also provides very generous pension benefits. In addition, SAG offers educational and professional development seminars to its members. To fund these services, SAG contracts stipulate that producers pay a surcharge, which amounts to as much as 30 percent of actors' base pay, into the Guild's benefits fund. In the construction industry, workers often move from firm to firm when they finish one project and go on to the next. To accommodate these circumstances, construction trade unions offer their members fully portable health and pension benefits. Members can maintain one health plan and continue paying into the same pension fund, regardless of which firm employs them on a project.

SAG and the construction unions can serve as models for other occupationally-based groups looking to play a role in the flexible workplace of the twenty-first century. Other groups that may play an interesting future role university alumni associations, as well as "alumni" organizations comprised of former employees of a firm.

Workforce Brokers

Many firms that serve as an intermediary between employers and workers, like the staffing firms and Web-based project brokers, have been been aggressive about offering benefits and training, as well as attempting to create a sense of community, in a bid to become the psychological workplace home for the workers who affiliate with them. Such efforts have to date been directed primarily at highly skilled workers, whose wages are sufficient to support the cost of such perks. Providing a comparable array of benefits to lower-paid workers has not proven as attractive to for-profit firms. As a result, non-profit community groups, sometimes aided by government subsidies, have been active at this end of the staffing market.

Regionally Based Organizations

Regionally based efforts often involve cooperation between non-profit community organizations, unions, and professional associations, local employers, state and local government agencies, and community colleges. Though the parties to these efforts have different agendas, their common interest in the economic prospects of the region frequently leads to innovative partnerships that result in win-win outcomes. A number of these efforts have been highly successful in maintaining and creating high-wage jobs by building worker skills. The most prominent have focused on the traditional manufacturing and services sector. Examples include the Wisconsin Regional Training Partnership, which involves more than 40,000 workers and 40 firms in the greater Milwaukee area; Project QUEST, in San Antonio, which offers long-term training to enable workers to escape low-wage jobs; and the San Francisco Hotels Partnership Project, which provides training and job referral services for 1,600 workers employed in 12 hotels (Carré 1998, Kazis 1998, Osterman 1999).

What May Emerge—Guilds as Personalized External HR Department

It is impossible to predict what might eventually emerge to take the place the firm in providing job security, benefits, career support, community, and identity for workers operating outside the old employment relationship. Among the factors that will shape the outcome are the individual preferences of workers and the circumstances of their work.

Regarding workers' preferences, an analogy to the varying styles exhibited by investors is useful. Some investors insist on handling every penny themselves, down to the last stock trade, while others are willing to hand over their affairs entirely to a financial advisor and not be bothered with any details. Many operate somewhere in the middle. Similarly, independent workers in the future are likely to have different styles in handling work-related benefits and careers. Some can be expected to choose self-reliance, researching to find the best temporary agencies and insurance providers, cultivating many affiliations to forward their career prospects. Others are likely to align primarily with one professional association or staffing firm, but maintain other affiliations as well. And still others will link up with a single organization that can meet all their needs.

Similarly, the extent to which workers of the future rely on guilds will be shaped both by the industry and by the part of the production process in which they are involved. Flexible employment practices are likely to have the most impact among workers involved in knowledge-intensive sectors and also those with a role in innovation efforts in traditional industrial sectors.

A likely future scenario is the emergence of networked guilds, in which a series of specialized organizations work together to provide a full range of services to workers. This is the model being pioneered by Working Today, which is linking up dozens of professional associations with providers of services needed by independent workers, like health insurance.

Regardless of how they obtain it, what workers will need from guilds will be a portfolio of services that replicate what the human resources department of a traditional firm provided under the old employment contract. Except this HR "department" will not be part of the firm, or more likely, firms, where the person actually works, but will be provided by guilds and be tailored to meet the requirements of individual workers. If this system works well, temporary workers—and even those who hold jobs on a more long-standing basis, but choose to align with a guild—will have access to personalized services that find them the best deals on health insurance and the right asset allocation for their retirement funds; determine which assignment will get them to the next stage in their career; and help them to land it through a dossier of recommendations and performance evaluations from past work.

Challenges Ahead

To create guilds that would play such a role requires that all the important constituents in the American employment system meet a series of significant challenges. Guilds, workers, and firms must effectively build a new employment system, operating outside of and across companies. Policy makers and educators can assist in this effort by providing enabling infrastructure and institutional support.

Challenges for Guilds

The major challenge guilds face will be to develop service offerings that appeal to mobile twenty-first century workers and figure out how to get paid for doing so. Portable health insurance and pension plans are among the most important services required by workers who lack ties to a traditional employer, and most of the organizations that aspire to fill the guild role are focusing much attention in these areas. Also important will be services that allow ready movement across firms and across industries.

The HR department of the traditional corporation maintained personnel files, job classification schemes, and salary scales that enabled workers to build careers and to move freely from division to division. Guilds will need to create similar tools to let workers build careers as they move from project to project across firms. Among the mechanisms required will be skills accreditation standards, industry-wide job descriptions and salary guidelines, even ways to build the equivalent of a personnel file over a career spent working for many firms.

The beginnings of cross-firm accreditation schemes are emerging. Web project brokering sites allow both buyers and sellers to submit evaluations on the quality of their experience during a transaction. On elance.com, for example, a customer who hires an e-lancer to create a Web page can rank the designer's performance along a 1-to-5 scale on such measures as "Timeliness" and "Quality Work." Companies and researchers are working on ways to make such on-line reputation systems more effective (Dellarocas 2000). Other innovative services that guilds could provide include screening of candidates for positions, "under"-employment or "income smoothing" insurance to cover freelancers who are temporarily unable to get enough work (Laubacher and Malone 1997), and test-based skill accreditation of the sort being provided today by Web sites such as brainbench.com.

Another area with great potential is developing innovative approaches for funding education and training. An interesting approach could involve providing loans in exchange for a portion of the future earnings of a pool of workers. This would be an extension of a 1990s Wall Street innovation—issuing bonds against future income from an entertainer's library of records or films. This practice began in 1997, when the rock star David Bowie raised $55 million through the sale of bonds backed by the expected flow of royalties from his recordings. Such bonds are now routinely issued by Wall Street firms (Orwall 1997). Extending the idea, securities could be issued, for example, to finance the education of a group of young software engineers from India, with the principal and interest paid for by a portion of the salary and stock options they subsequently earn (Davis and Meyer 2000).

Providing career-related services of this sort is a logical future step for professional associations and unions active in sectors where employer-worker ties have become more tenuous. In such industries, professional societies can be expected to take a more active role in keeping members' skills up to date and matching those skills with appropriate jobs. And trade unions are likely to move away at least in part from an exclusive focus on collective bargaining and offer help with training and placement. This shift has been foreseen by leading students of the American labor movement—Charles Heckscher touts "associational unionism" (Heckscher 1996); Thomas Kochan envisions a move to "full-service unionism" (Kochan 1996); and Richard Freeman calls for "open-source unionism" (Freeman and Rogers 2002).

New approaches are also likely in the temporary staffing industry. Some staffing firms today try to attract the best talent by offering generous benefits and career guidance. Innovative agencies could move even further along this path by declaring themselves advocates for talent, effectively assuming the role that Hollywood talent agencies now play for actors and directors. Aquent Associates is already doing this.

Guilds will also need to decide what range of services to offer and where on the worker services value chain to operate. At one extreme, guilds could offer a one-stop shopping experience, providing a full range of benefits, placement, and training, services under one roof. At the other extreme, they could specialize and operate only in areas where they have particular expertise. Even guilds that pursue the one-stop approach are unlikely to do everything themselves. Offering "shopping mall" convenience will involve bundling products from many providers—health insurance from an HMO or hospital group, pension plans from financial services firms, and job matching and career training from specialists in appropriate niches.

Emerging guilds are pursuing a range of approaches today, ranging from initial attempts at full-service offerings by some of the Web project brokering sites to highly-focused job matching/career development services being offered by professional associations. One possibility is that guilds will evolve in the same way many industry sectors have in recent years, with some organizations assuming primary responsibility for aggregating and maintaining contact with workers; others continually developing innovative services offerings; and still others running large-scale, high-volume operational functions—such as maintaining resume banks or cross-firm personnel files—at low cost (Hagel and Singer 1999). There will likely also be room for brokers, like the intermediary role Working Today plays today between a health insurance provider and specialized professional associations.

Regardless of what kinds of services guilds offer, there will be costs associated with providing them. Aspiring guilds will thus need to develop business models that allow them to pay these costs. One approach is to get employers to pony up. Unions active in industries with flexible employment practices, such as SAG and the construction trade unions, have collective bargaining agreements that were first negotiated in the heyday of the industrial era and today require employers to pay a premium above workers' base salary to cover benefits and administration costs. Staffing agencies charge employers a similar premium above base salary.

New types of arrangements are being tried out as well, including fee-for-service, retainer and membership approaches. For example, elance.com requires prospective buyers of services to pay a $50 fee to post a Request for Proposal on its site. Through its e.office service, freeagent.com assumes responsibility for invoicing and collect-ing from a free-lancer's clients and also offers access to group-rate benefits, for a monthly charge of $274. Working Today's members each pay $25 in annual mem-bership dues, and it also uses a small percentage of the health insurance premium paid by covered members to defray administrative costs.

Finding ways to cover the cost of benefits, placement, and training for lower-wage workers will be a major challenge. At some traditional employers, benefits and training are funded through a flat overhead rate added onto staff salaries.[3] Such systems have a redistributive effect—funds paid in on behalf of higher-paid workers effectively subsidize the lower-paid. Accomplishing a similar redistribution outside a traditional organizational setting will require convincing workers of varying income levels to band together or attracting government subsidies. Subsidized vouchers, which would allow workers to choose where to go for benefits or train-ing, could allow lower-wage workers to receive services comparable to those enjoyed by their higher-wage counterparts, while retaining choice and flexibility in the system.

Whatever package of services they offer and however they charge for those services, twenty-first century guilds will have to attract and hold onto workers' allegiance. For professional associations and unions, this will mean competing for members' attention and loyalty in new and unaccustomed ways.

Challenges for Workers

In moving from traditional to flexible employment practices, workers must find new places—likely a portfolio of formal organizations and informal networks—to invest the loyalty they formerly gave to the firm. This is understandably difficult now, since there are few viable organizations with a track record to which workers can confi-dently transfer their allegiance. For many, face-to-face work groups and networks are to a degree taking the place formerly held by the firm. In Silicon Valley, stories abound of such groups moving around as "tribes." This is a start. But such small groups cannot fill all the old roles played by firms. Just as new technologies require early adopters who will take a chance on something unproven and bring a novel invention into the mainstream, so emerging guilds will need early adherents willing to stake their allegiance before the payoff is certain.

The second challenge for workers will be envisioning anew how their work life might evolve over time. Specifically, workers will have to rethink the concept of career, seeing it not as a hierarchical progression within an organization, but rather, as ongoing skill development. Making a career no longer means moving "up the organization," to quote a popular management book from the 1970s. Instead, it involves progressing through a series of assignments that provide continual opportunities to learn and to apply that learning in practice. Those brought up with the old corporate-climbing mentality will need a new mindset and a new set of skills. In many cases, this will mean returning to a craft mentality, where progress is not measured by position, but by growing mastery (Denning 2002).

Challenges for Firms

With the dissolution of the old employment system, companies began filling important positions with outsiders. The practice of raiding other firms was at first confined to top management positions but has nowspread throughout the ranks. This is a major change from past practice, and many firms have yet to recognize its repercussions (Cappelli 2000b).

The first is that the old talent strategy—We'll get and keep the best—is no longer viable for every company. Such an approach may be possible for industry leaders with the ability to offer a compelling package of compensation and challenging work. But not every company has the assets to win this game. Those with limited resources will have to show the kind of resourcefulness that general managers of professional sports teams rely on when they face salary cap constraints. Firms will have to think hard about what positions are crucial and must be kept in-house and which might be filled by other means—by promoting promising young people on their way up, aided by coaching from experienced insiders or outside advisors; by bringing in a "rent-a-players" for certain periods; or by outsourcing work to specialist firms.

In the days of the old employment system, companies could solve their talent problems internally. Firms must now look outside, and the emerging guilds are promising potential partners. One important way firms can adapt to the new employment system is to begin developing relationships with the emerging guilds that are launching experiments to serve mobile workers.

Challenges for Policy Makers

At the federal level, one key challenge is creating a level playing field for guilds. Benefits and training funded inside firms currently enjoy significant tax advantages, and until these differences are redressed, the development of guilds that can operate outside of and across firms will be hampered.

Another challenge will be finding ways to support local experimentation. New Deal labor legislation and regulation arose in response to the needs generated by the rise of mass production and large bureaucratic organizations. The challenge in today's age of flexible organizations will be to create macro policies that set the overall rules of the game, while at the same time allowing for continual innovation. In the short run, the most promising approach may be providing training subsidies and grants to support creative grass-roots efforts. Out of grounded local experiments, success stories will emerge that can serve as models for subsequent changes to the macro-policy framework.

Policy makers will also want to attend to the needs of today's low-wage workers. In the past, getting hired by a large corporation provided lesser-skilled workers with a path to upward mobility. Such opportunities are much less prevalent today. One effective way to provide them in the new system is by a skills-building approach, where the goal is to increase low-wage workers' prospects by increasing their productivity. This requires investment in worker training and programs that link workers with real jobs.

Finally, diplomats and immigration officials will want to keep a lid on potential talent trade friction. During the late 1990s, to mitigate shortages of high-tech workers, the U.S. granted more than 100,000 special H-1B visas to computer engineers and technicians each year. Because the shortage of IT workers was so severe, the H-1B slots for 2000 were all filled before the end of March. European nations began to compete for these skilled foreigners as well, with Germany, the U.K. and Ireland all taking recent steps to ease restrictions on immigrant IT workers. At the same time, current exporters of high-tech workers, India in particular, is attempting to curb its talent outflow (Heavens 2000, Atkins and Gardner 2000, Brown 2000, Grande *et al.* 2000, Gardner 2000). But in sectors where output can take the form of bytes, the Internet allows overseas nationals to remain in their homeland and still undertake work for firms based in the United States or Europe. This practice, known as offshore development, is already common in the software sector (Filipov and Barnard 2000). During times of slack labor demand, tensions may also arise when high-wage domestic jobs migrate in this way to overseas workers.

Wealth today is generated primarily by brainpower, and not, as in the past, by the control of natural resources or physical capital. Given this, the global movement of knowledge workers has the potential to spark international tension, and even outright conflict, in the same way that rivalries over natural resources and immigration generated friction in the nineteenth and twentieth centuries. To reduce potential problems, policy makers will want to maintain enough movement of people and work across international borders to encourage diffusion of expertise and address talent market anomalies, but not so much as to cause tension. And to meet the IT skills gap, more effort could go into retraining U.S. workers.

Challenges for Educators

The primary challenge for the educational system will be to help workers to learn continually over the course of their careers. As a first step, schools can commit to lifelong learning as the educational model for the twenty-first century. Technology also offers opportunities for new forms of pedagogy, in which communities of like-minded practitioners learn from each other.

Educational institutions might also assume a leadership role in promoting cross-firm and industry- or occupation-wide learning and research. Twenty-first century business structures rely increasingly on workers holding skills applicable not only in a specific firm, but across firms within an industry, or even across industries. Educational institutions are well-positioned to develop and disseminate knowledge across industries and occupational groupings. Such efforts will involve schools working closely with organizations that are today assuming the guild role—unions and professional societies, as well as regional employers' groups, and even national industry associations.

Conclusion: A Possible Future

The erosion of the old employment contract has been lamented by many because it delivered—the system distributed the benefits of the post-World War II economic boom broadly enough that a vast middle class gained a share in the American dream. Even as it was providing prosperity, though, many social critics noted that the system undermined individual initiative and the craft ethic (Reisman 1950; Mills 1953).

The new, more flexible employment system has left in its wake the disruptions of downsizing and the anxiety associated with contingent employment, but it has also played a role in reviving initiative and the craft mentality. In the mass production era, many workers' jobs involved the performance of simple, repetitive tasks. Job security and a chance at being promoted were the rewards offered to workers for their acceptance of assembly line or forms-filled-out-in-triplicate drudgery. The newly-flexible organizations of today increasingly depend on all workers using their judgment and intelligence to the fullest. Work in restructured corporations and start-up firms, while less secure, has often proven more interesting and fulfilling than the typical job at a large firm in the 1950s and 1960s (Hammer 1999). In addition, to encourage a sense of accountability, firms operating under the new models increasingly grant workers a share in their financial success, through employee stock plans or profit-sharing.

The tradeoff for more interesting work and a shot at the upside has been greater risk. Workers now bear the brunt of their company's and the economy's misfortunes in ways they did not under the traditional system. The challenge is to create a buffer against the worst of the downside risk. This task initially appears daunting, since recent history suggests we must accept a tradeoff between innovation and engaging work accompanied by risk, on the one hand, or security accompanied by bureaucracy and drudgery, on the other.

In a different context, a similarly "inevitable" tradeoff existed a generation ago, among manufacturing engineers, who believed they had to choose between quality and low cost. Within the framework of traditional mass production techniques, this tradeoff was indeed all too real. But the quality movement showed that when the manufacturing problem was reframed, this seemingly inviolable tradeoff went away. Under new lean techniques, low cost and high quality could be achieved simultaneously, with major improvements in manufacturing productivity as the result (Womack *et al.* 1990).

The problems manufacturing engineers faced a generation ago were on a significantly smaller scale than those American society faces today in attempting to reconstruct its employment system. But the principles by which a solution might be found may not be so different. By combining nimble, quickly reconfigurable business organizations with stable, enduring guilds, the U.S. economy may be able to remain innovative and at the same time provide security, and even participation, for workers. If so, more Americans will be able to enjoy the very real economic benefits of twenty-first century business organizations.

Acknowledgments

This chapter is an updated version of MIT 21st Century Initiative Working Paper #033, August 2000, http://ccs.mit.edu/papers/pdf/21cWP033.pdf. The authors gratefully acknowledge the sponsorship of CDI Corporation, which funded the research on which this chapter was based. We also thank the e/free lancers and people at large companies, staffing agencies and emerging guilds who agreed to be interviewed for this study. Special thanks to Brian Delate, Jordan Dossett, Roy Lagemann, and Alan Singer; and John Vines of APESMA, Nick Bubnovich of Arthur Andersen, Mary Ann Jackson of Cisco Systems, Jeff Diegel and Walt Garrison of CDI Corporation, Hilary Krant of elance.com, Carlos Cashman of freeagent.com, Walter Buckley of Internet Capital Group, Gary Kaplan and Paula Paris of Jobs for the Future, John Featherstone of Sun Microsystems, and Poonam Arora and Sara Horowitz of Working Today.

Our initial thinking on the evolution of the employment relationship was developed as part of the MIT Initiative on Inventing the Organizations of the 21st Century. We thank the Initiative's sponsors for the funding that made this initial work possible.

We received perceptive comments on early drafts from Mitch Wienick and Tim Fitzpatrick of CDI Corporation; Barbara Leary and Domenick Argento of Ketchum; and Bill Hanson and Paul Gallagher of MIT's Leaders for Manufacturing Program.

Notes

1. For more on these changes, see chapter 1 of this volume and Cappelli *et al.* (1997); Osterman (1999); Cappelli (1999a).

2. The U.S. Bureau of Labor Statistics Household Survey for April 2000 indicated that out of 135.7 million working Americans, 22.1 million were part-timers (16.3 percent) and 10.1 million (7.4 percent) were self-employed; see U.S. BLS (2000a). The BLS Establishment Survey for the same month indicated that 3.5 million Americans were employed in the Help-supply services industry, SIC Code 7363; see BLS (2000b). Given slight differences between the Household and Establishments surveys, a conservative estimate is that of the 135.7 million working Americans, 3.5 million (2.6 percent) are temporary workers employed by staffing companies. Of this 3.5 million, 0.6 million are part-timers, and already included in the figures for part-time workers derived from the Household Survey. This leaves 2.9 million (2.2 percent) working as full-time temps. Thus in April 2000, 25.9 percent of working Americans were part-timers, self-employed, or full-time temps. In addition, for the same time period, 1.0 million (0.7 percent) were working in private households; see U.S. BLS (2000a). And the BLS survey on "alternative employment arrangements," conducted in February 1997, indicated that 1.6 percent of the workforce were on-call workers and another 0.6 percent were employed by contract firms; see Cohany (1998). When all six of these categories are included, 28.8 percent of American workers can be considered as not holding traditional full-time jobs.

3. MIT, for example, operates this way.

References

Atkins, Ralph, and David Gardner. 2000. Berlin's IT Employment Blues. *Financial Times*, April 18.

Benner, Chris. 1996. Shock Absorbers in the Flexible Economy: The Rise of Contingent Employment in Silicon Valley. Report for Working Partnerships USA, http://www.wpusa.org/publications/shockComplete.html.

Brown, John Murray. 2000. *Ireland Seeks to Plug the Software Skills Gap*. Financial Times, April 13.

Cappelli, Peter, Laurie Bassi, Harry Katz, David Knoke, Paul Osterman, and Michael Useem. 1997. *Change at Work*. New York and Oxford: Oxford University Press.

Cappelli, Peter. 1999a. *The New Deal at Work: Managing the Market-Driven Workforce*. Boston: Harvard Business School Press.

Cappelli, Peter. 1999b. Career Jobs Are Dead. California Management Review 42 (Fall): 146–167.

Cappelli, Peter. 2000a. Market-Mediated Employment: The Historical Context. In *The New Relationship: Human Capital in the American Corporation*, edited by Margaret M. Blair and Thomas A. Kochan. Washington: Brookings Institution.

Cappelli, Peter. 2000b. A Market-Driven Approach to Retaining Talent. *Harvard Business Review* 78 (January–February): 103–111.

Carré, Françoise, with the assistance of Pamela Joshi. 1998. Temporary and Contracted Work: Policy Issues and Innovative Responses. MIT Task Force on Reconstructing America's Labor Market Institutions Working Paper #WP02.

Cohany, Sharon R. 1998. Workers in alternative employment arrangements: a second look. *Monthly Labor Review*, November, 3–21.

Davis, Stan, and Christopher Meyer. 2000. *Future Wealth*. Boston: Harvard Business School Press.

Dellarocas, Chrysanthos. 2002. "The Digitization of Word-of-Mouth: Promise and Challenges of On-Line Reputation Systems." MIT Sloan School of Management Working Paper.

Denning, Peter J. Career Redux. *Communications of the ACM*. 45 (9): 21–26.

Filipov, David, and Anne Barnard. 2000. The Reversal of Russia's Brain Drain. *Boston Globe*, May 5, C1, C11.

Freeman, Richard B., and Joel Rogers. 2002. A Proposal to American Labor. *The Nation*, June 24, 18–24.

Gardner, David. 2000. India Takes on the Brain Drain. *Financial Times*, April 23.

Grande, Carlos, Ralph Atkins, and Andrew Heavens. 2000. U.K. Joins Fight for IT Workers. *Financial Times*, March 22.

Hagel, John III, and Marc Singer. 1999. Unbundling the Corporation. *Harvard Business Review* 77 (March–April): 133–141.

Hammer, Michael. 1999. Is Work Bad for You? *Atlantic Monthly*, August, 87–93.

Heavens, Andrew. 2000. U.S. Visa Quota Filled. *Financial Times*, March 22.

Heckscher, Charles C. 1996. *The New Unionism: Employee Involvement in the Changing Corporation*. Ithaca, New York: ILR Press.

Institute for Health Policy Studies, University of California, San Francisco. 1999. California Work and Health Survey (CWHS), http://medicine.ucsf.edu/programs/cwhs/.

Jacoby, Sanford M. 1985. *Employing Bureaucracy: Managers, Unions, and the Transformation of Work in American Industry, 1900–1945*. New York: Columbia University Press.

Jacoby, Sanford M. 1999a. Are Career Jobs Headed for Extinction? *California Management Review*. 42 (Fall): 123–145.

Jacoby, Sanford M. 1999b. Reply: Premature Reports of Demise. *California Management Review*. 42 (Fall): 168–179.

Kazis, Richard. 1998. New Labor Market Intermediaries: What's Driving Them? Where Are They Headed? MIT Task Force on Reconstructing America's Labor Market Institutions Working Paper #WP03.

Kochan, Thomas A. 1996. Full Service Unionism. *Boston Review* 21 (Summer).

Laubacher, Robert, and Thomas W. Malone. 1997. Flexible Work Arrangements and 21st Century Workers' Guilds. MIT 21st Century Initiative Working Paper #004.

Malone, Thomas W. and Robert J. Laubacher. 1998. The Dawn of the E-lance Economy. *Harvard Business Review* 76 (September–October): 145–152.

Mills, C. Wright. 1953. *White Collar: The American Middle Classes*. New York: Oxford University Press.

Orwall, Bruce. 1997. Wall Street Bets on Entertainment Idols' Earning Power. *Wall Street Journal*, September 26, B1.

Osterman, Paul. 1999. *Securing Prosperity—The American Labor Market: How it Has Changed and What to Do about It*. Princeton, N.J. Princeton University Press.

Riesman, David, in collaboration with Reuel Denney and Nathan Glazer. 1950. *The Lonely Crowd: A Study of the Changing American Character*. New Haven: Yale University Press.

Sennett, Richard. 1998. *The Corrosion of Character: The Personal Consequences of Work in the New Capitalism*. New York: Norton.

U.S. Bureau of Labor Statistics (U.S. BLS). 2000a. *The Employment Situation: April*.

U.S. Bureau of Labor Statistics (U.S. BLS). 2000b. *National Employment, Hours, and Earnings*, Series EES8076301, available at http://www.bls.gov.

Womack, Jim, Daniel Jones and Daniel Roos. 1990. *The Machine that Changed the World*. New York: Rawson Associates.

18 Unexpected Connections: Considering Employees' Personal Lives Can Revitalize Your Business

Lotte Bailyn, Joyce K. Fletcher, and Deborah Kolb

At a corporate retreat on organizational learning, the vice president of finance for a major manufacturer leads a discussion to raise the "real" issues that inhibit learning and growth. He promises to listen and asks his people to talk honestly, to "tell it like it is" instead of telling management what it wants to hear. To his surprise, nearly all the issues raised in each group—regardless of level or function—relate to work and family.

The director of a strategic business unit at a large high-tech company says, "After my heart attack at age thirty-seven, my doctor told me, 'Get a new job or you won't make forty.' I knew the important things in my life were health and family, but I loved my work and I couldn't face the prospect of giving it up. Isn't there any way to have a life and still do what I love to do?"

The president of a financial services company muses that past routes to success seem to be dead ends. He notes, "We've been tremendously successful, largely because of the hard work, energy, and commitment of our people. But I have the sense that we have pushed about as far as we can. The creative ideas and the energy to work on them seem to be coming from the top, and I know we can't sustain growth this way. We need to re-energize people and get those creative juices flowing from the bottom up if we are going to get to the next level of growth. And I am just not sure how to do that."

What can we make of this? It seems as if corporate America is caught in a dilemma. On the one hand, employees' personal lives are clearly an important issue. Integrating work and personal life is not just something that affects a small group of lower and mid-level workers for a short time but is an issue that affects many people—even at the highest levels in the organization—for a major portion of their lives. On the other hand, future growth depends on "getting more" from these same people. It is no wonder that leaders are bewildered and seem to say one thing and do another. As recent articles and commentaries in the popular press suggest, organizations like to *say* they are "family friendly," but, in fact, their internal workings indicate they don't "care" about family. Is it fair to say companies don't care? Or is it that organizations' current definition of the problem offers few alternatives?

Indeed, traditional thinking tends to pit employee goals and business goals against each other. Obvious responses to either goal seem to make the other worse: If you try to help families by putting in some benefits and special programs, there is a fear that too many people will use the benefits, costs will increase, and productivity will suffer. If you try to help the business by increasing demands for employee commitment and involvement, there is a fear that people will tune out and do only what is asked rather than bring new energy to their work. They might even leave and take needed skills and expertise with them.

The plethora of articles does little more than describe the situation and call for "fundamental change." Employee advocates long for socially responsible organizations; management longs for committed employees who have the passion and energy to stimulate new growth. Is it a tradeoff? Must we choose between the goals of the business and people's needs? We argue that the answer is a resounding *no*. Our research shows that the solution to this dilemma lies in *connecting* the two issues—people's personal lives and strategic business issues—rather than treating them as a tradeoff. It may seem strange and counterintuitive. But we have found that there is an untapped source of strategic innovation and growth that comes from making an explicit connection between personal needs and business goals. The payoff, it turns out, comes from refusing an either/or choice and instead connecting the two issues at the concrete level of local, everyday work practices at all organizational levels.

One Company's Experiences

A multiyear action research project, supported by the Ford Foundation, enabled us to work with a company known for its leading-edge employee benefits. Although the company had a full array of policies and procedures for flexible work arrangements, employees were barely using the policies and benefits for two reasons: First, employees assumed that family benefits applied only to a few people for part of their work lives (primarily women with young children), and, second, there were career repercussions for those employees who did take advantage of them. The result was that the benefits were underutilized, particularly by men, single workers, and career-oriented mothers.

We negotiated with the company to try a different approach that was not based on benefits and policies. We wanted to connect work to personal life (broadly defined to include both family and community) and to use this connection as a catalyst for changing work practices. We worked jointly with a corporate team to define:

• A current state—The culture unnecessarily creates conflict between work and personal life, which has negative consequences for the business and for the equitable treatment of employees.

• A desired state—The culture capitalizes on work-personal life issues as an opportunity to create innovative, productive work practices.

Using an action research method, we worked at a number of sites in the company that represented the major parts of the business. At each site, we collaborated with different groups to see if together we could change aspects of work to meet a double goal: Enable employees to better integrate their work with their personal lives *and* help the site meet its business goals. And in each case, we were able to make this productive connection.

Less Stressful On-Time Product Launch

The first group we worked with was a product development team that had a tough task: Produce a new product, using new technology, in a much shorter time than they'd ever done, but with no additional resources.[1] The group consisted of engineers, both men and women, single and married, with and without children. The engineers wanted very much to meet the ambitious schedule. They knew that this product was important for the company and that their careers were tied to its success. So they were working hard. In this group, working hard meant working long hours and coming in evenings and weekends. There seemed to be an unquestioned belief that, given the situation they were in and the importance of the product, they had no choice but to work additional hours.

People told us that they needed to put in long hours because they couldn't get their individual work done during the normal workday. Meetings, other engineers' requests for help, schedule checks, and management reviews—all deprived them of continuous, concentrated time needed to produce the systems that the product required. The result was that they were working in a continual crisis mode. Although people were aware that there were problems with this way of working, their attempts to address the issue through detailed process redesign usually made the situation worse.

Looking at the work patterns from the viewpoint of the engineers' personal lives uncovered different aspects of the problem. Many "interruptions" turned out to be unnecessary or unproductive. We also began to understand why the unit continued to work this way, even though almost everyone saw that it was less than efficient. For example, people noted that the norm was to reward individual heroics: Someone would get kudos for solving a visible problem even if that person had caused it in the first place! So there was no incentive in the system to prevent problems or to evaluate what were true emergencies and what could wait. Having a crisis to respond to actually helped a person be seen as a team player; it was an opportunity to demonstrate that he or she cared about the work.

We worked with the team in designing an experiment to change some of the work practices. With the double goal of changing work norms so the team members could get their individual work done during the day and reduce the tendency to proliferate emergencies, they came up with a plan to restructure their daily activities into "quiet times" and "interactive times." The results of the experiment were remarkable. The team achieved an on-time launch of the new product *and* received several excellence awards for quality. On the personal side, team members and their supervisor reported feeling more in control of their own time, less stressed, and less likely to take work and worries home with them at night. They also found themselves thinking twice before interrupting someone, even when it wasn't quiet time, and found that the interactions they did have were more productive and focused. Managers, trying to respect quiet time, reduced the number of status reports they requested and found that this made the engineers more, not less, productive.

What we learned at this site is that looking at work through the lens of employees' personal lives raised aspects of work that not only were creating individual stress but were also interfering with the attempt to shorten the time to market. Once everyone understood this connection, it was possible to introduce changes that helped both personal and business goals (see "Product Development Team").

Product Development Team

Type of work	Software engineering
Employees	Professional; the majority are men.
Business issues	Shorten time to market.
Personal issue	Long hours
	Stress
Diagnosis	Team operates in continual crisis situation.
	Rewarding of individual heroics undermines teamwork.
Experimental intervention	Analyze how time is used.
	Create quiet times and interaction times.
Business results	Launch product on-time, despite contrary expectations.
	Mitigate oversupervision by managers.
	Help engineers use time more effectively by distinguishing between interruptions and critical interactions.
Personal results	Less stress and pressure
	Less work during nonwork hours for some engineers
	More control over work and personal life

Reduced Absenteeism and Improved Customer Service

The second site, a customer administration center, dealt with customers on billing, scheduling, and so on, via computer.[2] To increase customer satisfaction, the site was trying to become an organization of multiskilled, self-managed work groups. The employees had had cross-functional training and had been reorganized into multi-functional groups, but management didn't know where to go next and was waiting for corporate empowerment training to make the change.

The workers were nonexempt, and their hours were not long, but rigid. The result was a lot of absenteeism and lateness, which, according to managers, reduced their ability to serve customers. So managers tightly monitored the way people worked, resulting in a highly controlled environment.

When we asked people what made the work difficult to integrate with their personal lives, they mentioned the rigidity. For example, despite the expressed need of many employees and an array of flexible policies on the books, very few of them were actually used. Most requests for flexibility were restricted to changing the beginning and end of the workday by a half-hour or so. Since managers felt they always had to oversee their employees, they were understandably reluctant to give more leeway. Moreover, employees who wanted to take advantage of the benefits had to submit a plan to management indicating their need and documenting how they would meet business goals. Reluctant to relinquish control, management typically sat on these plans or returned them, requesting more detailed documentation. Few requests were granted, and fewer and fewer requests were made, in a self-reinforcing cycle that systematically disempowered employees.

When we reported our findings to the senior team, it became clear that we had raised aspects of the work culture that not only made the working conditions difficult for the employees, but also undermined the managers' efforts to improve the unit's effectiveness. Their highly controlled, individualistic way of managing partly explained why they were having difficulty moving toward empowerment and self-managed teams.

In response, senior management proposed a three-month experiment: Each employee could establish any schedule that he or she wanted, as long as the work got done. After some confusion about what this meant, some dramatic changes occurred. First, almost everyone asked for different hours, men and women, single and married, managers and front-line workers. Given the various schedules proposed, managers realized they could no longer deal with the requests on an individual basis and had to bring the groups together to decide how to get the work done. Obviously, the groups had to compromise, which gave them their first experience in self-management.

Customer Administration Center

Type of work	Routine, clerical
Employees	White-collar; the majority are women.
Business issues	Improve customer service.
	Move to self-managed, empowered teams.
Personal issue	Rigid schedules
Diagnosis	Culture of control leads to zero-sum view of flexibility and productivity.
	Culture of conservatism interferes with the risk-taking required to move to self-managed teams.
Experimental intervention	All employees have flexible work arrangements.
	Teams learn about self-management by taking control of flexible arrangements.
Business results	Absenteeism reduced by 30 percent.
	Improved customer service from more coverage.
	Teams learn to work in empowered ways.
Personal results	Less stress and pressure
	Time to attend to family and community issues
	More control over work and personal life

A 30 percent reduction in absenteeism made managers see the value in relinquishing some of the control they had felt was necessary. Customer service improved as service hours were extended due to more liberal employee schedules. The organization was on its way toward the transformation it had sought but had not been able to achieve. Employees now had the flexibility to manage pressing issues in their lives.

What we learned from this example is that using a personal lens to understand working conditions helps to identify ways in which old cultural assumptions undermine new initiatives. In this situation, we found that letting work groups manage their own schedules helped them to develop as self-managed teams and serve their customers better (see "Customer Administration Center").

Cross-Functional Synergies and Predictable Schedules

Our work at the third site also produced benefits to both the employees and business goals, but in a different way. In a sales and service district set up to sell and service all the company's products, one product group in particular was consistently below target.[3]

The group was organized as a partnership, but the functions were quite independent. Salespeople, both men and women who were paid on commission, had very difficult selling targets and thus worked long hours. Service people, primarily blue-collar men, had to respond to service calls at all hours and were beset by uncertainty about their schedules. Neither group had much respect for the other and they had little experience working together.

Our analysis indicated that there were unrealized synergies between the two groups. Not only could they help each other be more productive, but they could support each other in ways that would ease the stresses in their lives. In collaboration with the district leadership, we decided to experiment with a cross-functional team. The team met for nine months and made a dramatic turnaround.

At first, all the old antagonisms surfaced, and the members did not understand how they could help each other. But when one service manager reported that three of his people were planning to retire, the salespeople realized that this would adversely affect their own ability to plan installations. Thus began a slow realization that working together could improve their performance. They discovered further synergies when the service people did the groundwork so the salespeople could close a big sale.

As a result, the group, which had not been able to meet its sales targets for some time, was among the highest revenue-producing units in the district. Further, the members found ways to support each other that led to more control and predictability in their lives.

What we learned from this site was that creativity and commitment are best mobilized in response to people's personal needs. This became clear when we discovered that management had once before tried to form a cross-functional team around this same product group, without positive results. What, the managers wondered, was different about what we had done? The significant difference was that we *began* by looking at the stresses in people's *personal* lives. We brought the members together to consider how they could ease their work situation to make their lives more livable, which motivated them to engage the issues more creatively (see "Sales and Service District").

Since this initial project, we have worked with many other work teams, at many different levels, and in many different organizations. The results are similar. Whether the situation involves scientists, purchasing agents, loan processors, line workers, or researchers, connecting the two seemingly incompatible aims of better integrating personal lives and more effectively meeting business goals leads to a win all around. When we re-examine work practices and organizational cultures through the lens of employees' personal lives, not only do formerly invisible inefficiencies and dysfunctional work practices surface, but creative, unforeseen solutions emerge. Making this unexpected connection is a powerful way to engage employee involvement and creativity. By adding personal payoff to organizational changes, employees are energized and motivated to undertake them. The bottom line is that implementing these

Sales and Service District

Type of work	Sales—individual, based on commission
	Service—individual, driven by calls
Employees	Sales—equal number of men and women
	Service—the majority are men.
Business issue	Increase revenues for poorly performing product group.
Personal issues	Sales—long hours driven by ever-increasing stretch goals in bad economic climate.
	Service—unpredictability of hours driven by promised fast response time.
Diagnosis	Sales and service work at cross-purposes.
	Failure to realize synergies in working with the same customers.
Experimental intervention	Cross-functional product team
Business results	Highest revenues in district
	Synergies recognized (service can help sell and sales can help on routine service).
Personal results	More control over hours
	More mutual support

innovations not only helps employees integrate work and personal life, but also leads to increases in productivity and effectiveness.

How to Capture the Benefits of Connection: A Dual Agenda

To capture the benefits of connection, managers need to develop a dual agenda: Identify and change work practices that have unintended negative consequences both for employees' personal lives *and* for the business. The approach has three major phases: viewing work through the lens of personal life, identifying leverage points for change, and designing and implementing work-practice interventions that meet the dual agenda of productivity benefits to the business and personal benefits to employees.

Viewing Work through the Lens of Personal Life

People tend to see their work and personal lives as separate spheres. While they recognize the conflicts between these spheres, they usually see them as their private responsibility to manage and contain. The purpose of the first phase is to challenge this tendency by making an explicit connection between work and personal life. We accomplish this by asking people to consider the impact of their work and how it is performed on their personal lives. One useful question is, "What is it about how work is done in your area that makes it difficult for you to integrate your work and personal life?" The question applies to individuals and to work groups from the lowest to highest levels of the organization.

Starting from the perspective of personal life generates a different kind of response from asking the same question with only a work redesign perspective. Typically, people focus on work practices they personally find unnecessary or inefficient—constant interruptions, rigid and inflexible rules, competitive approaches that lead to duplicated efforts, emergency meetings called late in the day, and so on. In probing deeper, people begin to discuss why they think the work continues to get done this way, despite the inefficiencies. At this point, some of the cultural assumptions that drive the work begin to surface, and people start to talk about how emergencies are glorified and the people who respond to them are seen as heroes, how staying late is a way to show you care about the work, how solving crises is rewarded while preventing them is not, or how a willingness to sacrifice personal time signals commitment.

As people explore how work interferes with personal life, the strategic benefits of changing these practices become obvious. As the group probes for underlying causes, it becomes apparent that the very same assumptions and work practices that make integrating work and personal life difficult are also a problem in meeting business goals.

People begin to see these issues as systemic. They realize that what they are experiencing—stress, overcommitment, family conflict—is not an individual problem that they can solve by themselves. Instead, they begin to appreciate how the structure of work contributes to those dilemmas. The frustrations they feel at being unable to deal with their own problems now are seen in a different context. People also realize that their issues are not unique; others in the work group or management team experience similar problems. Recognizing that identifiable features of the work contribute to these personal concerns increases the team's commitment to move to the next step and consider the leverage points for change.

Identifying Leverage Points

In the second phase, the group considers ways of changing work practices to meet the dual agenda of improving effectiveness and enhancing the integration of work and personal life. The kinds of connections that a group makes depends on many factors—the type of work the team does; the team's size, composition, and level; and the specific pressures, opportunities, and resource constraints that the team is experiencing. Whatever leverage points the team considers, it is important that the members evaluate them in terms of the dual agenda. If a certain change is made, how will it improve the group's ability to meet a key strategic challenge? How will it enhance the group's ability to integrate work and personal lives?

Identifying leverage points for change is not easy. It requires looking at unexamined practices and assumptions about how work is done, where it is done, when it is done, and who does it. The first step is to think expansively about how changing particular work practices would help the business and help employees. The purpose at this stage is to brainstorm and, for the moment, not let questions about feasibility overwhelm the discussion. Thinking out of the box on work issues is difficult because we tend to accept that there is no other way to do things. It is important to let ideas flow.

For example, in a purchasing organization, when the members looked at their work through the lens of personal life, they realized that they were operating in a continual state of crisis, leading to extremely long hours and unpredictability. With the business goal to cut costs, delays in getting supplies to the line organization were a big problem. Crises exacerbated the problem. Probing deeper, they began to understand the underlying causes of the crises. They saw that how they worked with suppliers contributed to the very crises that created business and personal life problems. Some of the negative practices included giving bonuses to managers who solved crises and ignoring suppliers who warned about problems because the group feared the suppliers would routinely ask for extensions. New understanding allowed the group to design a process to distinguish among suppliers, detect and respond to early warning signals, and map out a reward system based on the absence of crises.

Considering the possibility that there are other ways of working leads naturally to thinking about experiments. We found some critical factors to think about when designing experiments that will achieve the benefits we've described:

1. The experiments must focus on organizational, not individual, issues. It is not enough to hold the work as a constant and find a way to give certain individuals more time or flexibility to meet current demands. The work itself—and the organizational assumptions driving the way the work gets done—must be the focus.

2. The experiments must meet the dual agenda of business and personal life. It is not enough to find obvious solutions that favor one over the other. An on-site day care facility might help some people meet work demands. A reduction in head count might meet a cost-cutting goal. But an experiment that meets the dual agenda must move to nonobvious solutions that affect both personal and business goals.

3. The experiments must be connected to the deeper issues they are addressing. It is not enough to say, "Let's reduce the number of meetings," without understand-

ing how norms governing meetings are connected to broader issues such as reward systems, idealized behavior, promotion policies, or other organizational norms.

4. The group needs to define evaluation criteria for both parts of the agenda. If the change is implemented, what business measures should be affected? What personal life issues?

Implementing Work-Practice Interventions

In the third phase, the group tries to implement different ways of working. Invariably, some kinks need to be ironed out as the intervention runs into obstacles. While many interventions can seem simple and straightforward, in fact, they are by definition violating some basic assumptions and taken-for-granted norms. Had they been truly simple, they probably would have been implemented already! While this approach unleashes energy, creativity, and innovation, it can seem risky to those involved. It is important to deal with these risks to protect the intervention and enhance its chances for success.

Some team members may fear they will seem less committed or dependable if they suggest a change that would make it easier to integrate their work and personal life. They may have been unable to discuss problems in this area, so sharing them is difficult. At the same time, managers may fear that any suggested change is likely to incur productivity losses. Therefore, senior management must indicate that it is willing to suspend, if only temporarily, some of the operating procedures that were identified as barriers to the dual agenda.

For example, at one manufacturing site, a work group identified an inflexible operations review procedure as one factor that made it difficult for them to meet business and personal goals. The vice president's willingness to suspend some of the procedure's requirements for the duration of the experiment was important for many reasons. Not only did it help people see that management was serious about giving them authority to control significant conditions that affected their productivity, but it also helped them realize that change was possible and worth the effort. In addition, it protected the work group manager from bearing all the risks of innovation. In another organization, senior managers, who had previously insisted on unreachable stretch goals to motivate researchers, allowed them to establish and work toward "realistic" targets. At still another site, management agreed to modify some aspects of a short-term productivity measure. Senior management's willingness to create the conditions for success is important to this approach. Without support, even the best ideas that come from the dual agenda are unlikely to succeed.

As the group implements work-practice improvements and the benefits to the business become evident, a company may be tempted to keep the benefits for itself by increasing workloads or reducing head count. For example, one unit proposed realigning work responsibilities between on-site and remote personnel to reduce excessive travel demands on scientists. However, as the proposal moved forward, the company was tempted to increase the number of projects assigned to each scientist, thereby replicating both the business problem (missed opportunities from lack of time for reflection and analysis) and the personal issue (no time for nonwork activities). Only by evaluating the proposed change against the dual criteria did the company re-examine the indiscriminate increase in workload and preserve the dual goals. All experiments are fragile; without tangible benefits to employees and the visible support of key decision makers, they are likely to be only transitory.

Conclusion

The dual agenda makes it possible to increase productivity and effectiveness in the business, while enabling employees to better integrate their work and personal lives. But it is not easy to achieve. Connecting these issues is not the typical response. Faced with the business issues in our examples, most managers would try to re-engineer work processes, throw more time at the problem, or reduce the workforce to cut costs. Faced with the personal life issues, most human resource personnel would ask for additional benefits—like bringing in evening meals or giving extra vouchers for child care—to help people cope. These accommodations might leave both the workplace and families and communities worse off. When firms develop family-friendly policies and benefits that leave existing work practices and cultural assumptions about work and good workers intact, the conflict between the demands of the new workplace and the needs of families and communities is exacerbated. Only by connecting work and personal lives through a dual agenda can companies reframe the conflict into an opportunity for innovation and change.

How can an organization determine if it would benefit from a dual agenda approach? First and most obvious is to find out whether people are having difficulty juggling their work and personal lives. Signs of stress and fatigue, complaints about work demands and time, and dissatisfaction with work and family policies may emerge in satisfaction surveys, exit interviews, and off-line retreats. More critical may be the loss of valued employees or the sudden change in the performance of people who seemed to have great potential.

Such indicators may suggest that a company is ready for the dual agenda approach. They may explain why creative ideas are coming only from the top of the organization, or why repeated new initiatives show great promise but then disappoint. If companies undertake new initiatives to increase productivity, revenues, and general performance without looking at them through the lens of personal life, the very goals of the initiatives may be undermined.

Our work has identified some typical work practices and assumptions that are dysfunctional for both business and personal goals, for example, more time necessarily leads to greater productivity; time is an unlimited resource; the most committed workers are those who work the longest hours; individual competition and heroics are the best way to get the most out of people. When work is performed in an atmosphere of continual crisis or when the response to problems is to do the same thing, only harder, there are clear opportunities for innovation and change that can meet the criteria of the dual agenda.

Linking personal lives with strategic issues is an unexpected connection. But if we continue to deal with each area separately, in the long run, both individuals and organizations—if not society—will suffer. What we have outlined, however, is not a one-time fix. Rather, it describes a process of continually looking at the intersection of work and personal lives and using the connection as a lever to challenge work practices on an ongoing basis. The solution to one set of issues raises other issues that a company can subject to the same analysis and experimentation. Such an ongoing process results in changed mindsets and, ultimately, in the culture change that most companies seek but find so difficult to achieve.

This unexpected connection can revitalize your business.

Acknowledgments

This chapter is reprinted with permission from *Sloan Management Review* 38, no. 4 (Summer 1997): 11–20. It is based on a research project supported by the Ford Foundation. For a full report, see Rapoport, Bailyn, Kolb, Fletcher, *et al.* (1996). Others involved in the research project were Susan Eaton, Maureen Harvey, Robin Johnson, and Leslie Perlow. Rhona Rapoport was the consultant to the project. The Ford Foundation, in conjunction with the Xerox Corporation and Working Mother magazine, hosted a CEO Summit in New York on 15 September 1997 to discuss this research. This project, in conjunction with many others, is described and analyzed in Rhona Rappaport, Joyce K. Fletcher, Bettye H. Pruitt, and Lotte Bailyn, eds., *Beyond Work-Family Balance: Advancing Gender Equity and Workplace Performance* (San Francisco: Jossey Bass) 2001.

Our names are listed in alphabetical order. This article was a fully collaborative effort, as was, with other team members, the project itself.

Notes

1. For a full description of the work at this site, see Perlow (1995).
2. For a full description of this site, see Johnson (1994).
3. For a full description of this case, see Eaton and Harvey (1996).

References

Eaton, S., and M. Harvey. 1996. Re-linking Work and Family: A Catalyst for Organizational Change. MIT Sloan School of Management Working Paper 3892–3896.

Johnson, R. 1994. Where's the Power in Empowerment? Definition, Difference, and Dilemmas of Empowerment in the Context of Work-Family Management. Ph.D. dissertation, Harvard Business School.

Perlow, L. 1995. The Time Famine: An Unintended Consequence of the Way Time Is Used at Work. Ph.D. dissertation, MIT Sloan School of Management.

Rapoport, R., L. Bailyn, D. Kolb, J. K. Fletcher, *et al.* 1996. *Relinking Life and Work: Toward a Better Future*. New York: Ford Foundation.

19 Innovating our Way to the Next Industrial Revolution

Peter M. Senge and Goran Carstedt

Much of what is being said about the New Economy is not all that new. Waves of discontinuous technological change have occurred before in the industrial age, sparked by innovations such as the steam engine in the eighteenth century; railroads, steel, electrification, and telecommunications in the nineteenth century; and auto and air transport, synthetic fibers, and television in the first half of the twentieth century. Each of those technologies led to what economist Joseph Schumpeter called "creative destruction," in which old industries died and new ones were born. Far from signaling the end of the industrial era, these waves of disruptive technologies accelerated and extended it.

What would constitute the beginnings of a truly postindustrial age? Only fundamental shifts in how the economic system affects the larger systems within which it resides—namely, society and nature. In many ways, the industrial age has been an era of harvesting natural and social capital in order to create financial and productive capital. So far there is little evidence that the New Economy is changing that.

The industrial-age assault on natural capital continues. Vague hopes about "bits for atoms" and "demassification" are naive at best, echoes of talk about "paperless offices" 20 years ago. The rate of losing species has not slowed. Most New Economy products end up where Old Economy products do: in increasingly scarce landfills. Globalization is destroying the last remnants of stewardship for natural resources in industries such as forest products: Today, buy-and-sell decisions are executed by faceless agents living on the other side of the world from the people and ecosystems whose futures they decide. Moreover, New Economy growth stimulates related growth in Old Economy industries—along with the familiar pattern of suburban sprawl, pollution, loss of habitat, and competition for natural resources.

The New Economy's effects on social capital are more complex but no less disturbing.[1] Industrial progress has tended to destroy cultural as well as biological diversity, despite the protests of marginalized groups like the Provençal farmers who oppose the globalization of food production. Likewise, although changes in traditional family and community structures have brought greater freedom for women and many ethnic groups, the past decade also has brought worldwide increases in divorce rates, single-parent families, and "street" children. Global markets, capital flows, and e-commerce open up new opportunities for emerging economies, but they also create new generations of technological haves and have-nots. According to the World Bank, the poorest quartile of humankind has seen its share of global income fall from 2.5 percent to 1.25 percent over the past 25 years. More immediately, eroding social capital manifests in the isolation, violence, and frenzy of modern living. Individuals and small circles of friends carve out increasingly private lives amidst increasingly distrustful strangers, preferring to "bowl alone." We almost take for granted road rage, deaths of spectators at sporting matches, and kids shooting kids at school.[2] The "24-7" job has become the norm in many industries, the latest step in subjugating our lives to the clock, a process begun with the mechanization of work at the outset of the industrial era.

Judged by its impact on natural and social capital, so far the New Economy looks more like the next wave of the industrial era than a truly postindustrial era. Why should we care? Because the basic development patterns of the industrial era are not sustainable. As U.S. National Academy of Sciences home secretary Peter Raven says, quoting the Wildlife Conservation Society's George Schaller, "We cannot afford another century like the last one." Plus, there are other possibilities.

Corporate Heretics

"Is genuine progress still possible? Is development sustainable? Or is one strand of progress—industrialization—now doing such damage to the environment that the next generation won't have a world worth living in?"[3]

Those are not the words of the Sierra Club or Greenpeace, but of BP chairman John Browne. In 1997, Browne broke ranks with the oil industry to declare, "There is now an effective consensus among the world's leading scientists and serious and well-informed people outside the scientific community that there is a discernible human influence on the climate." Moreover, he argued that "the time to consider the policy dimensions of climate change is not when the link between greenhouse gases and climate change is conclusively proven, but when the possibility cannot be discounted."[4]

Equally important, BP looks at the situation as a business opportunity. "There are good commercial reasons for being ahead of the pack when it comes to issues to do with the environment," says Browne. Since 1997, the company has become active in public forums on global climate, has begun to reduce emissions in exploration and production, has started to market cleaner fuels, and has invested significantly in alternative sources of energy (such as photovoltaic power and hydrogen). All the while, Browne has led an effort to build a more performance-oriented culture, and company profits have been at an all-time high.

BP is but one example of the shift in thinking that is becoming evident in many companies and industries. Appliance maker Electrolux uses water- and powder-based paints (rather than hazardous solvent-based paints), prioritizes the use of recycled materials, and has introduced the world's first family of refrigerators and freezers free of the chlorofluorocarbons that contribute to ozone depletion. In 1999, Toyota and Honda began selling hybrid cars that combine internal combustion and electric propulsion, perform comparably to competitors—and can achieve up to 70 miles per gallon today, with prospects for two to three times that mileage in a few years.[5] In 1998, Xerox introduced its first fully digitized copier, the Document Centre 265, which is more than 90 percent remanufacturable and 97 percent recyclable. The product has only about 200 parts, an order of magnitude less than its predecessor. Its sales have exceeded forecasts. According to Fortune, remanufacturing and waste reduction saved Xerox $250 million in 1998. Some firms, such as Interface Inc., a $1.3 billion manufacturer of commercial carpet tiles, which saved about $140 million in sustainable waste reductions from 1995 to 1999, are even rethinking their basic business model. Interface's goal is to stop selling product altogether. Instead, it will provide floor-covering services, leasing products and later taking them back for 100 percent recycling. Assessing the environmental impact of the carpeting industry, chairman Ray Anderson says bluntly, "In the future, people like me will go to jail."[6]

These examples are all just initial steps, as each of these companies would readily admit. Ultimately, sustainability is a challenge to society as a whole. Nonetheless, business can play a legitimate leadership role as a catalyst for larger changes. We believe that a new environmentalism is emerging, driven by innovation, not regulation—radical new technologies, products, processes and business models. More and more businesses are recognizing the opportunities this creates. "Sustainability not only helps improve the world, but also energizes the company," says ABB's CEO Goran Lindahl.

The good news is that change through market-driven innovation is the type of change our society understands best. The problem is that much in today's business climate appears to run in the opposite direction. Short-term financial pressures, the free-agent work force, dramatic opportunities to start new companies and get rich quickly, often-cynical mass media, and industrializing countries aspiring to catch up to the industrialized world's consumption standards—these hardly seem like the conditions for increasing stewardship of the earth.

The challenge today is to develop sustainable businesses that are compatible with the current economic reality. Innovative business models and products must work financially, or it won't matter how good they are ecologically and socially. To explore how to achieve this, the SoL Sustainability Consortium was formed to bring together like-minded corporate executives experienced in organizational learning who also see sustainability becoming a cornerstone of their business strategy.[7] Together, we are asking: Can organizations committed to sustainability work with the forces propelling most of the New Economy in the opposite direction? And, can organizational-learning principles and tools help in realizing the changes that this will require?

Between Two Stories

The first reality confronting businesses that are serious about sustainability is ambiguity, starting with the question: What do we mean by sustainability? The ambiguity inherent in sustainability has deep cultural roots.

"We are in trouble just now because we do not have a good story," says cultural historian Thomas Berry. "We are in between stories. The old story, the account of how the world came to be and how we fit into it . . . sustained us for a long period of time. It shaped our emotional attitudes, provided us with life purposes and energized our actions. It consecrated our suffering and integrated our knowledge. We awoke in the morning and knew where we were. We could answer the questions of our children."[8] In a sense, sustainability requires letting go of the story of the supremacy of the human in nature, the story that the natural world exists as mere "resources" to serve human "progress." But most of us grew up with this story, and it is still shared by the vast majority of modern society. It is not easy to let it go, especially when we are uncertain about what the new story will be. Businesses seeking sustainability can easily feel like a trapeze artist suspended in the air. They have let go of a secure worldview without knowing what they can hang on to.

Yet the dim outlines of a new story are emerging. At its root are two elements: a new picture of the universe and a new sense of human possibility. "We are just beginning to explore what it means to be part of a universe that is alive . . . not just cosmos but cosmogenesis," in the words of Barry and physicist Brian Swimme. Moreover, the new universe story "carries with it a psychic-spiritual dimension as well as a physical-materialistic dimension. Otherwise, human consciousness emerges out of nowhere . . . an addendum [with] no real place in the story of the universe."[9] Echoing Barry, Roger Saillant, former Ford executive and now Visteon vice president, says, "The new story will have to do with personal accountability . . . new communities in business and elsewhere based on knowing that there is no parent to take care of us and that we have a stewardship responsibility for future generations." Saillant adds that gradually "a larger intelligence will emerge. Those special moments when we glimpse that our actions are informed by a larger whole will become more frequent." Interface marketing vice president Joyce LaValle foresees a similar shift: "I think this will actually get easier as we proceed. But first we must go through a kind of eye of the needle."

According to John Ehrenfeld, president of the International Society for Industrial Ecology, the challenge arises because sustainability "is a radical concept that stretches our current ideas about rationality. It has often been framed as environmentalists against business. But this generates polarization and misses the three very different worldviews needed to move forward: rationalism, naturalism, and humanism." Only by embracing all three can we begin to understand what sustainability actually means. (See "The Dimensions of Sustainability.")

The Dimensions of Sustainability

Rationalism, the belief in reason, has dominated society throughout modern times. It remains the dominant perspective in business and education. Yet it has limits. It cannot explain the passion that motivates entrepreneurs committed to a new product idea nor the imagination of scientists testing an intuition. Nor does it explain why a quiet walk on a beach or a hike into the mountains may inspire both. These can only be understood by seeing how naturalism, humanism, and rationalism infuse one another. Naturalism arises from our innate sense of being part of nature. Humanism arises from the rich interior life that connects reason, emotion and awareness—and ultimately allows us to connect with one another. Epochs in human history that have nurtured all three have stood out as golden ages.

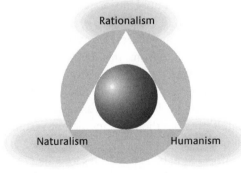

Figure 19.1
Three Worldviews Required for Building Sustainable Enterprises

Naturalism: Biomimicry and the Logic of Natural Systems

The diverse innovations that created the first Industrial Revolution sprang from the same guiding image that inspired the preceding scientific revolution—the image of the machine. "My aim," wrote seventeenth-century scientist Johannes Kepler, "is to show that the celestial machine is to be likened not to a divine organism but rather to a clockwork."[10] The assembly line became the prototypical organization—with managers as controllers and workers operating in rigid routines, all coordinated by bells, whistles, and production schedules. The assembly line was so successful it became the model for other types of organizations, including the nineteenth-century urban school system. Although the machine-age organization achieved previously unimaginable productivity, it also created a mechanized organizational environment that dehumanized and fragmented how people worked together.

If the machine inspired the industrial age, the image of the living system may inspire a genuine postindustrial age. This is what life-sciences writer Janine Benyus calls "biomimicry," innovation inspired by understanding how living systems work. "What is consistent with life is sustainable," says Benyus. For example, in nature there is no waste. All byproducts of one natural system are nutrients for another. Why should industrial systems be different? We would not ask engineers to build bridges that defy the laws of gravity nor chip designers to violate laws of physics. Why should we expect businesses to violate the law of zero waste?

All living systems follow cycles: produce, recycle, regenerate.

By contrast, industrial-age systems follow a linear flow of extract, produce, sell, use, discard—what "Ecology of Commerce" author Paul Hawken calls "take-make-waste." (See "Why Industry Produces Waste.")

Indeed, the primary output of today's production processes is waste. Across all industries, less than 10% of everything extracted from the earth (by weight) becomes usable products. The remaining 90 to 95 percent becomes waste from production.[11] Moreover, what is sold creates still more waste—from discard and from use (for example, from auto exhaust). So, while businesses obsess over labor and financial capital efficiency, we have created possibly the most inefficient system of production in human history.

What would industrial systems that conform to natural principles look like? First, they would be circular rather than linear, with significant reductions in all waste flows. (See "How Industry Can Reduce Waste.") This implies three specific waste-reduction strategies: resource productivity, clean products, and remanufacturing, recycling, and composting."[12]

LIVING SYSTEMS FOLLOW CYCLES

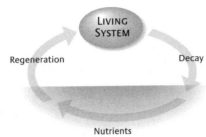

INDUSTRIAL-AGE SYSTEMS DO NOT

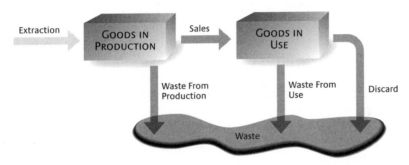

Figure 19.2
Why Industry Produces Waste

Strategy 1. Resource productivity reduces waste from production through ecoefficient production technologies and the design of production processes in which wastes from one process become nutrients for another.

Strategy 2. Clean products (say, hybrid cars) reduce waste from goods in use through nonpolluting product technologies.

Strategy 3. Remanufacturing and recycling (creating "technical nutrients") and designing more products that are biodegradable (creating "natural nutrients") reduce waste from discard.

Architect William McDonough and chemist Michael Braungart summarize the three strategies with the simple dictum: "Waste equals food."

Second, companies would invest in nature's regenerative processes. They would do fewer things that compromise regeneration, such as paving over wetlands, and would invest some surpluses in restoring natural capital—for example, companies

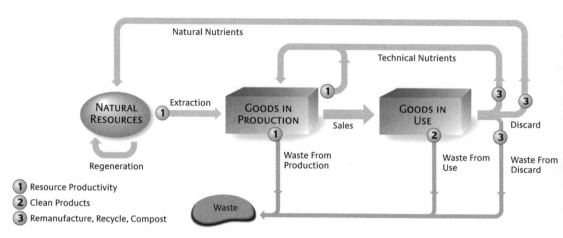

Figure 19.3
How Industry Can Reduce Waste

like Interface plant trees to match business miles traveled because increasing forest cover reduces greenhouse gases.

Third, following Buckminster Fuller's dictum, companies would "learn how to live on our energy income [solar, wind, hydrogen] rather than off our principal [oil and gas]." Living on our income would not only reduce resource extraction, but also eliminate the side effects of using minerals, like auto emissions.

Thinking in more systemic terms may appear simple, but it raises important questions about current corporate environmentalism. For example, ecoefficiency has become a goal for companies worldwide, with many realizing significant cost savings from eliminating waste from production. That is good in some ways, but troubling in others. Thinking about the larger system shows that ecoefficiency innovations alone could actually worsen environmental stresses in the future.

Ecoefficiency innovations reduce waste from production, but this does not alter the number of products produced nor the waste generated from their use and discard. Indeed, most companies investing in cost-reducing ecoefficiency improvements are doing so with the aim of increased profits and growth. Moreover, there is no guarantee that increased economic growth from ecoefficiency will come in similarly ecoefficient ways. In today's global capital markets, greater profits show up as investment capital that could easily be reinvested in old-style eco-inefficient industries.

To put it another way, nature does not care about the industrial system's efficiency. Nature cares about its impact in *absolute terms*. If a vastly more ecoefficient industrial system grows much larger, it conceivably could generate more total waste and destroy more habitat and species than a smaller, less ecoefficient economy.

The answer is not necessarily zero growth. The implications of naturalism are more subtle: We can sustain growth only by reducing total material throughput and total accumulated waste. Ecoefficiency gains are laudable but dangerously incomplete, as is any strategy that fails to consider the industrial-natural system as a whole. A systemic approach would reduce all sources of waste: from production, use, and discard.

Managers' faith in ecoefficiency also illustrates the power of mental models. Industrial-age managerial practice has always been about increasing efficiency. Increased natural-resource productivity that translates directly into lower costs offers a compelling business case, one that does not challenge established thinking deeply. However, focusing on ecoefficiency may distract companies from pursuing radically different products and business models—changes that require shifts in mental models, not just shifting attention within existing mental models.

This is unlikely to happen without mastering the human dimensions of learning and change.

Humanism: The Logic of Learning

"The prevailing system of management has destroyed our people," said total-quality pioneer W. Edwards Deming. "People are born with intrinsic motivation, self-esteem, dignity, curiosity to learn, joy in learning." Echoing Deming, anthropologist Edward Hall declares, "Humans are learning organisms par excellence. The drive to learn is as strong as the sexual drive—it begins earlier and lasts longer." The premise of work on learning organizations has been that thriving in today's knowledge-based marketplaces means reversing the destructiveness that Deming speaks about and cultivating people's drive to learn.

In fall 1999 the sustainability consortium was hosted by the Xerox "Lakes" team that had developed the Document Centre 265 copier. Already aware of the team's innovations in design for remanufacture (more than 500 patents came from the Lakes project) and the product's success in the marketplace, we learned about how the team's zero-waste vision translated into a manufacturing facility with virtually no waste and eventually became embraced by many of the team's suppliers. But it still wasn't clear how the team had achieved those accomplishments.

Late in the day, Rhonda Staudt, a young engineer who was one of the lead designers, was talking about the team's innovations when she was interrupted by David

Berdish, veteran of many organizational-learning projects at Ford. "Rhonda," Berdish said, "I understand what a great opportunity this was for you and how exciting it was. I work with engineers, and I know the excitement of pushing the technological envelope. But what I really want to know is why you did this. What I mean is: 'What was the stand you took and who were you taking that stand for?' "

Rhonda looked at David for a long time in silence and then, in front of many peers and a few superiors, began to cry. "I am a mom," she answered. We had all heard the Lakes motto, "Zero to landfill, for the sake of our children." But now we were in its presence. Roger Saillant of Visteon turned to Peter and whispered, "Seamlessness." Peter knew exactly what he meant: when what we do becomes inseparable from who we are.

We have all spent much of our lives in institutions that force us to be someone we are not. We commit ourselves to the company's agenda. We act professionally. After a while, we have lived so long in the house of mirrors that we mistake the image we are projecting for who we really are. The poet David Whyte quotes an AT&T manager who wrote, "Ten years ago, I turned my face for a moment . . . and it became my life."

Over the past decade, many companies have attempted to build learning organizations with little grasp of the depth of the changes required. They want to increase imagination and creativity without unleashing the passion that comes from personal vision. They seek to challenge established mental models without building real trust and openness. They espouse systems thinking, without realizing how threatening that can be to established "quick fix" management cultures. There is a difference between building more-sustainable enterprises because there is profit in it and because it is one's life's work. The journey ahead will require both.

If understanding natural systems establishes the guiding ideas for sustainability innovations, then learning provides the means to translate ideas into accomplishments. But, just as the logic of natural systems conflicts with take-make-waste industrial systems, so too does the logic of a learning culture conflict with traditional, control-oriented organizational cultures. To a controlling culture, a learning culture based on passion, curiosity, and trust appears to be out of control. In fact, it is based on a different type of control. "We are not trying to eliminate control and discipline in our organizations," says retired CEO William O'Brien, formerly with Hanover Insurance Co. "We are trying to substitute top-down discipline based on fear with self-discipline. This does not make life easier for people in organizations. It makes it more demanding—but also more exciting."

These two tensions—between natural systems and industrial systems on the one hand and between learning and controlling on the other—may appear to make sustainable enterprises impossible. However, deeper currents in the New Economy could also cause those tensions to become immutable forces transforming traditional industrial-age management.

A New Business Logic

Kevin Kelly, editor at large of *Wired*, observes that the "emerging new economic order . . . has three distinguishing characteristics. It is global. It favors intangibles—ideas, information, and relationships. And it is intensely interlinked." Kelly sees electronic networks generating new patterns of "organic behavior in a technological matrix." But he suggests that the real changes are not ultimately about technology but communication. According to Kelly, in the world that is emerging, "Communication is the economy."[13]

Today, perhaps the earth as a living system is communicating to us through increasingly turbulent weather patterns. Perhaps our frayed social structures are communicating to us through increasing acts of child violence. Are we listening? If the New Economy is revolutionizing communication, can it enable deeper listening? If so, we may discern a new business logic emerging, one that starts with rethinking how firms create value and continues by redefining "customers," "employees," "suppliers"—and ultimately the company itself.

From Things to the Value Provided by Things

"Production is increasingly not where value is created," says Ting Ho, vice president of strategy for global-logistics Internet startup Zoho. "The traditional company produced something that it then had to sell. Today, we must understand a customer and serve a genuine need."

At the heart of the industrial-age growth machine was a kind of mass hypnosis—convincing consumers that happiness meant owning a new thing. A new washing machine. A new computer. A new car. However, people do not want a hunk of steel in the driveway. They want the benefits it provides—whether they are tangible benefits like transport or intangible benefits like freedom or fun.

What does it mean to create new business models on the basis of that understanding? For Interface, it means shifting from selling carpets to providing floor-covering services, automatically taking back worn carpet tiles or replacing entire sections if a customer wants a different color. For Dow Chemical, it means leasing "dissolving services," then reusing the solvents. For Carrier, the world's leading manufacturer of air-conditioning equipment, it means renting cooling services rather than selling air conditioners. For IKEA, according to its published mission state-ment, it means providing services to help people "make a house or apartment into a home" rather than selling furniture. All these firms believe that "higher profits will come from providing better solutions rather than selling more equipment," in the words of "Natural Capitalism" authors Amory and Hunter Lovins and Paul Hawken.

From the standpoint of sustainability, providing services rather than just selling products creates a potential new alignment between what is sound economically and what is sound environmentally. A company's business model no longer requires designed-in obsolescence to push customers into buying new products. Instead, producers have an incentive to design for longevity, efficient servicing, improved functioning, and product take-back. Such design allows for maintaining rela-tionships with customers by continually ensuring that products are providing the services that people desire—at the lowest cost to the provider.

The shift from "the value is in the stuff" to "the value is in the service the stuff provides" also may lead to a radical shift in the concept of ownership. Swiss indus-try analyst Walter Stahel and chemist Braungart have proposed that, in the future, producers will own what they produce forever and therefore will have strong incen-tives to design products to be disassembled and remanufactured or recycled, whichever is more economical. Owning products forever would represent a power-ful step toward changing companies' attitudes about product discard.

Such ideas signal a radical shift in business models, one that will not come easily. It starts with how a company thinks of itself in relation to its customers: as a producer of things people buy or a provider of services through products made and remade? Marketing strategist Sandra Vandermerwe argues that such a view is essential to true customer focus, providing value for customers as well as obtaining value from customers.[14] It also shifts producers' time horizons. As Volvo discovered years ago, when a company is only selling cars, its relationship with the customer ends with the purchase. When it is providing customer satisfaction, it just begins.

From Producers and Consumers to Cocreators of Value

Focusing on the services provided by products also shifts the very meaning of "customer." Customers are no longer passive; they are cocreators of value. Thirty years ago, futurist Alvin Toffler coined the term "prosumer," people who actively participate in generating the value they derive from any product.[15] "Today, pro-sumers are everywhere," says Kelly, "from restaurants where you assemble your own dinner to medical self-care arenas, where you serve as doctor and patient." As Kelly says, the essence of prosumerism today is that "customers have a hand in the creation of the product."[16]

Prosumerism is infiltrating diverse marketplaces, especially those where Internet technology is strong. One of Amazon.com's most popular Web-site features is customer reviews of books, CDs, and other products. The five-year-old magazine *Fast Company* now rivals *Business Week, Fortune,* and *Forbes*, partly because of its "Company of Friends," a Web-site feature that allows subscribers to get together to discuss common concerns, form support networks for projects, or tell the magazine their interests. "I can go to our Web site and determine which are the 10 most frequently forwarded articles," says editor Alan Webber. "Our readers are no longer just an audience but cocreators of product."

How does that shift to prosumers relate to sustainability? It starts with activist customers who think for themselves. And activist customers are organizing themselves. "Thanks largely to the Internet," say C. K. Prahalad and V. Ramaswamy, "consumers have increasingly been engaging themselves in an active and explicit dialogue with manufacturers of products and services."[17] They add, "The market has become a forum." Or, as the popular "Cluetrain Manifesto" puts it, the market is becoming "a community of discourse."[18] With the inmates running the asylum, will they start to change the rules? What if people start talking to one another? What if they talk about the state of the world and how different types of products affect the quality of people's lives?

Leading Web-based companies, because they relate to their customers differently, also gain a different sense of what truly concerns customers. "Without a doubt, sustainability of our current lifestyle—personally and environmentally—matters to a lot of our readers," says Webber. "These were among the concerns that motivated us to start the magazine, and we've seen nothing to persuade us otherwise."

At this stage, it is speculation whether self-organizing networks of customers will unearth the deeper values essential to building sustainable societies. But it is no speculation that shifts in consumer behavior will be essential in creating such societies. One of the most significant concentrations of power in the industrial era has been the growth of a massive advertising industry applying psychological savvy to manipulate consumer preferences. "Soap operas" acquired their name because they were devised by Procter & Gamble and other consumer-goods companies to market soap. Could this be another form of centralized control that becomes history, the victim of the freer flow of information and interaction that allows people to know more and learn faster?

Homo sapiens has been around longer than *Homo consumer*. People still care deeply about the world their children will live in. Building sustainable enterprises will require tapping and harnessing that caring.

Many market-oriented companies sense just such a shift emerging in consumer preferences. For example, Nike has a host of recycled and recyclable products coming to market. For a company that sells the image of fitness, it is not surprising that Darcy Winslow, general manager of sustainable products and services, says: "Corporations in the twenty-first century cannot be fit if we don't prioritize and neutralize our impact on the environment."

From Compliant Employees to Committed Members of Social Networks

There are few companies today that do not struggle with the implications of the free-agent work force. The traditional employment contract based on good pay and benefits in exchange for loyalty is vanishing in many industries. Entrepreneurial opportunities are enticing, especially to young people. Most companies respond by trying to rework the old contract. They increase salary and benefits. They offer stock. They invent creative new perks. But in so doing, they miss entirely the change that might make the greatest difference: a mission worthy of people's commitment.

In 1991, IKEA faced the daunting challenge of extending its European business success to North America, the "graveyard of European retailers." It was clear from the outset that IKEA managers could not say, "Here's how we do it in Sweden," and expect much enthusiasm. Achieving strong returns for a distant corporate office was not enough. Being part of a proud and widely imitated European firm had limited meaning. It became clear that IKEA's North American management team had to find ways to truly engage people.

It turned out that North Americans, like Europeans, were concerned about the environment. Eventually, some 20,000 IKEA employees in North America and Europe participated voluntarily in a two-day training session on "The Natural Step," an intuitive introduction to the system conditions that must be met by a sustainable society. Not only did that engage people in selling the company's environmentally oriented products and creating related product and service ideas, it engaged them in working for IKEA. From 1990 through 1994, North American sales increased 300%.

The free-agent image connotes to many employers lack of commitment, people seeking a purely transactional relationship with a company. Perhaps the opposite is true. It may be a unique opportunity for organizations that truly value commitment. If we actually thought of people as free, we would have to approach them with respect, knowing that they can choose where to work. "It is amazing the commitment that people feel toward our focus on sustainability and the environment," says Vivienne Cox, BP vice president for marketing. "In a very tough business environment, it really matters to people who have many options in their lives."

Most industrial-age companies wanted what they regarded as committed employees. Today, the definition of commitment is changing, and paternalism is giving way to more adult relationships. "People stay with a firm, in many instances, because they see an alignment between their personal values and those they perceive the firm to be committed to," says Ged Davis, who is Shell's vice president for global business environment. If enterprises are not committed to anything beyond making money, why should managers be surprised that workers make transactional commitments?

Kelly also notes that in the competitive labor markets found in fast-growing industries, people change companies but maintain their loyalty "to advancing technology or to the region."[19] And to trusted colleagues. One key person may take groups of people from employer to employer like the Pied Piper.[20] Project teams form, un-form and then re-form like the teams of writers, actors, and technical specialists that make movies. Yet larger social networks remain intact. Increasingly, such networks are the keepers of values, commitments, and the subtle know-how that makes winners and losers. Longer-term relationships embedded in fluid but enduring social networks are a new phenomenon that most companies have not yet understood.

"Companies have felt that workers needed them more than they needed workers," says Peter Drucker. "This is changing in ways that most companies still do not seem to grasp."[21]

From Separate Businesses to Ecological Communities

"The great benefits reaped by the New Economy in the coming decades," says Kelly, "will be due in large part to exploring and exploiting the power of decentralized and autonomous networks," which in many ways now resemble "an ecology of organisms, interlinked and coevolving, constantly in flux, deeply entangled, ever-expanding at its edges."

"In traditional businesses, everything was piecework," says Zoho's Ho. "Now we are all part of larger systems, and our success depends on understanding those systems." For example, the traditional relationship between producer and supplier was neat and tidy. Producers wanted reliable supply at the lowest possible cost. Today, cost may be only one of several criteria that shape successful producer-supplier relationships. "Both as a supplier and with our suppliers, we are continually codesigning and co-innovating," says Ho. "There is no other way to keep pace with rapid changes and expanding knowledge."

Paradoxically, the realization that all enterprises are part of complex, evolving systems imparts new meaning to relationships and trust. As Webber has said, "The New Economy starts with technology and ends with trust."[22] People who are co-innovating must know each other and trust each other—in ways unnecessary in traditional relationships between providers and customers. That leads to the question: Can partners in complex supply networks co-innovate more-sustainable practices?

For example, Nike has programs in place with six of its material suppliers to collect 100% of their scrap and recycle it into the next round of products. The goal is to scale this up to all material suppliers. Similarly, all the big steps in design for remanufacture require intense cooperation up and down supply chains. "If you don't have suppliers hooked in, the whole thing will fail," says former Lakes chief engineer John Elter. The Xerox team hosted "supplier symposiums" where "we taught suppliers what remanufacturing means and gave them the basic tools for remanufacture," says Elter. Even more important, they assured suppliers that they would share in the cost savings—because used parts would go back to the suppliers for remanufacture. "The key is that suppliers participate in the economic benefit of remanufacturing because they don't have to make everything new. This is a big deal. Plus, they are developing new expertise they can apply with other customers."

Building the necessary alignment for product take-back among networks of wholesalers, retailers, and customers is equally daunting. "Without doubt, one of the biggest challenges with our 'Evergreen Service Contract' [Interface's model for selling floor-covering services rather than carpeting]," says chairman Ray Anderson, "is transforming mental models built up over generations"—such as those of purchasing departments in big companies whose incentives are based purely on cost of purchase, rather than on lifetime costs and aesthetic benefits.

Intense cooperative learning will never occur unless companies view their fates as linked. That is why the shift from seeing a world of suppliers and customers to one in which "we are all part of larger systems" is essential. Companies that do not recognize their interdependence with suppliers, distributors, and customers will never build the trust needed to shift established mental models.

"Tennyson had it only half right when he said nature was 'red in tooth and claw,'" writes Janine Benyus. "In mature ecosystems, cooperation seems as important as competition. [Species cooperate] in order to diversify and . . . to fully use the habitat." Companies that see one another only as competitors may likewise find their habitat disappearing as the world around them changes.

From Closed Doors to Transparency

The world in which key corporate decisions could be made behind closed doors is disappearing. In 1995, Shell encountered a dramatic and unexpected reaction to its plans to sink in the North Sea its Brent Spar oil platform, which was approaching the end of its productive lifetime. Despite the fact that the company had gone through a three-year process to identify the best environmental option and had the concurrence of the U.K. government, the situation became a public-relations nightmare when other governments objected to the plan. Shell had failed to realize that its private decision had become a public one, a harsh lesson learned by many other companies, from Nike to Ford to Microsoft, in recent years.

There is an old saying in the field of ecology: "There is no 'away.'" The old world of corporate inner sanctums isolated managers from many of their decisions' social and environmental consequences, distant in time and space from those who made the decisions. As transparency increases, these feedback loops are closing, and consequences must be faced. In this sense, transparency is a powerful ally to naturalism, and may drive many of the changes needed to implement more-naturalistic, circular business processes and models.

Growing transparency already has led to the inclusion of voices traditionally outside the inner circle. Several years ago, Greenpeace objected to the chlorides IKEA used in the printing of catalogs. Few in the industry thought there was any cost-effective alternative. But working together, Greenpeace and IKEA found a Finnish printing company that could produce catalogs without chlorides. IKEA presented its chloride-free catalog at an environmental conference in Washington and set a new industry standard. This experience showed that Greenpeace and IKEA could work together productively by focusing on tangible problems and by believing that breakthroughs were possible. Such trust can only be built over time.

Growing transparency is also leading to new accounting and performance-management practices. Shell and others are moving toward "triple-bottom-line" accounting—assessing economic, environmental, and social performance in a balanced way. The Global Reporting Initiative provides practical guidelines for such changes. "Adopting GRI guidelines and triple-bottom-line practices is an enormously difficult step," says consultant John Elkington. "But companies like Shell, Ford, and many others feel they must do this if they want to lead, rather than just react to change."

The path toward broader accountability is fraught with perils. Last spring, Ford's first "Corporate Citizenship Report," based loosely on GRI guidelines, was greeted with as much cynicism as appreciation. The *New York Times* ignored most of the report (which included lengthy sections on reducing emissions and radical redesign of manufacturing processes) to announce that "Ford Is Conceding SUV Drawbacks."[23] The article focused on a three-page section of the 98-page report that discussed the dilemma of having a profitable product line that had environmental and safety problems. The *Wall Street Journal* was more personal, suggesting that chairman William Clay Ford was a hypocrite for both making and criticizing SUVs, a "guilt-ridden rich kid" who should either embrace his customers' preferences or leave the business to those who do.[24]

Ultimately, transparency is about awareness. With increasing awareness will come pressures for greater accountability for social and natural capital as well as financial capital. Gradually, this will lead to innovations in the larger social context as well.

It is impossible to predict the range of social innovations that growing transparency will ultimately foster. Perhaps new collaborative action-research networks will create the right climate of objectivity and compassion, tough standards and fair reporting combined with a spirit of learning together. (See "The New Competen-

---

New Competencies

The challenges of building sustainable enterprises describe a strange new world few firms are equipped to understand, let alone navigate. The members of the SoL Sustainability Consortium came together believing that their preceding work with organizational-learning principles and tools might make a difference in meeting these challenges.

Today, Consortium members are engaged in projects on sustainability frameworks (from which the ideas on naturalism and humanism came), new energy sources, implementing new business models, and nurturing new leadership networks embodying competencies that build upon the leadership skills for learning organizations (published in the *Sloan Management Review* 10 years ago*):

• building shared vision,
• surfacing and testing mental models, and
• systems thinking.

Research on mental models and dialogue[†] needs to be scaled up to allow strategic conversations that involve hundreds and even thousands of people. As Juanita Brown, founder of Whole Systems Associates, says, "The questions we are facing will require members of organizations to learn together at an unprecedented rate, often on a global scale." Starting in 1999, Brown's colleagues Bo Gyllenpalm and David Isaacs helped several large Swedish organizations convene conversations on "Infocom (information and communications services) and the Environment." Convening and hosting such large-scale conversations require particular methodologies. But Brown believes that the key lies in "questions that challenge current experiences and assumptions, while evoking new possibilities for collective discovery." For example, "How can infocom technology and services support the evolution of a sustainable and renewable environment?"

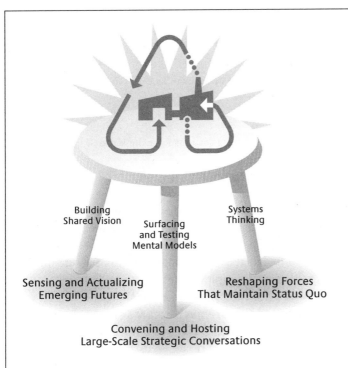

Figure 19.4
Core Learning Competencies for Building Sustainable Enterprises

Most attempts at large-scale change fail because otherwise competent leaders do not understand the complex forces maintaining the status quo. Getting a CEO to support sustainability is not enough. Bottom-up environmental innovations also often fail. Leaders at all levels must understand the multiple "balancing processes" that, on the one hand, make any complex organization viable, but on the other, consistently defeat large-scale change. Leadership strategies must address these balancing forces. For example: relevance (people asking, "What does sustainability have to do with my job?"), believers vs. nonbelievers (the polarization that passionate advocates for social and environmental causes can create), the tyranny of established metrics (most current metrics reflect take-make-waste mental models, and new metrics aimed at life-cycle costs are useless without changes in mental models), and purpose (if the company's core purpose is perceived as making money, people's commitment may be below the threshold required to lead significant change).[‡]

All meaningful work on shared vision rests on distinguishing "creating" from "problem solving." Problem solving seeks to make things we don't like go away. Creating seeks to make things we care about come into being. This is a vital distinction for innovation. When problem solving dominates an organizational culture, life is about survival rather than about bringing into reality things that people care about. Recent research on leadership among entrepreneurs and scientists reveals a particular creative capacity—sensing and actualizing emerging futures. Successful leaders see the world as "open, dynamic, interconnected, and full of possibilities."[§] They are both committed and "in a state of surrender," as cognitive scientist Francisco Varela expresses it. Economist W. Brian Arthur adds that "cognizing" in business today follows three stages:

- "Observe, observe, observe: become one with the world."
- "Reflect and retreat: listen from the inner place where knowing comes to the surface."
- "Act in an instant: incubate and bring forth the new into reality."

* Senge 1990.
† Isaacs 1999.
‡ These are four of ten basic challenges to sustaining deep change addressed in Senge *et al.* 1999.
§ Jaworski and Scharmer 2000.

cies") Perhaps more-participative media, building on successful experiments such as those of Fast Company, will enable new levels of collaborative innovation. It may even be time to question the traditional limited-liability status of corporations, which uniquely favors owners of financial capital. Today's world of abundant financial capital and limited natural and social capital differs profoundly from the world of a century ago, when there was a need to protect individual investors. "In a world where learning and knowledge generation are the basis for corporate survival and wealth creation, managers must see a company as a living being, a human community," says writer and former Shell executive Arie de Geus. "Yet, today's managers inherit a very different worldview, focused on the optimism of financial capital. Is it not inconsistent to emphasize knowledge creation, on the one hand, and then treat a company as a machine for producing money, which is owned by its financial investors on the other?"

Perhaps when we are able to rediscover "company" (from the Latin *companis*, sharing of bread) as "living community," we will also rediscover its place within the larger community of living systems where it rightfully resides.

The Logic of Revolutions

The New Economy is both not new and new. It continues industrial-age patterns, yet it also may hold the seeds for a truly postindustrial world. As such, it brings us to a crossroads. We can either continue moving ever more rapidly in a direction that cannot be sustained, or we can change. Perhaps no time in history has afforded greater possibilities for a collective change in direction.

"Creative engineers understand the role of constraints," says Elter of his Lakes experience. "Design engineers always deal with constraints: time, weight, operability.

These are all real. The extraordinary creativity of [our] team had its source in recognizing a different constraint—the constraint of nature, to produce no waste. Zero to landfill is an uplifting constraint. It's worth going after. It's not manmade." Constraint and creativity are always connected. No artist paints on an infinite canvas. The artist understands that rather than just being limits, constraints can be freeing, especially when those constraints that have genuine meaning are recognized. What if product and business designers everywhere recognized that their constraints came from living systems? What if they adhered to the simple dictums: waste equals food; support nature's regenerative processes; live off energy income, not principal; and, borrowing from Elter's team, do it for the children. As occurred with the Lakes engineers, might this not free everyone's creativity in previously unimaginable ways?

Such rethinking will not happen all at once. It will not arise from any central authority. It will come from everywhere and nowhere in particular. The first Industrial Revolution, according to author Daniel Quinn, was "the product of a million small beginnings. [It] didn't proceed according to any theoretical design [and] was not a utopian undertaking."[25] Likewise, the next Industrial Revolution, if it is to happen, will have no grand plan and no one in charge. It will advance, in Quinn's words, on the basis of "an outpouring of human creativity," innovations not just in the technological but in the human landscape as well—the only way a new story can arise.

Acknowledgments

This chapter is reprinted with permission from *Sloan Management Review* 42, no. 2 (Winter 2001): 24–40. Most of the ideas and many of the examples above come from the practitioners, researchers, and consultants in the SoL Sustainability Consortium, many of whom are quoted above. In addition, the authors would like to thank other consortium members who read the manuscript and offered helpful suggestions: Bernie Bulkin of BP, Amory and Hunter Lovins of the Rocky Mountain Institute, Otto Scharmer of MIT, Debbie Zemke of Ford, and Sara Schley and Joe Laur of Seed Systems, coordinators for the Consortium.

Additional Resources

Several authors have made compelling business cases for environmental stewardship in recent years, including Paul Hawken (1993), Amory and Hunter Lovins, along with Hawken (Hawken *et al.* 1999), and William McDonough and Michael Braungart (1998). For radical ideas on performance management, John Elkington (1997) explains triple-bottom-line practices, while accounting theorist Tom Johnson (2000), coinventor of activity-based costing, argues that companies with outstanding performance, like Toyota, mimic nature in their accounting practices, focusing on complex patterns rather than fragmented metrics. Janine Benyus (1998) offers a different slant on naturalism, suggesting that technologies in harmony with nature will arise when biologists work with product designers. Lastly, Arie de Geus (1997) and Dee Hock (1999) examine planning, leading, and governing when organizations are seen as living human communities.

To support those interested in building more sustainable enterprises, there are several Web sites focused on environmental education and planning (The Natural Step at http://www.naturalstep.org), natural capitalism and hybrid cars (the Rocky Mountain Institute at http://www.rmi.org), ecoefficiency (the World Business Council for Sustainable Development at http://www.wbcsd.org), triple-bottom-line reporting (http://www.sustainability.com and http://www.globalreporting.org) and organizational learning (SoL at http://www.SoLonline.org).

Notes

1. Social capital refers to "connections among individuals—social networks and the norms of reciprocity and trustworthiness that arise with them"; see Putnam (2000, 19). It is also the necessary context for developing human capital—skills and knowledge embedded in people; see Coleman (1988).

2. Why Is Everyone So Short-Tempered? 2000.

3. Browne 2000a, available from BP, London.

4. Browne 2000b.

5. See http://www.rmi.org/sitepages/pid175.asp for Rocky Mountain Institute publications about the Hypercar.

6. Gunn 1999.

7. The SoL (Society for Organizational Learning) Sustainability Consortium was established by BP and Interface and now includes established SoL members Royal Dutch/Shell, Ford, Xerox, Harley-Davidson, Detroit-Edison, Visteon, and the World Bank, along with new members Nike and Northeast Utilities. The group's current projects—on product development, innovation across complex supply networks, new energy sources, and leadership and cultural change—are described at http://www.SoLonline.org and are being studied through a National Science Foundation grant.

8. Berry 1990, 123.

9. Ibid, 131–132.

10. Boorstin 1985, 108–109.

11. See Hawken, Lovins, and Lovins (1999), 14, Ayers (1989), Lovins, Lovins, and Hawken (1999).

12. These three strategies, in concert with ideas below, relate closely to the four strategies of "natural capitalism," three of the four "system conditions" of "the natural step" described in Holmberg and Robert

2000 and McDonough 1992. (The last publication is available through McDonough Braungart Design Chemistry, Charlottesville, Va., by sending a request to info@mbdc.com, or can be downloaded from the World Wide Web at http://www.mcdonough.com/principles.pdf).

13. Kelly 1999, 2, 5, 31.

14. Vandermerwe 2000, 28.

15. Toffler 1980.

16. Kelly 1999, 121–122.

17. Prahalad and Ramaswamy 2000, xiv.

18. Levine *et al.* 2000.

19. Kelly 1999, 28.

20. Wysocki 2000.

21. Drucker and Senge forthcoming.

22. Webber 1993.

23. Bradsher 2000.

24. Yates 2000.

25. Quinn 1997, 200–201.

References

Ayers, R. U. 1989. Industrial Metabolism. In *Technology and Environment,* edited by J. S. Ausubel and H. E. Sladovich. Washington, D.C.: National Academy Press.

Benyus, Janine. 1998. *Biomimicry: Innovation Inspired by Nature.* New York: William Morrow.

Berry, T. 1990. *The Dream of the Earth.* San Francisco: Sierra Club Books.

Boorstin, D. 1985. *The Discoverers: A History of Man's Search To Know His World and Himself.* New York: Random House.

Bradsher, K. 2000. Ford Is Conceding SUV Drawbacks. *New York Times,* May 12, A1.

Browne, J. 2000a. Respect for the Earth. From a BBC Reith Lecture.

Browne, J. 2000b. Rethinking Corporate Responsibility. *Reflections* 1.4 (Summer): 48–53.

Coleman, J. S. 1988. Social Capital and the Creation of Human Capital. *American Journal of Sociology* 94: 95–120.

de Geus, Arie. 1997. *The Living Company.* Boston: Harvard Business School Press.

Drucker, P. F., and P. Senge. Forthcoming. Becoming a Change Leader. Video conversations, Peter F. Drucker Foundation for Nonprofit Management and SoL (Society for Organizational Learning).

Elkington, John. 1997. *Cannibals with Forks.* Oxford: Capstone.

Gunn, E. P. 1999. The Green CEO. *Fortune,* May 24, 190–200.

Hawken, Paul. 1993. *The Ecology of Commerce.* New York: HarperBusiness.

Hawken, P., A. B. Lovins, and L. H. Lovins. 1999. *Natural Capitalism.* New York: Little Brown and Co.

Hock, Dee. 1999. *Birth of the Chaordic Age.* San Francisco: Berrett-Koehler.

Holmberg, J., and K. H. Robert. 2000. Backcasting From Nonoverlapping Sustainability Principles—A Framework for Strategic Planning. *International Journal of Sustainable Development and World Ecology* 7: 1–18.

Isaacs, W. 1999. *Dialogue: The Art of Thinking Together.* New York: Doubleday/Currency.

Jaworski, J., and O. Scharmer. 2000. Leading in the New Economy: Sensing and Actualizing Emerging Futures. Society for Organizational Learning working paper, http://www.generonconsulting.com/Publications/Leading_in_the_Digital-Economy.pdf.

Johnson, Thomas. 2000. *Profit Beyond Measure*. New York: Free Press.

Kelly, K. 1999. *New Rules for the New Economy*. New York: Penguin Books.

Levine, Rick, Christopher Locke, Doc Searls, and David Weinberger. 2000. *The Cluetrain Manifesto: The End of Business as Usual*. Cambridge, Mass.: Perseus Press.

Lovins, A. B., L. H. Lovins, and P. Hawken. 1999. A Road Map for Natural Capitalism. *Harvard Business Review* 77 (May–June): 145–158.

McDonough, William. 1992. *Hannover Principles: Design for Sustainability*. New York: William McDonough Architects.

McDonough, William, and Michael Braungart. 1998. The Next Industrial Revolution. *Atlantic Monthly*, October (available on the World Wide Web at http://www.theatlantic.com/issues/98oct/industry.htm).

Prahalad, C. K., and V. Ramaswamy. 2000. Co-Opting Customer Competence. *Harvard Business Review* 78 (January–February): 79–87.

Putnam, R. D. 1988. *Bowling Alone*. New York: Simon & Schuster.

Quinn, D. 1997. *My Ishmael*. New York: Bantam Books.

Senge, P. M. 1990. The Leader's New Work: Building Learning Organizations. *Sloan Management Review* 32 (Fall): 7–23.

Senge, P. et al. 1999. *The Dance of Change: The Challenges to Sustaining Learning Organizations*. New York: Doubleday/Currency.

Toffler, A. 1980. *The Third Wave*. New York: William Morrow.

Vandermerwe, S. 2000. How Increasing Value to Customers Improves Business Results. *MIT Sloan Management Review* 42 (Fall): 27–38.

Webber, A. 1993. What's So New About the New Economy? *Harvard Business Review* 71 (January–February): 24–42.

Why Is Everyone So Short-Tempered? 2000. *USA Today,* July 18, A1.

Wysocki, B. Jr. 2000. Yet Another Hazard of the New Economy: The Pied Piper Effect. *Wall Street Journal*, March 30, A1.

Yates, B. 2000. On the Road: Pecksniffs Can't Stop SUV. *Wall Street Journal Europe*, May 19, A26.

V CONCLUSION

20 Prospects for the New Century

In 1879, Thomas Edison invented the carbon filament incandescent light bulb. Two years later, he unveiled another invention—the central generating station—that would make widespread usage of the electric light bulb possible. The great American inventor thus ushered in the electrical age. But as the economic historian Paul David has shown, it would take another forty years for electricity to have a significant impact on the overall economy. Though visionary engineers had extolled the potential of electricity as early as the turn of the century, it was not until the 1920s that all the necessary factors were in place for this new technology to be productively used on a large scale. One of the important developments, for instance, was the replacement of bulky centralized sources of steam power in factories by numerous small electric motors, which, in turn, allowed radical simplifications of factory floor designs. Once that point was reached, U.S. industry enjoyed an unprecedented jump in productivity, one that continued for nearly a half-century (David 1990, 2000).

In the case of electricity, nearly a half-century was required for a transforming new technology to have its first significant impact. Once that impact was felt, however, it turned out to be a sustained one, lasting another half-century. The story of electricity is a useful one to recall when contemplating the likely progress of the information technology-induced changes we are now living through. The changes we describe in this volume won't be completed in a year, or a decade. Instead, successive waves of change will continue to sweep through firm after firm, industry after industry, for many years to come.

One of the most effective ways to approach this period of change will be with an experimental, inventive attitude. Lots of new ideas will emerge and get tested in the continually evolving environment. Some will work the first time they're tried; many won't. In retrospect, we'll be able to look back on the winners and see a logic behind their success. But that logic will remain elusive in the maelstrom of uncertainty in which the bets will have to be placed.

Navigating through a turbulent time of this sort will require the imagination to see new possibilities, the willingness to try new things, the flexibility to improvise along the way, and the ability to learn from experience. Most of all, however, making wise choices in this uncertain environment will require a deep sense of what we want in the first place—for ourselves, our organizations, and our societies.

History has given us an unusual opportunity to make choices today that will lay the foundations for a new organizational era tomorrow. We hope this book can help us all make those choices as creatively, as intelligently—and as wisely—as we possibly can.

References

David, Paul. 1990. The Dynamo and the Computer: An Historical Perspective on the Modern Productivity Paradox. *American Economic Review* 80 (May): 355–361.

David, Paul. 2000. Understanding Digital Technology's Evolution and the Path of Measured Productivity Growth: Present and Future in the Mirror of the Past. In *Understanding the Digital Economy*, edited by Erik Brynjolfsson and Brian Kahin. Cambridge, Mass: MIT Press.

List of Contributors

Deborah Ancona
Deborah Ancona is Seley Distinguished Professor of Management at MIT's Sloan School of Management.

Lotte Bailyn
Lotte Bailyn is T Wilson (1953) Professor of Management at MIT's Sloan School of Management and Co-Director of the MIT Workplace Center.

Abraham Bernstein
Abraham Bernstein is Assistant Professor of Information Systems at the Leonard N. Stern School of Business, New York University.

Henrik Bresman
Henrik Bresman is a doctoral candidate in Organization Studies at MIT's Sloan School of Management.

Erik Brynjolfsson
Erik Brynjolfsson is George and Sandi Schussel Professor of Management at MIT's Sloan School of Management and Co-director the Center for eBusiness at MIT.

John S. Carroll
John S. Carroll is Professor of Behavioral and Policy Sciences at MIT's Slchool of Management.

Göran Carstedt
Göran Carstedt is leading the formation of the Society for Organizational Learning's global network. He was formerly a senior executive at Volvo and IKEA.

Kevin Crowston
Kevin Crowston is Associate Professor of Information Studies at the School of Information Studies, Syracuse University.

Chrysanthos Dellarocas
Chrysanthos Dellarocas is the Douglas Drane Career Development Assistant Professor of Information Technology at MIT's Sloan School of Management.

Michael J. Earl
Michael J. Earl is Professor of Information Management and Director of the Centre for the Network Economy at London Business School.

Charles H. Fine
Charles H. Fine is Chrysler LFM Professor of Management at MIT's Sloan School of Management and and Co-Director of MIT's International Motor Vehicle Program.

Joyce K. Fletcher
Joyce K. Fletcher is Professor of Management at Simmons School of Management and Co-Director of the Working Connections Project at the Jean Baker Miller Training Institute, Wellesley College.

Arnoldo C. Hax
Arnoldo C. Hax is Alfred P. Sloan Professor of Management at MIT's Sloan School of Management.

George Herman
George Herman is a Research Scientist at the Center for Coordination Science, MIT Sloan School of Management.

Lorin M. Hitt
Lorin M. Hitt is the Alberto Vitale Term Assistant Professor of Operations and Information Management (OPIM) at the Wharton School, University of Pennsylvania.

J. Debra Hofman
J. Debra Hofman is a Research Director at AMR Research. When she coauthored the chapter that appears in this volume, she was a Research Associate at the Center for Information Systems Research, MIT Sloan School of Management.

Bengt Holmström
Bengt Holmström is Paul A. Samuelson Professor of Economics, MIT.

Katrin Kaeufer
Katrin Kaeufer is a Visiting Scholar at MIT's Sloan School of Management.

Mark Klein
Mark Klein is a Principal Research Scientist at the Center for Coordination Science, MIT Sloan School of Management.

Thomas A. Kochan
Thomas A. Kochan is George M. Bunker Professor of Work and Employment Relations at MIT's Sloan School of Management. He is past President of both the Industrial Relations Research Associate (IRRA) and the International Industrial Relations Association (IIRA).

Deborah Kolb
Deborah Kolb is Professor of Management at the Simmons School of Management and Founding Co-Director of the Simmons Center for the Study of Gender in Organizations.

Nina Kruschwitz
Nina Kruschwitz is researcher, writer, and consultant based in Boston. She was formerly a Research Assistant at MIT's Center for Organizational Learning and is now the Managing Associate at the consulting firm, Reflection Learning Associates.

Robert Laubacher
Robert Laubacher is a Research Associate at MIT's Sloan School of Management.

Jintae Lee
Jintae Lee is Assistant Professor of Decision Sciences, College of Business, University of Hawaii.

Donald Lessard
Donald Lessard is Epoch Foundation Professor of International Management and deputy dean at MIT's Sloan School of Management.

Thomas W. Malone
Thomas W. Malone is the Patrick J. McGovern Professor of Information Systems and Director of the Center for Coordination Science at MIT's Sloan School of Management. He was Co-Director of the "Initiative on Inventing the Organizations of the 21st Century."

Elisa O'Donnell
Elisa O'Donnell is an independent consultant practicing in the Boston area. While at EDS/A.T. Kearney, she served as liaison to MIT's 21st Century Initiative.

Wanda J. Orlikowski
Wanda J. Orlikowski is Professor of Information Technologies and Organization Studies at MIT's Sloan School of Management and the Eaton-Peabody Chair of Communication Sciences at MIT.

Charles S. Osborn
Charles S. Osborn was Associate Professor of Information Systems, babson college. He died in December 2001 after a long illness with amyotrophic lateral sclerosis (ALS), also known as Lou Gehrig's disease.

Brian Pentland
Brian Pentland is Associate Professor of Information Systems at the Eli Broad Graduate School of Management, Michigan State University.

John Quimby
John Quimby is a Research Scientist at the Center for Coordination Science, MIT Sloan School of Management.

John Roberts
John Roberts is John H. and Irene S. Scully Professor in International Business Studies in the Graduate School of Business, and Professor, by Courtesy, of Economics at Stanford University.

John F. Rockart
John F. Rockart is Senior Lecturer Emeritus in Information Technology at MIT's Sloan School of Management. He was Director of Sloan's Center for Information Systems Research until June of 2000.

Jeanne W. Ross
Jeanne W. Ross is Principal Research Scientist at the Center for Information Systems Research, MIT Sloan School of Management.

George Roth
George Roth is a Research Associate at MIT's Sloan School of Management and Executive Director for the Ford-MIT Alliance, a partnership between MIT and Ford focused on engineering education, research, and environmental policy.

Michael S. Scott Morton

Michael S. Scott Morton is Jay W. Forrester Professor of Management Emeritus at MIT's Sloan School of Management and Co-Director of the the Cambridge-MIT Institute, an alliance between the University of Cambridge and MIT. He was Co-Director of the Initiative on Inventing the Organizations of the 21st Century.

Peter M. Senge

Peter M. Senge is Senior Lecturer at MIT's Sloan School of Management and Founding Chair of the Society for Organizational Learning.

John D. Sterman

John D. Sterman is Professor of Management, Director of the System Dynamics Group, and Chair of the Master's Program at MIT's Sloan School of Management.

Dean L. Wilde II

Dean L. Wilde II is Chairman, Dean & Company, and a Visiting Lecturer at MIT's Sloan School of Management.

George Wyner

George Wyner is Assistant Professor of Information Systems at the Boston University School of Management.

JoAnne Yates

JoAnne Yates is Sloan Distinguished Professor of Management at MIT's Sloan School of Management.

Index